God and Spirituality

**Hindsfoot Foundation Series on
Spirituality and Theology**

God and Spirituality

Philosophical Essays

Glenn F. Chesnut

iUniverse, Inc.

New York   Bloomington

God and Spirituality
Philosophical Essays

Copyright © 2010 by Glenn F. Chesnut

iUniverse books may be ordered through booksellers or by contacting:
iUniverse
1663 Liberty Drive
Bloomington, IN 47403
www.iuniverse.com
1-800-Authors (1-800-288-4677)

ISBN: 978-1-4502-6769-4 (pbk)
ISBN: 978-1-4502-2854-1 (ebk)

Printed in the United States of America
iUniverse rev. date: 9/29/2010

Table of Contents

Preface

As a child, I came to believe that the natural sciences could provide the answers to the basic questions about life and the universe. I started reading everything I could about physics, electronics, and astronomy from the time I was twelve years old. I concentrated on chemistry and nuclear physics when I did my undergraduate degree at the University of Louisville, and then went on to do half of the course work for a doctorate in physical chemistry with a subsidiary concentration in nuclear physics at Iowa State University. I decided to go to seminary at that point, at Perkins School of Theology at Southern Methodist University in Dallas, but not because of any fundamental unhappiness with all the important truths which the physicists in particular had taught me about the universe. It was rather that I had begun to see that my very deepest concerns lay in a different area: that dimension of reality where human beings encounter overwhelming beauty, the dark tragedy of human evil, the judgment of God, and a vision of life lived as a vehicle of the divine love. God was pointing me in a different direction from the one in which I had been going.

My four years at seminary, followed by doctoral work in theology at Oxford University, gave me my basic training in ancient Hebrew thought, the literature of the classical Greek period, and the world of the Roman empire: Jewish, Christian, Gnostic, and pagan. After I returned to the United States, both the University of Virginia and Indiana University asked me on occasion to teach courses which dealt with the middle ages, which broadened my experience yet further and enabled me to learn some of the things about medieval theology and philosophy which I have written about in the following pages.

Several years after I retired from university teaching, the various chapters of this book were composed and put into something close to finished shape. The major part of this work was carried out over a period of a year and a half or so, between the summer of 2006 and the beginning of 2008. At that point, copies of the whole work were run off, and ten of us met every Thursday evening in Milford, Indiana, for a number of months to read through the entire text, paragraph by paragraph. My friends of many years, William E. Correll, Frank Nyikos, John Stark, and Karen Zurawski, were there every week, and Elizabeth Ann Downs-Lewis, Patsy A. Doty, Alisa Pratt, Jerry J. Smith, and Jere A. Wendt joined in to help out too. Many of us had to drive more than an hour each way over narrow country roads running across the Indiana prairies, sometimes through driving rain or knee-deep snow, trying to keep from running off the road, dodging (or sometimes failing to dodge) an errant deer, or slowing down to avoid a wandering prairie wolf. One evening several of us were startled by a mountain lion dashing across the road in front of us. But we showed up every week, read the book, debated it, and discussed it, sentence by sentence. My copy ended up full of hundreds of changes and revisions.

What you hold in your hands now is the product of all those discussions. I hope you will find something in this volume which is useful to you. May God bless you.

Grace and peace,
Glenn C. (South Bend, Indiana)
March 1, 2010

Chapter 1

The X-factor in Conversion

St. Augustine in the garden

One of the most famous conversion stories from the ancient world was the account which Augustine, the great African saint, gave of his own conversion experience in his *Confessions*. It was August of the year 386, and he was in a garden, he tells us, lashed with internal torment, when suddenly he heard, coming from the other side of the garden wall, a small child singing over and over the same two words: *Tolle, lege* ("pick it up, read it"). Augustine went to a copy of the Apostle Paul's New Testament epistles, opened it at random, and read the passage at Romans 13:13-14. "In an instant," Augustine said, "as I came to the end of the sentence, it was as though the light of confidence flooded into my heart and all the darkness of doubt was dispelled." From this point on, he was a devoted Christian.[1]

Augustine abandoned his career at the imperial court and ended up as bishop of Hippo Regius, a small city on the coast of Africa, where he wrote numerous books on philosophy and theology during the years which followed. At the end of his life, the Roman empire in the western end of the Mediterranean began to collapse under the weight of barbarian invasions from the north. One German tribe, the Vandals, carved a path of destruction through France and Spain and then crossed the straits of Gibraltar and began conquering their way across North Africa. As Augustine lay on his death bed, these savage German tribesmen were attacking the very city in which he lay dying.

1

Augustine's books survived however, and during the long Dark Age which followed, his writings became the basis of all Roman Catholic theology. The Protestant Reformers in the sixteenth century saw themselves, not as innovators, but as conservatives who were putting western European theology back on its traditional Augustinian basis. In the modern period, anyone who knows Augustine well, who reads the first 164 pages of the Big Book of Alcoholics Anonymous, can see an almost pure Augustinian spirituality forming its underlying structure: a doctrine of sin and salvation in which pride and the human attempt to play God are portrayed as the root cause of all human misery. Augustine has been for centuries the most influential Christian thinker outside of the New Testament itself.

The first time I read Augustine's story of his conversion in the garden after he had turned to Romans 13:13-14, I went to my own bible and read that entire section of the epistle to the Romans, searching for something that might make sense of such a dramatic change of heart, and turned away feeling completely disappointed. It is true that, particularly if we read verses eleven and twelve as well, it is a call to changing one's life totally. And some of the specifics in there certainly applied to Augustine, who had been a great Latin lover, who could not stay away from the ladies, and knew that he would never be able to be faithful to a wife:

> And you know that this is the crucial moment, because it is already the hour for you to wake from sleep. For our salvation is very near .... the night is almost gone and day is at hand. So let us put aside the works of darkness and clothe ourselves in the armor of light. Let us walk about in the daylight like decent people, not partying and getting drunk, not sleeping around without sexual restraint, not quarreling and fighting. Instead, clothe yourself with the Lord Jesus Christ, and do not plan your deeds to satisfy the desires of your flesh.

But Augustine had read any number of biblical passages like this one before, and had also had his mother Monica preaching the same

2

kinds of things at him for years. I could not see any way that this particular passage could have conveyed any fresh new insight. It was not a revelation of any kind of new or profound idea, which could have perhaps opened someone's eyes and given that person a whole different perspective.

In the almost forty years since, I have read and heard any number of attempts at a psychological explanation for this decisive crisis in Augustine's life, and the nature of its resolution. Although the best of these add a measure of depth to our understanding of the psychological pressures that must have been present in his mind,[2] none of them would "explain" conclusively why his conversion took place at that precise moment, and in the direction it did—unless we assume, as some of these explainers unfortunately do, that Augustine was an extremely dull-witted and simple-minded person with little or no insight into either his own or anyone else's motivations and inner thoughts and desires.

But in fact, Augustine was one of the three or four most profound thinkers in all antiquity when it came to sorting out the complicated skein of the human psyche's inner tangle of conflicting desires and motivations and fears. He was up there with a handful of impressive figures like Plato and Euripides. He had come out of a small town in the interior of Africa and risen to become the man who gave the speeches for the Roman emperor, putting him in the middle of the greatest power circles in the entire Mediterranean world on the basis of his ability to intuit and shape human motivation. If he himself could give no logical explanation for that sudden dramatic shift in his perception of the world and in his perception of his own life, it would take a brave modern scholar indeed to claim that he or she was a more subtle and sophisticated analyst than Augustine was of the complexities of human purpose and desire.

The first time I read that part of Augustine's *Confessions* was when I was in seminary at Southern Methodist University during the early 1960's, before I went to Oxford. And as I say, it seemed simply a perplexing story which made no real sense to me in any kind of way. Obviously something truly dramatic had happened which had completely reshaped Augustine's mind. There was some strange sort of tantalizing x-factor present in that story, which was clearly real, because its effect had been decisive and sweeping in its consequences, but its nature completely eluded my understanding. I walked away totally dissatisfied, feeling like a failure, because I could not come up with any kind of satisfactory explanation for how and why that event in the garden had totally changed his life.

Now, some forty years later, I have come to the conclusion that I had read and understood Augustine's story far better than I realized at that time, and that a large part of my original reaction was completely appropriate! There are good reasons, I now realize, for why (in a genuine religious conversion) there must be some element of mystery, some x-factor present, which eludes the grasp of our human explanatory systems. Human lives are only changed in the way that Augustine's was by the power of divine grace. But that means that, in the same way that God's infinite being cannot be domesticated within the sphere of our ordinary intellectual concepts and scientific explanatory schemes, so too the acts of God share in his all-transcendent Mystery. Of necessity, a true act of God will be the impingement within our natural world of an alien power coming from outside the created realm. We cannot "explain" a genuine act of divine grace, because we cannot "explain" God.

John Wesley at Aldersgate

Another equally famous conversion story was John Wesley's. He was a scholar who taught at Oxford University at the time that the rise of modern science had first begun, a true Renaissance man with an enormous range of knowledge, including the most recent discoveries in psychology and the natural sciences. Just as with Augustine, we have an account in Wesley's own words of his conversion experience which, in his case, yanked him out of his book-filled Oxford study and turned him into one of the most famous revival preachers in history. It is given in his *Journal,* where he tells us that on May 24,

1738, he went to a small religious service at a place on Aldersgate Street in London, where someone read from Martin Luther's Preface to the Epistle to the Romans to the assembled group. In his *Journal*, Wesley said that suddenly "I felt my heart strangely warmed."[3] By 1739, this erudite and uptight Oxford University scholar had begun preaching, with enormous success, to English coal miners and factory workers and their families out in open fields and wherever else he could gather them together. He abandoned his university teaching and rode literally thousands of miles on horseback every year, through every conceivable kind of weather, preaching wherever he could gather an audience. The widespread Methodist movement was the result. He and the American theologian Jonathan Edwards became the two great theoreticians explaining how to preach the kind of revival sermons that produced the eighteenth-century evangelical movement and the later nineteenth-century American frontier revival movement—and also explaining how and why these sermons worked, both psychologically and theologically.

But again, when I was in seminary, I read Martin Luther's Preface in the attempt to gain some deeper insight into Wesley's conversion experience, and felt totally let down. There was nothing in that short writing that was any more useful than the passage from Romans 13:13-14, in terms of explaining why it should have had such an impact on John Wesley at that point. It was not one of Luther's more profound writings. And Wesley had been reading the great Protestant theologians for years. He could quote numerous sentences and passages from Calvin's *Institutes* by heart, and had made a thorough study of other early Reformation era theological writings, such as the Books of Homilies published by the great English reformer Thomas Cranmer, who had introduced the principles of the Protestant Reformation into the English church after the death of King Henry VIII. Wesley was intimately familiar with the Protestant theological literature of his own time, and unfailingly read from the New Testament every morning when he first got up, in the original Greek! There was nothing new in the short writing that was read at the Aldersgate meeting on May 24th.

But again, just as in the case of Augustine's conversion, in the years since then, I have read and heard numerous attempted "explanations" of what happened at Aldersgate, all of which seemed to start with the assumption that Wesley was a simple "folk theologian" who had never encountered the actual gospel message before, and who turned into a rather simple-minded but "warm-hearted" revival preacher after someone pointed out to him that we are justified by faith and not by works of the law.

His Aldersgate experience did not take place in a vacuum. There had been a series of preceding discoveries and psychological stresses building up to that decisive event.[4] Some twenty years after I graduated from seminary, there was a long period when I was teaching courses on Wesley and his theology to graduate students and giving lectures on his theology to various audiences. I went back over that part of Wesley's life in enormous detail. But even when an exhaustive catalogue of all that had taken place in his life during the two or three years preceding Aldersgate was taken into account, the effect of this further research only served to support my original impression, that what happened to Wesley at Aldersgate involved some mysterious x-factor—a hole in the middle of the narrative—which cannot itself be explained in terms of conventional psychological or historical explanation.

In fact, John Wesley was a priest of the Church of England, who taught Greek and Latin classics and the New Testament at Oxford University, which was one of the two great English universities. Even by Oxford standards he was a polymath and an extraordinarily (perhaps even dangerously) brilliant man. He knew the best psychology of his time—John Locke's explorations into conditioned reflex and the compulsive power of the human subconscious—and had an extraordinary knowledge of the inner workings of the human mind. And yet even he could give no explanation for what happened to him at Aldersgate, other than that some strange and quiet working of divine grace pushed him at that time, in some inexplicable way, into an entirely new perception of himself and of the world. Some mysterious x-factor was present, whose reality was obvious, because of the enormous changes it produced in his life, but which he could not explain in any kind of fashion other than to say that it was the hand of God intruding into our natural world and bringing him a new power and inner peace.

The twentieth century: conversion experiences in the twelve step movement

To move up to the present, the most significant spiritual movement in the United States during the past seventy years has been the twelve step movement first initiated by the formation of Alcoholics Anonymous in 1935-39. It has been at least as important in twentieth century American history as the Great Awakening was in the eighteenth century, and as frontier revivalism was in nineteenth century American history.

As part of the archival materials in the Alcoholics Anonymous offices in South Bend and Elkhart, Indiana, in 1993, I was able to gain access to a truly remarkable collection of tape recorded autobiographical accounts by the great spiritual leaders of the A.A. movement in north central Indiana during its formative period. These were much like the materials that Professor Starbuck provided to William James when the latter was researching his classic book, *The Varieties of Religious Experience*,[5] only even more detailed. The people who spoke on these tapes—as well as contemporary A.A. people who talked with me about their spiritual experiences in my later researches—were none of them trained theologians, but nevertheless spoke with a simple eloquence almost unmatched in my many years of reading and study, as they explained how they had experienced their personal encounters with the higher power who rules this universe, and how their own lives had been totally transformed by these experiences.

Nevertheless, the stories they told were no more illuminating in the final analysis, than Augustine's story or John Wesley's story. I learned a good deal from their stories about the descent into an inner hell of resentment and fear and guilt which occurs as untreated alcoholics get more and more ensnared by their drinking. And each of these people told of an event, or a series of events, which produced a radical soul change or psychic change, which not only enabled them to stop drinking, but also set them on the path to a new way of life where they could be happy, joyous, and free. But they otherwise left me just as puzzled as Augustine's and Wesley's stories.

The drunken English professor

As I was carrying out this research into the early history of A.A. in northern Indiana (which eventually ended up in my writing two books, *The Factory Owner & the Convict* and *The St. Louis Gambler & the Railroad Man*), I was invited to participate on one occasion, when a group of people were attempting to persuade a recently hospitalized alcoholic to start attending A.A. meetings and doing something about his drinking. And something the alcoholic said from his hospital bed suddenly provided the key to understanding why I had been unable to truly "explain" any of the conversion experiences I had been studying.

The story is a real one, but I will change the central figure's name and a few of the details about his life—although not the reference to his vast scholarly knowledge of English literature, because that is essential to the story—in order to preserve his anonymity.[6] Prof. Lewis Ruskin, let us call him, drove his car at high speed into a large concrete abutment at the edge of a college parking lot while extremely drunk. He said later, "I thought it was an empty parking space." He had numerous broken bones and had one leg crushed so badly that it had to be amputated above the knee. It was a great tragedy. I had great respect for the man, both as a scholar and as a kind and decent human being.

This was around ten or twelve years ago. Lewis was an English teacher at a little college with ivy-covered brick buildings in a small city in Indiana, and was a renowned expert on novels and short stories from the American South: William Faulkner, Robert Penn Warren, and so on. He himself had been born and brought up in Monticello, Georgia, where his family resided in a large but rather weatherbeaten antebellum mansion with faded white columns in front. He was a short, wiry little man with reddish hair flecked with gray and a ruddy complexion. He had developed a reputation over the years for drinking heavily at faculty parties, but at least during the earlier parts of the evening he could sit and spin yarns and tell fascinating tales, in his soft, educated southern drawl, for the younger professors. But often by the end of the party, another faculty member would have to drive him home, then watch as he wandered around in his front yard, trying to figure out where his own front door was.

His drinking unfortunately had gotten progressively worse, and by the time of the accident, he was showing up to lecture in front of classes obviously disoriented and sometimes slurring his speech. At the last graduation ceremony, he had been so drunk that he had staggered in a zig-zag as he tried to walk in the faculty procession; he caught his black robe on a stanchion, pulled until it tore loose with a loud ripping sound, then tumbled off the platform in front of all the assembled graduates and their parents. As he lay on the floor he blurted out, loud enough for half the auditorium to hear him, "But like the Southland, I will rise again!"

The automobile accident that crippled him came a month or so after that, during the summer vacation. Several people who were involved in alcoholism treatment showed up at his hospital room several days after his accident, figuring that now, if ever, Doc Lewis might be willing to admit that it could do him some good to join A.A. and begin doing something about his drinking! Calculating that he might, in his arrogance, simply brush aside an ordinary group trying to carry out an intervention with him, they had carefully assembled a blue-ribbon company composed of a retired Naval officer who had commanded nuclear submarines, a New Yorker who had been a major executive with the William Randolph Hearst newspaper chain, another man who was one of the three best psychotherapists in northern Indiana, and a woman who was one of the best psychiatric nurses in town. The first two men had helped found one of the best alcoholism and drug addiction centers in the South Bend area, and the two mental health professionals worked at another major treatment center in the region.

They also invited me to come along. They reckoned that, with this group, they could surely answer any question he threw at them!

Literary criticism and the stories in the Big Book

But Lewis threw us a curve none of us was prepared for. Someone had given him a copy of the third edition of the Big Book of Alcoholics Anonymous,[7] and he had read through the whole book. The first 164 pages lay out an outline of how the program works, but then the remainder of this rather large book is made up of a number of little stories, each one several pages long, in which various Alcoholics Anonymous members tell the story of how they were led into greater and greater horror and degradation by compulsive drinking, until finally they encountered A.A. and the spiritual program it offered, and were able, not only to stop drinking, but also to find a more peaceful and serene and joyous life than any of them had ever experienced before.

After all of us had gathered in Doc Lewis's hospital room, to everyone's surprise, instead of wanting to discuss alcoholism, he began giving us a lecture on literary criticism. "These will not work as short stories," he proclaimed disparagingly. "The person's life is terrible, then suddenly it gets wonderful, and there is no explanation, no advance setting up of the forces that will come together to produce this change. This does not follow acceptable canons of good writing."

Our attempt at an intervention continued to go downhill from there, I am sorry to say. He was in such deep denial about the seriousness of his problem, that he simply brushed aside all of the numerous examples that the group gave him of the troubles he had gotten into with his drinking. The psychiatric nurse pointed out that the frequent spastic jerky movements of Doc Lewis's eyeballs were evidence that brain damage had already occurred, but that too seemed to make no impression on him. At one point he began complaining about his long-suffering wife and declared that he would not be drinking the way he had, if he had just been able to get enough sex. In spite of the tragic nature of the situation, it was difficult for the group not to burst out with loud and boisterous laughter at that point—in fact, if he had said that in an A.A. meeting, that is probably what would have happened—because many an A.A. member had discovered by personal experience that even engaging in gross sexual promiscuity had not stopped him or her from drinking!

We finally gave us and walked away from his hospital room, totally unsuccessful in our attempt to be of help, and feeling very sad for him. Doc Lewis went back to his drinking, and with his mind once more befuddled by alcohol, returned to simply drifting along through life in the continual resentment, regret, self-pity, and feelings of futility and failure which accompany chronic alcoholism.

The mysterious x-factor

So the intervention was unsuccessful, and the outcome was sad. In the days that followed, however, that one comment which Doc Lewis had made stuck with me forcefully. He had in fact made a valuable point, even if he himself totally failed to realize the conclusions that he should have drawn from it. And it was not just the brief autobiographical tales at the back of the Big Book which were called into question, for in fact, across the board, real stories about real spiritual conversions do not fit the accepted canons of western literature. As Lewis himself complained, "The person's life is terrible, then suddenly it gets wonderful, and there is no explanation."

Going all the way back to Aristotle's *Poetics*, it has been understood in western literature that in a proper story, each separate event which is related in the telling of the tale, creates a situation which then logically and naturally leads into the next event, setting up a tight chain of cause and effect that leads from the beginning of the story all the way to its conclusion. After hearing the story, we then walk away feeling satisfied. We can explain everything that happened, so that whether it was good or ill, everything made sense. The *Poetics* is still one of the greatest philosophical discussions of the nature of good literary composition which has ever been written.

Now there is one odd little sentence in Aristotle's work, tossed in as an aside at one point, which hardly anyone ever notices or thinks about seriously. Aristotle commented that this kind of tight logical interconnection, where the entire story hangs together in strict cause-and-effect sequence, only happened in fiction. He went on to say that it was impossible to write a philosophical work about writing history—that is, writing about things that happened in real life as opposed to creating fiction—because real life, to his careful philosophical mind, was so often totally illogical.

The great Greek tragedies which were written back in Aristotle's time by authors like Sophocles, Aeschylus, and Euripides were fiction (not history or true stories), so the authors were able to follow the Aristotelian rule for setting up proper plots. At the beginning of the play, a situation is set up where the perceptions of the tragic hero—what the hero thinks is going on, and how the hero believes that he or she absolutely *must* act in that kind of context—are going to drive that poor person to a tragic doom. The cause and effect sequence is going to be totally logical and completely inexorable. Figures called "warners" always appear, who attempt to warn the tragic hero about what is going to happen, but the doomed hero, locked into his or her own distorted perceptions of the world, remains in total denial and pays these warnings no heed.

At the beginning of the *Oedipus Tyrannus*, for example, the warner Teiresias explains to Oedipus exactly what is going on and everything that is going to happen, but the tyrant is so locked into his own distorted perceptions of the world, that he cannot hear a word the prophet is saying. By the latter part of the play, poor Oedipus is the last person left in the play who cannot see the disaster to which his actions are going to lead.

Conversion stories on the other hand—all truthful accounts of successful conversions which take place in real life—are "anti-tragedies," if we might coin a phrase. Each of the alcoholics whose stories appeared at the end of the Big Book started out like the tragic figure of Oedipus, obviously doomed to a bitter end in a way which was totally logical, completely rational, and absolutely inevitable. Every human power to which that doomed soul had turned had proven unable to help, whether it was a spouse, a psychiatrist, a physician, or a pastor.

But then, as Doc Lewis noted, something unexpected and illogical happens: "The person's life is terrible, then suddenly it gets wonderful." And the issue for the literary critic is that "there is no explanation" for this totally unexpected turn of events. The most important part of the story appears to make no sense at all.

Some mysterious x-factor appears in the story at that point. Something intervenes "from outside" into the familiar this-worldly sequence of events, and produces something inexplicable.[8] That is the power of God's grace. Since God is not part of the natural world, but exists in a transcendent realm which is above and beyond the world of nature, God cannot be included in the this-worldly analysis of cause and effect. In the life story of a person who has undergone a genuine conversion or psychic change, the act of God's grace has to appear as an unexplainable divergence at that point from the logical course of events.

Only the *super*-natural in the original sense of the word (not Halloween-night ghoulies and ghosties, but that which transcends and goes beyond the ordinary laws of nature) can intervene in the *natural* course of the disease of alcoholism, where the person's mind and character and body progressively disintegrate until he or she is either dead or locked up in a sanitarium or penitentiary. And since *de supernaturalibus non est explicatio naturalis* (there can be no natural explanation of things which are intrinsically, in their very character, super-natural) the cryptic x in the x-factor must remain locked in mystery.

Karl Barth

The Swiss theologian Karl Barth, who was one of the two most important Christian theologians in the period right after the First World War, put this concept of the God who is the *ganz Anders*—the Wholly Other who intervenes into the story from without—at the very center of his theological system. His foremost American follower, Reinhold Niebuhr, was teaching at Union Theological Seminary in New York City at the same time that Alcoholics Anonymous was being founded in that city. The famous German-born theologian Paul Tillich was also teaching at Union by that point, and he too insisted that the real God was "the God beyond God" who appears after we have hit bottom, when the God of our childhood fantasies and facile intellectual theories collapses in ruins.[9]

The Scottish theologian John Baillie, in his oft-reprinted and very wise little book, *Our Knowledge of God*, was impressed by the similarities he saw between the ideas of Karl Barth and Frank Buchman, the man who founded the Oxford Group during the period when Barth was beginning his rise to fame. Buchman of course moved in the kind of world theological circles in which Barth's writings were well known and extremely influential. This observation is significant for A.A. history because the Alcoholics Anonymous movement began as simply a small circle of recovering alcoholics within the Oxford Group during the latter 1930's.[10]

In the book which first brought Barth to the world's attention, his commentary on the Apostle Paul's epistle to the Romans, he likened the act of God's grace (the "speaking of the Word of God," as he called it) to a bomb explosion. The historical analysis of the act, after the event, could provide no more than a description of the houses and buildings and landscape as it was before the bomb went off, and of the bomb crater and the totally changed landscape after the explosion. But the living experience of having seen the bomb go off could not be genuinely comprehended by anyone who was not there as a participant.[11]

Karl Barth went on in the *Epistle to the Romans* to state firmly that any attempt to produce a philosophical or psychological system which would totally "make sense" of the action of God's grace on the human spirit would therefore necessarily, in the process, turn God into an idolatrous figment of the human imagination. Whenever someone tries to domesticate God, to bring him into the fenced-in pastures of human concepts and this-worldly categories, what he invariably ends up with is no longer God but an idol, the work of human minds and hands. Worshiping idols never did anyone any good, even if the worshiper's self-delusion sometimes makes it temporarily seem so. For real human problems one needs real divine grace, which in turn requires a real God—a God who is (so to speak) wild and free, who will not just sit down where you place him, and turn this way and that at your bidding, in the manner of a stone statue in an ancient pagan temple.

The transcendent God

Let us look carefully at some of the reasons why the real God cannot be turned into an object in the natural world, the world which we investigate by means of the natural sciences, in case you the reader are still having difficulty grasping the real issue here.

The natural sciences provide us with logical explanations of why natural events happen, along with some predictive power, by setting up mathematical equations: $F = ma$, $E = mc^2$, and so on. Let us now look at the classical attributes of God. One of these is that God is infinite. But attempting to multiply or divide a number by infinity is mathematical nonsense. Infinity plus 365 is not "bigger" than infinity plus 7, if these statements mean anything at all. Infinity is not a number but a process which continues without limit.

In order to calculate how an event is going to take place, the laws of physics require us to indicate where an object is in space in terms of some kind of xyz coordinates. But in classical theology, God is omnipresent, that is, everywhere. Or more strictly speaking, God

15

is not in time and space at all, so that God is both everywhere and nowhere. Again we are left in the situation where, if God is involved, we have no way of indicating that in our mathematical equations.

Modern physicists tell us that the world of nature in which we live had a beginning in time. It burst into existence in what they call the Big Bang, where all the matter and energy in the physical universe—along with time and space itself—came simultaneously out of nothing. What was there before the Big Bang? That was the ground of Being, which has always existed, continues to exist as that which keeps our present physical universe in existence, and will always exist, for it exists by necessity.

This ground of Being cannot obey the normal laws of physics. The laws of thermodynamics—which everything in the physical universe must obey—include the law of entropy. This scientific law was first worked out when Watt and others were trying to build the first steam engines. Proof of its validity first appeared when they were able to engineer steam engines, using these newly discovered laws of thermodynamics, which were efficient enough to power railroad locomotives and paddlewheel steamboats. The law of entropy says that all energy sources eventually run down. As we use our flashlights, the battery progressively runs down, until finally the light dims and fades away. When we burn fossil fuels like oil and gas and coal for energy, even if we attempt to save all the ashes and gases which are the combustion products, we cannot reuse these materials to run our automobiles another few miles or produce another few kilowatts of electricity from our generators. Eventually the sun up in the sky will use up all its nuclear fuel and cease emitting light and heat, and finally everything in our universe will collapse into the random movement of particles which have used up all their free energy, so that nothing meaningful will ever be able to happen again.

The ground of Being however cannot be subject to the law of entropy, or else there would be no physical universe or anything else at all. So the ground of Being is omnipotent (to use the classical language), that is, seems effectively to have unlimited sources of energy.

The ground of Being is what the philosophical theologians of traditional western theism—in Judaism, Christianity, and Islam all three—have always called God.[12] So if it is acts of grace coming from the real God—the transcendent ground of all Being—which produce real conversion and genuine psychic change, sufficient to pull us back from our otherwise inevitable plunge down the path of tragic downfall, then of necessity any true act of grace must appear in the this-worldly narrative of events as a mysterious x-factor whose reality is obvious, but which cannot be portrayed as the logical consequence of the preceding events.

Creating a true theistic philosophy

Karl Barth, whom we mentioned earlier, made another interesting observation. He pointed out that over the preceding two and a half centuries, beginning with John Locke's *Essay Concerning Human Understanding* in 1690, the western world had seen the creation of a large number of philosophical systems which were constructed in such a way that there was in fact no room for any kind of God anywhere in the system. The definitions which were given about what counted as evidence and what was possible, removed any way of bringing God as an active participant into the system. They were cast in the form of what I would call "reductive naturalisms." Only things in the natural world were regarded as "real," and anything else was pushed aside as imagination, illusion, subjectivism, and wish fulfillment fantasy.

Barth went on to say that the history of Christian theology during those same centuries had seen theologian after theologian begin by accepting the basic ground rules of one of those reductive philosophical systems, and then exerting all of his or her intellectual ability in the attempt to smuggle God back into the system somehow. And of course it could not be done, other than by falling into fuzzy thinking, or by the kind of pure subjectivism which undercut any kind of attempt to talk about the world intelligently, or by a highly emotional sentimentality which reduced spirituality to the level of commercial greeting cards with pictures of furry bunnies and baby kittens and cute little elves peeking over toadstools.

If we are to create a viable philosophical theology for the modern world, then we must build the reality of God into the very framework of the system, as a basic and necessary constituent part of both its ontology and its epistemology. That is what this book will be attempting to do. We will not try to "prove" (on the grounds of a philosophical system which had no God in it in the first place) that conversions are produced by the grace of God acting on the human psyche. Instead we will say that a true empirical or pragmatic philosophical system must start with the observation that stories of real conversion experiences down through history—real psychic changes, or "changed lives," or spiritual transformations, or the major remaking of human character, or whatever you want to call them—display the intrusion, into the this-worldly sequence of events, of something totally alien and completely external to this world. And this other-worldly power—whose existence has to be real because the effects which we see are objectively real and totally concrete—we shall call God.

Science vs. fiction

For the past three centuries, innumerable self-styled intellectuals in the western world have attempted to explain away conversion experiences by giving facile psychological or sociological or even (in the case of the Marxists) economic reasons for why the sweeping changes in that human being's character occurred. My observation is that intellectuals of this sort are so desperate to believe that there is no God, that they are willing to grasp at the most naive kinds of pseudo-explanations. They will take an incredibly complex human personality, like St. Augustine's or John Wesley's or Bill Wilson's, and try to pretend that they have "explained" a total character change in that person—a person who was almost certainly far more intelligent and wise in the ways of the world than them!—on the grounds of something either truly trivial or totally unbelievable to an objective observer.

18

Only someone incredibly naive, or someone with a deeply pathological need to believe that God does not exist, could buy any of the intellectualizing pseudo-explanations that I have read over almost fifty years of reading that kind of thing. Or—and here is a third possibility—someone with a profound control neurosis who begins to feel panicky if he or she cannot give a full logical explanation about the way each event in the conversion story leads by strict cause-effect sequence into the next. A pathological control neurosis lies at the bottom of a good deal of human misery and unhappiness.

But let us remember what that shrewd observer Aristotle said in his *Poetics*. While claiming to be people who think about the world "scientifically," what they really want is fiction, not the real historical world. Because as Aristotle pointed out, it is only in fiction that the world proceeds so logically. It never does in real life.

The God who saves

So this is the path which we are going to follow in this book. Instead of trying to explain God away and create a fictional world in which everything proceeds in tidy, rational fashion at all times, where we can give a this-worldly reason for everything that happens, we are going to begin by accepting the reality of God and the demonstrated reality of the way God works in conversion.

The modern evangelical movement began when Jonathan Edwards, a Congregationalist pastor in colonial New England back in the 1730's, discovered—in spite of the fact that the best psychology of the period said that it was impossible—that he had devised a way of preaching which was producing real changes in human character. These changes in attitude and behavior were objectively verifiable. Every observer who looked at these men and women who had had conversions reported that they had been turned into a totally different kind of person. People who had been leading bad and destructive lives were now leading good and positive lives. When a copy of the book he wrote got across the Atlantic and fell into the hands of John Wesley, who was teaching at Oxford University in England (as we mentioned earlier), the latter tried out these new methods on coal miners and their families in Bristol, preaching to them in the open fields, and discovered to his amazement that people were also being changed before his eyes, and that the change was an objective reality, and was not imaginary or subjective.

The Oxford Group in the 1920's and Alcoholics Anonymous in the 1930's went back to what Edwards and Wesley had discovered in the 1730's and demonstrated that the same thing happened when one used their methods in the modern world. When men and women could be persuaded to call upon the help of a higher power who dwelt outside the natural realm, their lives were changed in dramatic ways. Particularly in the A.A. experience, men and women whose lives were clearly going down the path to a deeply tragic doom, experienced psychic changes so profound, that at first no one could believe it who had not seen it. It seemed impossible, but empirical evidence and pragmatic experience proved that it was real. Seeing is believing. One cannot deny the repeated evidence of one's own senses.

Nevertheless, continuously throughout the last sixty-five years, small numbers of psychiatrists and psychotherapists have attempted to explain away the A.A. experience, and replicate it through the use of psychological tricks that would not involve any appeal to a God or higher power. Again and again in the scholarly literature I have seen them claiming a 2% or 3% success rate for their secular, nontheistic recovery programs. On the other hand, I have personally known thousands and thousands of recovered alcoholics, and in all the cases I have seen, roughly 1% got sober by going to a Protestant evangelical church, another 1% got sober simply by an act of pure will power, and all the other 98% got sober through A.A. Neither I nor anyone in the field whom I have asked about this has ever seen a genuine hard core chronic alcoholic get sober and stay sober for a significant length of time (at least three years, and proof of a five year survival rate would be even more impressive) simply and only by going to a psychiatrist or psychotherapist.

I have no idea why psychiatrists and psychotherapists keep making the claim that they are able to obtain a 2% to 3% success rate in treating alcoholism, but I suspect that it is partly due to their doing no more than a six-month or nine-month follow-up on their patients, and partly due to their allowing the alcoholics themselves to tell them whether they are or are not doing O.K. The problem here is that one subgroup of chronic alcoholics can stay away from the bottle for a few month's time. The problem is that they always eventually go back to the bottle again, and each episode becomes progressively worse. And allowing the alcoholics themselves to tell you over the telephone whether they are doing all right is something that only a fool would believe! The head of one excellent and highly successful A.A.-based treatment program on the West Coast—a man who is himself a recovered alcoholic who descended to the point where he was living on skid row before he finally came into A.A.—once commented to an A.A. audience on that technique (the telephone survey) for measuring the success of a treatment philosophy: "They told the psychiatrist over the telephone that they were doing just fine, and he believed them? Hell, on my worst day drinking I would have told him that!" And the whole A.A. audience broke out into loud and uproarious laughter.

How do psychiatrists and psychotherapists of this sort fool themselves into believing this sort of flimsy evidence and convince themselves that it is significant? All we can say is that there are some self-styled intellectuals whose desire to deny God's existence is so great, that they can apparently delude themselves into believing almost anything that seems to support their denial. They want the comfort of a piece of fiction, not the harsh realities of the real world.

In the real world, nevertheless, countless alcoholics have gone to A.A. meetings, and have turned their wills and their lives over to the care of a higher power, a God who totally transcends the realm of physical nature. They will be glad to tell you the stories—completely verifiable if you desire to check them out—of the way they transformed their lives. You can talk to men and women who have been sober and living that way of life for twenty years, thirty years, forty years, fifty years or more, all the way to the end of their lives. That is the reality which this book will explore. God is real, and grace is real.

This book will explore what we *can* say about what God is and how we can know God, because there are in fact a good many things that we *can* say, and ways that we can make better sense out of what we can and cannot know about God. But we will build this philosophical system on two necessary starting principles: (1) God is real and grace is real and this has to be built into your system of thought from the very starting point. (2) God must nevertheless always remain to a considerable degree an "x-factor," a mysterious power who intervenes in our lives in ways that we can neither fully explain, nor predict nor control.

One of the best pastors I have ever known is an incredibly wise, silver-haired woman in Marion, Indiana, a woman filled with love and compassion for all, who speaks gently and with kindness to everyone she encounters. When you meet her, she almost seems to glow with light. She begins speaking to her congregation every Sunday with the simple words, "Let God be God. And let God's people be God's people." Let that be the motto of this book.

Chapter 2

Mount Sinai and the Burning Bush

In this second chapter, let us look at another very famous conversion story—and it begins as a conversion story, even though most sermons on it and theological discussions about it tend to forget that aspect of it. The central figure in this story is Moses. His two major encounters with God—first in the story of the Burning Bush, which occurred before he led the Israelites out of Egypt, and then in the story of his ascent up Mount Sinai to receive the Law, which happened after the Israelites had successfully made their escape—were central to the basic understanding of God in both Judaism and Christianity. We see Christian spiritual writers writing long commentaries on the ascent of Mount Sinai as early as St. Gregory of Nyssa and St. Denis in the fourth and fifth centuries.

When Moses encountered God for the first time, in the story of the Burning Bush, he was a man who had lost everything. He had once held a high position in the court of the Egyptian pharaoh, but was now a fugitive from justice, an escaped murderer who had been forced to seek refuge among the desert nomads, who were regarded in the ancient world as the lowest of the low. At this low point, where Moses' life seemed to have hit rock bottom, God reached out to him in an astonishing way. It is in fact a conversion story, because Moses did not know God at that point. Almost his first question was, "Who are you?" He knew that his ancestors had worshiped a God, but he seems to have had very little knowledge about who that God was. It was at this point in the tale that the mysterious x-factor spoke for himself. This is the part that we will need to focus on—the words which God spoke to Moses out of the Burning Bush, and what they imply about what we can and cannot know about him.

Moses' second major encounter with God has provided an extended metaphor for discussing the way we come to know God, for a long and fascinating series of Christian spiritual teachers over the past two thousand years. Along with the vivid images in the Song of Songs, it has furnished one of the three or four most important clusters of metaphors and symbols in the Christian spiritual tradition. Moses was going to have a much more profound experience of God this time, and in order to do that, he had to leave the normal world behind and walk into the dark cloud which now covered the slopes of Mount Sinai. The first time he met God on that mountain, it had been in bright daylight and he had seen a vision of an even brighter heavenly Light. But this time he met God in pitch blackness. And it was there in the dark that he heard God's voice giving him a much fuller message, the full message of salvation, both for him and for his people. An English spiritual writer from the medieval Catholic period (the fourteenth century) called this the Cloud of Unknowing. All of the authors who have commented on this story, in whatever century they lived, have stressed the way in which we must first enter a realm of ignorance and nothingness, in which all our previous claims of knowledge about ourselves and the universe and God have been stripped away, before we can begin to hear the fullness of God's message to us, and receive a totally new way of thinking about the world.

The x-factor which saves us is real, it turns our lives around and creates a new and far better kind of life for us, and it even allows us to enter its presnce, but it never loses its intrinsic mystery, not even for a spiritual giant like Moses. No human beings are allowed to climb the Mountain of God and truly speak with God, who have not cast aside all their claims to "explain" God in terms of the kinds of scientific reasoning and natural philosophy and psychology which we employ for analyzing and describing the ordinary events of this world.

Moses out in the desert sees the light

With this introduction in mind, let us now turn to the book of
Exodus in the Hebrew Bible (the Christian Old Testament) and see
how the story of Moses is told. The opening chapter explains how the
Israelites had been put into slave labor camps in Egypt, and forced to
make bricks for the pharaoh's building projects. Moses, even though
an Israelite, had gained a position in the royal court of Egypt, and had
escaped that fate. But when he saw an Egyptian forced labor gang
boss savagely beating one of his fellow tribesman, he fell into a rage
and attacked the Egyptian and killed him. He had to flee the country
and hide out somewhere out of reach of the Egyptian authorities. He
ended up finding sanctuary with a tribe of violent desert nomads called
the Midianites, who gave him a job herding sheep and serving in the
band of warriors which they used for fighting the other tribes in that
part of the desert.

In America and northern Europe, when we try to conjure up an
image of human beings living in the most primitive possible state
of existence, we think of cave men, a crude and brutish lot. Among
civilized people in the ancient Mediterranean world, it was the desert
nomads who were thought of that way They were regarded as thieves,
robbers, and murderers, who would slit your throat if they thought
you had a few coins in your purse, and steal anything that was not kept
locked or under guard. When a band visited your area, they traded
wool, goatskins, and cheese for wheat and olive oil, and perhaps a few
handfuls of raisins or dried figs or dates for a treat. You watched them
every second while the basic business transaction was carried out, and
then you encouraged them to be on their way back out into the desert
again, speedily.

When Moses appeared in the part of the desert where the nomadic
tribe called the Midianites held the water and grazing rights, dressed
in Egyptian garb, he must have been a strange and startling sight. But
when it finally came out that he was an escaped murderer, fleeing from
the law, they must have chuckled with glee, for a man who had already

made his first kill would be a welcome addition to their little warrior band which they used for raids on neighboring tribes.

From Moses' point of view, he had indeed hit bottom. He had once lived in a palace in the greatest civilization of the entire area, and now he was reduced to sleeping on the ground in a tent made out of cloth woven from goat hair, and reminding the occupant by the pungent odor, where the hair in the cloth had come from. It should also be noted that, except for the random moments of sheer terror when a war band from a neighboring tribe attacked, or one of the lions which still roamed the area in that century tried to seize a lamb or a kid and carry it off for dinner, the life of a shepherd, which mostly consisted of sitting on the rocky ground and watching sheep and goats munch grass, has to be one of the most boring ways ever devised for spending monotonous days and weeks and months, seemingly without end. The Sinai Peninsula is not a romantic desert of flowing sand dunes, but a stark wasteland of dark reddish rocks and crags and cliffs, where you pick your way on narrow pathways through the valleys and ravines, over fallen rocks and stones, in the midst of a constant oven-like heat.

We can easily imagine the thoughts which filled his mind, the bitter sense of a wasted life, of the futility of existence, of rage at the Egyptians, and rage perhaps also at himself, for having lost his temper so dangerously. And there was no meaningful future for him anymore, not for someone raised in the bustling civilized life of Egypt, with its great temples and palaces, and markets teeming with every delicacy, and books to read, and educated people to talk to.

It was while he was watching the flock of sheep and goats to which he had been assigned, on the barren, rocky slopes of Mount Sinai (Exodus 3:1), that the strange event occurred. He suddenly saw what looked, as best he could describe it, as a desert bush bursting into flame. When a bone dry desert bush is set on fire, it literally almost explodes, as the dry leaves and twigs burst into fiery fragments that go shooting through the air. But in this case, the flashes of sparkling light continued and continued.

One of my Hebrew professors in seminary once pointed out to us students, quite correctly, that "if anyone thinks he could have lit his cigar off the burning bush, he does not understand at all what the story was saying." The light metaphor, in one form or another, is frequently used in religions around the world to describe the encounter with the sacred realm. When a small Protestant evangelical congregation sings lustily at a Wednesday evening service out in the countryside, "I saw the light, oh, I saw the light! No more darkness, no more night," if someone suggested to them that they could therefore switch off the electric lights in the sanctuary and continue to read their hymnals and bibles with no trouble, they would stare at the person in blank amazement. The metaphor of "divine light" does not normally refer to the kind of visible light emitted by the sun, the moon, and electric light bulbs.

We are told that what Moses "saw" was an angel, a *mal'ak* or divine "messenger" in Hebrew. C. S. Lewis, in his Perelandra trilogy, describes the appearance of an angel on a couple of occasions, in language which I believe accurately sums up what the ancient Hebrew author was trying to describe to us. Lewis' angel was like small, swiftly moving jewels of glittering light, which you could "see" out "there" in front of you at one level, while simultaneously being aware that it wasn't really "there" in the sense in which physical objects are "there." But it was a presence whose emotions you could feel, and which emitted an aura of power so great that you would not dare do anything but stand quietly and listen with the utmost respect.

I am who I am

The conversation with God (speaking through this angel) had barely begun, when Moses asked what, to him, was the most important question of all: "What is your name?" Moses wanted to write a theology! He wanted to fit the voice from heaven into a nice, neat system of thought, where everything had labels and names and fit into proper categories, so he could then start figuring out how to manipulate and control the strange power. He wanted to be able to figure out all the rules, so that he could do such-and-such if he wanted the strange power to do thus-and-so, and would on the other hand, take great pains never to do such-and-such, which infuriated gods and goddesses and desert demons and genies and the other strange supernatural beings who lived out in the desert wastes.

We human beings, at all times and places down through history, believe that if we can put names and labels on everything, that we will be able to reduce all of these things to the natural order of reality with which we are accustomed to deal. We believe that if we can only do this, that we will be able to fit what is happening into a theological theory, or a philosophical theory, or a psychological theory, and then we will be back in control again. This can be a dangerous illusion, because the mysterious x-factor that saves us when we have fallen as low as Moses had fallen, can never be under our control. This was an illusion which God knew he had to disabuse Moses of, right on the spot.

So with a sort of divine shrug, the voice from the Burning Bush answered only, "I am who I am." (Exodus 3:14) The Hebrew phrase was *'ehyeh 'asher 'ehyeh*. The word *'ehyeh* in Hebrew is the first person singular imperfect of the verb to be, and the conjunction *'asher* is used in a way similar to English connectives like who, which, and what, so the three-word statement at first appears misleadingly simple. But ancient Hebrew did not have tenses like modern European languages do. In English, a verb has to be put in some form of the present tense, the past tense, or the future tense. In Hebrew, the two basic forms of the verb were very different, and were called the perfect and the imperfect. The imperfect form of the verb referred to something which was going on right now and had not been completed yet, or something which was not going to happen until sometime in the future, or something which happened in the past over and over again for a long period of time.

So in fact, in order to translate that simple three-word phrase into English, we would need at least three phrases:

I have always been who and what I have always been.

I am now who I am now.

I will become whoever or whatever I want to become.

Or in other words, the voice is telling Moses that he can appear under any name he wants to. It is made clear in the context of that part of the Bible, that he was already known under a variety of names to the Israelites and their kinsmen: some called him El Elyon, others called him El Shaddai, and the people of Jerusalem at that time called him Zedek. For Elijah on Mount Sinai many centuries later, he was the Bath Qol, the still, small voice, literally in Hebrew "the daughter of a voice." In later Judaism, people got around the problem in part by sometimes simply referring to him as Hashem, "the Name." It did not matter to the voice from the Burning Bush. And this in turn meant that God reserved the right to act in situations where the human beings involved did not even use the name "God" to describe what they were experiencing.

And yet at another level, the voice does tell Moses quite clearly who he is. He speaks in the first person singular, that is, he makes it clear that he is "I am" and not an "it." He is a deeply personal being. By the end of the story of Moses in the book of Exodus, after many subsequent adventures, he had become friends with the divine Voice, and talked with him all day long, throughout the day, "as a man speaks with his friend." (Exodus 33:11)

And the heavenly voice reveals himself as a figure of compassion. Almost the first words out of his mouth, at the beginning of the story of the Burning Bush, are the words "I have seen the misery of my people who are in Egypt. I have heard their cries under their taskmasters. I am totally aware of their sufferings, and I have come down to rescue them from the Egyptians." (Exod. 3:7–8)

So the mysterious x-factor who saves us is a person, not a thing, and a personal being who hears our cries of grief and sees our bitter sufferings and offers his help to lead us by his power out of our misery and suffering. Throughout the Hebrew Bible and the Christian New Testament, this higher power is portrayed as the one who hears and feels the cries of anguish of the downtrodden, the powerless, the enslaved, the hopeless, and the broken. The people he loves are the slave laborers in the prison camps, the widows and the orphans, the poor people without food or homes, the people who have to sleep in hedges and ditches and alleys, the resident aliens searching for jobs in a country where they barely know the language, the people dying with no one to hold their hands, the people rotting in dirty prisons, the prostitutes, the victims of abuse, and all the rest of the "outsiders." And the "proper people" in society look down on them with smugness and contempt, and murmur things like "but those people don't deserve help." And the voice from the Burning Bush says, "I didn't ask you that, I asked you to help them." And they murmur, "but they brought it on themselves because they were lazy and shiftless and immoral." And the voice from the Burning Bush says, "I didn't ask you that, I asked you to help them."

In our own world, the proper people in society looked down above all on drunks and drug addicts. "Punish them, scold them, fire them from their jobs, threaten them with hell fire!" They shouted at these alcoholics and addicts: "Just get hold of yourselves and show some will power!" But the light from the Burning Bush appeared once again in 1934, not to one of these proper people, simpering with their smugness, but to one of the lowest drunks in America, and said, "I am going to save you by sending you to save countless others. And I will lead all of you out of the house of bondage, and into a land flowing with milk and honey." And Bill W. was lifted up to the top of the Mountain of God, and felt the wind of the spirit blowing through him, and saw everything filled with the divine light. And he obeyed, and as is always the case—as with Moses or Mother Teresa of Calcutta or Albert Schweitzer or any of the others who have heard and obeyed the Heavenly Voice—it came to pass just as the divine power had promised.

The God of Abraham, Isaac, and Jacob

And the voice from heaven reminded Moses that his ancestors had been poor, struggling desert nomads just like the Midianites. Abraham, Isaac, and Jacob had been the ancient leaders of the little Israelite band which had wandered through the deserts of what is now Iraq, Syria, and Palestine. They had no money, they slept in tents on the bare ground, and everything they had smelled like sheep and goats. But he had gotten them through every difficulty that they encountered, as long as they trusted him, and were willing to venture into the unknown on his command, as a pure act of trust. Many centuries later, in the New Testament, the Apostle Paul used "the faith of Abraham" as his central example of the faith that saves. When Abraham was in the deserts of Syria, he told him to take his sheep and goats and "go south," down into the hill country of Palestine. And Abraham trusted God enough to pull up his tent stakes and head south, into the totally unknown. That is what the New Testament word "faith" really means, not believing in hundreds of theological doctrines and dogmas, but being willing to venture forth into the unknown, one step at a time, depending totally and utterly on God to tell us, when we have taken one step, what the next one is to be. The faith that saves is the faith of a desert nomad venturing into the unknown. That is the only way we can respond to a mysterious x-factor whose very nature is such that he must always remain locked in mystery.

During the early days of A.A. in northern Indiana, a colorful spiritual leader named Goshen Bill, a little black man with a glass eye and one wooden leg, and the longest, boniest fingers anyone had ever seen (he used to point them in your face or stick them in your chest), told the following tale. Once upon a time there were two men. One was a newcomer to the A.A. program, who kept on going back out and returning to the bottle, over and over again. He said that he was an atheist, and didn't believe in any kind of God. The other man was his sponsor, who had been sober for a long time, and prayed to God every morning and evening. "You have to pray if you want to get sober," he told the newcomer. "But who do I pray to? What? How?" And the newcomer kept on going back out and getting drunk. But finally one day, the newcomer fell down on his knees and looked up at heaven, and pointed at his sponsor and said, "Whoever it is helping that man, please help me." And Goshen Bill said that the newcomer never had another drink again after that day.

So the voice from the Burning Bush was telling Moses, "I'm the one who helped Abraham. I'm the one who helped Isaac. I'm the one who helped Jacob. That's all you need to know. If you want to say 'Whoever it was helped those three men, help me,' that's plenty good enough."

But it was time to quit trying to fit everything into names and categories and labels and theories. It didn't matter whether they were theological theories, or theories of natural science, or psychological theories. God was too big to fit into any of those. God is the power who disrupts and overturns the established order. As it says in the great revolutionary anthem called the Magnificat (Luke 1:46-53):

> My soul celebrates the Lord,
> and my spirit rejoices in God my Savior.
> For he has looked with favor
> on the humbleness of his servant.
> For see how, from now on,
> all generations will call me blessed.
> For the Powerful One has done great things for me,
> and holy is *Hashem*
> [the Name that is not a name].
> His *hesed* [merciful loving kindness]
> is for those who stand in awe of him,
> from generation to generation.
> He has shown the force of his arm;
> he has scattered the prideful
> in the thoughts of their hearts.
> He has cast down the powerful from their thrones,
> and lifted up the humble.
> He has filled the starving with good things,
> and the rich he has sent empty away.

We do not first figure out who and what God is, so that we can then decide whether or not we want to commit ourselves to him—or better yet, figure out a way around him so we can figure out how to save ourselves by ourselves. He is the power who disrupts all our careful plans, and sets to naught all our clever schemes. He is the x-factor which refuses to be domesticated and turned into our servant. And that is why, unfortunately, most human beings never take up the spiritual life with any real seriousness until they have lost everything they hold dear, and all of their most precious theories about the world and life have been proven to be utter failures. If it were not for our human pridefulness and arrogance—and fear of not being "in control"—this would not be necessary. But the only way to gain God's help is on God's terms, and his terms do not involve elaborate explanations about who he is and how he works. "If you don't want my help, there's the door."

The altar to the Agnôstô Theô, the Unknown God

Before we go back to Moses' story, let us insert another little story, this one from the New Testament. The book of Acts, in chapter seventeen, tells about the Apostle Paul's visit to the city of Athens in Greece. He noticed statues of all the Greek gods and goddesses everywhere he looked: Zeus, Athena, Apollo, Artemis, Aphrodite, and so on. These ancient Athenians were people who wanted to give names to their gods and describe them in detail, which is something we human beings almost automatically seem to want to do, including so many of the men and women who come into the twelve step program today. "Before I can turn my will and my life over to the care of God, first I have to know what he looks like! I need *a theory of God*. Otherwise, I'm not going to do that." The fallen human heart is a naturally pagan thing. What we need to remember however, is that if the A.A. old timers drew you a picture of God of the sort you keep on asking for, the picture they handed you would not be God. It would only be an idol, an image constructed by human hands and ideas. It would be incapable of giving you any help at all. "A theory of God" of that sort would do you no more good, in terms of getting you sober, than buying a little concrete statue of one of the Greek gods or goddesses from a roadside vendor, and setting it up in your back yard and planting flowers around it. It might look nice, but it wouldn't have the power to get you sober.

The Apostle Paul had been walking around the ancient city of Athens, and had noted all of these futile attempts that people had made to save themselves, by trying to figure out how to draw an accurate picture of God. And finally he got an opportunity to begin preaching to the Athenians. He noted that, amongst all this statuary, he had noticed that they had one strange little altar. There was no statue, no image, not even a name. Instead there was inscribed on the altar the simple words, *Agnôstô Theô*, "To an Unknown God." So he began preaching to them about this strange Anonymous God (Acts 17:23-28):

> What therefore you worship as unknown, this I proclaim to you. The God who made the world and everything in it, he who is Lord of heaven and earth, does not live in shrines made by human hands, nor is he served by human hands, as though he needed anything, since he himself gives to all mortals life and breath and all things .... He is not far from each one of us, for "in him we live and move and have our being."

And Paul's message makes some people uncomfortable, even to this day. You don't need to go to church to find God. The real God doesn't need a church building to live in. You don't need to put money into the collection plate at church in order to "pay" for God's services. The real God doesn't need money! You don't need to go into a church and sing special hymns and chants, and listen to music that sounds all "churchy." If you think that, you are as bad as the ancient Athenians whom Paul was scolding. You meet the real God in the desert, in the

34

marketplace at Athens, wherever you might be. We exist "in" God at all times, in the same way that fish live in the ocean. In the case of the fish, the ocean is always there surrounding them at all times. In our case, God's presence is always here surrounding us at all times: "in him we live and move and have our being."

The ancient Athenians believed themselves to be far too smart for that. They loved to discuss psychology and physics and philosophy. How ignorant this Paul fellow was! He couldn't explain anything to them the way they wanted it explained.

Most of these proud philosophers walked away, but one stayed, a man named St. Denis (Dionysius in Greek, see Acts 17:34). St. Denis understood what Paul was saying about the Anonymous God, the mysterious x-factor, the unknowable God in whom we live and move and have our being, who saves our souls from destruction. St. Denis was converted on that day. This is another little conversion story for us to think about. Newcomers to the twelve step program frequently badger the old timers continually, saying in effect, "If you would just explain to me adequately who and what this Higher Power is that you keep talking about, then I might be willing to be converted into becoming a believer in this Higher Power." But that was not what the Apostle Paul did when he was preaching to the proud intellectuals of ancient Athens, the intellectual center of the ancient world. Paul told them, "You're looking in the wrong place. It's over there, where that little nondescript altar is that you've been ignoring, the one with no picture of God, no description of God, just the simple words *Agnôstô Theô*. That's the real altar of God. The Anonymous God."

Paul was not being perverse, and these proud intellectuals to whom he was preaching were not nearly as intelligent and knowledgeable about the higher reaches of philosophy as they thought they were. The central theological problem arises here because no human language can ever adequately describe who and what God really is. The real God is infinite and eternal. You cannot stick "infinity" as one of the variables into a mathematical equation like the physicists use and get an intelligible answer. When one writes equations like $E = mc^2$ and $F = ma$, one cannot set one of the variables at infinity and calculate the value of the others. God's *ousia* (his essential Being) lies outside the box of space and time in which we human beings are compelled to think. The real God is far more powerful than the whole rest of the visible universe put together, and is not bound by the laws of physics which apply to everything else in the universe, such as the laws of thermodynamics for example, particularly the law of entropy.

If it is a real God that we are talking about—and that is the only kind of God who is going to have the power to save us when all our natural human abilities have failed us—then this will of necessity be a God to whom our normal scientific formulas and explanatory methods will not apply. That is the essential choice which is laid before a newcomer to the twelve step program. If you want a God whom you can explain and understand, this kind of God will not have the power to save you from your obsessive and compulsive drive towards total self-destruction. If you want a God who will have the power to stop your downward plunge and start lifting you back up again, it will have to be a God whom you would never have the power to fully explain or understand.

What can be done to help newcomers, lost and bewildered, and lacking any knowledge of where to turn next? What we can do is to come up with metaphors and symbols (like referring to God as the x-factor in conversion) which point towards God, and tell us which way to look and listen. If the metaphors and symbols are good ones, these newcomers will ultimately come into immediate personal contact with God's presence, in a way that they can feel and powerfully intuit.[13]

And perhaps even more importantly, we can tell them things to do. Pray in the morning and evening, do a moral self-inventory, make amends to those whom you have harmed, and so on. The twelve step program is a list of things to do, not a list of things to analyze intellectually. After we have done each of these steps—but only afterwards—we will understand what that step was designed to teach us. Action first, then understanding, not vice versa.

Of necessity, we must stand before the altar with the simple inscription *Agnôstô Theô*, the altar to the Anonymous God. When we ask his name, he simply tells us, "I am who I am." But we do know that he is a person who says "I" when he speaks to us, not some impersonal "it" which we can analyze and dissect and slice up and put on microscope slides. And we can walk into a twelve step meeting (particularly an A.A. or N.A. meeting) and say to ourselves, "Whatever this mysterious x-factor is, it has to be real, because there are people walking around here alive who should have been *dead*, and dead long before this point." Or we can read the Bible, and say to ourselves, "Whatever this higher power is, it was the power which guided Abraham, Isaac, and Jacob; it was the power which saved Moses; it was the power which grasped the Apostle Paul and St. Denis."

And at that point, all I have to pray is, "Whoever it was saved all these people, I'm praying to you now. Whoever you are, please save me too." This God—the Anonymous God—is the only God who actually has the power to save us, when we have hit absolute bottom and have no hope left in this world of any sort.

The Cloud of Unknowing: passing through the Dark Night of the Soul

But let us return to the story of Moses. After leading the Israelites out of Egypt, Moses guided them back to Mount Sinai. The mountain became covered with a dense, dark cloud (Exodus 19-20 and 24). Moses went up the mountain and into the thickest part of the cloud, where it was pitch black, with no light to see by at all. That was when God spoke to him, and gave him and the Israelites a *nomos*, a moral code, a new set of values to live by. It centered on the Ten Commandments and the Two Great Commandments: "You shall love the Lord your God with all your heart, and with all your soul, and with all your might," and "you shall love your neighbor as yourself" (Deuteronomy 6:5 and Leviticus 19:18).

In the western spiritual tradition, this part of Moses' story was for many centuries regarded as one of the key metaphors and symbols for talking about the spiritual life. As we enter the spiritual life, we too (like Moses) have to enter the dark cloud, metaphorically speaking, in order to climb up the mountain of God.

This image was at the very heart of the spiritual system taught by a Christian author who wrote a number of major works around 500 A.D. under the pseudonym of Dionysius the Areopagite. This pen name was a reference to the story of the Apostle Paul preaching in Athens about the Unknown God, where this was the name of one of the few Greek philosophers who was willing to pay serious attention to Paul's message. The Middle Ages knew this mysterious and anonymous author as "St. Denis." What makes St. Denis so important is that he was, along with St. Augustine, one of the four or five most formative figures in the history of Christian theology. A good deal of western mysticism followed in St. Denis' footsteps, not only throughout the Middle Ages, but later on as well, where figures like St. John of the Cross in the sixteenth century and Thomas Merton in the twentieth century were deeply influenced by St. Denis' ideas.

One of St. Denis' followers was a famous medieval English spiritual writer from the fourteenth century who wrote about the spiritual life in a work called *The Cloud of Unknowing*. This is such a nice term for referring to the central metaphor, that I will borrow it and use it in what I am writing here. It is also sometimes called the Dark Night of the Soul.

The first step and hitting bottom

In order to work the twelve steps, we first have to "hit bottom" in some way. Hitting bottom is entering the Cloud of Unknowing. We have to get to the point where all of our old ideas about the world and life and God have become totally unworkable, so that we see the very fabric of our life crashing down around us. The first step begins by talking about the dark thing that has enslaved us: alcohol, drugs, compulsive overeating, gambling, codependent relationships with other people, the absence of all anger control, a destructive sexual addiction, or what have you. But then it continues by talking about "unmanageability." Our ideas about life do not work anymore. No matter what we do, we seem to fail over and over again, and we suddenly realize that, honestly speaking, we do not have the slightest idea why. For years we have been blaming other people for everything that is wrong in our own lives, when suddenly we realize that, with this much calamity going on and the specter of further destruction looming ahead of us, there has to be something "wrong" with us too.

It is when it all comes crashing down and we no longer know which way to go, that we enter the Cloud of Unknowing. It is a state of radical disorientation. We may be flailing out in angry rages at everyone around us, or we may be lying under the covers whimpering and paralyzed, but we honestly do not have any idea what to do next. Nothing that we can see is going to work.

When newcomers to the twelve step program ask the good old timers to explain to them exactly who and what this God is whom they are supposed to pray to, they are simply trying to avoid going all the way into the Cloud of Unknowing. The problem is that they will not get the answer they are seeking—God will not "speak" to them metaphorically speaking—until they enter that cloud all the way.

We have to let go of, not only everything we think we know about ourselves and the world and life, but also everything we think we know about God. When Catholic priests and nuns and Protestant pastors come into A.A., they are sometimes among the hardest people to deal with. They are apt to think that they already know exactly who God is. One of the major crises that these self-styled "experts on God" will have to pass through, is coming to realize that their old ideas about God had fatal flaws in them, and that it is precisely these mistaken beliefs about God which have been destroying them. Sister Ruth, a Catholic nun in the A.A. fellowship who lives here in northern Indiana, said that in her case, she had to learn to read the Third Step in a different way. The actual words of the step talked about turning our will and our lives "over to the care of God *as we understood Him.*" And she heard other people in the fellowship talking about how working the steps had allowed them to find "a God of their understanding." But she said that for herself, she had to think about it as turning her will and her life over to the care of "the God of my nonunderstanding." She finally understood the point that the Apostle Paul had been making when he preached his sermon at the altar to the *Agnôstô Theô*, the Unknown God.

Most people have to let go of almost all of the theological doctrines and dogmas that they have learned. This includes even dogmas like the substitutionary doctrine of the atonement (the medieval idea that Christ died on the cross to pay the penalty to God for our sins), the doctrine of the incarnation, the doctrine of the Trinity, and other complex ideas like that. There is a fatal flaw in our theology somewhere, and we do not know where it is, so we have to let go, for now, of everything. We are seeking the God whom Paul Tillich, in *The Courage to Be*, called "the God beyond God, who appears when the God of theism has disappeared."

The most famous scene in the Big Book is the one on pages 10 to 12, where Bill Wilson is sitting at his kitchen table, telling Ebby Thacher that he has lost all faith in any kind of traditional Christian belief. He does not believe in any kind of loving personal God, he does not believe in the divinity of Christ, and he does not believe in the Devil either, but if any of these divine beings existed, he says, the Devil was the one who would seem to be in actual control of the universe. And what Ebby says back to him, in effect, is "Then drop it all. Let go of all those ideas." And it is only when Bill Wilson is willing to let go of the entire world of theological doctrines and dogmas that the scales fall from his eyes and he becomes able to actually encounter God. He had to enter the Cloud of Unknowing before the real God would reveal himself to him.

In order to work the twelve steps, it is also necessary to let go of all of our previous values and moral rules, such as they may be. "Good boys should always do this." "Good girls ought never do that." "Being praised and thought well of by other people is the most important thing." "Having lots of money is the most important thing." "If someone says such-and-such to you, you have to slug that person in the mouth, or you are not a real man." "Don't get mad, get even." "Obeying the laws is for those obnoxious church people with all their praying and screaming and carrying on." "If someone else is unhappy it must be my fault." "It is my responsibility to make sure that all the other people in the world do things right."

We have to lay all of these rules aside also, at least for now, in order to enter the Cloud of Unknowing. There will be fatal flaws, perhaps even many of them, in our present set of values and rules of behavior, and we do not know where these flaws lie. So we have to set all of them aside for now.

Am I allowed to take any beliefs at all into the Cloud of Unknowing with me? I will need some sort of faith or confidence that the God whom I will meet there, just might be willing to heal me and help me. I will not have the strength to step into that cloud until, somehow or other, I can get just the glimmer of the notion that there is a higher power who has helped people who were just like me. Bill Wilson saw Ebby Thacher sitting at his kitchen table, sober and happy, and he could not deny the evidence of his own eyes and ears. But in terms of going much past that point, I will need to strip myself of all my previous beliefs.

Hearing God speak from the Cloud

When Moses entered the Cloud of Unknowing, he heard God speaking to him. God's words laid out for him a *nomos*, a new set of values and guidelines for living, a new and different kind of moral code. We are talking about a metaphor here, a way of using symbolic language to talk about inner spiritual events. There are people in the twelve step program who have heard an actual voice speaking in their head, where God spoke to them in that kind of direct way. But that is not the way that God usually speaks even to these people, and most people in the twelve step program have never had an experience like that at all.

God speaks to us most often through other people. Someone at an A.A. meeting says something that I suddenly realize is God speaking to me, using that human being as a channel for communicating with me.

Or a single line in a book I am reading may suddenly, as it were, leap out at me. And I realize that this applies to me, and that the truth it contains will allow me to live my life in a much better way. In the New Testament, the "word" of God was the *Logos*, which means something logical that suddenly makes sense out of a part of my life that never made any real sense before. The *Logos* reveals *Alêtheia*, which is the Truth. It is the truth about the world and God and myself, coming in a moment of insight which strips away all the denial and alibis and excuses, and displays the real truth about things (which I have been trying so hard to avoid looking at) in the clear light of day.

This metaphor of the Cloud of Unknowing contains paradoxical qualities, for it talks about receiving Illumination by entering the Divine Darkness. It talks about hearing the Word of God by entering the Divine Silence.

When God touches me within the Cloud of Unknowing, it may not be conceptual knowledge that he will give me. It may not be words that I hear or read. It may be things that I see, like walking into a twelve step meeting, and seeing someone smile with pleasure to see me there. It may be someone giving me a hug when I need comforting.

It may be in the form of what the Germans call *Gefühl* and *Ahnung*, words which are translated into English rather weakly as "feeling" and "intuition" and other words like that. When Bill Wilson was sitting at his kitchen table talking with Ebby Thacher, and Ebby finally got Bill to let go of all of his preconceived notions about God and enter the Cloud of Unknowing, what popped into Bill's mind was the *Gefühl* of the sacred presence which he had felt while standing in Winchester Cathedral. It was a kind of awareness, a kind of real knowledge which was nevertheless not conceptual knowledge, not an intellectual theory. Ellen Lantz, one of the good old timers from northern Indiana, said that when she walked into an A.A. meeting, she could just "feel" the love. And when she and one of the young women whom she sponsored were sitting together chatting in her home, she could "feel" the love there too. That was what was going to heal the young woman's soul, in a way that was far more important than any kind of statements of ideas and principles that Ellen could give her.

Nomos

When God spoke to Moses in the dark cloud, he gave him the Law, the *nomos*, the Torah. As the letter of James says, the true *nomos* is not a set of mechanical rules which we can use for discriminating against other people and sitting in judgment over them and condemning them. The true *nomos* is what James called the Law of Freedom. As the A.A. old timer Raymond puts it, it is the simple rule that tells us to "do good and show love."

We will have to restructure our lives, and reframe the cognitive structures of our minds, in order to actually live the new way of life we are being given. A large part of the twelve steps, in fact, is simply a very well put together system for carrying out this process. It leads me step by step through the journey I must go through in order to remold and remake myself. I have to put away the old Me and wander for a while through the Cloud of Unknowing—the Dark Night of the Soul—confused and bewildered, while letting the twelve step program and the people in the program slowly help me figure out a new Me, one which I can live with inside my own mind without continual guilt, anxiety, fear, resentment, and remorse.

The first time God spoke to Moses, in the story of the Burning Bush, Moses wanted to know who and what God was, and what his name was. God spoke only those puzzling words, "I am who I am." We must complete our escape from Egypt (which stands metaphorically for the alcohol or drugs or lack of anger control or codependency or whatever it was which held us enslaved) and then enter the Cloud of Unknowing as we begin climbing up the Mountain of God. Going up one side of the mountain there are twelve steps, which can make the going much easier, although there are other paths up the mountain which will also work. By the time I get to the top of the mountain, I will realize who and what God is. God is the power who will heal me and give me a new self, built around the simple principles of love and service ("Do good and show love"). That is all I need to know about God, and all I will ever need to know.

If you who are reading this book today are a skeptic and a doubter, that is not necessarily a bad thing. It may make it easier to enter the Cloud of Unknowing, where everything at first must be cast into doubt and uncertainty. But if, amidst all your skepticism and doubt, you could perhaps have the tiniest bit of hope that, within that dark cloud, you might meet something which will heal you and give you a new and better self, it will be a big help. This is not an absurd hope. You would not be the first person in the world who climbed the mountain, immersed in the darkness of the Cloud of Unknowing, and like Moses, ultimately found the sunlight of the spirit at the top.[14]

Chapter 3

The Taste of Pineapple: Words and Meaning

We have talked about God as the mysterious x-factor in conversion stories, and as the "I am" who needs no name. He is the one, so we have said, who communicates with us after we enter the Cloud of Unknowing.

And yet some people continue to ask why, if the word "God" refers to anything meaningful at all, we cannot give a definition of the word. In serious talk about any subject, they say, we must necessarily begin by defining the basic terms, and not only that, but we must give some reasonably precise detail about what all these fundamental concepts mean. Then if we want to argue about whether God exists or not, at least no one will be in any doubt about how to debate this issue logically. Otherwise, it looks like we are trying to dodge serious questions by falling back into mysticism, obfuscation, emotionalism, and fuzzy thinking.

Now asking for this kind of clarification may seem at first like a perfectly fair thing to request. But there is a hidden presupposition buried there, which is the assumption that we cannot be said to "know something" unless we can give a word for it, along with a definition of that word, so that we can explain to someone else what that word means.

But this is not necessarily so. We need to look at the writings of two philosophers in particular, John Locke in the seventeenth century and Michael Polanyi in the twentieth century, to see some of the problems with that assumption. And then we will need to look in particular at how human beings learn the meaning of words, to see the problems that arise when we presuppose that it is definitions of words which tell us their meaning.

The impossibility of describing certain experiences to those who have not had them

John Locke (1632-1704), the founder of modern psychology and modern empiricist philosophy, published his major philosophical work, *An Essay Concerning Human Understanding*, in 1689. In that work he raised an interesting question: How could you truly describe the taste of pineapple to someone who had never tasted one? This was an especially intriguing question to the people in England at that time.

Pineapples came from South and Central America, and the Caribbean as well, where Columbus tasted that fruit for the first time in 1493 when he visited the Guadaloupe islands, so people in Europe had known of the existence of this tropical fruit for a long time. But this was the era of slow-moving sailing ships, long before airplanes or refrigerators or canning had been invented. Sailors and explorers who returned to England could talk about the marvelous taste of fresh pineapple to their stay-at-home countrymen, but found it impossible to explain how its distinctive flavor differed from that of apples, pears, cherries, currants, gooseberries, and other fruits that grew in the cold English climate.[15] Pineapples finally began to be grown in greenhouses in England around 1720, but that was over thirty years after Locke published his *Essay*, and even after that, for a long time it was only a few wealthy folk who had ever tasted one. This is one kind of instance of a quite ordinary experience, which is perfectly real, but which nevertheless could not successfully be described to someone else who had never had that experience.

How much more difficult it would be to explain the experience which Tennyson was describing in his poem "The Higher Pantheism," where he talks about feeling the divine presence immediately surrounding us, in even the commonest things:

> Speak to Him thou for He hears,
> and Spirit with Spirit can meet —
> Closer is He than breathing,
> and nearer than hands and feet.

Tennyson was here speaking about much the same sort of experience that the Apostle Paul was describing when he spoke of God as the one in whom "we live and move and have our being" (Acts 17:28) in the sermon which he delivered in front of the altar to the Unknown God.

Sigmund Freud spoke about that kind of experience of the divine presence in one of his writings. He said he had been given to understand that it was a sort of "oceanic feeling." Freud simply said that "he had never had that kind of feeling," making it clear that he regarded it as a batch of nonsense. And he had in fact probably always blocked it out of his consciousness, so that when he heard people who believed in God describing it, he assumed that they had to be talking about some sort of subjective illusion.

The problem here is that some very intelligent people, with sharp, critical minds, who were at least the equal to Sigmund Freud in their intellectual ability, have experienced the immediate presence of God, and many other things having to do with God and with his divine grace in action. They have seen the light of the divine illumination, sensed the warmth of his presence within their hearts, and felt the wind of his spirit blowing through their souls. The fact that there are also people like Sigmund Freud, who have never experienced any of those things, does not mean that those who have were simply giving way to overactive imaginations. It is like the taste of pineapple. The fact that one person has never tasted pineapple, does not mean that all the people who have tasted it were suffering from delusions.

Real experiences for which
there are no words

Locke also pointed out in *An Essay Concerning Human Understanding*, that there are experiences which we can recognize distinctly when they occur to us again at some later date, but for which there are no single, specific words at all.[16] This occurs in some areas of human experience much more than others.

We have names for most colors, so the problem does not usually arise in this area of human experience. We have literally hundreds of different color names in English: aqua, chartreuse, coral, cornflower blue, crimson, khaki, orchid, salmon, sea green, pink, lavender, ivory, fuchsia, turquoise, slate gray, maroon, violet, navy, orange, teal, burnt sienna, red, peach, and so on.

We have names for a great number of different kinds of flavors: beef tastes different from chicken, garlic tastes different from rosemary, and strawberries taste different from raspberries. We have names to describe all these specific flavors. But a good cook who is adjusting the taste of a broth will add a little bit of this and a little bit of that, until it tastes exactly "right," which usually means exactly the way the cook prepared it the last time. People who partake of her cooking regularly will also recognize that specific taste, although they likewise will have no name for it. A different cook will prepare the soup, and the diners will say things like, "The soup tastes different tonight." And they are not imagining this. All of them agree that the taste is not the same. This is real knowledge. But there will be no recognized word in English to describe "the way that my Mama's chicken soup tastes." And the same applies to a particular cook's spaghetti sauce and any number of other distinctive tastes.

In the case of sounds, there are even fewer names. We can recognize the sound of a given person's voice, and tell the difference between the sound of rain falling and the sound of paper rustling. Even when a number of babies are present, a mother can instantly recognize the sound of her own baby crying. People who own hunting dogs can tell one hound from another by the sound of its baying. But we have very few words to describe these differences: high pitched, low pitched, reedy, mellow, aggressive, plaintive, whispery, scratchy, and so on, do not even begin to be sufficient to distinguish between all the nuances which the human ear can identify.

And as Locke points out, it is particularly in the area of smells that we have real knowledge for which there are no words or names. In my own case, I remember from my childhood the special smell of the early morning out in the mountains of eastern Kentucky, when the dew is first melting off, coming from the pastures of grasses and aromatic herbs that spread across the open patches between the forested hills. I remember the equally distinctive smell of the dry leaves and grass, mixed with the smoke from a mesquite fire, when camping out in the live oak and mesquite thickets of central Texas. I remember exploring the ruins of ancient Rome in various places in Italy, where the wild flowers growing amidst the fallen stone columns smelled like rich honey under the hot Italian sun. And everyone who reads this will have memories of equally distinctive smells, which they could recognize instantly, but for which there are no recognizable names at all.

Most people have never gone deeply into the spiritual life, and therefore have never experienced any number of special experiences which are a regular part of that life. St. Teresa of Avila (1515-1582), in her great spiritual classic, *The Interior Castle*, began trying to create a language for discussing many of these experiences—the first time anyone in the Christian tradition had ever tried to go into the matter in that kind of detail—but even then, St. Teresa was barely scraping the surface. To this day, there are no real words to describe many of the common experiences of the spiritual life.

So when those who are newcomers to the spiritual life grow frustrated with the more experienced for "refusing to explain what it is all about," they should realize that these people are not deliberately refusing to explain, nor does their refusal to explain mean that they are talking about imaginary things. There really are no words in English to describe many of these experiences. Nevertheless, it is real knowledge.

Polanyi and the tacit knowledge
that comes from expertise

Michael Polanyi (1891-1976) was a Hungarian philosopher (and a scientist as well, for he also made notable contributions to the field of physical chemistry). He was teaching at the University of Manchester in England when he was invited to give the Gifford lectures in 1951–52 at the University of Aberdeen in Scotland.[17] The fruit of these lectures was a very important book, *Personal Knowledge*, which contained a number of insights into the way we know things about the world.

In particular, Polanyi discussed a kind of nonverbal intelligence which he called "tacit knowledge." He pointed to cases like that of the skilled wine connoisseur: the real experts can taste a sample of a fine French wine and tell you the area, and often the year, and sometimes even the specific vineyard where the wine was made. If the wine connoisseurs are asked to explain in words what the difference is between two wines, however, the words that they fall back on ("fruity," "robust," and so on) are so incredibly vague and general, that it is clear that their knowledge (though perfectly real) is not easily capable of being put into words.

We find tacit knowledge in many fields of human activity. There is real knowledge, for example, involved in being able to tell the sound of a French horn from a trombone playing the same note, or being able to tell an oboe from a clarinet—but how, Polanyi asked, can anyone put that in words?[18]

There are two things that are important about tacit knowledge. One is that it is based on expertise born of long experience. The other is that it can be verified empirically or pragmatically. When we test a real wine expert with an unidentified glass of wine, and he tells us what it is and where it came from and when, we can look at the label on the bottle which it was poured from and verify that he is correct. We can likewise check to see whether the musical expert has correctly identified which musical instrument was playing that note.

It is the same in the spiritual life. People with little or no experience will not be able to tell what is going on at all. But that is not because it is illusion or wish-fulfillment fantasy or fuzzy thinking, because there will be others who have developed some real expertise, which can ultimately be tested pragmatically.

In the Alcoholics Anonymous program, for example, we have a number of pragmatic tests which can identify those who have developed greater expertise in the spiritual life. People who had no control over their drinking whatever, will become able to maintain continuous sobriety for years, and those who are knowledgeable will say that this is because they have demonstrated, in this and other ways, that they have developed much greater spiritual awareness.

Before coming to A.A., the average divorce rate is far higher than the national average; after becoming totally immersed in A.A. spirituality, the divorce rate drops to far lower than the national average. We can make the same pragmatic check by observing how many alcoholics, prior to coming to A.A., bounce from job to job to job. Once they have begun to work the twelve step program, however, A.A. people in fact only rarely lose jobs. And when they lose jobs, it will be because the company they worked for folded, or some other factor totally out of their control. Learning how to maintain stable human relationships and stable employment involves a good deal more than just stopping drinking. Those who are knowledgeable will observe that success in these areas is closely connected with learning greater expertise in spiritual matters.

We are looking at real knowledge here, in which there are all sorts of degrees of expertise, including the truly great experts, who are looked at with admiration by those who have lesser knowledge. We can demonstrate that this is true knowledge by all sorts of pragmatic tests. Some of the greatest experts are able to sponsor large numbers of newcomers over the course of the years, and help these newcomers gain lasting sobriety. There is obviously an expertise about the spiritual life at work here. Other A.A. members have special talents in the area of helping others understand the program better. The people who have been helped by them display in their lives that the help was real and not just subjective.

Just as in the case of wine connoisseurs and skilled musicians, we can demonstrate that experts in the spiritual life possess a kind of tacit knowledge which can be tested empirically and pragmatically. And all three areas of knowledge have one thing in common: in each case we are dealing with subtle matters and delicate distinctions. Like identifying an especially fine wine or an exceptionally beautiful violin tone, God is not something gross and easily pointed out, like looking at a large tree or rock. In fact, a person has to *learn* how to identify many forms of the experience of God, and learning how to do this takes time.

People who have never seriously tried to live the spiritual life sometimes complain that those who do talk about the spiritual life must be talking nonsense, because they themselves cannot see or feel anything. But this is like an untrained person saying that "there is no difference between one wine and another because I cannot tell the difference." It is like an untrained person trying to say that "all the instruments in a symphony orchestra sound the same, because I cannot tell the difference," or that "all classical composers sound the same because I cannot tell the difference," or that "all violins sound the same because I cannot tell the difference." Their inability to tell the difference does not arise because they are more intelligent and knowledgeable than those who do understand these things, but the reverse.

And let us also remember that expertise in one area does not mean expertise in all other areas of human knowledge. Being an expert on football does not guarantee being an expert on classical music or fine French wines, and vice versa. Being an expert psychologist or physicist or sociologist does not make someone an expert on spiritual experience. In fact, unless psychologists and physicists and sociologists have spent years immersed in the spiritual life, and gaining real tacit knowledge in that area, they know no more about spirituality than butchers or bakers or candlestick makers. They will not understand a single thing that is going on when experts in the spiritual life are talking about their experiences.

Learning a new language:
the problem of meaning

When a beginner starts learning how to speak the language of the spirit, it is in some ways like learning a foreign language. Memorizing a verbal definition does you no good if you are a beginner who does not know what *any* of the words mean—we have surely all had the experience at least once of looking up a word in a dictionary because we did not know what it meant, only to discover that we did not know what the key words in the definition meant either!

Furthermore, we can understand the meaning of words without being able to give a logical definition of them. The twentieth-century philosopher Ludwig Wittgenstein once pointed out the window to the grass in the quadrangle in Trinity College at the University of Cambridge, and remarked, "Do you mean to say that I do not know what the word 'grass' means because I cannot define it?" When small children learn to speak, they do not learn what words mean by memorizing definitions of them.

Some philosophers have attempted to get around this problem by claiming that we learn words instead by what are called "ostensive definitions." One points at an object and pronounces its name. The idea here is that after being shown a number of objects, and being told that each one is a "leaf," for example, one will then know the meaning of the word "leaf." The problem with this theory is that, even after I have been shown an oak leaf, a maple leaf, a cabbage leaf, and a leaf from a gingko tree, all that I have are four very different pictures stored up in my mind. How can I tell, by looking at some new object and then comparing it with those four pictures, that an elm leaf is a "leaf" but that a woman's green glove is not? The glove has five points and is flat and green, so why is it not also a "leaf"? And yet even very small children learn the meaning of words very quickly, although obviously not by this method alone. Even if adults sometimes point at things and tell the child what that object is called, there clearly has to be something else involved beyond that. Having a series of pictures stored up in my mind is not the same as understanding the meaning of a word.

Let us imagine that I have landed on a tropical island, where I do not understand one single word of the native language, and they in turn do not understand one single word of mine. Pointing at objects with a questioning look on my face might be a way of at least beginning to learn that new language. I might, for example, point at a yellow wooden pencil lying on a table, and turn with an expectant and questioning look to one of the native speakers. Let us suppose that this person says, clearly and distinctly, "*ubunga, ubunga.*"

How much have I actually learned at that point? *Ubunga* may mean pencil. On the other hand, it may equally well mean yellow or long or cylindrical. The native speaker may have misunderstood and thought that I was pointing at the table on which the pencil was lying, so that the word *ubunga* may mean table in his language. There may have been an even deeper misunderstanding, and the native may have thought that I was asking, "When is dinner going to be served?" *Ubunga* may mean "this evening" in the language of that island.

Determining what words mean requires a good deal more work than just pointing at things and assuming that the first thing that comes out of someone else's mouth is the word I am looking for. We have to develop hypotheses and then ask further questions to see whether any of them are correct. Perhaps *ubunga* means the color yellow. I can check this hypothesis out by going over and picking up a lemon, and a piece of yellow cloth, and bringing them back and laying them on the table next to the yellow pencil, and saying, "*ubunga?*" If the native shakes his head, and points to the three objects and says "*babalooba,*" then it becomes clear that *ubunga* must not be their word for "yellow." Perhaps it is this new word *babalooba* instead which refers to the color yellow in their language. This could potentially be useful information if I am trying to learn their language. Of course, *babalooba* could also be an expression of disgust at my inability to learn their language, and could mean something more like "no, you idiot."

If I work long enough and hard enough at it, I will eventually be able to learn their language. But the important thing to note is that accomplishing this will require, not just passive listening, but *active involvement* on my part, carried out in real life contexts. And it will also necessitate long *practice and training* for me to learn the full *meaning* of the words in this new language.

Electronic computers and the problem of meaning

There have been long debates over most of my life as to whether electronic computers can "think." Part of this debate arises simply over what one means by the word "thinking." If adding 2 + 2 and calculating that the answer is 4 is construed as thinking, then there have been computers which could think ever since the middle ages. The medieval English treasury was called the Exchequer because there was a large table there, five feet by ten feet, divided up like a checker board. Whoever was doing the accounting placed counters on the squares to carry out addition, subtraction, multiplication, and division.

But if thinking means thinking like a human being, then humans have personal being. They have consciousness, including self-consciousness, and understand the meaning of what they are thinking about.

As of this date, there have been no electronic computers built which can truly understand meaning. Let me give an illustration. The Registrar's Office at the Indiana University campus where I taught once had its address included in a computerized mailing list (no one is quite sure how this happened) which was used by a woman's magazine for mailing out flyers advertising beauty products, including perfume and makeup and the like, and women's jewelry, and other things of that sort. They received an advertising flyer through the mail which had been "personalized" by the computer to make it appear as though it was a personal letter to the recipient. This letter was addressed to the Registrar's Office and began with the words "Dear Ms. Office." The computer program had been set up to take the last word in the first line of the mailing address and treat it as the last name of the recipient, who was assumed to be a female human being.

Now there have been computer experts who have argued, for years, that it should be possible in principle to construct a computer and a computer program which could handle problems like this. In this case the computer could perhaps be given a list of all the words of the English language, so it could recognize when the first line in the mailing address was not a personal name. This is more difficult than it may at first appear. Carpenter can be a last name, but can also be the description of a kind of job. There is one person in my local telephone book whose last name is Company. There are other people whose last names are Boys, Buzzard, Cook, Page, Rice, Sneeze, and Star, all of which can be words in the English language which are not personal names. Perhaps one could give the computer a list of all the possible first names in English, and set up the program so that the combination of first word and second word would only count as a personal name if the first word in the first line in the mailing address was one of these English given names. The problem here is giving the computer guidelines for recognizing variant spellings such as Jayne (for Jane), Barbra (for Barbara), Eolande (for Yolanda) and all the other variant spellings which are sometimes devised for personal names. Plus, in the modern United States, the computer would have to be given all the first names used in most of the languages of the world.

These "in principle" arguments can sound good until one actually tries to implement them. In actual practice, even when a computer has been loaded with the definitions for tens of thousands of words, there are so many limitations to what it can do with these words, that no sensible person would regard the computer as understanding the "meaning" of the words it was manipulating according to rote formulas.

Nevertheless, might it be possible someday to build a computer which could actually think in the sense of understanding the meaning of words? What the human mind can imagine, the human mind can eventually figure out how to build. Or at least our human ingenuity can accomplish this a good deal of the time. There is no way that anyone could say that it could never be possible. But the key point is that a computer which was able to actually understand meaning would have to learn the meaning of words by the same process which human beings use: not through being loaded with long catalogues of verbal and ostensive definitions, but through the computer taking an *active involvement* in real life contexts in the outside world, and slowly learning, through long *practice and training*, the *meaning* of the words which the computer was intended to be able to use.

Learning the meaning of a word takes place through a series of insights, in which the meaning of the word gradually becomes clearer and clearer. We can say that we truly have an adequate understanding of what the word means only when we can use it in real life contexts on a regular basis in ways which are appropriate in terms of the local language.

But we must be careful here. Understanding "meaning" sometimes refers to being able to master the usage of a particular word in a particular language. However, as we have noted at the beginning of this chapter, there can be "meaning" within my mind even when there is no word which is attached to this meaning in precise and literal fashion. Meaning is not the same thing as "correct word usage" and it is also not the same thing as a definable "concept" which I hold in my mind. Meaning is its own peculiar kind of thing, and cannot be reduced to some simpler kind of mechanism.

Plato said that we learned the "meaning" of a thing, we remember, by engaging in the Socratic dialectic, where we tested and discarded various formulations and definitions, until we finally arrived at a vision of the form (*eidos*) or idea (*idea*) of the thing. This was genuine knowledge, but not necessarily the kind of knowledge which could be put into words.

Learning to speak and understand
the language of the spirit

When we first enter the spiritual life, the words which we hear are in fact part of a strange new language. It is important to remember this, and to make a major effort not to fall into the trap of believing that I already know what the key words mean. There are a number of new words and terms which I must learn to understand, such as "grace," "faith," "spiritual experience," and above all, "God."

Even if it were possible to give an exact philosophical definition of what the word "God" meant, this would not help me experience God if I have never knowingly experienced him before. The connection between the words of the definition and real life experience will still be lacking, no matter how precisely the definition is framed. Even giving ostensive definitions ("I believe that what you are experiencing now is one way that God works") is capable of incredible misinterpretation unless the learner is given extensive *training* at the *everyday pragmatic level* by someone who does understand what the word God means.

Active engagement

In the 1960's, the United States Peace Corps discovered that volunteers could best be taught the language of the country to which they were going to be sent, through the total immersion method. Almost all the volunteers had to learn a new language, because the people in the countries to which they were being sent (Ethiopia, Thailand, and so on) usually spoke languages which were not part of the standard curriculum in American schools and universities. In this total immersion method, the students were given a couple of people who already spoke the language to act as guides, and kept for three months (ninety days) in a setting where they had to go about all their everyday activities without being allowed to speak any language except for the one which they were learning. And they were kept busy all day long in ways which forced them to speak. After three months of that, the volunteers were in fact able to speak the new language well enough to get by after they were sent to the host country.

Total immersion in the new language is the best and quickest way to learn it. That is why newcomers to A.A. are often told to immerse themselves in the program totally for the first ninety days. They are instructed to go to at least one A.A. meeting every day, and they are also told that they have to speak to other people at these meetings. If they try to remain just passive observers, they will not be able to learn the language very effectively. In fact, in my observation, the most important reason why the majority of failures in the A.A. program are unable to get sober and stay sober, is because they try to learn the program as totally passive observers, expecting to be handed everything on a spoon without any effort on their part.

Some newcomers to the twelve step program fall into the trap of insisting that they first be told what all the new words mean, before they will carry out any of the activities which are laid out in the twelve steps. They get nowhere, not because the twelve step program is "a bunch of old religious nonsense" (or some other kind of piece of silly foolishness), but because the only way to learn what the words actually mean is to carry out the actions specified in the twelve steps. It is in the process of working the steps that we learn what the words mean in this new language of the spirit. In this sense, it is no different than learning any kind of new language.

When external critics try to attack the twelve step program, their criticisms are usually so far off the mark that they are totally irrelevant to what really goes on in the program. I have seen this over and over again. The critics have never worked the steps themselves, so they have never learned what the words actually mean in context. They get in trouble because they assume they already know what these words mean, even though they are getting it all wrong. It is like English speakers who know only a few words of Spanish insisting that a Spanish speaker is stupid because they do not know Spanish well enough to understand what the person is actually saying. And vice versa. In the United States, which has been a land of immigrants, this has been a standing problem since the beginning, with people assuming over and over again that the new group of immigrants are stupid and ignorant people simply because they do not understand the immigrants' language and, at the beginning, the new immigrants do not understand English fluently.

I know that when I visit countries like Mexico, Italy, France, and Germany, I sound stupid and ignorant, because I cannot speak any of these languages with the fluency of a native. But at least I *knew* that I came across as very simple minded and dense when I was trying to understand what other people were saying to me! Unfortunately, most of the present day external critics of the twelve step program are arrogant people who totally fail to realize how ignorant and ill informed their criticisms of the program sound to those who actually know how to speak the program language through living it over a long period of time.

There are some people in the twelve step program who are in fact stupid and ignorant, and believe truly absurd things. One can encounter ideas in some factions of the A.A. fellowship at present, for example, which are simply destructive and wrong. I cringe inside every time I hear some of their misleading and spiritually dangerous statements. The same thing is true in the other twelve step fellowships, like Al-Anon and Overeaters Anonymous and so on. There are no large groups of ordinary people where everyone gets everything exactly right. But the only sure way to tell the difference between the wise and the foolish is to learn the language first, and this is what most of the external critics of the twelve step program arrogantly refuse to do.

Story telling

Active involvement is the best way to learn a new language, but sometimes this is impossible. For more than thirty years, I made my living by teaching history at Indiana University, and there was no possible way for my students to become actively involved in the everyday life of long dead eras like the Roman empire or the Italian Renaissance.

As the next best thing, I made it a practice to have my beginning students read one writing from a person who lived at that period (if possible) for each major section of each course. For Renaissance Italy, I had them read excerpts from both Machiavelli and Dante, to expose them to two very different kinds of personalities. For the period of the French revolution, I had them read from a short story which Voltaire had written, which was set in France in immediate pre-revolutionary times. For classical Greece, I had beginners either read excerpts from Herodotus' history or some of the Platonic dialogues describing the last days of Socrates.

I found that if I did not do this, the students would memorize the definitions which I gave them in my lectures, and then would write essays on the next exam which were filled (all too often) with total absurdities. They knew the words of the definitions and descriptions, but lacking any kind of knowledge of the living context, they were completely unable to grasp what these words really meant. So they would put together arguments in their essays and come to conclusions which appeared to be totally logical (based on the definitions and formal descriptions) but which had nothing to do at all with what was actually going on in that period of history.

Hearing stories and getting to know real people through the books which they wrote, is not as good as being able to become actively engaged in the world in which a particular language was spoken. But for ancient history, that is the best we can do. And it is a hundred times better, a thousand times better, than trying to memorize lists and definitions and "textbook" statements.

The Alcoholics Anonymous program has understood this from the beginning. The early parts of the Big Book have Bill Wilson's personal story woven through it at every point, explaining how he came from skepticism to belief. And then in the last part of the book we have a long series of shorter stories, recounting the experience of dozens of other men and women, and explaining how they came to terms with their alcoholism and found spiritual help sufficient to allow them to stop drinking and build new lives for themselves. One of the standard types of A.A. meeting is one where a speaker stands up and tells his or her life story.

Getting past our early religious training

When adults first decide to try to work out a meaningful higher power for themselves, those who had a fair amount of religious training during their childhood can sometimes be in worse shape than those who had little or none. Small children can often seriously misunderstand what religious authority figures were actually trying to tell them. Even worse, there are religious leaders who teach things that are seriously misleading or totally wrong. At a Roman Catholic parochial school there can be twenty nuns who both teach and display in their own lives a deep understanding of spiritual matters, and one nun who is so psychologically disturbed that she has truly horrifying ideas about God, and sadly enough, many of the children at this school will be so traumatized by her nightmarish vision of God that they will never even remember what the twenty good people told them. And exactly the same thing can happen in a Protestant Sunday School or a Jewish day school. A single teacher who distorts the religious teaching because of personal psychological problems can undo the work of a large number of deeply spiritual and totally sane teachers.

There are also religious groups, sad to say, where all of the authority figures are locked into highly destructive beliefs and behaviors, and where they all brainwash the small children under their care with a poisonous view of a cosmic tyrant who loves to torture and punish small children for the tiniest infraction of one of his thousands of absurd rules.

We can see the kind of problems which this can cause. If we imagined, for example, that the adults whom children encountered in the earliest years of their lives took even simple words like "green" and "leaf" and gave the children nothing but conflicting and often totally absurd information about what these words meant, we can see how we could easily produce children who eventually became either totally cynical and skeptical, or hopelessly confused, about what these two words actually meant, if anything. In the case of the spiritual life, similarly, the biggest problem for earnest seekers after God is often that they have been surrounded for all too many years by people who told them that evil things were good things, that black was white, that slavish submission to tyrannical human authority figures was saving faith, and that total nonsense was divine mystery. No wonder such people end up atheists, agnostics, or simply hopelessly confused!

Learning to see how God was always there, even if I did not recognize him

That is why growth in the spiritual life often means learning that I had been experiencing God all along, but had been putting the wrong words and labels on what I was perceiving. St. Augustine in his *Confessions* notes that, when he finally found a God of his own understanding at the end of his spiritual quest, he discovered that God had always been there, and that he had always known God.[19]

> Belatedly I loved you, O Beauty so ancient and so new, belatedly I loved you. For see, you were within and I was without, and I sought you in the outside.

The problem had been that he had been putting all the wrong words on his personal experiences. So for a considerable length of time in his youth, he was (at the intellectual level) a total skeptic who was extremely hostile to religious people. But in fact, as he came ultimately to realize, *God had always been there for him anyway, watching over him, guarding him, caring for him, and bringing him down the path that would ultimately lead to his discovery of the good spiritual life.*

Becoming a baby again

The vocabulary of the real spiritual life is surprisingly small, and the words it uses over and over are not only few in number but extremely simple. Some of the more important positive words would be surrender, gratitude, acceptance, grace, and detachment. Some of the major negative words would be resentment, self-pity, controlling, caretaking, and fear. Newcomers to the spiritual life characteristically either are totally mystified by these words, or give completely wrong meanings to them, or fail to connect these words with anything in their own everyday personal experience. They confuse the word "love" for example with sexual lust, or with having somebody else do everything I tell them to do, or some other distortion of that sort. In fact, it is in learning how to use these major spiritual words appropriately that we first truly start to understand what the word God means.

One of the good old timers in my part of Indiana is Raymond I., who began life as a gentleman burglar in Chicago. He also became involved with pickpocketing, robbing the federal mails, and other criminal activities during his youth. When he first came into the A.A. program, he was totally mystified by the concept of God. He kept plaguing his sponsor for explanations and definitions. He said his sponsor finally told him, "Raymond, you've never been nothing but a thief all your life. You want to *steal* spirituality from me. But this is one thing you *can't* steal. You got to work it out for yourself." He says his sponsor also told him early on, "Raymond, you're nothing but a baby." He answered his sponsor back angrily, "Who me? What you mean! I'm no baby." His sponsor responded, "*Spiritually* you are nothing but a babe in arms." He had to learn even the simplest things from scratch: what the simple little baby words meant when they were part of the spiritual life, how to walk in the spirit, and how to recognize even the simplest things with his spiritual eyes.

But Raymond stuck at it, and he did learn, and now is a person who almost glows with the light of the spirit. People travel regularly even from the surrounding states just to come in contact with his deep spiritual wisdom. And it works, because by being with Raymond, some of his wisdom and knowledge "rubs off," and you find yourself being able to cope with things in your life which you were never able to cope with before, and being able to maintain an attitude of peace and gratitude and love even in the midst of situations which used to drive you to wild rage or paralyzing fear. Raymond's spirituality works, and those who come in contact with him learn how to make it work for them too. This is real knowledge, even though it cannot be put adequately into words.

This is the whole message of this chapter. The language of the spirit has deep meaning, but we do not learn it by memorizing definitions and by mere passive observation. How do you explain the taste of pineapple? You have to taste some to find out. How do you explain what is meant by letting God grasp your hand, to comfort you, guide you, and carry you? You have to taste of God's love and grace over and over until you begin to find out. How do you learn the language of the spirit? You have to become like a little baby again. Little babies reach out and crawl and explore, and babble the few words they know until they can learn more. Learning a new language requires *active involvement* in real life contexts, and also long *practice and training*, before I can learn the *meaning* of the words in this new language. I must listen to the stories told by the old timers, and then try to carry out these same spiritual principles in my own daily life.

But if I do all this, I can in fact learn what the concept of God means. And I will be able to demonstrate that what I have learned is real knowledge, by the way in which my life is totally transformed. I will learn to trust and I will learn to love. I will stop attacking people and start helping people. But the majority of this will be "tacit knowledge," if we may use Polanyi's term. God will still remain the mysterious x-factor whom I can know but not explain. As Polanyi put it,[20] with the really important things in life, it is always the case that:

> We can know more than we can tell and we can tell nothing
> without relying on our awareness of things we may not be
> able to tell.

Chapter 4

The Realm of the Sacred

In the preceding three chapters, we explained a number of different reasons why the concept of God cannot easily be defined and explained in the way that we explain things in the field of the natural sciences. When God acts in our lives, he is always intruding into the this-worldly realm from the outside. His true Being lies in a realm which is prior to space and time and the law of entropy, a realm which is not governed by the kinds of scientific laws which physicists and chemists and biologists explore.

Furthermore, even in the case of ordinary this-worldly events, we experience many things for which we in fact have no words at all. Real knowledge is there, but the words to describe what we know do not exist. We have recognizable experts in certain fields—people whose skills can be objectively demonstrated—who operate on the basis of a kind of tacit knowledge which cannot be put into words.

And in addition, even when we do have words to describe our experiences and the things we know, we cannot necessarily give definitions for these words. But as we have seen, one cannot automatically conclude from this that we are talking nonsense, because understanding the *meaning* of a word is not at all the same thing as having memorized a definition, or having a catalogue of specific samples which we can refer to. So even when we have words for describing our experiences of God and the effects of God's grace, once we start trying to explain to other people what these words *mean*, giving them a list of definitions is not usually going to be very useful at all.

Anyone who does not believe me here should look at a textbook on later medieval scholastic thought, or seventeenth and eighteenth century Protestant scholasticism, where hundreds of definitions are given for various abstruse theological concepts, none of which are going to help anyone who does not already understand in advance who God is.

> For example, in Muller's *Dictionary of Latin and Greek Theological Terms: Drawn Principally from Protestant Scholastic Theology*,[21] one is taught to distinguish between three different kinds of faith: *fiducia* (faith as trust), *fides quae creditur* (a set of theological propositions which one believes by faith are true), and *fides qua creditur* (the faith by which these propositions are believed). And this in turn must be distinguished from *fides implicita* (implicit or blind faith in whatever the church teaches without even knowing what it teaches). One can also make a distinction between *fides informis*, which is faith which has not been given substance by love, as opposed to *fides caritate formata*, which is faith which has been instructed by love and produces good works. *Fides divina* refers to faith engendered in us by the action of God's grace, as opposed to *fides humana*, which refers only to the natural human ability to hold convictions on various subjects. *Fides historica* means acceptance of certain theological propositions (such as that Christ came to save the world from sin) without its having any spiritual effect. And one can go on and on, making fine distinctions and giving definitions of every conceivable theological term, and turn it all into a grand intellectual game which brings salvation to no one.

There are many of us who feel that this kind of scholastic approach ends up confusing and obfuscating the real issues instead of clarifying them. Even when one *can* draw up a list of such definitions, they do not necessarily end up being helpful. Eventually just about everyone becomes lost in the maze of complex and subtle definitions and distinctions, and totally loses sight of what the truly important words actually *mean*. People can read and memorize all the definitions of faith given in the paragraph above, and learn to recite them mechanically on command, and can then easily fool themselves into believing that they must have genuine faith, because they can reel out all the definitions which were given them by religious authority figures. People like this, even though they can say all the words, still do not really trust God. They still think of God as a tyrannical punishing figure, and remain unable to show real love and kindness towards their fellow human beings. They still have no notion at all of what the word faith *means*.

By the end of the middle ages, a whole host of theologians, from the Catholic author Thomas à Kempis (in the *Imitation of Christ*) to the Protestant Reformer Martin Luther, had rebelled against the late medieval attempt to teach theology by making endless definitions and distinctions. The real point—learning to love and trust God, and learning to do good and be of service to our fellow human beings—had ended up being totally lost, and what we ended up with instead was a vast number of totally terrified men and women who were mortally afraid that they would go to eternal hellfire if they failed to understand and perfectly follow every one of these hundreds and hundreds of definitions and the legalistic rules which were based on them.

The way we teach people about what the truly important words *mean* is to tell stories and get people involved in activities where they will learn the meaning of words in context, in the same way that small children learn to speak the language spoken in their homes. And we have to go about this, remembering at all times what Michael Polanyi said: "*We can know more than we can tell and we can tell nothing without relying on our awareness of things we may not be able to tell.*"

The holy as one of the categories
of the human understanding

In this chapter we need to talk about yet another area in which *it does not work at all* when we try to explain what we know about God by giving a list of technical definitions: the idea of the holy or the sacred. This is a concept which plays a truly major role in our knowledge of

God, which is radically different from anything we talked about in the first three chapters, because it is not the experience or perception of a particular individual thing. It is not like trying to describe an object like the maple tree in my front yard, or the experience of the taste of pineapple, or the specific flavor of a fine burgundy wine from a particular group of vineyards in a specific section of France.

In order to explain why we are dealing here with a totally different kind of knowledge, we will need to talk about what the philosopher Kant called the categories of the human understanding, which are the most basic ideas of all, which supply the framework and the tools for talking about everything else we know, and provide the epistemological basis for knowing anything about the world at all. The concept of efficient causality—that is, our human understanding of what we mean when we say that one event caused something else to happen—is one of the categories. The idea of logical classes—that is, our understanding of what we mean when we say, for example, that four different birds swimming in a river are all "swans" and belong to that logical class, rather than being ducks or geese—is another of the fundamental categories. The categories cannot be explained in terms of anything simpler, because we must first understand them before we can talk about anything else.

Rudolf Otto, the Idea of the Holy

The holy was not on Kant's list of the categories, but the philosophical theologian Rudolf Otto, who was one of the two greatest Christian theologians of the period right after the First World War, has shown powerful reasons why it should be included in that list. It is this category of the understanding which allows us to identify certain kinds of experiences as experiences of the holy and the sacred. In his theological masterpiece, *The Idea of the Holy*, Otto said that although the category in question was schematized by the human reason as "the holy" when we were talking about spirituality, it was also schematized by our minds in two other kinds of ways. When we were thinking about morality, we schematized it as "the good itself," and when we were talking about art and beauty, we schematized it as the concept of what Kant (in his aesthetic theory) called "the sublime."

Let us begin however by talking a little bit about what is meant by the "holy" or the "sacred" (the two words refer to the same thing), and what kinds of experiences this term refers to. We will not be able to explain why it must be regarded as one of the basic categories of the human understanding until we have a better idea of how and where this concept is used.

It is an extremely important category, because all of the human activities which we call "religion" are attempts to experience and deal with the holy and the sacred. This is what defines religion as such. Religion is not necessarily about God. There are human religions which have no gods. Nontheistic Buddhism, for example, rejects any kind of idea of a God or gods, and yet it is clear that this is a kind of religion. The Native American tribe who live in my area of the United States, the Potawatomi, have no God in the Jewish and Christian and Muslim sense. Instead, they worship what they call the Manitou. This word is sometimes translated as the "Great Spirit," but this is highly misleading, because it does not refer to any kind of personal supernatural being at all. The Manitou is the sacred and the holy itself, as we can experience it in the trees and mountains, the growing corn, and the deer and bears and eagles.

Rudolf Otto wrote his great masterpiece, *The Idea of the Holy*, in 1917, and scholars in the field of comparative religions quickly took up the idea and still use it as a fundamental concept in the study of world religions.[22] It was one of the most successful theological works of the twentieth century. It has never been out of print and is still available at bookstores around the world in twenty different languages. Anyone who is going to write about religion, and what religious language means, has to begin with this concept as the starting point. We cannot talk about how the human mind apprehends the presence of God, and why God is important, until we first understand what is meant by the holy.

The experience of the holy and the sacred

What do we mean by the experience of the holy or the sacred? Let us begin with some simple examples. People entering a church or synagogue or mosque—even if it is a place of worship belonging to a different religious group—show by the change in their tone of voice, and the expressions on their faces, that they have an awareness of some sort that they are entering the presence of something different from the everyday world. Some of the conversion experiences at Protestant revival meetings are best described as overwhelming encounters with the irresistible power of the sacred. In a much quieter way, a good Roman Catholic or Anglican praying before the various stations of the cross, or receiving the bread and wine at the eucharist, strives to use these occasions as a means to experience the holy within their hearts and minds at the deepest internal level. The reverent respect with which a good Jew handles the scroll of the Torah when preparing to read from it in a synagogue shows in like manner the awareness that here one encounters what to Judaism is the sacred; or as a pious Jew might put it, it is the Book of the Torah of "the *Holy* One, blessed be He."

In an Eastern Orthodox church, the painted image on a flat wooden panel of one of the saints with candles flickering in front of it is a *hagia eikôn*, that is, a *holy* icon; the worshiper praying in front of it is using it as a crossover point, where the sacred realm (as Mircea Eliade calls it) comes into contact with the profane realm (the ordinary, everyday world), and where in prayer the believer can enter into living contact with the divine realm.[23]

This is also part of what is involved in the experience of the holy. In addition to the three dimensions which the natural scientists talk about, there is a "fourth dimension" if we wish to speak that way, a realm of sacred time and sacred space. Using Jean Piaget's terminology, we could say that this realm of sacred time and sacred space is *in correspondence with* the this-worldly realm—sacred events take place in conjunction with this-worldly events in such a way that they are in certain respects isomorphic—but we must also say that the sacred realm is not *interdependent with* the this-worldly realm in such a way that sacred events are reducible to this-worldly events, where the sacred events can be totally explained in terms of cause and effect within the this-worldly realm.[24]

The story of Bill W., co-founder of Alcoholics Anonymous

In the Big Book, the basic book which lies behind all the twelve step programs, Bill Wilson used this metaphor of a fourth dimension to describe the way in which he and the other early A.A. people had discovered the spiritual life: "We have found much of heaven and we have been rocketed into a fourth dimension of existence of which we had not even dreamed." Within that sacred realm of existence, that "fourth dimension," they were "to know happiness, peace, and usefulness, in a way of life that is incredibly more wonderful as time passes."[25]

In fact the experience of the holy lay at the very heart of the Big Book's description of what spiritual experience was basically about. Bill W. illustrated this from his own life. In the first chapter of the book, which was him telling his own story, he began by talking (in his distinctively sparse and simple prose style) about how he, as a young army officer during the First World War, first landed in England. He had a moving experience of the sacred, which he immediately brushed aside, and then a warning of the fate towards which his drinking and his contempt for the spiritual life was going to lead him, which again he also immediately brushed aside:[26]

> We landed in England. I visited Winchester Cathedral.
> Much moved, I wandered outside. My attention was caught
> by a doggerel on an old tombstone:
>
> "Here lies a Hampshire Grenadier

Who caught his death
Drinking cold small beer.
A good soldier is ne'er forgot
Whether he dieth by musket
Or by pot."

Ominous warning—which I failed to heed.

Over a decade and a half later, Bill W. had hit bottom, and was in total despair, when one of his old drinking buddies, a man named Ebby, came to visit him. Ebby was not only sober, he seemed to glow with love and serenity and a deep inner confidence. He explained how the Oxford Group had helped him find a God who had healed his life and his spirit. Bill W. was reminded of his experience of the sacred in its medieval Catholic expression at Winchester Cathedral, and also in the way that it was expressed by the small-town New England Protestant preachers of his childhood[27]—whom he had listened to only from a distance!

> [Ebby] talked for hours. Childhood memories rose before me. I could almost hear the sound of the preacher's voice as I sat, on still Sundays, way over there on the hillside . . . . That war-time day in old Winchester Cathedral came back again.
>
> I had always believed in a Power greater than myself . . . . How could there be so much of precise and immutable law [in the discoveries of the natural scientists] and no intelligence? I simply had to believe in a Spirit of the Universe, who knew neither time nor limitation. But that was as far as I got.
>
> With ministers, and the world's religions, I parted right there. When they talked of a God personal to me, who was love, superhuman strength and direction, I became irritated and my mind snapped shut against such a theory . . . .
>
> Despite the living example of my friend there remained in me the vestiges of my old prejudice. The word God still aroused a certain antipathy. When the thought was expressed that there might be a God personal to me this feel-

ing was intensified. I didn't like the idea. I could go for
such conceptions as Creative Intelligence, Universal Mind
or Spirit of Nature but I resisted the thought of a Czar of the
Heavens, however loving His sway might be. I have since
talked with scores of men who felt the same way.

My friend suggested what then seemed a novel idea. He
said, "*Why don't you choose your own conception of God?*"

That statement hit me hard. It melted the icy intellectual mountain in whose shadow I had lived and shivered
many years. I stood in the sunlight at last . . . . Scales of
pride and prejudice fell from my eyes. A new world came
into view.

The real significance of my experience in the Cathedral burst upon me. For a brief moment, I had needed and
wanted God. There had been a humble willingness to have
Him with me—and He came. But soon the sense of His
presence had been blotted out by worldly clamors, mostly
those from within myself. And so it had been ever since.
How blind I had been.

We need to note first of all one of the phrases which Bill W. used, in
the next to last paragraph above, about scales falling from his eyes. To
Americans of his generation, most of whom knew the Bible extremely
well, this was an obvious reference to the story of the Apostle Paul's
conversion on the road to Damascus (Acts 9:18). Bill W. was trying to
make it clear to us, in his use of this biblical reference, that this was his
fundamental conversion experience that occurred at that point.

And then we need to note one phrase in the final paragraph:
it was *the sense of the sacred presence* which he was able to focus on,
coupled with Ebby's suggestion that he stop worrying about traditional
theological definitions and doctrines and dogmas. Bill W. suddenly
realized that all the intellectual theories—about who or what this sacred
presence was—were secondary, and should be disregarded if they kept
one from feeling that presence. The force that could transform and
heal the ailing spirit was encountered by learning to *feel* once again
the primordial sense of the sacred. You could cast aside the entire
complex world of ecclesiastical doctrines and dogmas and still cling to

the foundational awareness of the holy and that alone, and be led by it out of the land of Egypt, out of the house of bondage, and successfully make your way to the divine light which shone out from the peak of the Mountain of God.

The sense of the presence

The "sense of the presence" can be felt in other contexts as well. People entering a cemetery find themselves unconsciously muting their voices. A professor of comparative religions at a university near mine was frustrated by the difficulty he was encountering in getting his cynical and worldly-wise undergraduates to take the concept of the holy seriously, until he came up with an interesting project for them. At the beginning of the semester, he required each student in the class to spend an entire night alone in a graveyard, with a pen and notebook, simply taking notes on what they *felt* as the night progressively wore on. He chuckled when he told me how well this worked at making even the most skeptical admit to feeling eventually some powerful awareness of the uncanny, or of the great mystery which lies beyond this world and this life and its concerns.

Being present at the birth of one's own child and actually seeing the infant born can make even many a hardened skeptic realize suddenly what the experience of the sacred is. The view of the planet earth from space had that effect on some of the first American astronauts: one of them, James Irwin, had such a profound spiritual experience that he afterwards founded a Christian ministry called High Flight, named after the famous poem by John Gillespie Magee, Jr. (the official poem of the Royal Canadian Air Force and Royal Air Force, it is also required to be recited from memory by first-year cadets at the United States Air Force Academy):

Oh! I have slipped the surly bonds of Earth
And danced the skies on laughter-silvered wings;
Sunward I've climbed ....
   Where never lark, or even eagle flew.
And, while with silent, lifting mind I've trod
The high untrespassed sanctity of space,
Put out my hand, and touched the face of God.

Back in the ancient world, the Roman essayist and dramatist Seneca commented, in his little epistolary essay "On the God Within," on the way the experience of the holy can suddenly come upon a person deep within the shadows of a forest filled with ancient, over-towering trees: a cold chill down the back, or a sense of uneasiness, or of awe at a kind of nonhuman grandeur that makes one feel one's own smallness and the transitory character of one's passage through that place. Or, Seneca said, deep within the arches of an enormous subterranean cavern, the same awe-filled awareness may come upon the visitor, or it can steal upon a person while staring into the unfathomable depths of a cold, dark, volcanic lake high on a mist-covered mountain.[28]

In William James's classic book, *The Varieties of Religious Experience*, numerous examples were given of encounters with the sacred that were even more overpowering, quoted verbatim in the actual words of the various people who had had the experiences. One of these autobiographical narratives is frequently quoted in detail, because it pulls together so well, in condensed form, a range of motifs that appear over and over again in so many other of the first-hand accounts in James's book:[29]

I remember the night, and almost the very spot on the hill-top, where my soul opened out, as it were, into the Infinite, and there was a rushing together of the two worlds, the inner and the outer. It was deep calling unto deep—the deep that my own struggle had opened up within being answered by the unfathomable deep without, reaching beyond the stars. I stood alone with Him who made me, and the beauty of the world, and love, and sorrow, and even temptation. I did not seek Him, but felt the perfect unison of my spirit with His.

The ordinary sense of things around me faded. For the moment nothing but an ineffable joy and exultation remained. It is impossible fully to describe the experience . . . . The perfect stillness of the night was thrilled by a more solemn silence. The darkness held a presence that was all the more felt because it was not seen. I could not any more have doubted that *He* was there than that I was. Indeed, I felt myself to be, if possible, the less real of the two.

Then, if ever, I believe, I stood face to face with God, and was born anew of his spirit . . . . Since that time no discussion that I have heard of the proofs of God's existence has been able to shake my faith . . . . My most assuring evidence of his existence is deeply rooted in that hour of vision, . . . and in the conviction, gained from reading and reflection, that something the same has come to all who have found God.

Since this person came from a Christian background, when he was attempting to identify intellectually what he had confronted, he spoke in Judaeo-Christian terms of this experience as an encounter with *God*— but when he instead spoke simply about *feelings*, in phrases like "the darkness held a *presence* that was all the more felt because it was not seen," any person who had had a profound encounter with the sacred, from any of the world's religious traditions, whether theistic or nontheistic, would have understood immediately what the feeling was that the writer was trying to describe.

The holy as the experience of the "numinous"

Having given some examples of what is meant by the holy and the sacred (these two words are interchangeable in English), we need to start looking in more detail at this idea, and the obvious place to start is with the classic book on this topic, *The Idea of the Holy*, which as we have mentioned, was written in 1917 by the German theologian Rudolf Otto.[30] He had made a systematic study of religions all around the world and through all periods of history, searching for how each religion described the *experience* of the sacred or holy. He had assumed when he began his researches (based on an important idea[31] he had picked up from the German philosopher Jakob Friedrich Fries) that he was going to find a rather simple sense of awe in the face of "the infinite" lying at the heart of religion, but instead he came up with a surprisingly long list of elements which all religious feeling, all over the earth, seemed to have in common. It was a much fuller and richer kind of experience than he was expecting to discover when he first began his project. And he concluded that referring to it simply as a sense of the infinite was not good enough—in fact it was something which was actually quite different from what Fries had theorized about—so he decided to refer to it as "the holy."

He began his book with a warning: there have been many religious systems where human beings experienced the sacred with no moral or ethical component attached to the experience at all. Now it is true that in many of the more developed religions, including Judaism, Christianity, and Islam of course, the concept of the holy is given strong moral and ethical content. In fact, in modern popular Christianity, the adjective "holy" can even degenerate into nothing more than a term for a rigorous (even fanatical) obedience to a set of rigid moral rules.

But there have been and still are religions where no strong moral component is present in the idea of the holy. An Aztec Indian felt the immediate presence of the sacred as he stared in fascinated awe at the still throbbing heart of a human sacrificial victim, held aloft in the blood-drenched hands of the priest who had just ripped the victim's chest open with a jagged flint knife. The Santería rituals carried out in Hispanic neighborhoods in some cities in the United States, where chickens and goats are sacrificed to a pantheon of Afro-Hispanic deities and powers, are sometimes concerned with quite selfish and non-moral purposes (love charms, the magical blessing of new building construction, hostile spells cast upon enemies, and so on). There were many stories in classical Greek mythology which were obviously grossly immoral: there was rape, castration, homosexual child abuse, adultery, diabolical revenge, lying, defrauding, theft, envy, and a host of other despicable deeds.[32]

Even in the more morally developed religions, there was always "something more" in the concept of the sacred than simply moral perfection—what Otto called an *Überschuss*, something surplus, something additional left over at the bottom of the balance sheet —and this "something more" was itself totally *ethically neutral*.[33]

From the Latin word *numen* (meaning the power of the divine) Otto coined the word "numinous" to refer to this ethically neutral component of the holy.[34] It was seemingly the only element in some primitive religions, but was nevertheless also strongly present in the ritual language and spiritual experience even of heavily moral religions like Judaism and Christianity. This word numinous was so useful that it has become part of the standard working vocabulary of theologians ever since.

In all the religious traditions of the world, Otto observed, this numinous reality was regarded as being (at its deepest level) a *mysterium*, the ultimate Mystery of reality—something hidden, something inexpressible, something intensely private and non-public, something which could not be conceptualized and intellectualized (*nicht Begriffene und Verstandene*), something not a normal component of the everyday world, something which was not part of the familiar and well-known.[35]

Metaphors, analogies, and ideograms

If the sacred is a *mysterium* which cannot be turned into a precisely defined intellectual concept (*Begriff*) which can be described directly—using the sort of literalistic language we would expect in a book on physics or chemistry or biology—then how can we talk about it at all? Otto said that religions all around the world have dealt with this problem by resorting to the use of symbols, metaphors, images, and analogies in order to describe the experience of the sacred numinous. When Christians describe God as the rock of ages, for example, or as our shield against the stormy blast, these are obviously metaphors.

When, in Hinduism, a god is portrayed as having many arms and legs and many mouths, this is likewise just a metaphor, in this case referring to the god's ability to go many places and do many things all at the same time, and so on.

And there was another way that language about the sacred could be symbolic, Otto said. Ordinary words in the language, which were used to talk about everyday things, could be used as "ideograms."[36]

Let us explain what he meant by the term ideogram, because this is apt to be an unfamiliar concept to most people in the western world today. Most writing systems used in the modern world employ an *alphabet* for writing (the Roman alphabet, the Russian alphabet, the Arabic alphabet, and so on) where there is a small set of twenty to forty letters (each one standing for a different short sound) which are used to represent phonetically all the words in the language. But there are other writing systems, like the one still used in China, which require the memorization of hundreds and hundreds of separate symbols (called ideograms), where each symbol stands for an entire word. In the ancient world, Egyptian hieroglyphics and Assyro-Babylonian cuneiform were written in this same kind of way, where each symbol represented an entire word.

To keep the list of ideograms from becoming impossibly huge (tens of thousands of symbols at the very least), it is the regular practice in languages which use this form of writing to use each picture or stylized symbol to represent several different words. Each symbol can be used, for instance, to first represent the word for some concrete, common object, but then used also to represent various transferred meanings which the common object might suggest. In ancient Egyptian hieroglyphics, the ideogram which represented the Egyptian word for musical instrument (a little picture of a musical instrument) also meant, by extension, the word for music, and even the word for joy.

In reading a language that is written in ideograms, the reader must therefore first decide what level of meaning is being used in the passage. Sometimes the pictures or stylized symbols are meant to be taken literally, but at other times, trying to read them in this fashion would produce nonsense.

A skilled writer however can write a series of ideograms which can be read at several different levels, where the sentence means something different at each level, but where all of these possible meanings make sense. This is part of the technique of writing poetry in Chinese (and is also the reason why it is impossible to truly translate Chinese poetry into English). In Chinese Taoist philosophy, even a short passage can often be translated "correctly" in two or three or more different ways, depending on the level at which one chooses to read the Chinese characters. Quite often, *all* the readings may be regarded as true within the Taoist philosophy of the world and life. Anyone who doubts this should obtain several different English translations of a Taoist philosophical work and compare them against one another, and notice how the same sentence says something totally different in each of the English translations. The odd feature here is that all of the different English translations are correct in so far as they go.

The main point here however, is that all languages which are written in ideograms use characters which represent simple, concrete things to stand for things which are not concrete objects or actions. In one version of ancient Mesopotamian hieroglyphics, the symbol for the word mouth can also stand for the verb that means to speak and the verb that means to eat. It can also stand for the noun that means hunger, or the noun which means a speech which someone gives, depending on the context.

Otto brought up this topic, because he discovered that traditional religious language all over the world used metaphors and terms which sometimes could appear extremely naive or even foolish if read at their simplest literal level. Those who scoffed at religion could use this phenomenon to make fun of religious people, and portray them as simpletons. This was not fair, Otto said, because these scoffers were not reading the words correctly. One could easily make a Chinese Taoist philosophical text appear like the work of a childish and stupid author if one insisted on going through the work and translating each Chinese character at its lowest level of meaning.

In order to understand religious language properly, the reader had to learn how to read its words as "ideograms" referring to higher or more subtle feelings or awarenesses. That was the only way their real meaning could begin to emerge. This was true not only for obvious metaphors, such as referring to God as the Rock of Ages or as our shield against the stormy blast, but also for apparently simple terms like *fear, happiness, mercy,* and *love.* Even words like these functioned in the language of spiritual experience as ideograms, as metaphors or symbols, and did not mean the same thing that they did in their ordinary everyday usage.

This-worldly fear, for example, is what I would feel if I were in a jungle and a tiger suddenly appeared, charging towards me with his fangs bared, or what I would feel if I woke up in the middle of the night and discovered a burglar standing over my bed with a gun in his hand. When we say however in religious language that "the fear of God is the beginning of all wisdom," this is referring to a quite different feeling, where the everyday meaning of the word fear is only being used metaphorically. "Fearing God" is an ultimate existential dread and an awe in the face of infinitely overwhelming power which strikes us at a completely different level of our souls.

When people are first being introduced to the spiritual life, summoning up the courage to deal with the fear of God in that sense is one of the biggest hurdles which they have to get past. In C. S. Lewis' children's story, *The Lion, the Witch, and the Wardrobe,* the figure of Aslan, the mighty lion, represents the power of God and the sacred realm penetrating into our ordinary material world. When the children who are the central figures in the story see Aslan for the first time, one of them, in terror, asks one of the villagers, "Is he safe?" The villager, who is one of the good and truly spiritual people in the story, smiles and says, "Of course not. But he is good." That is what newcomers to the spiritual life have to learn. Because God and those whom he sends have a goodness which includes compassion, kindness, forgiveness, and mercy, we can approach the throne of God to ask for help, with a full trust that this help will be given. This is what the word faith *means.* But God is not "safe" in the sense in which the child was asking, and neither are the ones whom God sends into the world as the channels of his grace.

Can you see here how we are using stories, symbols, metaphors, and ideograms to talk about real things and true knowledge? Aslan the lion is obviously a symbol, and the story of the children's encounter with him, and the way they come to understand the meaning of sacrifice and salvation and the way that good triumphs over evil, is obviously a metaphor. Children cannot really walk through the back of a wardrobe and enter a fairytale land, and ordinary lions in Africa do not act at all like Aslan. But let us not be misled: the words "safe" and "good" are not being given their ordinary meaning either. They are being used here as ideograms, which also stand for something beyond their literal everyday meaning.

Chapter 5

The Mysterium Tremendum

Rudolf Otto, the nature of our
encounter with the Holy

In ancient Rome, the word *numen* referred to the power of the divine as such. All the gods and goddesses and nature spirits within the Roman pantheon—Jupiter, Juno, Mars, Venus, Silvanus, Vesta, the Lares and Penates, and so on—were simply different expressions of this single mysterious power. Rudolf Otto took the word *numen* and used it to coin a new term, "the numinous," which he used to refer to that mysterious power. This was what the sacred was, at its heart, the power of all the gods and goddesses and spiritual forces which human beings had worshiped throughout history. Or better put, when the power of the numinous came in from the outside and intruded into our everyday world, we human beings felt it and experienced it as the holy and the sacred.

In his book, *The Idea of the Holy*,[37] Otto made a long, detailed list of six different basic kinds of ways in which the various religions of the world had spoken about the numinous. I have added a seventh motif to the end of Otto's list, one which I believe is also important: the idea of the sacred as a force producing illumination and enlightenment. It should also be included in this list, not only because it appears in religions all around the world in a great variety of different forms, but also because it will help us to understand the idea of God as the x-factor in conversion, where God appears as the divine power which enlightens us and produces authentic psychic change.

1. *Tremendum:* the feeling of awe and dread

The numinous is above all the *mysterium tremendum*. It is a mysterious presence which in its fullness can make us tremble (Latin *tremo*) with dread. In all our encounters with the sacred, we will at the very least feel a strong sense of *total awe*. As we enter more deeply into the sacred realm, we may *stand aghast* at the prospect of going into it any more deeply, and in fact we may turn and "run back out of the experience" in *panic fear* and *phobic terror*. Nevertheless, over the long-term process of spiritual growth, we become progressively able to actually take delight and find pleasure in experiences of the numinous.[38]

This is not the same thing at all as the artificial fears and anxieties which some religious systems attempt to indoctrinate into their members. In religions of this sort, the leaders, in order to maintain their power and authority, devise hundreds of complex mechanical rules which they insist that everyone must follow. Members become terrified in a manner which is very different from an authentic encounter with the sacred, because they are led to believe that if they violate even a single one of these arbitrary and absolutist rules, their souls will suffer in eternal hellfire, or they will be reincarnated as worms or frogs, or they will suffer some other painful divine punishment. This distortion of the authentic experience of the *mysterium tremendum* can work its way into any kind of spiritual system.

It requires a certain kind of neurotic authoritarian mentality to make and enforce these rules, or to passively accept them and attempt to obey them, but this is a perverted kind of pseudo-religiosity which has appeared over and over again in human history. The authoritarian mentality—both in the case of those who make the hundreds of rules and in the case of those who attempt to follow them—is in fact an attempt to avoid the authentic experience of the sacred and "domesticate it" in a way that gives us an illusion of control over God and the sacred. We come to believe (falsely) that if we can work out all the "correct rules" and follow them perfectly, God will be compelled to grant us whatever we want, and we will have gained control over him.

The real sacred power is so overwhelmingly powerful, however, that there is no way that a human being could ever gain control of it in this fashion, so people who become involved in legalistic religions of this sort invariably end up worshiping a fantasy God created in their own imaginations. This imaginary higher power can give us a comforting illusion of being in control over our own lives—we convince ourselves that all we have to do is follow a set of mechanical rules—and if we can rise to leadership positions, it can give us the egotistical thrill of control over the lives of others, who will be forced to obey us blindly. The problem is that, in the process of freeing ourselves from authentic awe at the overwhelming and uncontrollable power of the *mysterium tremendum*, we also find ourselves no longer able to share in its healing and power. The imaginary rules of an imaginary God cannot save anyone.

All spiritual systems can fall into this trap, if people are not perpetually vigilant. By the beginning of the twenty-first century, the twelve step program—which had gained its enormous healing power during the mid-twentieth century from its rebellion against the authoritarians and the rule-makers, and by its demonstration of the true route to an authentic experience of the sacred—found increasing numbers of members who were trying to create just as many arbitrary and mechanical rules for the twelve step program as there were in the legalistic religious systems from which they had fled. Now the authoritarian mentality was expressed in the neurotic belief that saying the wrong words at the beginning of a twelve step meeting, or allowing the wrong person to speak to a conference, or reading something which was not "conference approved" (i.e., dictated by the authority figures who, in their blind egotism, claimed "to know better" than everyone else), would send people back to drinking or drugging or codependency or gambling sprees, or whatever the compulsion was which that twelve program was designed to deal with.

Why would people fall for that kind of obvious nonsense? Any sensible person can see that, in A.A. for example, parroting exactly the right phrases at the beginning of a meeting is not going to get an alcoholic sober. If only it were so simple and easy! Alcoholics do not get sober by magically repeating certain words or by blindly turning their lives over to the complete control of egotistical authority figures, whether these figures are called delegates or service representatives or members of the intergroup committee or whatever. A domineering authority figure is a domineering authority figure, whether you call the person a priest, a cardinal, a pastor, a rabbi, an imam, or an A.A. delegate to New York. But there are lazy people, searching for the easier and softer way, who will grasp at this kind of mechanical nonsense in order to avoid taking authentic responsibility for their own lives, and in order to flee from an authentic encounter with the *mysterium tremendum*. And once these people start volunteering for a role of blind and servile obedience, there will also unfortunately be other men and women who will gladly and gleefully sit around pontificating and making up rules for them to follow, because being "the stage director" gives the prideful and arrogant an enormous ego thrill.

These kinds of imaginary fears and anxieties over breaking rules drawn up by pompous authority figures have nothing at all to do with the authentic experience of dread and awe in the face of the sacred, which is a force of nature itself. When the experience of the sacred bursts in upon us, it confronts us with something which we could never ever manipulate or control. Until we can learn how to live in the awareness of the *mysterium tremendum* without coming to pieces psychologically, we will never be able to truly live.

The real problem is that, even after we relieve newcomers from the fear that violating some mechanical rule will doom their souls for all eternity, the real power of the sacred will still loom before their eyes. Some of us are so scared of God and holy things when we first enter the twelve step program, that we will do anything to avoid praying to God or talking about God at all. A certain percentage of the newcomers who claim to be atheists are not atheists at all, at least down in lower levels of their minds. They spend large amounts of time trying to devise intellectual reasons for doubting God's existence, up at the top of their minds, in the attempt to quiet their overpowering fear of God down in the bottom of their hearts. To put it very crudely, an awful lot of people who claim to be atheists, are not atheists but wimps and cowards.

No newcomer is totally immune to this fear. At the beginning, whenever we start to have a powerful experience of the numinous, our natural tendency is to become frightened and pull back out. Proceeding more deeply into the spiritual life means confronting a series of additional things which will frighten us in a way which goes far deeper than any this-worldly fear. It takes a long time before we become able to tolerate long periods of immersion in the experience of the numinous presence.

Nevertheless, I know people in the twelve step program who are some of the most courageous people I have ever met in my life. They have managed to cope with and survive catastrophes in their personal lives, which would have crushed and destroyed most human beings. I suspect that the reason why they are able to manage this-worldly fears so successfully is because they have been schooled, in their spiritual lives, in dealing with experiences of dread and awe and terror which surpass any kind of this-worldly fear.

Why would we want to experience the holy at all, if it is so frightening? It should not be forgotten that we human beings can learn to turn certain kinds of fear into pleasure. We can learn to love going on roller coasters, jumping with parachutes from airplanes, racing on horseback, and riding fast motorcycles. The hint of danger is a vital part of the thrill. Real spiritual people (as opposed to the phoneys) are not stuffy, and the real spiritual life is never boring.

2. *Majestas:* the call to
total surrender

Even in the modern world, when we speak of the *majesty* of a great king, or a noble lord, or grand lady, some of the ancient numinous feeling still clings to this word. The sacred demands our *respect*. We can ridicule it or make fun of it only for so long as we can avoid having to actually experience it, and can keep well away from any authentic contact with it.

In its majesty, the sacred requires my *surrender* to it, and the *submission* of my own egotism. The Arabic word *islam* means surrender to the will of Allah in that fashion. The heart of Islam as a religion is this acknowledging of the overpowering majesty of God, who stands above all things and rules all things. Christianity and Judaism likewise proclaim a God before whom all creation will have to bow the knee at the end of time, when God will become all in all.

In the twelve step program, we are forced to learn that "either God is everything or else He is nothing."[39] The psychiatrist Harry M. Tiebout, who was one of the first psychiatrists to take the twelve step program seriously, wrote a famous journal article with the title, "Surrender Versus Compliance in Therapy: With Special Reference to Alcoholism."[40] Tiebout was struggling for words which would describe what he had noted in his work with alcoholics. Alcoholics who came for treatment could sometimes be totally "compliant." By that he meant that they were polite and listened and did what they were told, but they were still unable to stop drinking (and there was no real progress in the other parts of their psychotherapy either). No progress was made until something mysterious happened, which Tiebout called "surrendering." Alcoholics who *surrendered* turned themselves totally over—mind, heart, body, and soul—in a way that went far beyond merely following rules and passively listening to authorities and experts lecturing at you and preaching to you. At the spiritual level, they finally became willing to acknowledge the *majestas* of the numinous power, the overpowering demand which the numinous power made

89

on us, to become part of something much bigger than ourselves. This total surrender then liberated them to experience the sacred at all sorts of other levels, and that in turn allowed the divine healing power to actually enter into their hearts for the first time.

In some of the spiritual disciplines within what is called the mystical tradition (St. Denis the Areopagite, the Hindu philosopher Shankara, the Sufi mystics in Islam, and so on) this idea is taken much further: believers are asked to submerge their own self-identity so completely that they become a part of the numinous themselves. Mystical systems of this sort speak of attaining a "union with God" (or with the supreme divine reality) in which there is a total annihilation of the ego and the self, to such an extent that I lose all consciousness of being a separate self. I am God, in the same way that all is God.

It should also be noted, however, that there are many other spiritual traditions in which any talk of "becoming one with God" in this kind of fashion is regarded as not only silly but in fact blasphemous. They tell us that this kind of language lessens God and attempts to pull him down to our level. Rudolf Otto, however, points out that this language, used properly, does not at all imply a lessening of God's *majestas* but the reverse. Union with God in the mystical sense comes only when our awareness of the majesty of God finally grows so great that it totally overwhelms us with its numinous power.

Nevertheless, rather than become hopelessly entangled in this argument (which has been going on for thousands of years) over whether a human being can enter into this sort of union with God and the divine (where different religious traditions come to such completely different conclusions) Rudolf Otto says that it is sufficient to state that in all higher spiritual teachings, the follower must at the very least ultimately learn to say of the numinous reality, "thy will, not mine, be done."[41]

This phrase was originally spoken by Jesus, when he was praying to God in the garden of Gethsemane immediately before his arrest. Luke 22:42 says that he prayed, "Father, if thou be willing, remove this cup from me: nevertheless not my will, but thine, be done." Matthew 26:39 gives Jesus' prayer in closely similar words, "O my Father, if this cup may not pass away from me, except I drink it, thy will be done." This simple prayer of surrender to the divine *majestas* then became one of the central themes in the A.A. Big Book, which said that this must be part of every prayer to God: "How can I best serve Thee—Thy will (not mine) be done."[42]

3. *Energeia:* power, energy, love and Eros

It is strange, but a good many of the philosophers and theologians who have talked about God and the divine over the course of history, have portrayed the higher power as something static, as some sort of absolute which remains unchanging for all eternity. The higher power they describe may be grand and glorious, but it dwells in a realm where there is no emotion or feeling. We may admire this eternal and unchanging absolute from a distance, and look on it with awe, but there is in fact no logical and coherent way that we can combine that kind of idea of God with the idea of a God who reaches out to each of us with acts of grace, where each individual act of grace is different and tailored to exactly where I am or you are, at that particular moment in time.

Rudolf Otto was originally inspired to begin his phenomenological study of the idea of the holy by his research on the philosopher Jakob Friedrich Fries,[43] who said that our awareness of God was an experience of the Infinite and the Absolute. That implied the traditional static concept of the supreme being, the one which had appeared in the writings of so many other philosophers down through history.

But when Otto looked at the actual experiences of religious people, all around the world and at all periods of history, he discovered that the sacred was not experienced in that fashion at all. The numinous reality was always in practice—at the actual phenomenological level— apprehended as something which was full of force, vital passion, and *energy*. To most of the peoples of the earth, at all periods of history, the sacred was seen as something that could *act* in this world, and act with overwhelming power.

When we look at their stories and rituals and instructions for actually living the spiritual life, we observe the numinous reality being portrayed as capable of passionate *love*. At the lowest, crudest level, the myths of the ancient Greeks spoke of the amorous affairs of the god Zeus; in India the Hindu religious tales of Krishna's exploits tell of his erotic exploits with the cow-maidens.

But the divine capacity for love can also be spoken of, in some spiritual traditions, at a higher level, such as when the New Testament speaks of a God "who so loved the world, that he sent his only-begotten son" (John 3:16). The mystical spiritual writings of St. John of the Cross, St. Gregory of Nyssa, St. Teresa of Ávila, and Hannah Hurnard—spiritual authors writing at all periods of history—describe the spiritual life as a love affair between God and the human soul.[44]

I have chosen the word *energeia* to describe this aspect of the sacred (what Otto calls the urgent, fiery, passionate, sometimes also frighteningly wrathful element), because it links into one of the most important themes of this book. Prior to the twentieth century, western theology and philosophy usually spoke of God as a static and unchanging Absolute, who was totally divorced from the world of time and change. God was the "Unmoved Mover," who served as a passive attractive force, putting the world into motion by pulling it towards himself as the ideal goal of all processes. But the revolutionary realignment of western thought produced by the discoveries of twentieth century science forces us to develop a different kind of concept of God, one which sees God as an active and dynamic force, exploding with energy, change, and continuous creativity, presiding over a universe which is likewise continually dynamic and changing and immersed in the flow of time and process—a universe peopled, at least on the planet we live on, by human beings who, by their free choices and driving passions, enliven the universe with the same perpetual creativity and blossoming of newness.

There are different kinds of energy, which is very important to note. All of the physical energy in our universe is derived from the explosion of energy which we call the Big Bang, which took place around 13.7 billion years ago. The natural sciences study that kind of physical energy, including all the natural forces of attraction and repulsion.

But there is another kind of energy, which also involves both attraction and repulsion, which operates as a kind of "higher harmonic" of the kind of energy which the scientists study. This different kind of energy, which operates at the level of higher meaning, is love. Even though speaking of love gives us no help at all when we are talking about rocks and electrons and galaxies and the other sorts of things which natural scientists study, human beings understand (and are motivated at all times by) this kind of love, so we have to talk about this other kind of attractive energy field in order to make any real sense of human behavior at all. "Love" as a kind of energy is only relevant to beings which have a higher consciousness, but it is an essential part of their makeup, and hence is a real part of the universe.

The ancient Greeks spoke about three different kinds of love, a distinction which is extremely useful to make. God can act towards human beings with all three of these different kinds of love: The Bible tells us that God wants to be our friend (*philia*), and that he will treat us with *agapé*, a kind of dependable and compassionate loving kindness, a "welcome home love" which will express itself in concrete help.[45] But Christian mysticism goes beyond that, and says that God also desires us with a divine *erôs*, where he wants us for his own.

As the contemporary Irish-American writer Father Andrew Greeley puts it in a whole series of interesting novels (over fifty of them at last count),[46] the divine Eros continually showers us with countless gifts in truly exuberant fashion. One galaxy would be an incredible thing to create, but the divine Eros creates millions. A single flower would be an extraordinary thing to create, but the divine Eros scatters them everywhere, dandelions and wild roses and honeysuckle and all the marvelous tiny little blossoms we see scattered through the grass in Spring. And the divine Eros uses every wile in its power to gently and subtly seduce us into believing that we are the ones who are trying to find God, when in fact it is the other way around.

What makes Father Greeley's novels especially interesting is his portrayal of the feminine aspects of God. The preceding Christian mystical tradition liked to quote from the Song of Songs in the Old Testament and portray the human soul as feminine, while portraying the divine Eros as a masculine love. Greeley however reverses this, and says that the divine Eros is not masculine at all, but the kind of feminine love which young women know so well—the art of acting in ways which make the young man of her choice believe that he is the one who chose to pursue her, where the young man is often filled with great fear and trembling at the thought that she might reject him, little realizing that it was her (the young woman) who actually chose him and not vice versa.

This is one aspect of the ancient figure of God as "Sancta Sophia," Lady Wisdom, whom we meet in the Bible at various points, as in Proverbs 8:1, 23-25; 9:1-6.

> Does not Wisdom call,
> and does not understanding raise her voice?
>
> At the first, before the beginning of the earth,
>   when there were no depths I was brought forth,
>   when there were no springs abounding with water.
> Before the mountains had been shaped,
>   before the hills, I was brought forth.
>
> Wisdom has built her house,
>   she has hewn her seven pillars ....
> She has sent out her servant-girls, she calls
>   from the highest places in town,
> "You that are ignorant, turn in here ....
>   Lay aside ignorance and live,
>   and walk in the way of insight."

In the vernacular, Sophia (Lady Wisdom) is sometimes referred to as Mother Nature or the creative and healing power of nature, but she is also identified in the Christian tradition with the Holy Spirit, and sometimes even with the indwelling power of Christ.[47] She is also essentially the same power as is represented in the figure of Our Mother Mary as the Gate of Heaven.[48] The huge domed church of Sancta Sophia in Constantinople (modern Istanbul) was for almost a thousand years the largest Christian church building in the entire world.

The numinous reality can display other emotions as well, such as joy, anger and grief.[49] In Alcoholics Anonymous, people regularly report that the higher power they have discovered also has a well-developed sense of *humor*. Sometimes for example he plays little tricks on us, they say, to get us laughing at ourselves until we are laughing so hard that we truly come to realize how foolish one of our old destructive behaviors actually was—and in that very moment, we become freed from its deadly power.

This is a place where we need to ignore all the philosophers who have attempted to turn God into a static, unchanging Absolute, devoid of all emotion and feeling, and pay attention to what ordinary men and women have discovered—people from all parts of the globe and all periods of history—as they went about the day-to-day business of actually leading the spiritual life. A careful phenomenological study of the idea of the holy, like the one Rudolf Otto made, makes this clear. Learning to feel the power of the energy flowing forth, in God's continually outpouring love for us, is one of the most important parts of the experience of the holy at its higher level.

4. *Alienum:* the divine abyss lying behind the surface illusion of understandability

The sacred is a *mysterium*, Rudolf Otto said, a mysterious reality which cannot be talked about in the same kind of language that we use in speaking of houses and chairs and cabbages and nuclear reactors and space missiles and choosing the best laundry detergent and what the new duties are that my boss gave me at work.

But that negative description does not go nearly far enough. *The numinous confronts my soul as the completely Alien.* We are struck with blank wonder, numb amazement, or total astonishment. A chill runs down our spines.

In Rudolf Otto's German phrase the numinous reality is *das ganz Andere*, the "Wholly Other." Karl Barth borrowed that phrase from Otto, and pointed out its consequence: "you cannot speak of God by speaking of man in a loud voice." God (or Allah or Brahman) is not like a human being, except that he is just more intelligent and more powerful and in more places. Instead, the numinous reality is *totally different* from anything in this world.

When I move to the very edge of the structures of my own mental world, and look "over the edge," I may attempt to describe what is there as *das Nichts*, the infinite Nothingness which is the existential abyss. In one sense it is correct to say that this is a No-thing-ness, because the numinous reality is not a thing in the way that the things of this world are things. But it is not truly an empty void, because it is the surrounding presence of something totally alien but nevertheless there, which stretches out forever.[50]

All of the plethora of different atheistic systems which began to be developed in the western world in the 1840's were attempts to domesticate the universe, and turn all of our human experiences into things which we could explain and control. Human beings wanted to be their own gods, and turn everything into this-worldly experiences, which thereby became "comfortable" and manageable.

One of the major points which this present book was making in its first three chapters was that, paradoxically, we cannot turn even this-worldly experiences into "safe" and totally explainable this-worldly experiences. Everywhere we turn, gaps appear in our explanatory schemes, fissures open up in the seamless façade of logical interconnections, and through the gaps and rents we see the completely Alien lying below the fragile surface of our definitions and scientific laws.

When I look around my study, I can focus on the comforting illusion of normality: my desk, the bookcases filled with books, the walls and ceiling of the room, grass and trees which I can see through my windows. And when I do so, I can comfort myself with the illusion of things which are solid and stable and unchanging. But all of this is no more than a tissue laid over an alien abyss stretching forever, and my life (with all its schemes and plans) is no more than a tiny chip laid on top of this insubstantial fabric.

And yet herein lies salvation and healing. Once I truly see how frail and fragile the surface of "normality" actually is, I can also see that it is plastic and malleable. I can learn to use the power of the underlying Alien reality to take apart the distorted and destructive ideas which dominate my life, and remake the surface layer of my world so that I can live triumphantly and successfully. Instead of frantically trying to patch and cover over every rift and tear in this surface layer, I can learn to relax and float upon the surface of the infinite ocean of the eternal Mystery which lies below me.

This was the secret of the New Thought movement—Emmet Fox, James Allen, and so on—which had such a powerful effect upon the thinkers who put together the twelve step program. I can change my world in dramatic and sweeping fashion by changing the way I think about my world.

The alien quality of the numinous may send a shiver down my spine and raise up the hairs on the back of my neck, but it is the power of New Meaning which can rescue my soul when all the meaning which used to structure my life seems to have fallen into the fires of destruction. It is what Paul Tillich, in *The Courage to Be*, called the power of the New Being, and what Viktor Frankl (a survivor of the Nazi death camps) called the power of meaning (*Logos*) to rescue our spirits and keep the flame of our humanity alive in even the most desperate of circumstances.[51] *Das ganz Andere*, the "Wholly Other," tears apart the fabric of our old lives, but contains a power which will give birth to a new and better life, *as long as we give it its power* by not attempting to domesticate it.

5. *Fascinans:* salvation itself as living in the continual presence of the sacred

In spite of the fear and awe which one feels before its sheer otherness and its overwhelming majesty and power, the experience of the numinous nevertheless fascinates us so deeply that it draws us in. People pursue the spiritual life because they want to drink more and more at the spring of this experience.

In the higher religions, it is found that living in the presence of the numinous in the right way conveys a sense of peace and overwhelming joy and gratitude. It gives power to us far beyond the normal human limitations. It gives a sense of being loved—in spite of anything that we have done, or have not done, or may not ever do—with a total trustworthiness and dependability and an infinite well of compassion and mercy.

In the highest and truest form of the spiritual life, as this is described in all of the higher religions of the world, living in the continual presence of the numinous *is salvation itself.* Experiencing the numinous (here and now in this life) is in fact the blessedness or beatitude that is the real spiritual goal. This is "being saved" or "experiencing Nirvana" or "achieving satori."

This is also what is meant by the Christian teaching of salvation by grace alone and faith alone, rather than by works of the law. There is no way I can feel the experience of the sacred and the holy simply by following a set of mechanical and arbitrary regulations. I cannot achieve this goal by doing things like not going to movies on Sunday, not eating meat on Fridays, not harming the sacred cows wandering through the streets, not eating pork, wearing my hair or my clothes in a certain way, following all the rules devised by overenthusiastic and authoritarian A.A. delegates, or anything like that. I also cannot automatically feel the experience of the sacred by donating food and clothes to the poor, showing sympathy towards someone who is grieving, or taking faithful and responsible care of my family. The experience of the sacred is simply something "wholly other" from these concerns.[52]

On the other hand, it has been found repeatedly that people cannot be in close contact with the realm of the numinous when their minds are totally taken over by resentments that will not go away, by unrelenting self-pity, by worldly fears that gnaw and nag at them continuously, and by anxieties that keep them perpetually on edge. Once people are far enough along in the spiritual life, they take great pains to act as morally as they can, not because they are afraid that God will not love them if they do not do so, and not because they believe that God will reward them for acting morally, but because they have found that only by acting morally can they keep resentment, self-pity, fear, and anxiety from blocking them from the full experience of the sacred. There is a kind of paradoxical quasi-selfishness to this, because it is only by acting in a totally *unselfish* manner that I can gain real peace and joy and the experience of the numinous *for myself*.

6. *Augustus:* the power which condemns us but then washes us clean

The sacred represents the power of what Rudolf Otto called the *augustus*, which he understood as a kind of numinous value which makes itself regarded as the supreme center of all worth. It is that which commands our ultimate reverence. He said that in the higher religions which have well-developed moral systems, this is what is being schematized in their ethical precepts. The numinous in this aspect is what the ancient Greek philosopher Plato called the *bonum ipsum*, the Good Itself.[53] It is our awareness of that ultimate transcendent goodness which creates the criterion for the basic distinction between good and evil.

In this section of *The Idea of the Holy* however, where Otto is talking about the *augustus*, he only talks in detail about one aspect of this way of apprehending the holy, that is, the holy as the vision of the *bonum ipsum* which condemns the evil in our hearts and deeds, but also paradoxically washes us clean and heals us. So I am going to add a seventh section (under the heading *illuminatio*) where we will look at the important part he left out, which is the way this vision of the *bonum ipsum* also shines its light on goodness and beauty, in a way which makes them so attractive and desirable that we become willing to turn our lives over to the pursuit of the new goodness and beauty which has been revealed to us.

For now, however, let us confine ourselves to what Otto said about the sacred as that feeling of the *augustus* which at first seems only to condemn us. In the presence of the sacred—because it contains within itself an all-surpassing goodness and beauty—all the things inside our souls which are evil will appear to us as things of horror and total revulsion.

Our ability to sense the sacred in this aspect is what creates the *scintilla conscientiae*, the little spark of what we might call deep conscience, which is buried down in the bottom of our souls. We are not talking here about the Freudian superego, which is made up of introjected parental and societal admonitions, and is essentially no more than a set of arbitrary guilt-laden rules. We are looking here at something far more primordial, which has nothing to do with the hundreds of rules and arbitrary should's and ought's which various authority figures tried to impress upon us when we were children. The *scintilla conscientiae* (the divine "spark of conscience" within our souls) is based on something much deeper, that is, the ability (which all human beings share) of being able to understand the infinite qualitative difference between true evil and true good.

Since we cannot avoid being aware of the presence of the sacred all around us, at the subconscious level at least, after we have done something that we know is enormously evil, we feel dirty and unclean. Pontius Pilate and Lady Macbeth both tried compulsive hand washing, but this never really works. People who have done something which they know was dirty and perverted, and a betrayal of all decency and all their self-respect, will sometimes go home afterwards and try to spend an hour in the shower, scrubbing themselves with soap over and over and trying to wash off the sense of being stained and fouled which continues to cling to them.

Sometimes, Otto said in this section of *The Idea of the Holy*, we may feel almost sick at our stomachs, in a kind of inner spiritual nausea at the memory of the ugly deeds which we did. We feel somehow that if we could "throw it all up," we could somehow get the poisonous and damning awareness out of our systems.

We remember Jean-Paul Sartre's novel, *La Nausée*, which came out in 1938, and quickly became one of the defining works of the early twentieth-century atheistic existentialist movement. Even though we try to deny the existence of the sacred, we will still feel its presence at some level, although usually it will be an extremely negative feeling. The atheistic existentialists saw the sacred ground of being, but denied its sacredness and claimed that it was only an abyss of nothingness. Trying to deal with it that way, what they could not truly explain was why, if it was only nothingness, their immediate reaction was to draw back in nausea and a sense of pervasive guilt. Nearly all of the atheistic existentialists spoke of the feelings of continual floating guilt which still plagued their lives. They tried to explain the guilt away by claiming that it was only an "existential anxiety," a natural part of human existence itself, which had to be resolutely ignored and rejected. But they never could get rid of the feelings of guilt that way.

We can run from the feeling of the sacred, but we cannot hide. This is why any good spiritual system requires some means of *atonement*, some way of "washing ourselves clean" spiritually, some method of admitting or confessing our wrongs, some way to make amends when possible, or some other kind of way to take away the sense of dirtiness, pollution, shame, and humiliation.[54] The English word atonement means quite literally at-one-ment, healing and cleansing our relationship with the sacred, so that we can be "at one with it" again, able to immerse ourselves fully into the feeling of the sacred again without continually wanting to throw up or flee in horror.

There is a great paradox here. When people first begin the spiritual life, they fear the experience of the sacred because they feel so morally unclean, yet the only thing which can truly wash us clean is the numinous power itself. Only the force of the Good Itself can overpower that which is truly evil. But that means we first have to appear before this sacred power while we are still in our dirtiness before the process of washing us clean can even begin. And we have to be willing to remain in the presence of the holy while it cleanses us, in spite of our feelings of guilt and nausea and dirtiness.

This is why a good deal of time needs to be spent on reassuring newcomers to the spiritual life that the force of the numinous will not destroy them, no matter how it makes them feel at first. Instead, it is going to wash them clean and heal them. They need to be told over and over, that God accepts us just as we are, and that God loves us long before we learn to love back. The self-hatred and self-loathing which is created by my sense of guilt over the truly evil things I have done, is part of the evil which needs to be washed away. But I have to confront it courageously, and allow myself to feel it, before it can be washed away.

What people do not seem to realize is, that God's response to finding a human soul that can be cleaned is like that of an antique dealer who discovers an old table at a garage sale, covered with peeling paint, and filthy and dirty, and realizes that it is in fact a fine Louis-the-whatever piece of antique furniture that can be restored perfectly. But every human soul at bottom is the little child of God, made in his image,[55] so none of us are truly irredeemable, and all of us can be turned into something of infinite worth and value by God's restorative techniques, even if it takes months to begin seeing the fine lines of God's original handiwork beneath all the accumulated grime and cheap, garish paint. So God does not mind me appearing before him, still dirtied with shameful deeds, but on the contrary is delighted to see me, as long as I allow him to start healing and restoring me, one little step at a time, and at a pace that I can tolerate.

Nevertheless, if I wish to continue standing in the presence of the holy, I must begin doing some work myself right away, in order to cleanse my life. There is a synergism at work: only the power of grace can save me, but even the power of grace cannot save me unless I am willing to do my own small part to help it. And if I wish to continue in the spiritual life, I must continue this cleansing process at deeper and deeper levels. In the twelve step program, this is what is being done in the fourth through tenth steps, where I begin in the fourth step by identifying my character defects, then confess them to God and another human being in the fifth step, and next ask God to start freeing me from their power. When I finally get to the tenth step, I learn that I must continue this process for all the rest of my life on earth, because as I "peel the onion" and get down to deeper and deeper parts of my being, I will continually find new levels where I need cleansing and healing. Once I am past the stage, however, of being a raw newcomer, I will learn that the process of continuing to work on my soul and my character is in fact a joy and a triumph. No matter how good my life becomes, I can always make it even better, going on (as the Apostle Paul said in 2 Corinthians 3:18) "from glory to glory," *apo doxês eis doxan*, from one eye-opening revelation of new life and light to the next. Walking this journey into greater and greater insight and wisdom, with new depths of happiness opening before me without end, produces an extraordinary feeling of joy.

In traditional Christian mysticism, this journey was called the Purgative Way (*via purgativa*), the cleansing of the ingrained evil in the soul. The great mystics like St. Teresa of Avila and St. John of the Cross made clear that we had to work at that part of our spiritual lives in order to obtain the higher spiritual gifts, as we progressed to walking the Illuminative Way (*via illuminativa*) and ultimately the Unitive Way (*via unitiva*), where God's spirit and the power of the divine love came to totally fill our hearts.

As St. Teresa said, in the *Interior Castle*, when talking about the first of the seven sets of mansions (the seven stages of the spiritual life), which is the entryway into the spiritual life:[56]

> You must note that the light which comes from the palace occupied by the King hardly reaches these first mansions at all ... because there are so many bad things—snakes and vipers and poisonous creatures—which have come in with the soul, that they prevent it from seeing the light. It is as if one were to enter a place flooded by sunlight with his

eyes so full of dust that he could hardly open them. The room itself is light enough, but he cannot enjoy the light because he is prevented from doing so by these wild beasts and animals, which force him to close his eyes to everything but themselves.

But we must pass through St. Teresa's seven sets of mansions in order, and this is where we must begin, at the first one, where we are still horrified at our own evil and wickedness, but must begin to use the power of prayer and divine grace in order to cleanse ourselves of the character defects which have made us think and act in that kind of destructive, dirty, resentful, and fear-centered way. This is the beginning of the *via purgativa* (the cleansing way) in St. Teresa's teaching about the spiritual life.

In the section of *The Idea of the Holy* where Rudolf Otto discussed the holy as the *augustus*, he began by talking about this, the first of the traditional Three Ways: the *via purgativa*, where the encounter with the sacred fills us with horror at our own evil. But he also explained why we had to walk this way before we could begin walking the *via unitiva*, the Unitive Way, where our souls could be united with the Good and the holy, and we could obtain *atonement* for our guilt by washing ourselves in the light of the holy, and once again become "one with God."

7. *Illuminatio:* inspiring us to pursue the true goal of the spiritual life

Once we recognize that what Rudolf Otto called the feeling of the *augustus* was what the Platonic tradition called the vision of the *bonum ipsum*—the sunlight of the spirit, which shows us all the goodness and beauty of the world, and the path to true serenity and "feeling good about ourselves" again—we realize that we must add a seventh section to his discussion of the human awareness of the holy and the numinous. Because in Plato, as we see in his parable of the cave, the Good Itself is the power of divine light.[57]

Or as St. Teresa and the mystical tradition put it, there are three ways which we must follow in order to obtain true serenity and peace. In between the *via purgativa* (where we see the evil lurking within our souls and begin to cleanse it) and the *via unitiva* (where we atone for the evil deeds in our past and are allowed to become one with God again), there lies the *via illuminativa*, the Illuminative Way.

The vision of the sunlight of the spirit in Plato is an awareness of that ultimate transcendent goodness which creates the criterion for the basic distinction between good and evil. At first we feel a sense of guilt and condemnation, because our deeds have been such that we cannot bear to see them in the full light of day. That is the feeling of the sacred as the *augustus*, to use Rudolf Otto's terminology.

But it is not enough simply to see the wickedness of my old way of life. That is the problem with a good deal of religious preaching. People are harangued and condemned and told over and over that they are evil wrongdoers, but they are given no power to change. The human soul cannot be changed at its deepest level by preaching a negative. A true psychic change can only be produced when human beings are given positive motivation for thinking about the world in a different way. We must be inspired and given a vision of something so wonderful and marvelous that we would be willing to do anything at all in order to obtain that kind of beauty and goodness of life.

We must see the sunlight of the spirit shining, not only on the dark side of the street, where we have been living, but also on the sunny side of the street, so that we can be motivated from within ourselves to walk over to that side of the street.

A.A. spirituality begins with the recognition that a practicing alcoholic will do anything at all to obtain alcohol. Alcohol is dearer to them than job, family, social approval, freedom, health, and even life itself. If you tell practicing alcoholics that you will lock them up if they continue drinking, they will continue to drink. If you tell practicing alcoholics that they will die if they continue to drink, they will continue to drink. To non-alcoholics, this is impossible to comprehend or imagine. How could human beings conceivably continue to drink when competent physicians (and elementary common sense) are telling them that they will be dead within a few weeks or months, from a heart attack or a stroke or liver failure, or something else of that sort? And yet that is exactly what real alcoholics do. Alcohol is their Higher Power, and they will sacrifice even life itself in order to persist in their drinking.

The only way to stop alcoholics from drinking permanently is to give them something so much better that they will voluntarily stop drinking. They will no longer want to drink. But nothing earthly will be big enough to do this. Only the vision of the sacred and the infinite itself will be great enough to overcome their desire for alcohol. And the same thing applies in all the other twelve step programs. We find people literally destroying themselves with narcotics, gambling, dangerous sexual addictions, food (because we can literally eat ourselves to death, and many food addicts actually do that), caretaking (because people in Al-Anon will tell you how they were driven to the point of suicide by their obsessive need to "save" other people), and inability to control their anger. They *know* that they are destroying themselves, yet in their despair, even then they cannot quit.

So we need to add a seventh section to our discussion of the sacred, where we talk about the way the sacred gives us saving insight, enlightenment, illumination, and a quality of luminosity that shines out in all the universe. We see this kind of light metaphor being used in religions all over the earth. The Buddha, we are told, grants us true enlightenment. The Dead Sea Scrolls tell us how to stop being Children of Darkness, and how to start becoming Children of Light. In a little Bible church in Marion, Indiana, I love to listen to Steve C. and Sister Neese strumming their guitars and leading the congregation in a rousing rendition of "I saw the light, I saw the light, no more darkness, no more night ...." You can just feel the love in that little church, and Steve C. in particular will gladly tell you how the combination of A.A. and that church led him out of all the raging anger that had filled his soul after the horrors he had experienced as a foot soldier in the jungles of Vietnam—a rage that had led him down the path into alcohol and drugs, and had been destroying him.

The Navajos in Arizona and New Mexico arise at dawn, and chant sacred hymns while they scatter corn pollen as an offering to the rising sun, which is the symbol of the light which illumines all that is good and beautiful and harmonious. The Navajos do not talk about God in the Judeo-Christian sense, but instead use the word *yo'zho'* to refer to the saving power which they find in the experience of the sacred. *Yo'zho'* is a Navajo concept which takes several different English words to translate fully: it means beauty, harmony, the smooth natural flow of things, peace, and serenity, all viewed as a sacred and holy quality which we can sense and feel in the natural world around us—the mountains, the valleys, the deer, the sky, the clouds—and which we can also sense within ourselves, when we have attuned our emotions and attitudes to it. Their traditional prayers ask us to visualize this sacred beauty and harmony all around us: "Beauty in front of us, beauty behind us, beauty beside us." "Peace in front of us, peace behind us, peace beside us." What is important to note here however, is that in the offering to the rising sun, and in the campfires which they light to perform some of their most important rituals, they are using the light metaphor to symbolize the way that the experience of the sacred illumines their spirits and shows them the healing path.

In traditional western spirituality, when we enter the Cloud of Unknowing, the power of the sacred topples and dissolves all our old preconceptions and dismantles the framework of our old cognitive structure. New insights however begin to show us new ways of framing our basic thought structure. Sometimes this can take a long time. I may hear something at a twelve step meeting 453 times without understanding what people are telling me, and then suddenly, the 454th time, I suddenly understand what the words mean, and how they impinge on my life.

But receiving an insight into a new and different way in which I could live my life will not, in and of itself, motivate me to change the way I have been living my life. We often find ourselves knowing what we ought to do in order to live a good life, but being totally incapable of making ourselves actually do it. As the Apostle Paul said in Romans 7:15-24:

> I do not understand my own actions. For I do not do what I want, but I do the very thing I hate. Now if I do what I do not want, I agree that the law [of God] is good. But in fact it is no longer I that do it, but sin that dwells within me .... I can will what is right, but I cannot do it .... For I delight in the law of God in my inmost self, but I see in my arms and legs another law at war with the law of my mind, making me captive to the law of sin that dwells in my arms and legs. Wretched man that I am! Who will rescue me from this body of death?

Jonathan Edwards, in his essay on "A Divine and Supernatural Light,"[58] explained that real soul change will only occur when the divine light shows me "the excellency of the things of God," as he put it in eighteenth century language. I have to see the new way of life as a shining goal which pulls me towards it by its own intrinsic beauty and goodness. Its appealing quality has to become so great that I will, by my own deepest internal wishes and wants, leave my old way of life behind and turn to it instead. It will then become, not some rule or requirement imposed on me from outside myself, but something which I authentically desire inside myself.

Alcoholics in A.A. who have become genuinely sober do not stop drinking because they hate alcohol and its effects, but because they have found something which their hearts desire even more. Newcomers to A.A. are sometimes disturbed when one of the old timers tells them, "Why don't you go back out and drink some more? I don't think you're ready for this program yet." These newcomers expect the A.A. old timers to scold them and preach to them about the evils of drinking. Instead they tell the newcomers that they have no objection at all to other people drinking, and that they are not anti-alcohol in any way whatsoever. That is because they know that these newcomers will never become able to stop drinking (and stay stopped) until they see something in the eyes and faces of these good old timers that they want even more than they want alcohol, and until they find a higher power whose holiness and goodness and beauty will turn them into *willing* sober people, getting sober because they themselves want to dwell in the presence of this sacred reality, instead of doing as they used to do when they were continually attempting to befuddle and confuse and darken their minds into an alcoholic stupor.

> Spirit creative, give us light,
> Lifting the raveled mists of night;
> Touch thou our dust with spirit hand
> And make us souls that understand.[59]

The experience of the sacred: the source of true serenity and the healing of the spirit

In conclusion, what will save the lost soul is learning to experience the sense of the sacred once again. It can be perceived in a church or a religious ritual, or even in a graveyard for that matter, but it can also be encountered in many other contexts. Many people can feel it the same way that many of the Native American people used to encounter it. So for example, I know people in the twelve step program who experience it by going out for walks in the woods, and soaking in the beauty and peace which surrounds them. I know a woman who begins every day by quietly drinking her morning coffee and silently meditating while looking out over a peacefully flowing river. There is an A.A. old timer in my part of Indiana, a retired nuclear submarine commander, who was in the Navy alcoholism treatment center at Great Lakes, and made his first entry back into the awareness of the sacred when he looked up into the sky after he had been there a number of days: he saw wild geese flying overhead and marveled at the sight of these birds flying hundreds of miles and somehow knowing where to go in their annual migration, and suddenly realized that there was something far bigger than himself, and that it was grand and awe inspiring.

Some Christians experience the sacred while going through elaborate communion rituals, with long liturgical prayers and chants and incense, in churches with organs and stained glass windows and robed priests. Quakers and A.A. people experience it when a small group of people sit together quietly in a room, and simply talk honestly about their spiritual lives—whether we call it the Holy Spirit or the Inner Light or the spirit of the tables, it is the numinous power which is quietly but unmistakably present when people gather together to surrender themselves to the power of the sacred.

Someone beginning the spiritual life merely needs to experiment. Where can I, at this point, experience some sense of the sacred in a way that seems healing and restoring? This is not an exercise in working myself up into a frenzy or some other highly abnormal emotional state, nor is it an exercise in seeing how much I can beat myself up with guilt and shame and blame, with endless penitential prayers, or by listening to condemnatory sermons or lectures. No, what I should be looking for is a context in which I can find awe and wonderment and the sense of the infinite and all-powerful, but also healing, peace, a calm mind, and a sense of quiet empowerment for whatever has to be coped with. What works for me will not necessarily work for you, and vice versa, which is why you will just have to experiment with different things until you find what works for you.

But if you wish to walk the spiritual path, it is important to find something, and preferably something that you can do regularly and consistently as part of your normal life schedule. Remember, living in the continual presence of the sacred *is salvation itself.* In the highest versions of the spiritual life, this brings along with it true self-esteem and inner confidence, the end of self-sabotage and self-betrayal, serenity, inner quiet, peace, joy, and a comforting sense (at the end of every day) that "the day has been satisfied." But more than that, it brings the blessed presence of the sacred itself into the heart of our lives. This is where all the rewards are, and they are amply worth it.

Chapter 6

The Ground of Being

Let us talk a little about trees and the ground they grow in. The maple tree which grows in my front yard shades my lawn throughout the Indiana summer with its multitude of many-pointed leaves. The tree and its branches form a totally concrete and tangible thing. One can put one's hand on its trunk and feel the roughness of its bark and its sturdy solidity. One can hear the summer breezes rustling its leaves. Birds fly down—little twittering sparrows, brilliant red cardinals, colorful blue jays—and perch on its branches. The tree is a reality which I can know and depend on, and is part of a larger physical world which is familiar and understandable.

In the fall, the maple's leaves turn a beautiful yellow and red, and seem almost to glow against the clear blue of the sky. Autumn in Indiana is a season of incredible beauty. One can see the furry gray squirrels scurrying up and down the tree's trunk, beginning to prepare a nesting place in which to shelter for the frigid months ahead.

Then comes winter, when I can look out at the tree and its now bare twigs covered with white snow. The birds are gone now, except for occasionally a few little snowbirds (the bird books call them "juncos") with their dark slate gray backs and white breasts, pecking around the base of its trunk on sunnier days. The only thing separating us here from Canada and the Arctic is the vast expanse of Lake Michigan, so as the frigid wind howls in, we feel grateful for the warm, snug house and the fire flickering in the fireplace. On some winter days the twigs and limbs of the maple tree become coated with ice, but then they twinkle like little diamonds whenever the sun comes out. We drink hot chocolate and pop popcorn as we sit in front of the fire and look out the window at the snowdrifts piled against the porch.

In a few months though, spring comes again: bird songs fill the air once more, and one can smell the wet earth and the fresh growing things. First the daffodils planted around the base of the maple tree come out in brilliant yellow flowers, and then the first light green leaves start to appear on the tree itself. The little children come out once again, riding their bicycles and tricycles up and down the sidewalk which runs past the maple tree, laughing and calling out to one another.

An important part of spirituality is learning to appreciate the beauty of the universe again, from the grandeur of its mighty heights to the ordinary little things which surround us every day. When those of us who were locked into self-destructive behaviors first start noticing the world outside our own heads and enjoying it once more—with all of our five senses—we know that our souls are beginning to be healed of all the self-centeredness which had driven us into that grim place inside our minds. But to continue growing spiritually, we must go beyond simply enjoying all these things which we can see and hear and smell and touch and taste, and ask where all this beauty and goodness came from, and in what ultimate source it is grounded.

Using this metaphor of the tree and the ground in which it is planted, it is true that we could continue to study every part of that maple tree for all the rest of our lives: the leaves, the twigs and branches, the trunk, and the roots which extend deep down into the ground. But what about the ground it grows in? The ground is something different from the tree. Yet that tree could only sprout and grow when its seed was first planted in the ground many years ago, and the tree will continue to grow and prosper only as it remains firmly planted in that ground.

This enables us to make an important observation about science and the universe. If the physical universe which we study in the natural sciences is like a tree, then the ground from which it sprang into being—which is a different kind of reality—is what we can call "the ground of being."

The ground of being and the Big Bang

Modern physicists tell us that the world of nature in which we live had a beginning in time, around 13.7 billion years ago. It burst into existence in what they call the Big Bang, where all the matter and energy in the physical universe—along with time and space itself—came exploding simultaneously into being. But what was there before the Big Bang? That was the ground of being, that infinite Mystery which has always existed, continues to exist as that which keeps our present physical universe in existence, and will always exist, for it exists by necessity.

The ground of being—whatever it was which existed before the Big Bang—cannot be analyzed by the same scientific laws and methodologies which we use for investigating the universe which it created. Everything in the created universe, for example, is compelled to follow the laws of thermodynamics. These laws were first worked out when James Watt and others began designing new and improved steam engines during the 1760's. Proof of the validity of these newly discovered laws of physics appeared when they were able to use these principles to engineer steam engines which were efficient enough to power railroad locomotives and paddlewheel steamboats. The first internal combustion engines (which were later to enable us to build the first airplanes and efficient automobiles) also came out of their experiments and their discoveries about the laws of thermodynamics.

One of the these laws of thermodynamics which Watt and his coworkers discovered was the law of entropy, which says that all energy sources eventually run down. When we use flashlights to find our way around after dark, the battery progressively runs down, until finally the light dims and fades away. When we burn fossil fuels like oil and gas and coal for energy, even if we attempt to save all the ashes and gases which are the combustion products, we cannot reuse these materials to run our automobiles another few miles or produce another few kilowatts of electricity from our generators. Eventually even the sun up in the sky will use up all its nuclear fuel and cease emitting light and heat, and finally everything in our universe will collapse into the random movement of particles which have expended all their useful energy, so that nothing meaningful will ever be able to happen again.

Nothing in the physical universe is immune from the law of entropy, nothing at all. Our universe came into being 13.7 billion years ago, and in another few billion years it will have run down. Nothing within our physical universe can escape this fate. And yet the law of entropy cannot apply to the ground of being, because this ground has to have existed from all eternity. If this ground could run down and run out of energy, it would already have done so at some time in the infinite past, long before the Big Bang which created our universe. The ground of being is therefore omnipotent, in this sense. Its extraordinary reserves of energy can apparently exist forever.

And in addition, the ground of being is by necessity something even more extraordinary yet. Space and time were not created until the Big Bang occurred, which means that the ground of being lies outside of the box of space and time. Our human minds are so imprisoned within the box of space and time that we can barely even imagine such an alien reality: it confronts us as *das ganz Andere*, the "Wholly Other," and sends a shiver down our spines.

This ground of being is the infinite itself, the boundless, what the pre-Socratic philosopher Anaximander called the *apeirôn*, that primary existent out of which everything else in the universe came into being and was formed. In Ancient Near Eastern religion, it was the Primordial Abyss which existed before the creation of the world, what the ancient Greek creation myth called Chaos, the gaping void which was all that existed at the beginning of all things. It was the all-swallowing gulf which the ancient Babylonians mythologized as the she-monster Ti'amat.

Our ordinary laws of science cannot be applied to the ground of being, because they are all phrased in the form of mathematical equations which make no sense when infinity is introduced into the formulas. What happens to equations from mathematical physics like

F = ma and E = mc² when we try to introduce infinity into any of their terms? We get nothing which makes any sense at all. The concept of infinity does not work that way. Is X plus infinity bigger than just infinity by itself? The question itself is mathematically meaningless. Multiplying X by infinity is mathematical nonsense. Infinity is not just an extremely big number, but something quite different: a process which proceeds without limit and goes on forever.

God is the ground of being

Let us think about the traditional attributes of God. For thousands of years the theologians have said that God is *eternal,* in the sense that this ultimate reality (unlike the physical universe) has no beginning or end. The theologians have said that God is *omnipresent,* which actually means that—since this reality lies outside our box of space and time—it is everywhere and nowhere. The word "where" we remember refers to physical location at a specific point in space. The ground of being is *immaterial* and *incorporeal,* because it is not composed of the electrons and protons and neutrons and other types of matter which form our physical universe. It is *omnipotent* because it is not subject to the law of entropy, and can never run down or decay. It is also *ineffable,* which means that we cannot talk about it in ordinary human words, because even the greatest scientists cannot fit it into their mathematical equations and precise definitions. It is not just a matter of cleverer scientists coming along and working out new laws of physics which will enable us to analyze the ground, because that which is truly infinite cannot be constrained within the kind of mathematical equations which would have to be drawn up in order to bend it to our manipulations.

In calculus and in the construction of infinite series, mathematicians can sometimes talk intelligibly about processes which are infinite in the sense that they proceed without limit, but the only processes which give us useful information are those which *converge toward a finite limit.* The ground of being cannot be described by mathematical formulas of this sort, because it involves infinite processes which do not converge toward any finite limit.

The ground of being not only created all the matter and energy in the physical universe, it also supplied—and continues to supply—the laws of nature which the physical universe is constrained to follow. The electrons and protons and various kinds of energy which make up our physical universe do not create these underlying laws of nature which the scientists explore. This realm of scientific law was also supplied by the ground at the time of the universe's creation, and it is this underlying ground which continues to maintain and enforce all these fundamental laws of physics.

What this means is that the ground of being not only created our physical universe 13.7 billion years ago, but that it is still there today, and that it is still connected to our physical universe today, in such a way that if our physical universe lost its link to the underlying ground, it would blink out of existence on the spot.

The ground of being is what the philosophical theologians of traditional western theism—in Judaism, Christianity, and Islam all three—have always called God. In classical Hindu philosophy, this ultimate ground was referred to as Brahman.

Whether regarded as personal or impersonal, the ground is the ultimate divine Mystery

In ancient pagan Greek Neo-Platonism, the ground of being was called the One, the single and unitary divine Mystery which stood above everything else: the gods, the human soul, and even the power of reason itself. It was regarded as a completely impersonal transcendent ground. It was not a personal being because it was above and beyond all multiplicity, above and beyond all thoughts and concepts, and above and beyond everything which could constitute a distinct personality filled with individual cares and concerns and desires.

In Hindu philosophy down through the centuries there have been a variety of interpretations of this ground of being. In the philosophical system called Advaita Vedanta for example, Brahman (the ground of being) was described as a kind of infinite "cosmic consciousness" (an ecstatic absorption in an awareness of the unity of all reality), which formed an infinite field of bliss from which shone the infinite radiance of the outpouring of pure knowledge itself. But this was not the same as a truly personal God, since it was believed that Brahman possessed no specific personal attributes. It functioned simply as a universalized ultimate ground from which other lower forms of being could emerge. Vedantist philosophers of this school taught that a fully personal understanding of God, where God was personified as one of the particular Hindu gods like Vishnu or Shiva—a specific god or goddess with his or her own individual personal characteristics and traits—was simply a reflection of Brahman (like the reflection of the moon in a pool of water) down into the realm of Maya (the domain of the illusions which rule the material world). So it is clear that they regarded any kind of belief in a deeply personal God as part of the realm of ignorance, illusion, and fantasy from which good spirituality was supposed to save us.

In early and medieval Christian theology, we see the full gamut of interpretations. In the early Christian period, St. Macarius (the author of the *Fifty Spiritual Homilies*) and St. Augustine taught a deeply personal God. But during that same period of history (the fourth and fifth centuries A.D.), St. Denis (the early Christian theologian who wrote under the pseudonym of Dionysius the Areopagite) gave an interpretation of God which was even more impersonal than the Hindu system described in the previous paragraph, and St. Gregory of Nyssa asserted that the ultimate vision of God was that only of a bottomless abyss of No-thing-ness which threw us into vertigo and total disorientation.

Theism vs. atheism: personhood
not the issue, but Mystery

The real issue which has divided theism from atheism down through the centuries had not been a debate over whether God is personal or not. That is important to recognize. What is fundamentally at stake is something very different. Theism recognizes that the ground of being is a Mystery of which the human mind can never grasp more than hints and reflections. Atheism—the kind of repudiation of God which has flourished in the modern western world since the 1840's—is, on the other hand, above all *an attempt to deny that mystery.* Modern western atheists want to reject the notion of human powerlessness in the face of anything at all. Human science, they desperately want to believe, will ultimately be able to explain all things. The universe will eventually be proven to be an adequate explanation of itself. Human beings will then be able to control all things and solve all of their worldly problems—on their terms, not God's terms—with machines and scientific instruments, and with pills which we can swallow, which will fill our minds with sanity and bliss.

And back the other way around, theism in all of its forms recognizes that whenever we attempt to describe our service at the altar of the *Agnôstô Theô*, the Unknown God whom we encounter within the Cloud of Unknowing, we will always end up having to be involved with what the Hungarian philosopher Polanyi called tacit knowledge, and various kinds of indirect ways of knowing and speaking: metaphors, symbols, allegories, and other such devices. As we saw from Locke's example of the taste of pineapple, we will always eventually run into real experiences of God's reality for which we have no words, where we know that God is there but cannot explain what it is we know to those who have never felt or sensed it. We will be able to see the concrete evidence that God's works of saving grace have been manifested in the world, when we observe human beings undergoing major psychic changes as part of their encounter with God's grace, but in our scientific accounts of what happened, all we will be able to talk about is some kind of strange x-factor at work, disrupting the normal sequence of cause and effect.

And above all, whenever we approach that ultimate power which heals and saves us, we will be thrown into awe and overpowering wonder at the numinous reality which shines through, the *mysterium tremendum* which is the power of the sacred and is incomparably greater than anything in the created world.

So is the ground of being a personal God who thinks and wills and is conscious of the world and us human beings who live in it? I think so myself, but let us wait until the latter part of this book to discuss the reasons why. For now, the most important thing to say in response to the kind of modern western atheism which has swept the globe since the 1840's, is that God is real—something out there, distinct from us and the scientifically observable universe—which can be shown to exist. God is the Great Mystery out of which the universe emerged in the Big Bang. God is the power of the numinous shining out of that primordial abyss and filling all the created world with the light of the holy and the sacred. Full God-consciousness—fully sensing that sacredness and bringing its numinous power within ourselves—is what we mean by salvation.

For over two thousand years it has been demonstrated all around the world, that a very satisfying and effective spirituality can be devised—one which will heal the human soul and bring us lives filled with peace, joy, and love—as long as belief is present that the ground of being is the great sacred Mystery underlying all things, regardless of whether that ground is regarded as personal or not. So for the next few chapters, that is what we will be primarily talking about.

The prelude to the rise of modern atheism: eighteenth and nineteenth century attacks on the infallibility of the Bible

In the Middle Ages and Early Modern period, the greatest thinkers were willing to turn to the Bible as a source of infallible truth on a vast range of issues. St. Thomas Aquinas, for example, the greatest Christian philosopher of the thirteenth century, believed that it was impossible to prove that the universe either did or did not have a beginning in time using natural science and philosophy. But since the Bible said that the world in fact had a beginning in time, he believed that we could take this as a dependable truth.

In the Early Modern period, the Anglo-Irish theologian James Ussher, who served many years as Archbishop of Armagh and Primate of All Ireland, made one of the most famous attempts at calculating the age of the universe using biblical texts, producing a date which was still printed in Gideon Bibles in hotels and motels all across the United States when I was a child. In his *Annales veteris testamenti, a prima mundi origine deducti* ("Annals of the Old Testament, deduced from the first origins of the world"), which appeared in 1650, and in its continuation, *Annalium pars posterior*, which appeared in 1654, Archbishop Ussher calculated the date of creation to be the nightfall preceding October 23, 4004 B.C.

But by the end of the next century, the rise of modern science and modern historiography had begun to show increasing problems with any kind of attempt to use the Bible in that way. Thomas Jefferson for example, the principal author of the Declaration of Independence and the third president of the United States, wrote a book in 1781 entitled *Notes on the State of Virginia*, in which he commented on the bones of an elephant-like creature which had been dug up in Virginia, the remains of a prehistoric animal which we would today describe as a mammoth or mastodon. Jefferson noted that no known species of modern elephant could survive the cold of a Virginia winter, which led him to speculate that either this was a different kind of (now extinct) elephant-like species or that the climate of Virginia had been far different in the distant past. Today we know that both of these speculations were correct.

A man named James Hutton presented a paper entitled "Theory of the Earth" to the Royal Society of Edinburgh in 1785. In that paper, he argued that the planet earth must be far older than had previously been supposed in order to allow enough time for mountains to be eroded and for sediment to form new rocks at the bottom of the sea, which in turn were raised up to become dry land. The idea that the beginning of the universe only dated back to 4004 B.C. was rapidly coming to appear more and more preposterous.

Following up on observations of that sort, geologists and paleontologists over the course of the next century began to estimate the true age of the earth at anywhere from 100,000 years old, up to even perhaps billions of years old. At the end of the century, in 1899, John Joly of the University of Dublin calculated the rate at which the oceans should have accumulated salt from erosion processes, and determined that the oceans were about 90 million years old.

> As a brief note, in the last half of the twentieth century real precision finally began to be obtained. The mass spectrometer was invented in the 1940's and began to be used in radioactive dating techniques in the 1950's. The oldest known minerals on the surface of the earth were determined to be 4.404 billion years old. Numerous meteorites have been discovered however which are slightly older, 4.567 billion years old, so modern scientists push the creation of the earth back to that point, and regard that as the date when the planet earth would first have begun to form as part of the same process which created those meteorites and not only the earth, but also the other planets which circle our sun.

The important thing to note is that the date of the creation which is implied in the Judeo-Christian Bible could not conceivably be correct, and that this date was already being seen to be impossible by the early nineteenth century. Other ancient sacred texts, from India and elsewhere, fared no better than the Bible. Their guesses were wrong too, and the accumulated evidence discovered by modern science over the past two centuries shows overwhelmingly that none of them were even remotely correct.

Adding to the problems raised for the biblical account by the geologists and paleontologists, Charles Darwin in 1859 published his book *On the Origin of Species by Means of Natural Selection, or The Preservation of Favoured Races in the Struggle for Life*, which brought the theory of evolution into the fray.

Moreover, between 1820 and 1860, western scholars began figuring out how to read ancient Egyptian hieroglyphics and ancient Mesopotamian cuneiform writing, and that, coupled with the beginnings of modern archeological excavation, began to show other kinds of discrepancies in the Old Testament accounts of ancient historical events.

The New Testament also came under attack by modern historians. Research by numerous scholars on the synoptic problem increasingly showed that the three synoptic gospels (Matthew, Mark, and Luke) reported the words, deeds, and even the chronology of Jesus' life so differently in some places, that there was no way to reconcile them. Rarely do we have a saying of Jesus reported verbatim, in exactly the same words, in all three of these gospels (even though his basic teaching can be reconstructed, I believe, with a good deal more accuracy than some of the more recent radical New Testament scholarship acknowledges). Nevertheless, by the end of the nineteenth century, it had become clear that none of the gospels were written by eyewitnesses, and that the gospel accounts of what Jesus said and did during his active ministry, which took place around 30 A.D., were based on oral traditions passed on from person to person, which were not fully put down in writing until around 80-90 A.D., which meant that they could and did contain errors and distortions (and sometimes even the purely legendary) in the form in which we now have them.

It was a traumatic period for traditional Jewish and Christian belief at every level. More and more intellectuals in the western world began realizing that the Judeo-Christian Bible was a product of an ancient world which knew nothing about modern science or the modern historical method. Any kind of belief in God based solely on the idea that the Bible was inerrant and infallible in all of its statements began to crumble quickly during that period of western history.

The rise of modern atheism in the 1840's

Atheistic and quasi-atheistic ideas had begun to appear on occasion in public contexts by the end of the eighteenth century. David Hume's *Dialogues Concerning Natural Religion* in 1779 demolished any hope of drawing up a conclusive proof of the existence of any clearly defined God within a Lockean philosophical system (the system of thought which was assumed at that time to provide the simple and common sense basis of the modern scientific method), and Immanuel Kant's *Critique of Pure Reason* in 1781 appeared to demonstrate that even if God existed—which he argued was unprovable one way or the other—we could know nothing at all about him. Completely atheistic ideas surfaced temporarily during the most radical phase of the French revolution, with the abolition of the worship of God on November 10, 1793 and the formation of a short-lived governmentally-sanctioned alternative called the Cult of Reason.

Nevertheless it was not until the 1840's that modern western atheism began to spread widely among European intellectuals. At the beginning of that decade, in 1841, Ludwig Feuerbach published a book called *Das Wesen des Christentums* (The Essence of Christianity), which laid out some of the most important assumptions of the new atheistic theory of the universe (it was translated into English in 1853 by the famous Victorian novelist Mary Anne Evans, better known by most under her pen name of George Eliot). Feuerbach said that what religion calls "God" is simply our minds' projection onto the universe of what are only subjective human goals, ideals, and fears. There is no real God out there, merely an impersonal universe running according to scientific law.

In the years which followed, a long string of atheistic thinkers built their ideas on Feuerbach's theory. Sigmund Freud claimed that God was only a fantasy image of our human fathers which our subconscious projected onto the universe. The sociologist Émile Durkheim said that "God is society, writ large"—that is, the gods whom we worshiped on social occasions were simply symbols of our own culture, so that religion was actually the group worshiping itself. Karl Marx argued that religion was a projection of the class structure and economic structure of a society onto the material world, used as a tool for maintaining the subjugation of the lower classes.

Modern atheism as control fantasy and utopian fantasy

Modern western atheism, on the surface, was made up of theories like these: God is only ancient primitive superstition, or my father, or society, or a tool for subjugating the masses. But to truly understand the power of this new atheistic movement and the way it came to grip so many people's hearts and souls in the nineteenth and early twentieth century, we need to take a deeper look into the atheistic mind.

It was believed by these dedicated atheists—deeply and devoutly believed—that modern science would eventually be able to account for everything, including the origins of the universe, on the basis of mathematical laws that were completely understandable to the human intellect, without anything "left over" that would fall outside complete analysis by the modern scientific method. We would be able to explain everything that happened by scientific law, and with that, we would gain total control of Nature.

That was what was really at stake to the devotees of modern western atheism. It was a control neurosis, a control fantasy, where they talked themselves into believing that, as we human beings made more and more scientific discoveries, we would eventually be able to take over from God and run everything ourselves. If one reads contemporary science fiction novels, one can see the full atheistic fantasy coming out in a number of these works. We will live surrounded by electronic gadgets of every sort, with all the hard work being done by computerized robots which never break down or malfunction or refuse to come online. Modern medicine would conquer death, so that we would no longer get sick and die, but would live forever. And so on and so forth.

Already by the time I went to university, there were psychiatrists claiming that we would soon be able to fix any problem which afflicted the human mind—any kind of disturbance or unhappiness, any sort of neurosis or psychosis or addiction—by having the patient swallow the right kind of pills. There was no longer going to be any need for God or religion, atheists proclaimed, because physics and chemistry and biology and psychology were going to become the new gods, and replace all the old religious systems with completely scientific methodologies which were totally under rational human control. Modern atheism was going to bring in a Brave New World[60] in which human beings were going to be happy, healthy, free, and fulfilled.

It is interesting to note that the principles of the twelve step program, which appeared at the end of the 1930's, were a rebellion against this sort of atheism. This was made clear from the very first two steps in their spiritual program: First "we admitted we were powerless ... that our lives had become unmanageable." Then we "came to believe that a Power greater than ourselves could restore us to sanity." We had to learn to quit playing God. We had to learn that this never worked. Could I as a human being ever have the power to create an entire universe, with all of its stars and planets and galaxies, out of empty space? This is a fantasy so silly that it is difficult to see how an intelligent adult could be taken in by it.

In addition to control fantasies, modern western atheism became involved in utopian fantasies as well. I remember back during the 1960's and 70's, first I was a student at Oxford University where some of the Communists among my fellow students were proclaiming that their politico-economic system would bring happiness and prosperity to human beings all over the earth. Then I obtained a teaching position at Indiana University, where some of the behaviorist psychology professors were teaching their students that, if only the government could be persuaded to allow them to put all the children in the country in Skinner boxes for the appropriate behavioral conditioning, they would be able to produce utopia on earth. It should be clear to anyone who looks at them carefully, that these atheistic utopian theories are just another kind of control neurosis. The reality was that neither the Communists nor the Skinnerian psychologists were actually able to produce what they promised.

Modern western atheism is built on the fantasy that we can use modern science to literally control everything: that we will learn how to remove all uncertainty and chance, bend everything around us to our will, and turn ourselves into the all-powerful Masters of the Universe. Their grandiosity is without bounds. Theism on the other hand points to the fact that the universe arose out of Mystery, that it will vanish back into Mystery at its end, and that this Mystery which underlies all things may bring chance and uncertainty into the universe, but also produces creativity and novelty. The x-factor which appears in our lives over and over again is the tiny Mystery that lies inside me (the miracle of free will) interacting with the grand universal Mystery in a way which brings grace and new life.

How the scientific discoveries of the twentieth century tore away the supporting pillars of modern western atheism

There is a great and infinitely tragic irony in the survival of atheism among many intellectuals in today's world. The classical western atheists of the 1800's knew nothing about the discoveries that were going to be made by twentieth-century science and philosophy, and for that one supposes they can be forgiven. They thought they could remove all the Mystery from the world, and in the process, put themselves into godlike control of all things. But we know better nowadays, or at least we ought to.

During the course of the twentieth century, further advances in science and philosophy truly revolutionized the human understanding of the world, but contrary to the expectations of the previous century, the most important discoveries brought the Mystery back into the universe—that Mystery which the nineteenth century had tried so hard to remove. It began with the discovery of statistical thermodynamics (Ludwig Boltzmann's *Lectures on Gas Theory* was actually published slightly before the beginning of the twentieth century, in 1896), which made it clear that the element of chance and randomness could not be removed from the universe. Einstein published his famous initial studies in 1905, and introduced the strange world of relativistic physics, where the fabric of space and time itself could be stretched and bent. Quantum theory (Niels Bohr developed his model of the atom in 1913) led eventually to wave mechanics and the discovery of the peculiar way in which electrons can function both as waves and as particles (deriving from Erwin Schrödinger's publication of the Schrödinger equation in 1926). The uncertainty principle (discovered by Werner Heisenberg in 1927) made it clear that science would never be able to explain all things in the universe with infinite precision. Gödel's proof (published in 1931) showed that in any reasonably complex scientific theory of the universe, it would be possible to ask questions to which the theory could not give an unequivocal yes-or-no answer. Scientists found themselves in a strange new world where threads of Mystery ran through the entire fabric of the universe.

The atheists of the nineteenth century had believed that scientific knowledge would automatically keep growing more and more complete and precise until finally all the possible questions about the universe had been answered, with no uncertainties, mysteries, or loose ends left over. We human beings would be in possession of godlike knowledge, and would become our own gods. By the end of the twentieth century however it had become clear that what actually happened in real life was that we human beings were continually called upon to make creative and novel responses to an ever-changing universe which was shot through with Mystery from beginning to end. Where we got into trouble was when we fooled ourselves into believing that we knew more than we really did, or that we could control more than we were really able to. God—the great, eternal Mystery—was the real ruler of all.

An eternal universe, or one
with a beginning in time?

The theory of the Big Bang, which said that the universe had a beginning in time, went back to the beginning of the twentieth century: Edwin Hubble published his first observations on the red shift in 1929.

But in reaction to this, some physicists and astronomers tried to come up with arguments which would show that the physical universe had no beginning in time, and that it was eternal and had always existed. Many of them openly acknowledged that their primary motivation was to undermine the idea of God. If the universe had always existed, then (they believed) there would no longer be any need for a God.

So what was called the steady state theory, for example, defended by scientists like Fred Hoyle, Thomas Gold, and Hermann Bondi, argued that the universe has been kept in existence from all eternity, in spite of its perpetual expansion, by the continual spontaneous appearance of new matter in empty space. Other astronomers and physicists tried to devise cyclic models, such as the theory of an oscillatory universe, in their attempt to deny any beginning to the universe. In theories of this sort, it was argued that each Big Bang introduced an expansionary phase which continued until gravitational attraction finally halted the expansion and started a period of contraction which ended in a Big Crunch. But out of that, another Big Bang would explode, followed by another contraction into a Big Crunch, and so on, in such a way that the universe would continue to exist—alternately expanding and contracting—for all eternity.

The discovery in 1964 of the cosmic microwave background radiation which had been predicted in the theory of the Big Bang[61] put an end to these particular attacks. It is now generally acknowledged that the Big Bang theory is fundamentally correct: that our universe had a beginning in time around 13.7 billion years ago (according to most current calculations), where it exploded into existence at a point in space and began an expansion which is still going on.

Atheistic physicists and astronomers who upheld the theory of the Big Bang tried to fend off any talk about God at work in this event by referring to it as a "singularity," a word which gave a quasi-scientific aura to that part of the theory. But what the word singularity means is an event which is like no other events which science has ever observed and which seems to violate the laws of nature at the most basic level. In old-fashioned English an event of this sort is called (and has been called for many centuries), not a singularity, but a *supernatural* event. That means exactly the same thing, but makes it far clearer that the present universe came into existence out of the great eternal Mystery, that ground of being which Jews, Christians, and Muslims call God.

Attempts are still being made by physicists and astronomers to devise theories which would account for the existence of the universe where *everything* could be explained, without exception, on the grounds of natural physical law, without bringing in any concept of a supernatural ground. But all of these theories involve the claim, at one level or another, that one has successfully devised a perpetual motion machine. By one strategy or another, the theorists end up claiming that they have gotten around the problem of the first law of thermodynamics (the conservation of energy) as well as the second law of thermodynamics (entropy and the arrow of time problem). But a perpetual motion machine is still a piece of hokum, the sort of thing that is only peddled by con men and frauds, even if you build one as big as the entire universe.

How the utopian fantasies of modern
western atheism turned sour

Modern atheism has in some situations been able to liberate people from some of the intolerance, bigotry, authoritarianism, and stupidity of the past. And in addition, in parts of the globe, we live today with more food and material belongings, and far better health care, than any previous century of human history was able to enjoy. But there are also numerous places where human beings are still starving to death.

All in all, modern atheism tends to have too good a conscience. In writings promoting atheism, there is still apt to be an absence of any admission of the evil that has been done in the name of this philosophy of life. Even if some good has been done in some small parts of the world, it is difficult to exaggerate the negative effects which modern western atheism has also had over the history of the last century and a half. It produced Hitler's Nazi Germany, Stalin's Soviet regime in Russia, the deaths of millions of Chinese as the effect of Mao Zedong's theories, the proliferation of nuclear weapons (and other weapons of mass destruction) beyond all reason, the genocidal murder of millions of human beings in Europe and Africa, and a whole series of other catastrophic effects.

The kind of atheism which began sweeping through the western world in the 1840's should have a very guilty conscience indeed. Its defenders are in no position to deliver moral lectures at people who hold other beliefs.

The ground of being as the
basis of real spirituality

So let us not be duped by the more grandiose promises of modern atheism, and instead use the idea of the Big Bang and the ground of being to create a spirituality which respects the findings of modern science, but which also recognizes the presence of Mystery and the numinous power of the holy. Only in this way will we be able to bring out the true goodness and beauty of human life, and learn how to link ourselves with the life-giving power of freedom and creativity rather than the dark power of fate and destruction.

Chapter 7

The Sense of the Infinite

One group of people to whom I would like to speak in this chapter, are those scientifically minded people who understand what is meant by the ground of being (as that out of which the Big Bang occurred) and who understand why this ground must be regarded as eternal, omnipresent, immaterial, incorporeal, omnipotent, and ineffable, but who simply cannot make themselves believe that this ground could be identified as a personal God.

I have total sympathy with these scientifically minded people, and the first thing I want to say to them is that you can create a very good spirituality based on belief in a totally impersonal ground of being. There is in fact a rich tradition of spiritualities of this sort, in both the eastern world and the western world, going back thousands of years.

So why not begin by admitting frankly that you do not believe that the ground of being is any kind of personal God, but then go on to look at it instead as something like what is called the Brahman in Hinduism, or the One in ancient pagan Neo-Platonism? Although the ground of being is regarded as impersonal in a philosophy of this sort, it is nevertheless recognized as the source from which all other being derives its existence. And what is even more important, a profound and workable spirituality can be built upon this basis.

Down at one level, I always believed in a personal God myself, but my undergraduate degree was in physical chemistry and nuclear physics, and I went on to do half of the coursework for a Ph.D. in that field. I worked as a research scientist in an Atomic Energy Commission laboratory, and also in a chemical factory that made rocket fuel. So—

although, God be thanked, I always realized down in my heart that there was a personal, loving God at all the significant turning points in my life, and actually acted on that basis at the concrete level, even during those years—throughout my twenties and even my thirties, if you had asked me just to theorize about who and what God was, I would have given you a set of intellectualizations which fundamentally explained away all the personalistic language as "ways of talking" that we should not take too literally. I would have told you that referring to God as a person was simply a metaphor or analogy or useful way of speaking at the figurative level. I do not think that what I was doing was bad, however, because explaining things away in this fashion got me through those early years of my life. And it is also the case that intellectual philosophies of this sort have given untold numbers of human beings a full, rich spiritual life over the past three thousand years.

The blackness between the stars
and the unmeasured distances beyond

Good spiritual systems which employ an impersonal concept of the ultimate are often built upon what we might call *the sense of the infinite*. This is what needs to be discussed in this chapter. When we look up at the starry heavens, for example, on a clear and moonless night, what we are able to see with our naked eyes extends many light years into space, yet that magnificent sight, we know, represents only a small portion of the known universe. We are keenly aware of how much more of the universe there is which extends beyond the range of our eyesight. When a group of us were reading an earlier draft of this book, Liz commented on this passage:

> I feel awe when looking at the night sky and I can feel God.
> But it is the blackness between the stars which makes me feel
> God. It is not like the blackness of a dark cave—the black-

ness between the stars is in fact alive with even more stars
which we cannot see, out even further.

And if we were able to go even further, venturing beyond or even
outside our universe, we would find that the apparent nothingness was
alive with the presence of the ground of being, that ultimate reality
which keeps everything else in existence by its extraordinary power.

The universe we know is a finite part of infinite processes, where
God dwells in the unmeasured distances. We cannot picture God as
a thing, but we can in fact understand, at another level, the existence
of that which has no finite boundaries. The word *infinitum* in Latin
meant that which had no *finis*, that is, no end, no boundary, no fence
around it. In ancient Greek likewise, the word *apeiron* (the infinite,
the unlimited, that which was inexhaustible, vast, endless, boundless)
meant that which had no *peras* (no limit or boundary, no end or
termination or conclusion, no "other side" to which we could cross).[62]

We can neither imagine nor understand, in their totality, all the
length of the infinite processes which make up reality, but we can
know of this infinite, bustling reality indirectly, at least in part, through
our knowledge of the universe around us, which participates in those
infinite processes.

The sense of the infinite
and the Kantian problem

The philosophy of Immanuel Kant has undermined western
theology since the appearance of the first edition of his *Critique of
Pure Reason* in 1781, and has made it almost impossible to come up
with a coherent and workable concept of God. This has been so for
over two centuries, even among theologians and philosophers who
would deny that they were Kantians, because they have unconsciously
assumed certain presuppositions about God and the world and the
nature of human knowledge, which can ultimately be traced back

to that philosopher. I regard this as the greatest single cause of the demoralization which affected most of the theological authors of my own lifetime, and left them often grasping at frail straws in an attempt to salvage something to keep the theological enterprise going. At one level, one could regard this present book as a deconstruction of the Kantian philosophy, a progressive dismantling of its fundamental structural members and presuppositions, a discourse *Contra Kantium* (were we to give it a medieval Latin title), in which we can discover where Kant went wrong, so we can start building a philosophy that will make sense out of God again. We will therefore need to talk about Kant over and over again, in order to see how we can get things working smoothly again and undo the damage that his ideas caused.

One of the important ways in which Kant's philosophy prevented workable understandings of the spiritual life from being developed over the next two centuries came from his denial that human beings could talk and think meaningfully about the infinite. In his *Critique of Pure Reason*, he imprisoned the human mind in a box of space and time, and argued that the human mind could not even imagine anything that lay outside of that realm of three-dimensional Euclidean space and chronological time (what the ancient Greek philosophers called *chronos*, time understood as a series of objectifiable phenomena arranged in their sequence of occurrence). A real God, even if one existed, would have to lie outside the box of space and time, which would mean that our human minds could have no contact with such a being. There is no way of either proving or disproving the existence of something about which one can know nothing at all.

What Kant was *de facto* saying in his *Critique of Pure Reason*, if one reads it closely, was that it was the soul being trapped in a physical body which imprisoned us in that box of space and time. We could not penetrate through the veil of the phenomena as they were apprehended through our five gross physical senses, and come into direct contact (via that route) with either the noumenon (the realm of the eternal ideas) or with the great mystery which lay beyond. (We could in fact enter the world of the pure ideas, according to Kant, only when we set up categorical imperatives for the governance of our moral stances.)

Those who know their history of philosophy will immediately recognize this as a motif which went back to Plato, and even before that, to the religious ideas of the quasi-shamanistic movement referred to as Orphism. The Orphic movement, which used a pun on the Greek words *sôma* (body) and *sêma* (tomb), stated that the human body was in fact a tomb which imprisoned the soul, and prevented it from realizing freedom, true happiness, and the clear and direct knowledge of the eternal ideas.

Kant declared that the human mind could not even imagine any kind of object other than one which was in space and time, and on the surface, his position looks like one which could be argued successfully. I can go to a zoo and perceive a real elephant through my five senses. I can imagine an elephant in my mind which is much larger or much smaller, a pink elephant, a blue elephant, an elephant standing on its head, or an elephant balancing on a large ball and attempting to play a saxophone. But I cannot imagine an elephant which is not in space. Moreover, this imaginary elephant also has to be in time, because I can only imagine it as either moving or standing totally motionless. If it is moving, then it is moving through time. But it is equally true that an object which is imagined as remaining unmoving over the passage of time, is still being thought of as an object in time, namely as a phenomenon which continues to show the same characteristics over repeated slices of chronological time.

Infinity is a process, not an extremely big number

When Kant says that it is impossible for the human mind to have any kind of sense of the infinite, his arguments may at first glance seem very powerful. But he is using what is in fact an incorrect understanding of the infinite, which tricks us into asking the totally wrong question.

Even very good philosophers can find themselves unconsciously thinking of infinity as an extremely big number. It is an easy thing to do, and can creep up on us very quietly and unobtrusively, if we do not force ourselves to remain perpetually aware of the dangers of this fallacy. And Kant pushes this a bit further, and leads us from that point into thinking of infinity as "a number too large even to imagine." And there he has us. Once we have become trapped by this false notion, the real God disappears over the epistemological horizon and is never seen again.

But as Aristotle pointed out well over two thousand years ago—and as any good modern mathematician would likewise state—infinity refers, not to any kind of number at all—even an extremely big number, one "too large even to imagine"—but to a *process*. Let us take as an example a simple kind of infinite series, where I start out by laying down one grain of wheat. Then right next to it, I lay down two grains of wheat. Then next to that, I lay down four grains of wheat, and then eight grains, and then sixteen grains, and then thirty-two grains of wheat, and so on. It is the process itself—one which can go on forever—which is infinite. The individual numbers which make up the process are always finite, no matter how far I carry out the process:

$$1, 2, 4, 8, 16, 32, 64, 128, 256 \ldots.$$

In one of his works, Aristotle gave the famous example of the chicken and the egg. In order to have the egg, we first need to have a chicken to lay it. But in order to have that chicken, we need to have a preexisting egg for that chicken to have hatched from. And so on, *ad infinitum*, going back into the infinite past and forward into the infinite future. In Kant's argument, you see, he tried to get us to believe that we could have no sense of something like this kind of Aristotelian chicken-and-egg series as an infinite process unless we could imagine, in one simultaneous vision, all of the chickens and all the chicken eggs that had ever existed or ever would exist on the planet Earth.

But in order to have "a sense of infinity," an awareness of the presence of the infinite, all our minds have to grasp is that what we are sensing is some sort of interconnected series of events which must, by their very nature, extend further in one or more directions than we could even imagine, with no reason to believe that the sequence would ever come to an end.

Sensing part of a thing, and then using our minds to extrapolate the rest

But it is also important to realize that we are talking here, not just about infinite series, but also about other kinds of realties we can encounter, in which we can reconstruct the whole from the part.

At a very early stage in childhood, the human mind develops the ability to "fill in the missing gaps" in what our five senses are presenting us. This was necessary for survival itself in primitive times. An early human walking through the jungle, who saw the tip of a leopard's tail sticking out from behind one side of a large bush, and the tip of that leopard's nose sticking out from behind the other side of that bush, had to instantly construct an inner mental image of the entire leopard, and decide whether to heft his stone ax and fight for his life, or take to his heels and hope he could run fast enough to save his skin.

I see half of a pencil sticking out of a pencil cup, and my mind extrapolates the existence of the other half of the pencil. The minds of students watching their professor lecture from behind a podium in a college classroom automatically supply the hidden parts of the teacher's body (lower body and legs) which they cannot see.

We do not even need to bring in the concept of the infinite in the technical sense in order to see how we can use this natural human mental ability to grasp something about the magnitude of the divine ground of being. According to present day calculations, the visible universe (looking outward as far as the theoretical limits available for astronomical telescopes) is a sphere of about 46.5 billion light-years in radius. It has also been calculated that the observable universe contains about 10^{80} atoms. These are extremely huge numbers, but they are nevertheless finite numbers. They are not "infinite." And as we have already noted, human beings, gazing up at the starry heavens on a clear night, can see even less than that with their naked eyes, only a tiny fraction of all these stars and galaxies. Nevertheless, the mind can "fill in the gaps" and think about all the additional stars and drifting cosmic dust clouds which our naked eyes cannot see, and the mind can, beyond that, think about the ground of being as something which would have to be, in some fashion, larger or more powerful even than all of that.

St. Anselm: God is that than which nothing greater can be conceived

St. Anselm (c. 1033-1109), an important Catholic theologian who lived at the beginning of the High Middle Ages, developed a proof for the existence of God, in which he defined God as "that than which nothing greater can be conceived" (*aliquid quo nihil maius cogitari posit*). The basic idea was taken by him from St. Augustine, who in turn had borrowed it from the pagan Roman philosopher Seneca (a famous Stoic author of the first century).[63] There is a two thousand year tradition, in other words—both Christian and non-Christian—of talking about the supreme being in this fashion.

So even if a clever philosopher should wish to argue that we cannot logically extrapolate from what we know about the universe and prove the existence of something truly infinite lying behind it—using the word infinite here in the fully technical sense—it is nevertheless clear that we can demonstrate the existence of a supreme being, that is, an ultimate reality which is above or beyond everything else in some meaningful sense.

This is important to note, because we do not in fact have to prove that God (or the ground of being) is infinite in order to demonstrate that this extraordinary reality is worthy of our awe. It is only necessary to show that our minds can (and do) extrapolate from what they can perceive of the marvels of nature, to an understanding that all of this is only a small part of that ultimate reality which is *that than which nothing greater can be conceived.* If this is the case, then it is worthy to be honored by us as the ultimate grandeur and majesty of all reality.

The aesthetic experience of the sublime

Kant, in his *Critique of Judgment* (1790), spoke about the human reaction to what he called "the sublime," which was the feeling of awe and wonder which we experienced when we observed the greatness and vastness of certain kinds of impressive natural phenomena. The concept of the sublime was a topic which arose in the study of aesthetics, that is, the philosophical investigation of beauty, as it occurred both in human works of music and art and architecture, and in the delights and wonders of nature.[64]

Kant noted that when we stood on a cliff overlooking a beach with a wild and furious storm raging, and mighty waves pounding on the beach, we felt a sense of extraordinary awe at the power of the forces we were observing. This was what aesthetic theory called the experience of the sublime, which was our human response to one kind of natural beauty. The human mind (he argued) tried to think of what it was perceiving as though it was "infinite," even though these forces were not. Kant tried to explain away our human awe at the sacred dimension to the universe, the sense of marvel which we felt in situations of this sort, as being no more than an illusion. What we were feeling might be an emotionally moving aesthetic experience, but it was not any direct perception of something which was truly infinite.

Kant was certainly correct at one level. The enormous power of an ocean storm is so great as to be terrifying large, if I am a human being in a boat, battling for my life at sea. But even though the forces driving the towering waves are giant and prodigiously huge, scientists can in fact put a number on the amount of energy being released, so it is not truly infinite.

There are many situations in which we can experience the sublime: We may be gazing at the starry heavens above and pondering the immensity of the universe. Or perhaps we are standing in the middle of a deep forest, surrounded by trees which were planted in the earth long before we were born. There are oak trees which are well over a thousand years old, and beyond that, we know that huge forests covered the earth over a hundred million years before the first human beings appeared.

Or we might be standing in front of a powerful particle accelerator at a nuclear research facility, and thinking about the tiny subatomic particles moving at speeds near the velocity of light and colliding with their targets with explosive energy. Scientists who study nuclear physics, and astrophysics also, are confronted with the enormous depths and utter strangeness of the universe on a regular basis. I have never known any of these researchers who did not inwardly marvel at the extraordinary nature of what they were studying. Once we begin peering out at astronomical distances, or attempting to peer down into the world of subatomic phenomena, we quickly find the assumptions of our commonsense everyday world turned topsy-turvy, and the deeper we explore, the stranger and more awe-inspiring the universe becomes.

It may sound strange to non-scientists to speak of the "aesthetics" of science, but real scientists—and mathematicians too—all understand in their hearts that there is a beauty and elegance to what they are studying, and a thrill that accompanies the journey into new discovery and the outer limits of human knowledge. This aesthetic drive is what actually motivates them to commit their lives to such difficult researches. Good scientists and mathematicians are in fact artists, in a different way from painters and sculptors and composers and architects, but artists nevertheless, who are driven to discover things and create things with their own kind of beauty.

The experience of the sublime as a
signpost pointing to the infinite

But let us remember our example of the caveman looking at the leopard hidden behind the bush. Seeing part of the leopard—the end of its nose peeking out on one side of the bush, and the tip of its tail sticking out on the other—is sufficient for his mind to understand the nature of the hidden portion of the leopard which he cannot directly perceive. We do not have to see the entire leopard to know how big it is. My mind knows that behind these quasi-infinities—these giant and prodigiously huge numbers—lie the forces that brought the universe itself into being, and that behind all that lies the ground of being itself, where truly infinite forces and powers occur.

While standing on a beach and looking out at a storm-tossed sea, I know that the ocean is huge, but that it is not truly "infinite" in the technical mathematical sense. Nevertheless, the immensity of the ocean and the power of the storm *participate* in the infinite. That means that the ocean and the storm act not only as signposts pointing to the infinite power and might of the ultimate ground of being, but also are themselves component events within the infinite chains of cause and effect which that ground of being set into motion. As Paul Tillich said, the Platonic concept of participation means that the symbol is itself part of that to which it points.

The ocean existed before life even existed on this planet. But we know that both the ocean and our planet were brought into existence by prodigious forces of nature, which arose as part of the formation of the stars and galaxies at the beginning of our universe. And we likewise know that the universe itself was created by the Big Bang, which emerged out of a ground of being which was and is infinite in the truly precise sense. This ultimate ground of being can have no beginning or end in time. It must be immune to the laws of thermodynamics, which means that it possesses in effect infinite energy and power.

The part of the ocean which I can see is huge, and the storm raging across its surface is enormous, even though they are not themselves infinite. But they point in back of themselves to even greater and more powerful forces, all the way back to the truly ultimate, which is in fact infinite. Kant is correct at one level: I cannot "see" the totality of an infinite sequence of events. But I can look at processes as simple as a chicken yard full of chickens laying eggs and hatching out of eggs, and understand (from the part which I can see) that I am looking at a process which is, at least in principle, infinite.

When we feel what Kant called the awareness of the sublime, we are not falling under an illusion when we say that this experience gives us a sense of the infinite. We are, so to speak, seeing the tree limb, halfway up the tree, bend under the weight of the hidden leopard crouching upon it. Only in this case, the leopard is infinitely big.

Human beings can and do sense the hint (the *Ahnung*) of the infinite lying behind and beyond and also deep within the things which we *can* directly see and investigate scientifically. It is this sense of the infinite, combined with the sense of the sacred which this *mysterium tremendum* arouses in us, which is one of the most important factors in true spirituality.

Chapter 8

The Spirituality of an Impersonal Ground

Jesus' God

Jesus presented a picture of a warmly personal God, who was good and loving and compassionate, and who reacted emotionally to events in the same way that human beings do, only without our human tendency to excessive grudge-holding, and selfishness and pettiness, and the desire to hurt others simply to make ourselves feel more powerful. In his parables, Jesus presented God in a number of highly personal ways: as a woman at one point, as a man giving a dinner party, frequently as the wealthy owner of a large estate, but also in some of these parables as a loving and forgiving father. In the well-known prayer which he composed, called the Lord's Prayer, he took the traditional preface which is used in so many Jewish prayers, "Blessed are you O Lord our God, King of the Universe," and turned it into something which was probably, in the original Aramaic or Hebrew, "Blessed are you *Hashem*, our Father in Heaven" (already by this time Jewish culture had begun to refer to God simply as *Hashem*, "The Name," as many pious Jews still do to this day).

The important thing that Jesus did here at the beginning of the Lord's Prayer was to replace the word *king* with the word *father*. That is, he removed the traditional distant figure of the mighty king seated in judgment, and substituted for it the warm and intimate image of a good and loving father who would hold his little children in his arms and comfort them when they were hurt and crying. In the Greek translation of this prayer in the Sermon on the Mount (Matthew 6:9-13)—the form in which the prayer is recited today—this opening line was rather awkwardly rendered as: "Our Father who art in heaven, hallowed be thy name." But the word "Father" was preserved, so that Jesus' warmly personal view of God remained even in somewhat modified Greek translation.

The later New Testament and second-century Christianity

In spite of Jesus' emphasis upon the image of a highly personal God, we can see a progressive depersonalization of God rapidly taking place in many Christian circles during the first century or so after Jesus' death. In fact, we can see the figure of God already becoming more and more distant and impersonal even in the later parts of the New Testament itself. In the gospel of John, for example, which was written c. 90-100 A.D. (no more than fifty or sixty years after Jesus' execution by the Romans), God the Father was turned into the Unknowable Father, a distant and unapproachable figure, locked in eternal mystery, with whom we could never come into any direct contact at all. All our dealings with this high God had to be carried out through the intermediary of the Logos (the Cosmic Christ Principle) that had provided the laws of nature, and had revealed itself to the great Hebrew patriarchs and spoken through the prophets. The great Greek philosophers had also known the Logos, and indeed to this day, many of our natural sciences embody the concept of the Logos as part of their names (bio-logy, geo-logy, psycho-logy, socio-logy, and so on). The gospel of John began (1:1-4) with the words:

> In the beginning was the Logos [the eternal Cosmic Christ Principle], and the Logos was with God, and it was the God-Logos. It was in the beginning with God; all things were

made through it, and without it was not anything made that was made. In it was life, and the life was the light of men.

This Logos was embodied in the words and deeds of the historical Jesus, but the gospel of John gave permission to early Christians to discover this Cosmic Christ Principle displayed also in the writings of the wisest of the philosophers.

In the Epistle to the Hebrews in the New Testament (which was most likely written around 150 A.D.,[65] about half a century after the gospel of John), the high God has been totally turned into the *mysterium tremendum*, the primordial abyss out of which all other being emerges and comes into being, which can only be approached with the aid of Jesus the Heavenly High Priest who can console us and comfort our fear and terror, and lead us gently by the hand into the sense of the infinite and the fullness of the numinous reality.

And the writings of St. Justin Martyr, the first Christian philosophical theologian, who was active about the same time (mid-second century), portrayed the high God (who stood at the top of the Christian three-fold vision of the divine) as identical basically to the ground of all being which the pagan Middle Platonic and Neo-Platonic philosophers called the One, and regarded as the primordial infinite abyss out of which everything else came into being.

St. Gregory of Nyssa and the vision of the primordial abyss

How do we form a spirituality built upon the sense of the infinite, the sacred *mysterium tremendum*? One of the great Christian Platonists of the ancient world was St. Gregory of Nyssa (c. 330 - c. 395), who lived in Cappadocia, among the rocky cliffs and vast deserts of the Anatolian plateau, in what is now central Turkey.[66] There is a stark beauty and an unbelievably rich color to the landscape, where one sees a vista painted in reds of various hues, ochre, sienna, tan, cream, butterscotch, blinding white, dove gray, charcoal, and misty blue. In the central part of the region, one can prowl through the ancient rock churches and monasteries of Ürgüp, cut out of the living stone, down to the benches and tables in the monastery refectories. Gregory of Nyssa and the other great Cappadocian Fathers (St. Basil the Great and St. Gregory of Nazianzus) who lived in the middle of that scene of stark and arid beauty in the middle of the fourth century, provided the basis for a good deal of subsequent Christian spirituality, not only in the Eastern Orthodox Church, but also (as mediated through St. Denis and John Scotus Erigena) western Catholic spirituality as well.

We can find the hint of infinity revealed, Gregory said, at all levels of our human experience of the world. We can look at the vastness of the heavens, the power of the ocean waves, and the ground-shaking might of the earthquakes, and sense the infinite power of the ground of being from which they all emerged. We can look at a tiny ant, and marvel at how the human mind, in attempting to understand nature, is drawn into equal marvels as we journey down to the infinitely small.

When the sense of the infinite depths of the universe strikes us with special force, we feel something almost like vertigo, Gregory says. It is like looking over the edge of a cliff and seeing an abyss lying below which literally stretches to all infinity.

In twenty-first century language, we can look into the starry heavens and realize that those stars and galaxies extend as far as the most powerful telescope can peer, but there is something yet "beyond" that, the ground of being itself, which is infinite and unfathomable, and has always been there. The planet Earth is hardly worthy of even being called a speck of dust at that level, and an individual human being is an even tinier speck of inconsequential cosmic dust. And all of that is as nothing compared to the ground of being from which the universe emerged in the Big Bang.

We feel something like vertigo, Gregory says, a giddiness and disorientation. We stand over an infinite abyss of what, to the human mind, is sheer nothingness, held up only by frail supports. And at death we will go plunging into that abyss.

Or we might imagine ourselves standing on the banks of a mighty river, the river of eternity (*aiôn*),[67] and as we look downstream, we can see countless human faces and stories being swept back into the forgotten past. Some of those faces are my own face, at earlier points in my life. There I see myself struggling with other people perhaps, trying to control an event which even now, a few years later, is totally irrelevant to anyone today. A seventy-year-old like me can look back and see myself, when I was a young man, believing that the world hung upon a conflict I was having with people who are all dead now, and not only dead, but forgotten by almost everyone else in the world except me! As the river of eternity flows on, the currents of time bring us to the point where nothing we were fighting over exists any longer, or has any measurable effect on anything happening today.

And back in the past there may be the ghostly figures of people screaming in agony and undergoing pain and torture, and episodes when I was myself scared to death and suffering incredible physical pain, or being treated abusively by other people in situations where I was helpless to defend myself. And looking upstream, I can see nothing clearly, but know that episodes of pain and suffering are probably on their way, and that my own death in particular is coming towards me and will arrive sooner or later. The universe is a place of incredible beauty and indescribable horror, often simultaneously, but in the overall scheme of things—from the viewpoint of infinity—none of it at first glance seems to mean anything, particularly my own tiny little life, no matter how important my own cares and wants and desires may seem to me.

The universe refuses to remain stable or constant. And it is not just the sweep of time. The universe around us shifts continually with every change in our own mental framework. A moral inventory forces us to realize the selfishness and tawdriness of our own past motives, and all the events in our life stories suddenly look completely different. We find ourselves compelled to realize, perhaps, that the person who seemed to be our most implacable enemy was in fact all along the greatest friend we ever had. What appeared to be an insoluble problem in our lives suddenly turns into the key to opening new doors into a greater and more satisfying world than we ever could have imagined.

That which had seemed ordinary and commonplace suddenly reveals an incredible beauty and charm.

Or vice versa, deliberately shutting our eyes to moral considerations changes the way everything around us appears. Good turns into evil and evil turns into good. An act of what is in fact insane self-destruction appears to our deluded eyes as a golden opportunity which will shower us with riches and success, while a fellow human being who needs our help becomes transformed, in our minds, into a fool whom we should harm or take advantage of.

When a good teacher appears and shows me a different perspective, a literary work which had seemed boring and trivial suddenly comes alive and begins disclosing an endless fount of insight and wisdom. I take a course in science, and it makes my head swim when I first realize that the apparently solid wood of the desk I am writing on, and the wall opposite my desk, are actually (from the physicist's point of view) not solid at all, but composed of tiny electrons whirring around atomic nuclei in what is mostly empty space.

What is the world of the five senses really like? I see it, hear it, touch it, taste it, and smell it, but it is nevertheless as insubstantial as a dream. How things look totally depends on how we look at things. At one level, there are brute realities which remain unchanging, but at all other levels, the phenomenal world around us is infinitely plastic.

The French existentialist Jean-Paul Sartre, as a young man, spoke of his feeling of nausea when he began to realize fully that his mind could imbue the world around him with any kind of meaning that he wished to impose upon it, but that this was simply his own subjective projection upon a universe (which was totally unfeeling and did not care) of values and desires which he himself could change whenever he wished, without accomplishing anything that would not be swept away by the great river of time.

St. Gregory of Nyssa described this same feeling as being more like the way one perceived the world after too much wine. Things swim around in your vision, and nothing seems to stay quite solid, where the thing will stay where you put it, and where you will be able to grasp it again without fumbling and falling.

This is the sense of the infinite. At the higher levels, in both the east and the west, among Hindu philosophers and Christian mystics and ancient pagan Neo-Platonists, but also among atheistic existentialists like Sartre and Heidegger, this is the mystical vision of the higher reality which is the starting point for a good deal of higher spiritual teaching.

St. Denis

Building upon Gregory of Nyssa's ideas, a mysterious figure living in Syria around 500 A.D. wrote a series of books on Christian mysticism which formed the basis of a good deal of Christian spirituality for the next thousand years. We do not know St. Denis' real name. The author wrote under the pseudonym of Dionysius the Areopagite, using the name of the Greek philosopher who was converted to Christianity by the Apostle Paul's preaching before the altar to the Unknown God in first century Athens. I strongly suspect, but cannot prove, that St. Denis was a woman, since the only ancient analogies that I know of where works of this sort were written under a pseudonym,[68] were writings authored by a woman, such as the work called the *Sixteen Revelations of Divine Love*, where the author's name was given as "Julian of Norwich," since she was a nun at a convent attached to the church of St. Julian in Norwich, over on the east coast of England.

In St. Thomas Aquinas' *Summa Theologica*, which was the basis of what was regarded as correct Roman Catholic theology and doctrine in Catholic universities for many years, the two most cited earlier theologians are St. Denis and St. Augustine, both of whose ideas and arguments are cited on almost every page.

In St. Gregory of Nyssa, God was still technically speaking a personal God, because he believed that God in some sense had both *logos* (reason) and *thelêma* (will). But the only kind of vision of God which we human beings could attain was that of an infinite and incomprehensible abyss, devoid of all personality. St. Denis pushed this further, and argued that since the ground of being was beyond both being and essence, even the word "God" (with all its residual personal associations) could be regarded only as a metaphor or symbolic way of talking. A ground of being which was literally indescribable in any kind of human concepts or language, could not be regarded as a person who was conscious in the way that human beings were. St. Thomas Aquinas, in his adaptation of St. Denis' ideas, made it clear that God could not possibly feel emotions. God likewise could not be conscious of the universe (and the human beings who lived on the planet earth) in the way that human beings were conscious, because human knowledge is mediated through the five physical senses, and God does not have flesh-and-blood eyes and ears and other physical organs. Some medieval Christian theologians argued that God "knew" the universe in the sense that a creative source contains within it the pattern of what it is creating, but that would certainly not be personal consciousness in the way in which human beings observe the things in the world around them.

For a thousand years, a good deal of Christian theology in both the east and the west moved within that basic range of alternatives: St. Denis, St. Gregory of Nyssa, and St. Thomas Aquinas. They continued to speak (by reflex action) of "God the Father" as the high God within their three-fold vision of the divine. They sometimes argued that in some kind of attenuated technical sense, God had *logos* (reason) and *thelêma* (will), and could be said to "know" the physical objects which made up the material universe. But the vision of God of which so many of the Christian mystics spoke through all those centuries was the vision of the ground of being, which was simply the impersonal abyss of the *mysterium tremendum* which lay behind and beneath the surface world of sense impressions.

In Eastern Orthodox Christianity, the important Hesychast tradition also spoke of a vision of divine Light which mystics could sometimes obtain, but this vision of light was also not a personal God.

Over the past two thousand years, rabbinic Judaism has attempted to stay away from speculation about these issues, but the great Jewish philosopher Philo Judaeus (20 B.C. - 40 A.D.) simply identified God with the Platonic concept of the "One" as the incomprehensible and infinite ground of being, and the Jewish Kabbalistic tradition taught about the same kind of mystical visions of an indescribable Ultimate Mystery which we encounter in Christian mystical writings. In the hierarchy of being in the Kabbalah, personal attributes only begin being applied to God when we descend downwards from the highest vision of God, where our minds begin shaping the idea of God into something that is more understandable to human beings, but further and further removed from the ultimate divine reality, which is totally impersonal as it is in its ownmost being.

The great medieval Muslim philosophers like Averroes (Ibn Rushd, 1126-1198) simply stated point blank that Allah was not a personal God, but was simply the pinnacle of a perfectly natural process by which beings of various sorts emerged into existence out of the ground of being. Allah did not have a personal will, and some of these medieval Islamic philosophers argued that it would be impossible for such a ground to have any kind of consciousness of individual human beings or any other individual things in the realm of time and space.

It is important to explain all this to modern men and women, because it is vital that they understand that, when I speak here of a spirituality based upon the idea of an impersonal ground of being (that out of which our universe exploded into being in the Big Bang, around 13.7 billion years ago), I am not pitching my tent in the campsite of modern western atheism, or trying to undermine the traditional western religious beliefs of the past two thousand years with all sorts of "newfangled modern ideas." I have no truck with the kind of atheistic ideas which began appearing in the western world in the 1840's, and believe that they have been conclusively proven to be destructive in the long run to everything human beings hold dear.

I am attempting to speak here with the tongue of Philo Judaeus, the Kabbalah, Averroes, St. Gregory of Nyssa, St. Denis, and St. Thomas Aquinas, because in the modern scientific world, no one is going to be able to understand that the ground of being IS God in the traditional western meaning of that concept, until someone starts explaining clearly that the basic vision of God in the western tradition, among most theologians and philosophers of the past two thousand years, has been the vision down into the bottomless depths of the infinite abyss that existed before our present physical universe came into being. At most, for the majority of these figures, this *mysterium tremendum* was only vestigially personalized in some highly technical and attenuated fashion, and for many traditional theologians and spiritual writers was not personified at all. If you the reader are a scientist who is afraid that talking about a personal God would land you in the middle of all sorts of superstitious beliefs and wishful illusion and the ignorant pious babblings of the uneducated, then stop worrying about that, and start looking more seriously at the many different ways that the western tradition has provided for developing the spirituality of an impersonal ground.

A spirituality of the abyss in the language of the twelve step program

How can one build a spirituality upon such a dark and disconcerting vision as the one which St. Gregory of Nyssa described (and St. Denis and Philo Judaeus and Averroes)? Although most of the people in the twelve step groups believe in a personal God, it is nevertheless true that a good deal of twelve step spirituality, as practiced and taught by the great spiritual masters of the program, is based on this vision, and can be explained in a way which can sometimes make more sense to modern men and women, I believe, than the older traditional ways.

The most successful spirituality of the twentieth and twenty-first century was that developed within the twelve step program. 95% of the alcoholics who began attending A.A. meetings during that period (and most of the men and women also who became involved in the other twelve step programs) were at that point hostile to all organized religion, and most of them were atheists or agnostics, at the practical level if not at the theoretical level. Ways had to be devised to talk about God to people who had given up on God, and were never going to accept freely (at the beginning of their attendance at meetings) that there was any kind of loving and personal God whom they could pray to and depend on. Because of that, the early A.A. people began developing a way of talking about spirituality which was put in modern terminology, and which eliminated most of the traditional religious doctrines and dogmas, because they had found that either believing or not believing in these really did not make any difference to people's observable spiritual progress in the program.

One did not have to pray to Jesus Christ to get sober and stay sober. One did not have to believe in the substitutionary doctrine of the atonement (the idea devised by Anselm of Canterbury in his *Cur Deus Homo* in 1098, that Jesus' death on the cross paid the penalty owed by us to God the Father for our sins). Buddhists, Jews, and Muslims likewise could all get sober and display all the fruits of the good spiritual life (love, compassion, peace, and so on) whether they did or did not follow all the detailed doctrines and dogmas of their religious systems.

The early A.A. people developed a "bare bones" spiritual system that required only those things which had been proven in actual practice to be absolutely essential. And it was discovered from the very beginning, that even people who regarded themselves as atheists, because they totally rejected all of the traditional God language used by the simple pious, could get sober and gain real serenity in the twelve step program. That was why the phrase "as we understood Him" was added to the third and eleventh steps when the Big Book of Alcoholics Anonymous was being written in 1938-39:

> Made a decision to turn our will and our lives over to the care of God *as we understood Him.*

> Sought through prayer and meditation to improve our con-
> scious contact with God *as we understood Him* ....

Within the A.A. historic heritage, that little phrase "as we understood Him" has always been interpreted as not only allowing those who walk that spiritual path to use some word other than "God," but also allowing them to declare themselves as outright atheists if they so choose. So let us look at how much of the twelve step spiritual program is totally independent of whether we do or do not believe in a personal God. The spiritual teachings which I am discussing here are ones which one encounters in A.A. meetings on a regular basis, because even the men and women who do in fact believe in a personal God, seem to feel much more comfortable if they can phrase the spiritual teachings in a way where they would still be true and still have equal healing power, even if God were only the impersonal and infinite ground of being out of which the Big Bang occurred. There is so much skepticism and cynicism among twelve step people (based on their past experiences of the way the world really works) that everyone feels much "safer" living a spirituality which would still lead them to healing and serenity and the revival of the ability to *lieben und arbeiten* (love and work), even if it turned out that God in fact was only an impersonal infinite.

Twelve step spirituality starts with the observation that what actually makes our lives miserable and intolerable is resentment and fear. We build up resentments which we rehearse over and over in our minds, with a thread of overwhelming fear running through them. Resentment means not only anger, rage, and feelings of hurt at wrongs which we believe were done to us in the past, but also self-pity, which might be described as simply a more cowardly form of resentment, where we stop fantasizing revenge (or "fixing" that past wrong) and collapse into a feeling of helpless futility. Fear can take the form not only of continual anxiety and worry, but also can appear as shame (the fear of being found out and discovered by other human beings) or guilt (the fear of being totally condemned by some cosmic force of right and decency).

The libido dominandi, the
fundamental control neurosis

Our resentments and fears are built upon character defects. One of the commonest of these is what Augustine, the great African saint, called the *libido dominandi,* the lust to control all the people and events going on around us. In the Big Book of Alcoholics Anonymous,[69] right after the statement of the twelve steps to recovery, this is presented as the greatest barrier to spiritual wellness. All the world's a stage, as Shakespeare said, and we are invariably tempted into trying to take over the role of stage director.

> Each person is like an actor who wants to run the whole show; is forever trying to arrange the lights, the ballet, the scenery and the rest of the players in his own way. If his arrangements would only stay put, if only people would do as he wished, the show would be great. Everybody, including himself, would be pleased. Life would be wonderful. In trying to make these arrangements our actor may sometimes be quite virtuous. He may be kind, considerate, patient, generous; even modest and self-sacrificing .... What usually happens? The show doesn't come off very well. He begins to think life doesn't treat him right. He decides to exert himself more. He becomes, on the next occasion, still more demanding or gracious, as the case may be. Still the play does not suit him .... He becomes angry, indignant, self-pitying.

Or if we do not try to play the role of stage director, we tend to at least fall into the fantasy of believing that our task in life is to play the role of chief drama critic. As Dr. Paul O. said in one of the most-read stories in the Big Book:[70]

> Shakespeare said, "All the world's a stage, and all the men and women merely players." He forgot to mention that I was the chief critic. I was always able to see the flaw in every person, every situation. And I was always glad to point it out, because I knew you wanted perfection, just as I did.

Great scientists fall into this spiritual trap just as frequently as alcoholics or any other human beings on the face of this earth. St. Augustine, who lived at the time the Roman empire was falling, and who had served at one point in his life as the public spokesman for the Roman emperor, commented in his *City of God* that in his observation, the rulers of the Roman empire and the savage tribesmen who ran the German war bands which were invading the empire, were equally prey to this fantasy.

In fact, the whole underlying drive behind the kinds of western atheism which began appearing in the 1840's was based on this kind of control neurosis. If we could dispose of God, then we could be in control of human life, and produce heaven on earth.

So in twelve step spirituality, the first goal, as laid out in the first step, is not to get newcomers to believe in God, but to get them to quit thinking that they are God, and to get them to quit thinking that they could remove all their resentments and fears if they could only work out some way of obtaining God-like control over their surroundings. That is where the good old-timers, the great spiritual masters, begin trying to get them to peer over into the infinite abyss, and attempt to get them to look a little further downstream at the great river of eternity. One of the great spiritual masters will listen to a newcomer talking in agony and frustration about the situation that is driving him to desperation, and then say quietly, "How important is it, really?" Brooklyn Bob Firth, when he was in his eighties, once commented wryly, "All the people I used to fight with are dead now! And even the huge corporation in New York City where we were officials no longer exists." Seen from the viewpoint of eternity, not only are all our attempts to control everything around us doomed to ultimate futility, but are not even worth that much inner misery and unhappiness in the short run. On the old A.A. room walls, one would often see the slogan "Easy Does It." That was a warning to remember that trying to over-control the world around us was insane.

Or in a moment of saving insight, a comparative newcomer would say, at the tables, "I asked myself, why did this happen to me? And then I thought," the newcomer would say while laughing, "why not me?" This is disconcerting to people who walk into their first twelve step meeting. Other people around the tables utter truly grim truths, and then everyone laughs. But that is the twelve step formula for obtaining true sanity and real serenity, to learn to recognize the truth about reality, and then learn how to laugh about it, as best we can, because wishing that the world was different than it is will not make it so.

The desire for the glory of the world

The second way in which St. Augustine said that *superbia* (insane egotism) destroyed our lives was through the desire for the *gloria mundi*, the glory of this world. A scientist who has just come upon what he or she regards as a truly epoch-making discovery wants all the other scientists to proclaim this as the greatest scientific discovery of the century (or at least wants the university administration to give him or her a full professorship as a reward!). We want the lead article in the most important professional journal, and invitations to speak at international conferences, and to be praised and applauded. Or, in the twelve step program, our desire for the *gloria mundi* may just take the form of continual people-pleasing, where we betray our true selves over and over again, in the hopes of "being liked" or admired or accepted by some other person.

The vision of the infinite tears the foundations out from under that kind of false way of life as well. The question of how other people respond to us is not worth driving ourselves to total desperation over, and it is never worth betraying who we really are.

Notice how many of the greatest evils in history emerge from the attempt to deny the power of the infinite and the eternal. We kill millions of other human beings, and suffer and die ourselves, in the attempt to create mighty world empires which will eventually disintegrate and disappear just like all the others on this tiny speck of dust that we call the planet Earth. Is it worth maiming one single young man or killing one innocent baby for the sake of something as pointless as that? For the love of empty glory? I lie and cheat and steal in the attempt to gain money to make me look important, or for some other pointless reason like that, where everything involved is only going to be swept down the endless river of eternity and disappear into the mists.

Another of the mottos on the walls of the old A.A. meeting rooms was "One Day at a Time," for today is the only day we have in which to feel satisfaction and joy. I remember some old-timers listening to a newcomer complain about the way the roofers had done one part of the job of putting a new roof on his house (one of our Indiana tornados had toppled a tree on his roof), and finally saying to him, "Would you rather be right or happy?" And he looked back at them and said plaintively, "Couldn't I be both?" The old-timers just grinned and walked away.

When people in twelve step programs do their fourth step moral inventory, which is an analysis of all their obsessive resentments and fears, they regularly discover that the character defects which are making them react in that unnecessarily unhappy way, are almost invariably good old-fashioned moral defects like selfishness, dishonesty, lack of humility, lack of courage, failure to feel gratitude and appreciation for what we do have, a lack of simplicity, too much impatience, a failure to develop a spirit of fairness, an unwillingness to go to work and really work, materialism, envy, jealousy, vengefulness, meaningless rebelliousness, uncontrolled lust, and so on.

Since this is a *self*-inventory of course, where (unlike in most religions) no one gives the newcomer a list in advance of religious rules and laws which external authority figures have set down, they become willing to take these issues seriously for the first time. In my own life I can see that acting on these kinds of character defects produced nothing in my own soul but overwhelming resentment and fear by the time all the consequences of my actions had played themselves out. So if I want my life to be happy, joyous, and free, I will have to stop acting on the basis of these character defects, and quit pretending that I have God-like powers (or God-like responsibilities) and can and must control the infinite and the eternal. Instead, I must start living one day at a time, seeking true serenity and satisfaction within myself.

And what comes out of this are some very good people, who obtain a great sense of satisfaction out of life, and are no longer frightened or driven to desperation by the vision of the infinite which looms over everything, or the continually shifting panorama of our surface sense impressions.

The courage to be: the second clause of the Serenity Prayer

The kind of spirituality I have described here is a part of a number of world religions, including religions and philosophies in the Hindu and Buddhist traditions, along with Christian figures like St. Gregory of Nyssa and St. Denis in the ancient world, St. John of the Cross in the early modern period, and the Protestant theologian Paul Tillich in the twentieth century.

But some religious forms of this teaching can give beginners the false impression that the way to salvation is through the total renunciation of the world, and a passive acceptance of everything that life and other people do to us. The twelve step program gives a much clearer view, I believe, of the other side of the coin, because although some things just have to be accepted (as serenely as possible under the circumstances), there are other even more important things which must be attacked courageously. The most famous twelve step prayer is usually called the Serenity Prayer, but it just as well could have been called the Courage Prayer or even the Wisdom Prayer, for all three are equally important. Let me give the long version of that prayer, which is essentially just an epitome of the basic beliefs of the Roman Stoic philosopher Epictetus,[71] to remind the reader of what it says:

> God grant me
> [1] the serenity to accept the things I cannot change,
> [2] the *courage* to change the things I can,

[3] and the wisdom to know the difference.

Living one day at a time,
    enjoying one moment at a time;
    accepting hardship as a pathway to peace;
taking this sinful world as it is,
    not as I would have it:

trusting that you will make all things right
    if I surrender to your will;
so that I may be reasonably happy in this life
    and supremely happy
        with you forever in the next.

Remembering the vision of the infinite and the onward sweep of the river of eternity helps to sort out the things in life which fall under the first clause, where a good deal of our human misery arises from frittering away all our energies attempting to change the unchangeable in order to obtain goals which would be at best merely temporary bubbles in the eternal flow of things, the kind which float away and burst, leaving nothing behind them.

Once having set these fantasies and illusions aside, we can then be freed to devote our full energies to identifying and struggling courageously for things which fall within the purview of the second clause. The young Einstein, instead of paralyzing himself with self-pity over the fact that he had not gained a professorship at a university, instead courageously worked on his own and in 1905 published his three great works which changed the whole direction of modern science. The young William James managed to obtain a minor teaching post at Harvard University, and instead of bemoaning the fact that there were no people standing around praising him and urging him on, *created* the science of psychology as an American university discipline. Sigmund Freud had 600 copies printed of his first major work, and it took years to sell them all. Since none of the leading scientific journals would publish any of the articles which he and his followers were writing, he started his own scientific journal.

The four great early A.A. authors, instead of sitting in paralyzed self-pity because there were no publishers who wanted to print their books, set up their own publishing arrangements. Bill Wilson sold stock to other A.A. people to obtain the money to print the first edition of the Big Book. Richmond Walker used the printing press at the county courthouse in Daytona Beach, Florida, to print the first copies of *Twenty-Four Hours a Day*, which he distributed from his own home. Ed Webster, author of *The Little Red Book*, teamed up with his good A.A. friend Barry Collins, and they paid for printing the book themselves, calling themselves the "Coll-Webb Company." Father Ralph Pfau and the three nuns who were his assistants called their little operation "SMT Guild," and printed and published the Golden Books from the Convent of the Good Shepherd in Indianapolis, Indiana, where Father Ralph held the post of confessor.

Mother Teresa of Calcutta, as a young nun, saw people dying in the gutters of that city, with no one to hold their hands or wipe their foreheads with a damp cloth, and instead of railing at the universe and its inequities and unfairness, decided to do it herself. "But they are going to die anyway." She knew that. "But there are too many of them." She never thought that she could save the entire world, or even help all the people dying in Calcutta. What one young woman could do however, was to stay by as many of them as she could, and try to comfort those poor people a little. That was all her namesake, St. Therese of Lisieux, had ever tried to do—to live the true spiritual life, which implies showing love and compassion for all around us—within the limits of what one little girl could do, but to do that with a total and outrageous courage, fearing nothing.

And when I act this way—following the path of the true saints and Hindu gurus and Buddhist masters—I show that I am paying attention to the final clause in the long form of the Serenity Prayer. I act in this way "so that I may be reasonably happy in this life" (which those who have tried it report is enormously happy indeed for the greater portion of their lives) instead of weeping because I am not God, or leading myself (and sometimes thousands of other human beings) to destruction, because I have deluded myself into believing that I have discovered the secret of making myself the Master of the Universe who can control all things and will be remembered forever as the Savior of the Universe and the discoverer of the Ultimate Truth of the Universe.

Only fools go that route, but the world is full of fools. Turning to the vision of the infinite and standing on the banks of the river of eternity, and thinking just a little bit about what all this means, is the best antidote to this kind of foolishness, and the entry way into a full and rich spirituality which can give life and blessing.

Learning that I am not God

The good old-timers in the twelve step program tell the newcomers to relax and go at their own speed in working out a concept of God over the months and years after they come in, because they know that these newcomers will have to internalize the most important spiritual message first, the one contained in the first step, which talks about powerlessness and unmanageability. One of the best of the twelve step authors from the second generation was Ernest Kurtz, who summed up the most important teachings of the program in the titles of his two most important books.[72]

The first, which came out in 1979, was entitled *Not-God*, for we must grasp at least enough of the vision of the infinite to understand that *we are not God*, before we can learn anything else at all about the true spiritual life. That is the wisdom of the first of the twelve steps.

Kurtz's second book, which came out in 1992, was called *The Spirituality of Imperfection*, because we must quit trying to become Masters of the Universe, and attempting to gain perfect control of everything, including ourselves. The universe is too big for that game to be winnable. The ground of being is the only truly infinite and eternal reality. The human attempt to gain perfect control of anything, even our own minds and emotions, will drive us insane (which is the wisdom of the second of the twelve steps) and prevent us from attaining even a tiny speck of what lies at the heart of the best and highest kind of spirituality, which is the development of real compassion for the other human beings around us, as well as ourselves. This means a kind of compassion which includes the recognition of other people's inescapable imperfection and finitude, as well as our own.

Richmond Walker

The second most published early A.A. author was a Boston businessman who wrote a little meditational book in 1948, called *Twenty-four Hours a Day*, which was printed at the beginning by the A.A. group in Daytona Beach, Florida, on the printing press in the local county courthouse. There were periods when more A.A. people owned copies of this little pocket-sized book, with its plain black cover, than owned copies of the Big Book. Now it is not totally fair to include him in a chapter on the spirituality of an impersonal ground, because he was equally much influenced by the ancient spiritual tradition which went back to the fifth-century author St. Macarius and *The Fifty Spiritual Homilies*, with its image of the loving hand of a deeply personal God holding our souls up over the abyss, never letting us fall, and giving us continual personal guidance and direction. Rich loved to quote Deuteronomy 33:27, "and underneath are the everlasting arms." But he also interwove the vision of the infinite and incomprehensible divine abyss with this personalistic Macarian spirituality in the meditations in the *Twenty-four Hour* book, and gives us one of the best descriptions in the spiritual literature of any era, of the way our souls can find comfort and calm and new strength from contemplating the infinite and absolute.

Rich, who knew his Kantian philosophy well, insisted that our minds were not in fact totally imprisoned within the box of space and time, but that we could experience the vision of the infinite and the eternal Mystery which lay outside this box. The most important thing he said however, was that this experience, which he called entering into the Divine Quiet or Silence,[73] was not ultimately one of terror, vertigo, nausea, and the plunge into an abyss of nonbeing, but (once we became more used to it) was the entry into a realm of peace and calm, where all the fears and anxieties and resentments which had plagued our minds and thrown us into a chaos of warring thoughts and terrifying emotions, would be washed away in the cleansing waters of this experience. We would emerge with our hearts serene and filled with calm, and empowered with a new energy to automatically do what we knew was spiritually right. Even in the midst of the greatest this-worldly fears, we would find ourselves able to function without panic.

Paradoxical in the extreme? Allowing ourselves to feel the infinite abyss below as a source of profound peace? Putting back to sleep all the personal demons in our closet of anxieties by entering that which spiritual newcomers find even more frightening? Did that not sound paradoxical to the point of absurdity? Indeed, yes. But he and thousands of others found that this kind of meditation did in fact work that way. And how could such an experience cause us to emerge from it with new power? Rich did not attempt to explain it, but just observed that it was so, and thousands of others tried it and found the same thing.

The message we are preaching here is not one of fear and despair and the descent into helplessness and hopelessness. It is a message of peace and hope and new life. We are explaining here how to find the path which leads to functioning with clear heads and stout courage in the face of anything at all that life can toss at us. Read from the fine print section at the bottom of the page in the reading for the day in *Twenty-four Hours a Day* every morning for a while (the top of the page is just for alcoholics, but the bottom of each page is applicable to everybody), and you too can verify that it does in fact work. That is how the famous spiritual masters of the past rose to the great spiritual heights which they achieved.

Remaking the human heart

The twelve step program put these ancient ideas into modern language. In fact none of the basic ideas behind the program were new or original. Anyone who has studied traditional spiritual systems will have been nodding over and over again, as he or she recognized old familiar spiritual truths.

The question which may well be asked at this point however, by some modern western atheists, is why it would be necessary to regard the ground of being as divine in any kind of way. The answer is that the root of our human problems always lies, when we first begin the spiritual life, down in the subconscious, where we have buried all the real issues under a thick layer of alibis, excuses, lies, and evasions. The power of the sacred, however, as Rudolf Otto talked about it, has the ability to drive itself down into the deepest depths of the human subconscious. Years of Freudian psychoanalysis may be able to bring much of this subconscious material up to the level of conscious awareness, but long experience shows that most human beings, even when they know what the subconscious forces are, still are left with precious little ability to change what these forces are continually whipping and goading them to do.

Allowing ourselves to feel the full sacredness of the experience of the *mysterium tremendum* forces us, for the first time, to start changing. We must immerse ourselves into the experience of the awe, the majesty, the raw *energeia*, the totally alien, the Wholly Other, and the pull of the *fascinans*, and finally allow ourselves to receive the illumination and enlightenment which transforms us in the depths of our souls and remakes our hearts.

The ground of being IS the God of the western Jewish, Christian, and Muslim tradition, the One of the ancient pagan Neo-Platonists, and the Brahman of the Hindu philosophers. We do not have to view it as a personal God. But we do have to acknowledge it as the Sacred Itself, and meditate upon its depths, in order to heal our souls when our lives have gone astray, and we are left wandering blindly through the darkness of this world "as atheists, without hope and without God."[74]

Chapter 9

The Cosmological and
Epistemological Grounds

The cosmological ground of being

I began this book by talking about the cosmological ground of being, which is that out of which the universe came into being in the Big Bang around 13.7 billion years ago. I did that because the kinds of atheism which began to appear in the western world during the 1840's got their power by arguing that God existed only in our minds: as an illusion, or an ignorant superstition, or some other kind of subjective creation of our emotions. The best way of undercutting that kind of attack is to link God firmly with something which is absolutely concrete and undeniably there in a way which is totally external to our own inner emotions and feelings, something whose existence can be proved by good scientific methodology. The cosmological ground—that out of which the Big Bang occurred—has to exist, and is not just a fuzzy subjective "feeling" or emotion on our part, but it has all the attributes traditionally assigned to God. It is infinite, eternal, and incorporeal (it is not itself made up out of matter which can be measured in terms of grams and kilograms), and is prior to the creation of space and time. It is ineffable (it cannot be described in words past a certain limited point) and incomprehensible (its behavior cannot be described by mathematical equations in the kind of exhaustive way that we can do with the matter and energy in the observable universe). It is also omnipotent (all powerful), at least to the extent that it does not have to obey the laws of thermodynamics, in particular the law of entropy, and cannot run down and cease to have the power necessary to do what it does. We know this, because if it were possible for the cosmological ground to run out of power, then—since it has existed since infinite times past—it would already have run out of power before it could create our universe.[75]

<h2 style="text-align:center">The sublime and
the vision of the infinite</h2>

When we start trying to construct a spirituality, we also need to talk about the experience of what Immanuel Kant, in his *Critique of Judgment* (1790), called the sublime. This is the kind of experience we have when we are standing in a safe place, looking down at the ocean, and are overcome by the power of a storm breaking in driving waves on the beach. Or we might be gazing in awe down into the depths of the Grand Canyon, or marveling up at the starry heavens above.

This can be a vision of the infinite, because the particular sights we are seeing are not infinite in themselves, but are very much constituent parts of something which is infinite, and extends back to the incomprehensible power of the cosmological ground which created them.

Infinity is not a specific number or thing, but a kind of process. With anything that is infinite, the human mind can never perceive the infinity as a whole. In fact even talking that way is incorrect, for infinity can never be "a whole," which implies that we could come to the end of the process. But by definition, a true infinite can never actually contact a limit which can serve as the end of the process. What the human mind can perceive is therefore *the process itself,* which we can see is necessarily infinite from the parts of the process which we can in fact apprehend.

At a simple minded level, look at the following series: 1, 2, 4, 8, 16, 32, 64, 128, 256, 512 .... We create this series by starting with 1, and then doubling the number each time. This is an infinite series, because no matter how far you take it, you can always add an additional figure. But to say that the human mind cannot comprehend infinity is misleading, if we mean that our minds cannot comprehend how and why that particular number series must necessarily go on forever.

So when we experience the sublime in nature, we are looking at one part of a series of powerful events which extended back all the way to the Big Bang, and beyond that, to whatever mysterious things were going on in the infinite ground of being out of which the Big Bang occurred. In that sense, the experience of the sublime can be a vision of the infinite.

The sublime and forces
outside our control

When we are constructing a spirituality, the experience of the sublime also makes us powerfully aware that our lives will always be, at times, very much at the mercy of powers outside our control. The classical Greek world was very much aware of this ancient wisdom. They symbolized it by speaking of the power of Fate and Fortune, and by talking about gods and goddesses whose whims and jealousies and petty quarrels brought woes innumerable upon the heads of us poor human beings. Aphrodite was the uncanny power of the natural sexual urge, which drives even the most intelligent human beings at times into doing unbelievably foolish and self-destructive things. Hephaestus was the power of the volcano, such as the one which destroyed Pompeii and Herculaneum, and killed so many of the inhabitants of those two cities. Poseidon was the power of the ocean, which could leave sailors tossing helplessly in a raging storm which was going to smash their ship to pieces and drown them all, no matter what they did.

The kind of western atheism which began appearing in the 1840's denounced God as a product of fantasy and illusion and wishful thinking. That kind of western atheism derived a great deal of its power from replacing the mythological thinking of the ancient world with what was only a different kind of fantasy and illusion and wishful thinking, namely the claim that modern science would tame the entire universe and bring it all under human control. It was a control fantasy and a control neurosis. They made good on some of their promises. I would not be alive to write this book, were it not that, at two points in my life, modern medical science saved me from something that would have killed me only a century or two ago.

But let us look at all of the record, and not just the parts that atheists of this sort want us to look at. Modern science gave us no power to divert the hurricane which destroyed so much of the city of New Orleans in 2005. When Mount St. Helens erupted into a volcano on May 18, 1980, and the eruption cloud exploded twelve miles high, there was no human science which could control that event. For many years now, countless human beings all over the world have died from the AIDS virus. Will we be able to find a real cure for it some day? Perhaps, but what happens if some other new mutant disease organism appears and spreads so fast that the entire human race is killed by it before a cure is discovered? Mutant forms of tuberculosis have already developed, which cannot be controlled by the kinds of medication which once promised to totally eradicate that disease.

It may be possible to save the American chestnut tree, which has been rendered nearly extinct by a fungus called *Cryphonectria parasitica* which has been running rampant for over a century, but only by crossing the American trees with blight resistant Chinese chestnut trees, so that the new trees will not really be genetically the same. The same strategy is also the only thing that has been developed so far for dealing with Dutch elm disease, which has devastated European elms and has already destroyed many of the elm trees which used to shade American streets. Complex hybrids of European and various types of Asian elm trees may be able to resist the disease. A tree's life can sometimes be prolonged for five or ten years with medication, but so far nothing has proven permanently effective in blocking the disease from developing and spreading. The point here is that the power of modern science is not always as great, even at best, as the fantasies of modern western atheism would have us believe.

Current calculations show that no large asteroids from the asteroid belt are going to come dangerously close to the planet earth in the next century or two, but in spite of juvenile fantasies, there is no technology currently available which could possibly send enough nuclear weapons by rocket to fragment a truly large asteroid. And it should be noted that some of the asteroids are in fact on orbits which can pass through the orbit of the earth. A large one hitting our planet would wipe out nearly all life, as the dust clouds lingered in the atmosphere and prevented nearly all the warming sunlight from penetrating.

Modern western atheism loves to foster fantasies about reversing the aging process and enabling human beings to live forever. The principal problem here is that medical science already has developed many more ways of prolonging human life than the economy can pay for. We literally cannot afford to provide all of the life-prolonging medical techniques which we already know about, to all of the human beings on the planet. We could endeavor to beef up the economy all over the world, to provide more money to spend on modern medicine, but so far, only by filling the air with emissions which are going to render the earth's climate ultimately unable to support life. Atheists who point towards the continual progress of modern science in order to spin fantasies of some day obtaining total control over nature, do not like to be reminded of economics. But the study of economics is also a science, which uses mathematical formulas and careful analysis of data. Atheists of this naive sort like to think of themselves as "materialists," but the study of economics is a materialist view of the world *par excellence*.

In spite of the scientific advances of the last three centuries, human beings still remain at the mercy of forces over which they have no control. The ancient Greek philosopher Plato spoke of the power of what he called *anankê*, "necessity," which meant that in the material world, attempts to produce a better situation in one aspect inevitably ran into problems at another level, so that the best we could ever do would only be a compromise which produced what we decided were the least bad consequences. No matter how much progress science makes, there will always be brute realities over which we will still be left powerless.

The experience of the sublime forces us to look at the reality that human beings will always be powerless over forces over which they have no control. Acknowledging this brute reality is a necessary part of any sophisticated, adult, and ultimately workable spirituality. In this area, it is the modern western atheists who are the ones falling into childish fantasies.

The river of eternity

The ancient Greeks already made use of the image of the river of eternity,[76] which in its infinite flow immerses us in the process of "the coming to be and passing away," as they put it. Things change and we cannot prevent them from changing. Anything we create will ultimately pass away and disappear into the mists of times past. And unfortunately, where human life is involved, "passing away" can involve enormous suffering and terror. The science fiction writer Robert Heinlein wrote a series of novels about a small group of human beings who had discovered how to live forever, and these should be mandatory reading for all those atheists who believe that such a discovery would produce heaven on earth. Change and loss still occur. And in Heinlein's vision, the longest lived member of this group eventually becomes so bored on the one hand, and so saddened on the other (over all of the things that he has had to grieve as they disappeared forever down the river of time) that he loses his will to live.

And at an even deeper level, the physical universe which came into existence at the time of the Big Bang, around 13.7 billion years ago, is subject to the Law of Entropy, and will eventually run down. There will still be a universe left, but a universe made up only of the random motion of particles where there are no energy differentials left enabling anything significant to happen at all. In fact a lot of current calculations seem to show that we may be much nearer the end of the universe than its beginning. The ancient Greek author Hesiod said that the universe came into existence out of Chaos. Modern science teaches us that Chaos is inescapably where the universe will end.

The cosmological ground, the sublime, and the river of eternity

Strictly speaking, the human problems which we can sense in the experience of the sublime and in our awareness of the ceaseless flow of the river of eternity, are not direct experiences, in and of themselves, of the cosmological ground of being. But all three become linked together when we start trying to talk about spirituality, and the problems which the spiritual life is designed to deal with.

What all three have in common is first, our awareness of the enormous forces of nature and our inability ever to control them totally, and second, the fact that all three talk about brute scientific fact. We are not spinning comfortable little illusions and fantasies about an imaginary God inside our own minds, and we are not falling into blind subjectivity and wishful thinking and superstition.

The epistemological ground of being

The biggest difficulty we have in appropriating some of the wisdom of the past, is the fact that in much of the western tradition, if we go back into the ancient and medieval period, philosophers and theologians were not talking about the cosmological ground of being (that out of which the Big Bang occurred), but about what I would prefer to call the epistemological ground of being.[77]

The human mind receives data from all the five senses, and constructs a picture of the external world by fitting that data into a preexisting cognitive structure. I see a chair, and feel it as I sit in it, and my mind's cognitive structure tells me not only that this is what is called a "chair" in English, but that it is for sitting on, and that it keeps me from hitting the ground (under the force of gravity) when

I sit down on it correctly, and it also tells me what color it is, and all sorts of other things.

There have been many mystics however, down through the centuries (not only in the western world but also in India, China, Japan, and the Muslim world) who have believed that they could go into a meditative state where they could eliminate all conceptual thought and all thinking, and block out all the mind's cognitive structures, and have what would be in effect a vision of the pure flux of sense perception in totally unstructured form.

But we must note that they were not, and could not, be in direct contact with the cosmological ground of being by using that strategy. Nevertheless, to the degree to which it was in fact possible to block out all conceptualization and all the higher cognitive structures of the mind, they would in fact be in some sort of contact with what I am calling the epistemological ground.

One perceives no universe full of "beings" (like chairs and trees and objects perceived as moving under the force of gravity and so on) in that mental state. This is the ground of being in the epistemological sense, because "beings" appear only when we reopen the conceptual and cognitive structures of our minds.

The cognitive structures of our minds have a profound effect on the kinds of beings that will be perceived. This was one of Immanuel Kant's most important contributions to philosophy. There is a major school of psychotherapy called cognitive therapy which further develops what Kant discovered and turns it into a highly useful therapeutic tool. It has helped enormous numbers of people by teaching them how to reframe the cognitive structures of their minds. In treating chronic depression, the success rate for cognitive therapy alone is just as high as the success rate for medication alone. The world literally becomes a totally different place when we reframe the cognitive framework of our minds.

The Irish philosopher Bishop Berkeley, in the early eighteenth century, stated the basic philosophical principle of subjective idealism, which is *esse est percipi*, "to be is to be perceived." The only beings of which we can ever be directly aware are those which we are aware of through immediate sense perception. Something which we would call a material object is simply a cluster of ideas, involving the solidity which we perceive when we push on it, the effort it requires to lift and move it, its extension in space, and so on. But all these are ideas in our minds which arise from our sense perception.

To the degree to which a philosophical position involves some form of idealism, defenders of that position will argue that the *epistemological* ground of being (the raw sense data which pours into our minds in unstructured form) is therefore also the *ontological* ground of being (*epistêmê* in Greek means "knowledge," while the word *onta* means "beings"). This means that if we ask where and how beings come into being (as beings which we can understand and think about inside our minds), then the epistemological answer is that they come into being out of the epistemological ground of being, not the cosmological ground of being.

There has been an idealistic cast to much of modern philosophy, although one must also distinguish between a variety of different strategies for dealing with the problem of where our ideas come from, and their ontological status. Immanuel Kant's philosophy for example is usually described as transcendental idealism, which is more sophisticated than Bishop Berkeley's subjective idealism, but it too is nevertheless a form of philosophical idealism. Some of the twentieth century existentialists, including both the atheistic philosopher Martin Heidegger[78] and the Christian theologian Paul Tillich, were idealists at least to a degree.

Both/and: the river of eternity and the
epistemological ground in a single system

But the attempt to define precisely what kind of philosophical idealism we find in Heidegger and Tillich is neither here nor there. What is important to note for our purposes here, is that both of these thinkers presented a mixed package, where the human problem was discussed in terms of what we have called the "river of eternity" model, while the solution was proclaimed to lie in the contemplation of the epistemological ground of being.

We had to come to terms with the fact that the onward flow of time would inexorably sweep our lives and our creations back into the oblivion of Nonbeing. As Heidegger put it, rather grimly, we had to project our lives onto the reality of our oncoming deaths, in order to attain authentic existence. Because if we attempted to "flee" from that necessary vision of our own mortality, we could do so only through denial, evasion, self-deception (what Jean-Paul Sarte called *mauvaise foi*), and attempting to hide within the conventionalities of "what one does," huddling within the illusory safety of Nietzsche's herd mentality. "Fleeing" in this fashion, Heidegger said, condemned us to an inauthentic existence which was a lie to its core. In order to attain authentic existence, we had to begin by grasping the vision of Nonbeing, death, and destruction.

And with Tillich likewise, part of what he meant by the term "ground of being" was the abyss of Nonbeing into which the flow of the river of eternity swept our lives. He once commented wryly that, during the first part of his life, which was spent in Germany, since he read Shakespeare in the classic German translation, he unconsciously assumed that Hamlet, in his great soliloquy was talking about this issue. That is because "to be or not to be" in German came out as *Sein oder Nichtsein*, "Being or Nonbeing." He admitted that after he had to come to America, and started living in an English-speaking society, he finally realized that Hamlet in the original English was not talking about existentialist philosophy at all! But Tillich still insisted that the fundamental existential question was *Sein oder Nichtsein*, "Being or Nonbeing," and that what he called the ground of being first confronted us with the abyss of Nonbeing.

Both of them however (Heidegger and Tillich alike) turned to the epistemological ground instead in order to find the solution to the human problem. For Heidegger, a human being is basically *Dasein*, "being here and now" at a particular time and place, surrounded by beings which my mind has brought into being by applying the cognitive framework of my mind to the sense impressions I am receiving. The defining axis of this cognitive framework will be supplied by my *Entwurf*, the sketch or basic plan or rough draft of what I want my future to be, the "throwing forth" into the future of the fundamental life goal I want to attain, which in turn will define all the beings which surround me in my world here and now, as either aids or hindrances in attaining this goal. My *Entwurf* can be changed, and in doing so, new being will appear, where things I had disregarded will suddenly become transformed into opportunities for creative purpose.

And Tillich likewise proclaimed that the seeds of the New Being could emerge from the abyss of Nonbeing, and give me new purpose and meaning in my life, even when it felt like everything I had ever accomplished had plunged into the dark abyss.

"Mixed packages": combining four different factors in a spiritual system

I am making this long excursus here because, in order to speak clearly about a spirituality based on an impersonal ground of being, it is necessary to note that there are really four different factors involved: the cosmological ground of being looming in the background, the experience of the sublime, the motif of the ceaseless river of eternity, and the epistemological ground of being from which the answers emerge. Good theologians and philosophers have tended to present mixed packages, where they included more than one of these issues under the general heading of coming into contact with the ground of being. I am going to be mixing all four into the package I am presenting in this book, because all four of those motifs are part of the history of western thought.

There is nothing subjective about the first three. They are concrete and really there, and they can be investigated scientifically. The fourth—the epistemological ground of being—contains what some might call a subjective element, in that I can in principle arbitrarily choose to change my cognitive framework and view the world through any set of presuppositions which I choose. This was one of Kant's positive contributions to philosophy, for he was the first philosopher in the modern period who realized that our human freedom could be returned to us by our ability to frame categorical imperatives (as he called them) as new guiding principles around which to restructure our lives. Some might argue that this introduces a subjective element into the spirituality we are attempting to construct, but when I am locked into total despair over my life as it is now, and filled with resentment and fear and self-pity, and see only futility and hopelessness all about me, it is the epistemological ground of being, and the possibility which it offers of finding New Being (and new hope and new meaning and new purpose) to which I am going to have to turn in order to find the answers to my problems.

We can choose to regard this as the introduction of a subjective element, but we could equally well see this as the place where true human individuality and authentic freedom and creativity can enter into our lives. And although this is not the place to argue this, it is also the case that Plato (in his myth of Er) and the twelve step program both argue that this is not a totally subjective decision, because in choosing new lives for ourselves, based on a different set of goals and presuppositions, we always have the choice between selecting good lives or bad lives. We could in principle choose any kind of new goals and presuppositions that we wanted to, as we began trying to climb up out of the pit of destruction into which we had fallen. But some kinds of lives put us on a path that leads up out of the pit, while other kinds of lives just dig us deeper. And the twelve step program in particular teaches that this is not a matter of pure subjectivity and individual taste, for the accumulated wisdom of human experience and the primordial vision of what Plato called the Good Itself, can guide us into choosing new lives for ourselves with wisdom and discernment.

Radical idealism and New Thought

When the twelve step program was being formulated during the later 1930's and the 1940's, it was often deeply influenced by the world of New Thought and its cousins (including Christian Science).[79] In this sort of idealism, in its most radical form, it was taught that all human diseases and illnesses were the product of wrong thinking, and it was believed that by learning to understand the idealist position, we could not only heal illness but block threatened law suits and all sorts of other human problems, simply by restructuring our thoughts.

To borrow (and expand upon) an example from Heidegger's *Being and Time*, it is certainly true that an object like a carpenter's hammer can in fact be many different things, depending on the mindset of the observer. To a skilled carpenter, the hammer provides a way to build a house. To a sculptor, it could be used if necessary, along with a good chisel, to carve a beautiful marble statue. To a newly divorced woman who has never used one before, and who is suddenly confronted with the necessity of hanging pictures and so on in her new apartment, it may be a source of anxiety and apprehension. To a small child, it may become a dangerous object which the child can drop on his foot or use to break the glass topped coffee table. To a crazed murderer, searching around for a weapon, it might present itself as an appropriate blunt object to use in order to bludgeon his victim to death.

Nevertheless, since we want to keep the natural scientists on board, it must be pointed out that there is also a kind of "brute thereness" to the hammer, where it *cannot* be turned into all things. One might hack a board in two with it, but any good carpenter will tell you that a handsaw works much better and more smoothly. There is no way one could put a neat quarter inch hole in a piece of lumber with a claw hammer. That takes a drill instead. There is no way that even the most skilled painter could paint a fine, detailed portrait by trying to apply the paint with a hammer. That takes a brush instead.

So our working assumption in this book will be that the New Thought people do have a good point, and that the world around us can be totally transformed in extraordinary ways just by learning how to think about it on the basis of a different kind of cognitive framework. And it is amply proven that how a patient thinks about himself and about his disease, will often play a major role in whether he will get well or not, sometimes to an incredible degree, including everything from getting rid of warts to obtaining one of those rare spontaneous remissions of cancer (where good data exists showing that this never occurs except in patients who are engaged in some sort of spiritual meditation or spiritual activity).

On the other hand, as all good scientists know, there is also a "brute thereness" to the world around us. Electrons cannot be turned into protons by thinking about them differently. The speed of light in a vacuum can neither be slowed down nor speeded up by the mood or subjective feelings of the experimenter who is attempting to measure its velocity. Chemists who are living saints and chemists who are dangerous villains will have exactly the same results from mixing a solution of silver nitrate with a solution of sodium chloride, that is, the same amount of insoluble silver chloride will precipitate to the bottom of the beaker.

So when we begin talking about how we can transform our lives, and make them much happier and better, by pursuing the spiritual life, we are going to attempt to maintain some practical common sense about the limitations of what we can do. That is the essence of the Serenity Prayer, learning the wisdom to tell the difference between the things we cannot change and the things that we can change. The vision of the New Being only comes after we honestly confront the abyss of Nonbeing which is created by the "brute thereness" of time and death and destruction, and things that science both can and cannot do to change the course of events.

Nevertheless, the world around us is much more plastic than most people realize, and the best of the New Thought teachers help us to realize the extraordinary degree to which we can change both our own lives and the world around us. They do in fact have something valuable to teach the physical scientists, about a dimension of reality which is never included in scientific calculations. Even if it is only learning how to accept the inevitable with serenity and calm, and learning how to take things one day at a time, and seek in each day for things that we can be grateful for, and appreciate, and feel joy about, this is a major part of learning to live the good life.

A fifth factor: the experience of the sacred

We have talked about the cosmological ground of being, the experience of the sublime which confronts us with the reality of forces which we cannot control (and points us towards the vision of the infinite), the experience of living within the river of eternity (whose flow sweeps everything ultimately into the abyss of Nonbeing), and the possibility of finding new life and New Being by opening our minds to the epistemological ground of being.

But in finding new life and new meaning and purpose in the midst of destruction and uncertainty, the most important life-giving vision arises from a fifth factor, the experience of the sacred. Rudolf Otto, in *The Idea of the Holy*,[80] gives a series of excerpts at one point from pieces that a variety of people wrote about the life-giving nature of the experience of the sacred, excerpts which he drew from William James' *Varieties of Religious Experience:*

> For the moment nothing but an ineffable joy and exaltation remained. It is impossible fully to describe the experience. It was like the effect of some great orchestra, when all the separate notes have melted into one swelling harmony, that leaves the listener conscious of nothing save that his soul is being wafted upwards and almost bursting with its own emotion.

> The conceptions which the saints have of the loveliness of God and that kind of delight which they experience in it are quite peculiar and entirely different from anything which a

natural man can possess or of which he can form any proper notion. [Jonathan Edwards]

But I can neither write nor tell of what sort of Exaltation the triumphing in the Spirit is. It can be compared with nought, but that when in the midst of death life is born, and it is like the resurrection of the dead. [Jacob Boehme]

And in particular, those who feel that their lives have been destroyed, and that they are surrounded by nothing but failure, hopelessness, pain, torture, and death—the dark side of reality which so preoccupied Carl Jung during his youth—should hear the words which Rudolf Otto drew from St. Catherine of Genoa.

O that I could tell you what the heart feels, how it burns and is consumed inwardly! Only, I find no words to express it. I can but say: Might but one little drop of what I feel fall into Hell, Hell would be transformed into a Paradise. [St. Catherine of Genoa]

What is the meaning of suffering? It is pointless to engage in endless philosophical discussions and arguments and attempts to make sense of God and the universe at the intellectual level. Thomas Merton said that he learned from St. John of the Cross that the only way to learn the meaning of suffering is to go through suffering. These are the wisest words I have ever read on the subject, but I do think that what St. Catherine of Genoa said should be added to them. The way to understand the meaning of suffering is to go through suffering while lifting our eyes upward to the experience of the numinous which St. Catherine had learned to cling to:

Might but one little drop of what I feel fall into Hell, Hell would be transformed into a Paradise.

A very wise woman who spoke the truth. That is the only answer that ultimately works.

Chapter 10

Paul Tillich: An Impersonal Ground of Being

In a later chapter, I am going to talk about reasons for regarding the ground of being as a fully personal God. But given the peculiar situation which has developed at this point in history, where the rise of modern atheism during the 1840's still casts its shadow over the western world, it seems useful to begin by explaining some of the ways in which many of the great thinkers, over the past three thousand years, have linked a *personal* spirituality to an *impersonal* ground of being. It has been demonstrated repeatedly through the ages that we do not need to regard the ground of the universe as a highly personal God-figure in order to create a method for dealing with the sacred and the infinite which will enable us to handle the traumas of life and heal the overpowering burden of resentment and fear which can otherwise build up and destroy all of our happiness and satisfaction. I am going to start at this point in particular, because I want to get the scientifically minded on board first, before going any further in this book.

I remember what I was like when I was in my twenties and was a scientist myself, working in research labs and atomic energy facilities, when I was a good-hearted young man who would have been delighted to have some of these ideas explained to me. I had been brought up believing in a warmly personal God, and never truly let go of that at the bottommost level of my heart, but it no longer seemed to make any sense in terms of all of the physics and chemistry I was learning. So if you like, you can understand this and the immediately following chapters as myself at age sixty-seven talking respectfully and helpfully to myself at age twenty-two. It is a debt, if you will, which an old man needs to pay to a young man, and other young people who think today as he thought then, because there was nothing mean-hearted or trivial about that young man. I was thirsty and seeking for knowledge about the ultimate nature of things. That was why I went into science in the first place.

And I can still remember the thrill which I felt in the summer and fall of 1961, right after I turned 22, when I first opened Paul Tillich's two books, *The Dynamics of Faith* and *The Courage to Be*, and then the book Charles Hartshorne did (with W. L. Reese), called *Philosophers Speak of God*. That was the first time I had ever read anything by people who knew and understood about the world of modern science, who were talking intelligently about God and the ground of being, instead of simply uttering pious platitudes. The ideas they discussed were as sophisticated and complex as anything which the theoretical scientists investigated, and I discovered that philosophical theology could be as intellectually rigorous a discipline as nuclear physics or physical chemistry.

Both Tillich and Hartshorne had helped take care of the wounded and ill soldiers in the First World War, the one as a military chaplain on the German side and the other as a hospital orderly in France on the American side, and neither man tried to prettify or deny the enormous evil and suffering which we can encounter in this world. When I read Tillich describing "the God beyond God" who appears when we have lost all faith in the personal God of conventional western theism, I found his vision an extraordinarily frightening one. In fact, the first time I tried to read *The Courage to Be*, I found that it dug so deeply into our fundamental human existential anxieties that I ended up having to put it down before I was finished. But eventually I built up my nerve and picked it up again, and ended up learning that even a totally impersonal ground of being—if we recognize its true sacredness and its implications for the way we need to live our lives—can provide a spiritual basis which can enable us to deal with anything which life throws at us.

The story of Tillich's own life, including not only his World War I experiences, but also what happened to him after Adolf Hitler's rise to power fifteen years later, made it clear that he was not just talking words but laying out the structure of a faith that we could actually live by, no matter what happened to us. And in fact the best way to get to the heart of Tillich's teaching is to explain it in the context of his own life story.

Tillich's childhood and youth

Paul Tillich was born on August 20, 1886, in a small German village called Starzeddel, where his father Johannes Tillich was the Lutheran pastor. For almost seven hours, the little baby struggled at the point of death before he turned the corner and it became clear that he was going to survive.

Otto von Bismarck, who had created the modern German state by his conquests and acquisitions of all the surrounding German-speaking parts of Europe up in the north, was still Chancellor of Prussia (a position he held from 1862 to 1890). Kaiser Wilhelm II became the new emperor in 1888, when Tillich was around two years old. It was the height of nineteenth-century German power and prestige.

When Tillich was around four, his father was made Superintendent of the diocese of Schönfliess-Neumark, where he was in charge of a number of pastors and parishes, serving a role similar to that of an assistant bishop or coadjutor bishop. They moved to Schönfliess, a town of three thousand, which was still surrounded by its medieval wall and towered gates, and governed from the old medieval Rathaus or town hall. The atmosphere of the Middle Ages and the sense of being in the presence of centuries of tradition were still alive when Tillich was a child.

When he was twelve, he began his studies at a "Gymnasium," as it was called in German, a secondary school which emphasized a kind of strongly humanistic education which involved learning to read the pagan Latin and Greek classics, and also the study of German philosophers like Kant and Fichte, who would be regarded by anyone who believes in a strongly personal God as being, both of them, nearly total atheists. Any residual discussion of God in Kant and Fichte pertained only to their idealized discussion of the presuppositions of the moral life, and even then, merely at certain peripheral points.

This is important for understanding Tillich's thought later on. The greatest challenge to his father's and mother's belief in God did not come from popularizations and accounts in school textbooks of what were believed to be the necessary implications of modern scientific knowledge, but from this kind of much more ancient humanistic education, which indoctrinated students with both the old paganism of the ancient Greco-Roman world and the neo-paganism of the Renaissance and Enlightenment eras. The results however were much the same. Any kind of belief in a personal God was made to seem incompatible with being an educated person.

In 1900, his father took up a position in Berlin. The young Paul, who was now around fourteen, was introduced for the first time to life in a big city, and fell in love with city life instantly. He never ever wanted to go back to what he regarded as the stultifying and boring life of the small towns and tiny rural villages where he had spent his early childhood. The only positive thing which he found coming from his forced move to the United States later on was the opportunity to live in what he regarded as the most exciting city of them all, New York, the city which surpassed all others in its excitement and variety and cultural opportunities.

Not long before he finished at the Friedrich Wilhelm Gymnasium in Berlin, when he was only seventeen, his mother died of cancer. It was a devastating blow which left a permanent mark on his soul. He nevertheless somehow pulled himself together well enough to pass his final examinations in 1904, and started university at the normal age.

As was commonplace among German students, he attended lectures at several different universities, so he could hear as many of the great scholars as was possible. In spite of the antireligious atmosphere of his humanistic secondary education, he studied Protestant theology at the University of Halle from 1905 to 1907. He also attended lectures in Protestant theology at the Universities of Berlin and Tübingen, and finally received his Dr.phil. degree at the University of Breslau in 1910.

He also completed the requirements for a Licentiate in Theology at the University of Halle in 1912, which enabled him to be ordained as a pastor in the Evangelical Lutheran Church.

He had gotten through the death of his mother and the challenges to faith posed by his humanistic secondary school education, where most of the curriculum had been based on skeptical and atheistic authors, and was nevertheless willing to commit himself to a life of service as a pastor.

The First World War

He was now to be assaulted however by challenges to faith that far surpassed anything he had ever been subjected to before. The First World War began, and Tillich was called to serve as a German army chaplain on the Western Front from 1914 all the way to the end of the war in 1918. The horrors of the trench warfare were unbelievable. Those who know nothing of the massive slaughter and helplessness of those sent to their doom in continual pointless human wave attacks and counterattacks should read the classic account in Erich Maria Remarque's novel, *All Quiet on the Western Front*. In its original German, the novel bore the title *Im Westen nichts Neues*, "Nothing new happening on the western front," a grim reference to the fact that all the fighting and dying accomplished nothing, as the two sides remained locked in conflict along essentially the same battle line for month after month, with neither side able to gain any military advantage or "win" the war.

Tillich had two nervous breakdowns during those years. Everywhere he could hear the sound of the shells exploding along the line of battle, the groans and screams of the dying as he rode in the ambulances bringing the wounded back from the front, the weeping of those who had lost limbs, or been blinded, or had their lungs destroyed by gas attacks. Instead of preaching sermons, he spent his time saying the prayers for the dead over and over as the bodies of thousands of young men were shoveled into their graves. There was no "nice God" who would make sure that "everything turned out for the best." There was no true joy or kindness to life which he could see anywhere, no cheerful comradeship of brothers in arms, only raw fear, bitterness, and despair all around him, and the knowledge that anyone who refused the order to mount a suicidal mass charge on the enemy's trenches and die in the mud of no man's land, would instead be shot to death on the spot by his own commander.

Even when I met him, almost fifty years later, Tillich still had what Vietnam war veterans call the thousand yard stare, the look in his eyes which told of the unbelievable horrors that he had witnessed.

Then during that same period, he was hit by yet two further blows. He had married a young woman named Grethi Wever shortly before the war. They had a child, but the child died in infancy. Then at the end of the war, Paul discovered that Grethi had had an affair with his best friend, Richard Wegener, and was pregnant with that Richard's child, a little boy, who was to be named Wolf, to whom she gave birth in June 1919. Then six months later, in January 1920, Paul's sister Johanna died. She had been the only family member with whom he had been truly close since the death of their mother.

The Dark Night of the Soul

The Dark Night of the Soul is not a romantic poetic term for a vague intellectual disquietude or a polite intellectual skepticism. It describes the entry into a kind of hell on earth, a period of overwhelming terror and despair, where everything which seemed to give meaning to our lives collapses under us. The term comes from a strange and nightmarish episode in the ancient Hebrew poem called the Song of Songs, in verses 2-7 of chapter 5. The young woman in the story hears her lover knocking on her door in the middle of the night, and sees his hand reaching in, trying to touch her. She arises from her bed, opens the door, and goes out into the sleeping city to try to find him, but he has inexplicably vanished. She calls out to him and no one answers. As she wanders through the dark streets, she comes upon the night watchmen, who are supposed to be the city's protectors. But instead they beat her savagely and rip off her clothes, and leave her to wander half naked, wounded, and stunned through the pitch black streets. Where had her lover gone, the one to whom she had committed her soul, the one who should have been there to protect and save her? She loved him and trusted him, and he seems to have only turned on her and abandoned her with total treachery. Far better would it have been for her, she thinks with total outrage, if she had never loved him at all, let alone trusted him with her soul and life.

Young Paul Tillich believed that he had been called by God, the Lover of our Souls, to serve as a pastor, and in fact, for the first two or three weeks after he had begun his work as an army chaplain, he still believed that he could hear God knocking on the door of his soul, and see God's hand beckoning to him. Instead, as the full reality of the war broke upon him, he found himself cast into an overwhelming nightmare that only kept getting worse and worse.

That is what any truly deep spirituality has to overcome. When the naive beginning stage of our love affair with God seems to totally collapse, and all the good things which we believed about him seem to be betrayed by bitter reality, we have only two ultimate choices. We can choose to live the rest of our lives in bitterness, cynicism, and anger, or we can somehow open up our spiritual eyes and ears to see and hear a higher understanding of the meaning of life and the divine light of God.[81] Those who go the first route, often destroy themselves totally, with alcohol, drugs, cynicism, angry attacks on other people, and a soul-destroying bitterness. The ones who go the other route embark upon the path of the saints, and develop a new and different kind of courage and faith. Their eyes are in fact even clearer than those who fall into everlasting bitterness, for they see human imperfection with even greater clarity, and yet somehow they are not destroyed by it, but rendered more compassionate and filled with an enormous depth of personal humility. They emerge from their suffering filled with a divine light which makes them sometimes almost visibly glow with light. You can sense it the minute they walk into a room and begin to speak. Where did they get that courage and that divine light within?

Not from going back into the old naive and childish beliefs about a "nice" universe, and not from clinging to sentimentality and wishful thinking.

Thomas Merton, when commenting on St. John of the Cross's writings about the Dark Night of the Soul, noted that second and third-rate philosophers and theologians often put together long, wordy, and complicated attempts to make sense out of "the meaning of suffering." If God is all powerful, all knowing, and all loving, then how can evil exist? And so they write lengthy books on the subject, and come out with nothing useful by the end of it all, if the reader has any common sense. But what St. John of the Cross said was short and simple: *the only way one learns the meaning of suffering is to go through suffering.* That is a truly profound statement. The only thing I would add is, that the only way one learns the meaning of suffering is to go through suffering and nevertheless discover, at some point along the line, *how to reach out and touch God in spite of the pain and suffering.* And this discovery lifts us up into a new dimension of existence, as we discover how to climb up out of that miry pit, and live by a new set of rules and a new and different kind of meaning.

In the twelve step program, no one has to be taught about the Dark Night of the Soul, for no human beings truly commit themselves to working the steps until they have descended so deeply into the pit of rage and anguish and despair that life seems impossible to maintain any longer. No one is going to truly work the steps the way they were intended, until they have no choice but to work the steps or die. The twelve steps are twelve things to do, which will enable us to climb up out of that pit and find that new dimension of reality which works by its different kind of divine and eternal rules.

But whether we use the twelve steps or some other spiritual discipline, one of the most important things that happens, if we are able to walk through the Dark Night of the Soul successfully and ascend back up into the light again, is that we are given by grace a vision of a new meaning for our lives, to replace the old meaning which was destroyed.

University teaching

Tillich did successfully get through his Dark Night of the Soul, and began building a new life for himself. He began to realize that he had important things to teach people about the relationship between theology and culture, and especially theology and the arts. Many years later, he would take his American students in New York City and give them guided tours of the great art museums in that city. In the art of various periods one could see painters and sculptors giving expression to the deepest existential anxieties of their eras. Among the ancient Greeks and Romans, one saw the anxiety of fate and helplessness and the confrontation with powers beyond any possible control. In the later Middle Ages, one could see the anxiety of guilt, death, and condemnation. In mid-twentieth century art, one could see the anxiety of emptiness and meaninglessness. There was a kind of catharsis which could be achieved, as Aristotle called it in his *Poetics*, a kind of cleansing that came from realizing that other human beings had felt the same things that we are feeling. For people who have been suffering in lonely and isolated anguish, who believe that no one else has ever experienced the torment that they have experienced or done the terrible things that they have done, the simple realization that *we are not alone* can be a saving message of new life and new hope.

And Tillich also realized that the old authoritarian German way of life had to be replaced with a spirit of democracy and social responsibility for all segments of society, all the way down to the poorest and worst abused segments of society. He began to realize for the first time what the Hebrew prophets had been talking about when they preached about our social responsibility for the widows, the orphans, the poor people, the resident aliens, and the other people on the neglected fringes of our society, and why Jesus had devoted himself to the poor and the outcast.

So it was a new kind of theology which he began developing, a theology of culture combined with a kind of political activism that had him speaking out forcefully for a new kind of social and political order in post-imperial Germany. It was a theology based on a new kind of profound compassion which he had learned from his own sufferings and from observing the sufferings of those around him. It was a powerful message, based on a new and deeper understanding of the meaning of life.

In 1919, the year he turned thirty-three, Tillich obtained a post at the bottom of the academic ladder, serving as a Privatdozent at the University of Berlin. He lectured on the philosophy of religion, the theology of culture, and the relationship of religion to politics, sociology, art, and the new Freudian depth psychology, which made it clear that the capacity for massive evil lurked at the bottom of every human heart. Under sufficient pressure, as the experiences of war made clear, all human beings were capable of murder, rape or prostitution, lying, theft, abuse of power, enormous atrocities of revenge, and every other kind of evil under the sun. We could not build a truly moral society until we came to grips with the extraordinary power of the demonic forces which would constantly work to corrupt it.

A docent in the German university system was roughly equivalent to a non-tenure-track lecturer in an American university. Docents had university positions but were not considered faculty members in the proper sense. The German doctoral degrees in those days did not require quite the same level of competence as an American Ph.D., so docents had to continue their studies on their own, and publish scholarly works to establish their worthiness of being given a professorship. Because there were so very few openings at the higher teaching level, most of them did not make it, including unfortunately even some of the brightest and best. There were many very good scholars who never obtained a real position on a university faculty, and ended up spending the latter part of their lives teaching in secondary schools.

In spite of the odds against him, after five arduous years, Tillich was called to a post as Extraordinarius (roughly equivalent to an American associate professor) at the University of Marburg. This was in 1924, the year he turned thirty-eight. There were two other very brilliant young men on the faculty, of roughly his own age. Martin Heidegger (1889-1976) was Extraordinary Professor of Philosophy at

Marburg from 1923 to 1928, and published *Being and Time*, his great work on existentialist philosophy, in 1927. Rudolf Bultmann (1884-1976) had come to the University of Marburg in 1921, and was to remain a professor there for thirty years. He had already established his reputation with his book on the *History of the Synoptic Tradition* (1921), which used a new technique called form criticism to analyze the sayings of Jesus in the gospels of Matthew, Mark, and Luke. New Testament scholars at most major American universities still use variations of this basic method to this day. But Bultmann was also an existentialist, and had begun developing his idea of demythologizing the New Testament, where the basic message was reformulated in terms of existentialist philosophy. Heidegger was an open atheist, who saw the ground of being as an empty abyss of nothingness into which we were being led to our deaths.

At that point in his life, Tillich found himself rebelling against all of these existentialist ideas, even though he was eventually to incorporate a good many of their existentialist terms and ideas into his own theology. Also, the position he had been given at Marburg had him teaching systematic theology, which was not his real goal. But probably even more important, Marburg was a beautiful and charming little medieval town, with an emphasis on the word little. Tillich wanted to live in a big city, and he quickly decided that he was willing to pay a price for it.

The next year he accepted a position as professor of the philosophy of religion and of social philosophy in the philosophical faculty of the Technische Hochschule at Dresden. This kind of institute of technology did not have the prestige of a university position, but as Tillich said in an autobiographic memoir later on, he wanted "the openness of the big city both spatially and culturally. Dresden was a center of visual art, painting, architecture, dance, opera," and this was what he needed to feel that he was truly alive.[82] In 1929, the year he turned forty-three, Tillich finally got what he was looking for. He was given a full professorship (in philosophy and sociology) at the University of Frankfurt, a good university in a decent sized city, teaching exactly what he had always wanted to teach. He began to be a well-known theologian in Germany, and he also used every opportunity to speak out on German political issues. In particular, he began to develop a reputation as a major and effective public opponent of the rising Nazi movement.

On January 30, 1933, Adolf Hitler was made Chancellor of Germany, and on April 13 Tillich was fired from his teaching position and replaced by a philosopher who had just joined the Nazi party.

Coming to America

Tillich turned forty-seven that summer. Everything that he had worked for all those arduous years had been destroyed. He was a man not only without a job, but also apparently without a future. Providentially however, Reinhold Niebuhr, the leading American theologian of that time, happened to be spending that year in Germany, and invited Tillich to America. Niebuhr taught at Union Theological Seminary in New York City, which at that time was considered one of the three top graduate theological institutions in the United States (along with Yale and the University of Chicago). It was located right across the street from Columbia University.

Tillich and his family arrived in New York on November 4, 1933. He did not have even a minimum knowledge of the English language, and he also found out almost immediately that the Americans were not impressed by his reputation back in Germany. Neither Union nor Columbia regarded him as good enough to teach on their faculties. He was finally somewhat grudgingly given a position at Union as a Visiting Professor of the Philosophy of Religion and Systematic Theology, but it was made clear to him that he was only given that as an act of charity, and that they wanted him to find some other teaching position somewhere else in the United States, at an institution more in keeping with what they regarded as his somewhat limited abilities. Duke University eventually brought him for an interview, but did not regard him as good enough for their faculty either, and no place else in the United States was interested in giving him a teaching position.

Meanwhile, the news from home made it clear that Hitler was going to destroy Germany and be responsible for the deaths of millions.

Again Tillich was forced to walk through the Dark Night of the Soul. Again he had to start from scratch to develop new meaning for his life, when all the old sureties and so many of the things he loved in life had been destroyed. He was in a strange and alien world, where he was regarded with contempt, and did not even speak the language, trying to start over again. When Tillich spoke in his theology about the power of the New Being to bring new life and meaning out of the abyss of Nonbeing, he was not talking glib theories but reporting what he had learned from his own life struggles. He did not mean that climbing up out of the pit was easy, but he did proclaim over and over that the ground of being was a source of grace and the possibility of New Being. Two of his most important later books were entitled *Dynamics of Faith* (1957) and *The Courage to Be* (1952).[83] Faith was necessary to walk through the Dark Night of the Soul and emerge into the sunlight on the other side, but so was courage. In his autobiographical memoir, Tillich talked about how he served for many years as the chairman

> ... of the Self-help for Emigres from Central Europe, an or-
> ganization of refugees for refugees, giving advice and help to
> thousands of newcomers every year, most of them Jews. This
> activity brought me into contact with many people from
> the Old World whom I never would have met otherwise,
> and it opened to view depths of human anxiety and misery
> and heights of human courage and devotion which are or-
> dinarily hidden from us. At the same time it revealed to me
> aspects of the average existence in this country from which I
> was far removed by my academic existence.

His new American students were the brightest of the bright. But their faces remained blank and uncomprehending when Tillich would sprinkle his lectures with his customary references to German authors like Fichte, August Wilhelm Schlegel, Schelling, Goethe, and Hegel. This turned out not to be a bad thing in the long run. Had Tillich remained in Germany, in spite of the fact that he was a recognized figure in German theological circles, I do not believe that he would have been remembered for very long after his death, and in particular it is difficult to see how he could have risen to the stature of one of the four or five most important theologians of his century.

But in America, Tillich had to learn how to explain his ideas all over again, working from the basics all the way up and giving all of the details in the process. In the course of doing this, he was forced to sharpen his thought and develop even greater depths of profundity, as he searched for explanations and examples which would make sense to any intelligent person from any culture or part of the world.

If I were asked what I thought made a work a perennial classic, I would point to three necessary features. First, a real classic is a work of such depth that one can read it multiple times over the course of one's life, and still gain new and valuable insights each time it is read, and obtain yet further food for one's own creative thoughts. The greatest classics produce, not disciples mechanically reproducing the master's ideas, but people who are inspired to produce great creative achievements of their own. Second, a work which is too tied into the current fads and the passing fancies of its own period cannot achieve that status, because one of the measures of a true classic is that it can and will still be read and treasured, even centuries later, by men and women from totally different cultures. Third, it must be written on two levels, where it can be read equally well by ordinary people or advanced scholars. Shakespeare's plays, in their time, had to compete in the same kind of commercial market which we have for contemporary television and film productions, and supply the completely ordinary people who flocked into his theater with a kind of drama and action which they could appreciate, and which would make them also think about the meaning of life and the nature of human existence in a way which was in fact quite deep and profound. St. Thomas Aquinas's *Summa Theologica* was written by him to be used as a beginner's textbook for people who knew little or nothing about the complexities of advanced philosophical theology, and in fact many sections of it can still be used effectively for that purpose today, in the hands of the right teacher.

Tillich's struggle through this second Dark Night of the Soul forced him to write true classics, so that the new meaning he forged for his life during those early years in New York City turned him from a very competent man into a truly great thinker.

In 1937, Union Theological Seminary finally gave him a permanent position on their faculty, albeit as only an Associate Professor of Philosophical Theology. But as Tillich continued to adapt his ideas to expression in English, Americans slowly began to understand how brilliant his theological system really was, and Tillich in turn had been forced by his American experience to articulate his ideas with all the supporting philosophical framework attached. In 1940 he was finally awarded a full professorship. It had taken him seven years of struggle to win full acceptance there in New York. He became an American citizen that year, and committed himself to the New World and his new life, without ever looking back again.

To sum up the final years of his life fairly quickly, Union required mandatory retirement at age seventy, so in 1955 he went to Harvard as University Professor. *Time* magazine for March 16, 1959, had Tillich's portrait on the front cover, which was an honor that he richly deserved. The only other American theologian with his philosophical skills had been Jonathan Edwards, two centuries earlier. The works which he published during this final period of his life are all true classics, including especially his three-volume *Systematic Theology* (1951-63),[84] *The Courage to Be* (1952), and the *Dynamics of Faith* (1957).

In the American theological world of that time, Harvard was in fact a slight step down in terms of prestige. But in 1962 he was made Nuveen Professor of Theology in the Divinity School of the University of Chicago, and was back in one of the top three places again. He remained teaching there until his death in 1965, at the age of seventy-nine. He was buried at New Harmony, a tiny little town in southwestern Indiana which had been the site of an experimental utopian and communitarian community founded by a man named Robert Owen in 1825. Tillich's gravestone, a large chunk of rough granite with a simple inscription on it, is placed in the midst of a tiny but beautiful garden enclosed by evergreen trees.

Paul Johannes Tillich
1886-1965
And he shall be like a tree planted by the rivers of
water that bringeth forth his fruit for his season.
His leaf also shall not wither and
whatsoever he doeth shall prosper.

Chapter 11

Tillich and Einstein

The famous scientist Albert Einstein had spoken on "Science and Religion" at The Conference on Science, Philosophy and Religion held in New York City in September 1940, strongly attacking the traditional concept of God. Tillich's response to these arguments was published as one of the chapters in his book on the *Theology of Culture*,[85] and is especially important to look at, because it shows us one of the greatest theologians of the century responding to one of the greatest scientists of the period.

The title which Tillich gave to his response was "The Idea of a Personal God," because he saw that this question was at the true crux of the many issues separating the theologians and the scientists. As Tillich sums up the great physicist's position:

> Einstein attacks the idea of a personal God from four angles:
> [1] The idea is not essential for religion. [2] It is the creation
> of primitive superstition. [3] It is self-contradictory. [4] It
> contradicts the scientific world view.

Tillich's response to this was very interesting, because he in fact acknowledged that he, just like Einstein, did not believe that the ground of the universe was in fact a personal being. But against the scientist, he insisted that a certain amount of the personalistic language in the traditional Jewish and Christian prayers and texts was in fact necessary, even if it was only being intended as metaphor and analogy.

1. Spirituality cannot be reduced to only a system of humanistic ethics

The first criticism assumes, Tillich says, that religion and spirituality can be understood in a way which leaves out everything except ethical issues, which Einstein said in that speech can still be talked about meaningfully on a completely humanistic basis, with no reference to any kind of religious belief. Tillich says that this ignores the experience of what Rudolf Otto called the numinous aspect of reality and the reality of the enormous depths which we encounter when we approach the ground of all being and meaning, and the effect that has upon our moral perspective. It also assumes that a moral perspective on our personal relationships with other human beings can be constructed upon the basis of a neutral sub-personal view of the universe, which is not possible, because our scientific beliefs (when based upon this kind of foundation) depersonalize our entire view of the world and always end up undermining and negating the validity of any moral principles we then try to maintain.

2. Primitive superstitions can nevertheless refer to things that actually exist

The second criticism points to the abuse of the idea of God in previous eras of human history by primitive imaginations which converted it into ignorant and superstitious beliefs and tried to use it to justify grossly immoral behavior. As Tillich points out in his essay, the fact that an idea has been abused by some people does not mean that the underlying idea is totally invalid, and without foundation. If primitive people foolishly believed that volcanoes were caused when the god Vulcan, the smith who made metal objects for the other gods, began hammering on his forge under the earth, and if these primitive folk out of fear then began burning sacrifices to Vulcan to try to prevent volcanoes from occurring, this does not in fact mean that volcanoes do not exist or that the ground of being does not exist. It simply meant that they had an ignorant and faulty science and an ignorant and faulty theology both. And Tillich goes further, and cites the philosopher Descartes: "the infinite in our mind presupposes the infinity itself." Uneducated and primitive notions about the infinite ground of being does not mean that there is no infinite ground.

3. Omnipotence as symbol of an unthreatenable cosmic source of power and grace

Einstein's third argument, that religion is self-contradictory, is directed at the often heard religious concept of "an omnipotent God who creates moral and physical evil although, on the other hand, he is supposed to be good and righteous." But the idea of omnipotence, Tillich says, is a symbol, not a statement that God is an object who is active in terms of physical causality, as simply one object among all the other objects in the physical universe. As a religious symbol, we see the correct understanding of omnipotence in biblical passages like the famous one from Deutero-Isaiah (Tillich here cites Chapter 40 in the book of Isaiah). To put this in context, we need to remember how the ancient near east had been swept by bloodshed and slaughter over and over again for two entire centuries, as first one imperialistic power and then another sought to gain control over the entire region: the Assyrians (the Nazis of the ancient near east), the Babylonians, and finally the Persians. Through all of this the Jewish people had somehow survived, and were now going to be given the opportunity to return to Palestine and rebuild Jerusalem and the Temple. The passage to which Tillich refers was written at this point, shortly after the Edict of Cyrus was issued by the King of the Medes and the Persians (modern day Iran) in 538 B.C. Since a good many of the people who are going to read this book are not great biblical scholars, I believe it will be useful to give an extended selection from Isaiah 40, so the reader can get a better idea of what Tillich meant by the image of omnipotence as a powerful symbol for talking about the structures of reality:

> A voice says, "Cry!" And I said, "What shall I cry?" All flesh is grass, and all its beauty is like the flower of the field. The grass withers, the flower fades, when the breath of the LORD blows upon it; surely the people is grass. The grass withers, the flower fades; but the word of our God will stand for ever.

> Have you not known? Have you not heard? Has it not been told you from the beginning? Have you not understood from the foundations of the earth? It is he who sits above the circle of the earth, and its inhabitants are like grasshoppers; who stretches out the heavens like a curtain, and spreads them like a tent to dwell in; who brings princes to nought, and makes the rulers of the earth as nothing. Scarcely are they planted, scarcely sown, scarcely has their stem taken root in the earth, when he blows upon them, and they wither, and the tempest carries them off like stubble.

The real God is far above all the meaningless battles of ignorant kings and dictators struggling for power. The real God is the power revealed in all the countless stars and galaxies which came into being out of the infinite ground of all being in what modern physicists call the Big Bang, 13.7 billion years ago:

> To whom then will you compare me, that I should be like him? says the Holy One. Lift up your eyes on high and see: who created these? He who brings out their host by number, calling them all by name; by the greatness of his might, and because he is strong in power not one is missing.

The symbol of divine "omnipotence" means that the force which created the galaxies can never be threatened or overthrown by puny human beings, even so-called mighty kings and world conquerors, who are like tiny grasshoppers madly jumping about on a planet that is but a speck of dust in a universe which extends as far as the largest astronomical telescopes can peer.

After passing through any kind of historical cataclysm, however, this passage from Isaiah proclaims that human beings can turn to the realm of the sacred and the infinite, and draw power and grace to rebuild their lives. If Solomon's Temple has been destroyed and Jerusalem lies in ruins, this does not mean the end of the people of God. They can turn to the source of all spiritual power again, just as their ancestors did in the midst of earlier historical periods of destruction and calamity, and build the Second Temple and the New Jerusalem.

> Have you not known? Have you not heard? The LORD is the everlasting God, the Creator of the ends of the earth. He does not faint or grow weary, his understanding is unsearchable. He gives power to the faint, and to him who has no might he increases strength. Even youths shall faint and be weary, and young men shall fall exhausted; but they who wait for the LORD shall renew their strength, they shall mount up with wings like eagles, they shall run and not be weary, they shall walk and not faint.

The symbol of divine "omnipotence," Tillich says, does not refer to a mechanical system where God is purported to be a this-worldly physical cause (an object among all the other objects in the universe) who somehow or other prevents bad things from ever happening to good people, which would simply be total nonsense anyway to any human being of even moderate intelligence. It was obvious to the biblical authors too. Of course, vast numbers of innocent human beings died when the cruel Babylonian army took the city of Jerusalem in 586 B.C., and even more died during the thousand mile death march which followed, when the survivors were forced to cross the burning deserts under armed guard, to concentration camps and resettlement camps in Babylon.

As a religious symbol, omnipotence means that the word God refers to something so huge and powerful that the existence and integrity of this infinite ground can never be threatened by anything human or earthly, no matter how cruel or evil or powerful. And it also means that God always remains as a source of power and grace and courage for finding new meaning and creating new structures of being, which can be called upon by human beings in any kind of possible situation. Tillich had had to do that during two different periods in his own life, first during the period of the First World War, and later during the period just before the Second World War when he was having to rebuild his whole life in the new country of America.

But we cannot get involved, Tillich says, in trying to argue that the sufferings of young men in the trenches of the First World War, lying maimed or blinded and screaming in fear and pain, were the direct causal result of a decision made by some imaginary God. And theology turns into nonsense when we try to use logical trickery and special pleading to insist that this cruel imaginary being could nevertheless somehow or other be construed as good and loving. As Tillich says in forceful language in his essay:

> The concept of a "Personal God," interfering with natural events, or being "an independent cause of natural events" makes God a natural object beside others, an object amongst objects, a being amongst beings, maybe the highest, but anyhow a being .... No criticism of this distorted idea of God can be sharp enough.

4. A supra-personal ground of being does not contradict the scientific world view

On Einstein's fourth criticism, that belief in a personal God contradicts the scientific world view, Tillich quotes the physicist against himself, and then makes a careful and important distinction (absent from the scientist's talk) between the personal, the sub-personal, and the supra-personal. Einstein said that there was a kind of religious perspective, if one wished to call it that, which could be held within the modern scientific world view, without contradicting any of the fundamental principles of science. A man or woman who held that kind of scientific religious perspective "attains that humble attitude of mind towards the grandeur of reason incarnate in existence, which, in its profoundest depths, is inaccessible to man." But in these words, Tillich says, Einstein is admitting all of the basic underlying assumptions of a good and authentically traditional theology.

> If I interpret these words rightly they point to a common ground of the whole of the physical world and of superpersonal values, a ground which, on the one hand, is manifest in the structure of being (the physical world) and meaning (the good, true, and beautiful)—which, on the other hand, is hidden in its unexhaustible depth. Now, this is the first and basic element of any developed idea of God from the earliest Greek philosophers to present day theology.

Since humanistic values emerge when intelligent minds come into contact with the ground of being and the infinite depths of reality—something which Einstein held at the heart of his own belief and tried to act on in his own activities as an opponent to the cruel and inhuman Nazi view of the world—we must say that the ground of being is *higher* than the personal (not *lower*) because, though not personal itself, the ground of being has the power to give rise to personal values involving the entire sphere of goodness and beauty. Furthermore, Tillich points out that when Einstein refers to both the "grandeur" of the divine Logos (Reason Itself) which is "incarnate in existence" and also to the "profoundest depths" of this incarnation which are "inaccessible to man," he himself admits that "the manifestation of this ground and abyss of being and meaning creates what modern theology calls 'the experience of the numinous.'" Einstein himself in fact *knows* and *acknowledges* that the grandeur and the sense of infinite depths, along with the wonder and awe which these arouse, are all really there. They are not imaginary. And this, Tillich points out, is what Rudolf Otto called the awareness of the numinous, and this in turn means that religious language (properly understood) is not as foolish as Einstein would have us believe.

The need for symbolic language and metaphor

We cannot talk literally about the infinite without falsifying its infinite qualities, so there are few (if any) fully literal statements which we can make about the divine ground. St. Thomas Aquinas said that the only literal statement that we can make about God is to state that the divine ground is Being Itself, the pure act by which all other beings come to be. In his *Systematic Theology*, Tillich at first said that the only literal statement that we can make about God is that it is impossible to make any literal statements about God, but he eventually came to the position that even this statement could not philosophically qualify as a literal statement *about* God.

This creates great theological difficulty. How can we write or think intelligibly about spiritual issues, if all that we are allowed to say is that the ground of being is Being Itself, or one or two other abstract and theoretical propositions of that sort? How could we write meditations or give talks that would help people who are dealing with real spiritual problems, and may have fallen into blind panic or total despair? People who may perhaps have given up on life and are in a state of final psychological and spiritual collapse? We have to speak to these people, and try to help them.

But what kind of language is left to use? On the one hand, the ground of being itself cannot, by its very nature, be turned into an *object* for the objectifying language of normal scientific inquiry. On the other hand, speak we must, because compassion requires us to help these people if we can. "But since it is 'inaccessible' to any objectivating concept," Tillich says, the idea of who and what God is "must be expressed in symbols."

That is what all the great spiritual traditions of the earth have done at all periods of human history, that is, to build up vast repertoires of symbols and metaphors for helping people who are in great psychological and spiritual need. The psychiatrist Carl Jung has shown that these symbols are not only verbal but also visual, and include many things with profound but deeply hidden meanings. Jung showed, for example, that the Christian cross is a universally found religious symbol called a mandala, with the same underlying kind of symbolism as that which is found in the sand paintings of Tibetan Buddhism, the Chinese yin-yang symbol, the six-pointed Jewish Star of David, the five-pointed star of the American flag, and the designs used on some of the old Native American shields (as for example on some of the painted, round leather shields created by the Lakota, the Crow, and the Blackfoot tribes). If we walk into a place of worship in any religion of the world, we will hear and see hundreds of symbols and metaphors in the chants and religious phrases and sacred texts and pieces of art. All these different human religions introduce us to the great truths of spirituality and the sacred by using symbols and metaphors, because that is the only way they can speak about the real spiritual issues.

There are an incredible number of symbols used in the Judeo-Christian tradition, but Einstein's criticism (Tillich says) focused on one of these in particular, and singled it out for attack.

> One of these symbols is "Personal God." It is the common opinion of classical theology, practically in all periods of Church history, that the predicate "personal" can be said of the Divine only symbolically or by analogy or if affirmed and negated at the same time.

A symbol, in Tillich's theological system, is a signpost pointing our attention to something else. But we must remember at all times that the symbol is not that to which it points. The signpost pointing our eyes towards the Grand Canyon is not itself the Grand Canyon. I prefer to use the term metaphor instead of symbol in my own theological writings, because it makes it easier to understand how so many religious texts, like the passage from Isaiah 40 which was quoted earlier, consist of vast numbers of vivid metaphors: human lives are like tiny blades of grass or like grasshoppers jumping about, but they can use the power of divine grace "to mount up with wings like eagles," to mention just a few of the colorful images used. But my choosing to use the term metaphor instead of symbol is mostly just personal preference, because I am pointing to the same kind of religious language to which Tillich refers.

The cataphatic-apophatic method

Religious symbols and metaphors have to be analyzed by what early Christian theologians called the cataphatic-apophatic method. The Greek verb *kataphêmi* means to say yes or assent to something, so the Greek noun *kataphasis* which is derived from it means an affirmative statement. The *kata* prefix can also be added to a word to mean that whatever is being done, is being done throughout and thoroughly, from one end to the other, so this is also implied in the theological use of the term cataphatic in early Christian Greek. The other word, *apophasis*, meant negation, saying no, denying that something was true. In a paradoxical sort of way, in order for us to use religious metaphor properly, we have to do both, and say both "yes" and "no" to the contents of the symbolic elements.

When we apply the cataphatic-apophatic method to analyzing religious metaphors, we have to begin by using the cataphatic approach and discussing the internal structure of the metaphor in detail, exploring the context of its meaning if it were taken literally. So when Isaiah 40 says that the Jews who were now going to be allowed to return from the Babylonian concentration camps "shall renew their strength, they shall mount up with wings like eagles, they shall run and not be weary, they shall walk and not faint," we can use the cataphatic method to discuss the eagle metaphor and try to visualize more clearly what it means to talk about eagles flying through the air, taken as a totally literal visual image. When we watch an eagle soaring overhead, we are impressed with the grace and ease and total freedom with which the eagle sweeps through the heights. The eagle's wings are strong and capable in themselves, but the eagle also knows how to use them to ride the powerful air currents in the upper atmosphere, and be borne upwards even further. Above all, the eagle is lifted up above the creatures who creep and crawl and hop upon the surface of the earth, and can ignore their petty battles and concerns. Eagles do not bother themselves about tiny grasshoppers fighting for the same blade of grass.

But then, to appropriate the metaphor for spiritual purposes, we must use the apophatic method, and make it clear that when we are reading the Bible, we are not studying a biological textbook about the habits of eagles. We must see how to apply the metaphor to our own lives. The higher meaning of the metaphor is a message about freedom, rising to new heights, receiving an exuberant new power, and being able to leave behind all the old earthly constraints which had us crawling miserably through the rocks and thorns of existence. But this higher meaning has to be grasped intuitively, and cannot itself be put literally into words, because as the reader can see, all I really did in the preceding sentence was to use a different set of metaphors in the attempt to illuminate the meaning of the eagle metaphor. Freedom vs. being locked up, high vs. low, references to "the rocks and thorns of existence," and so on, are also metaphors and not literal statements, when we are attempting to describe a spiritual state of mind.

The analogy of being

The concept of analogy is one that Tillich drew from St. Thomas Aquinas, and is important enough that we will have to devote part of a chapter later on to the Thomistic concept of the analogy of being.

The important thing to note here is that Tillich insists that talk about a personal God is symbolic language (a metaphor) and not a literal description of a being which thinks and acts exactly like a human being, except that he is much bigger and stronger. When we start thinking that way, Tillich says, we have confused the signpost with that to which it was pointing. And he is also correct in saying that in most periods of Christian history, the top ranking theologians have regarded the idea of a personal God as an image which is totally or almost totally metaphorical, not literal.

The supra-personal vs. the sub-personal

Einstein insisted that a humanistic religion had to talk about the "supra-personal," and cannot get bogged down in myths and fantasies about personal gods drawn from primitive religion. And Tillich agrees with him, and says that this may be the best way of putting the most important issue here. Only we must look much harder than Einstein did, at how one must go about this.

We must remember that the supra-personal is not the same thing as the sub-personal. "The depth of being cannot be symbolized by objects taken from a realm which is lower than the personal, from the realm of things or sub-personal living beings. The supra-personal is not an 'It.'" If we try to avoid using any personal symbolism at all in talking about the ground of being, we will of necessity turn this ground into an It. When the only tool we possess for talking about the ground of being and meaning is construed as only a bare "It," this always ends up turning our understanding of human existence into a sub-personal one:

> The "It" element transforms the alleged supra-personal into a sub-personal .... And such a neutral sub-personal cannot grasp the center of our personality; it can satisfy our aesthetic feeling or our intellectual needs, but it cannot convert our will, it cannot overcome our loneliness, anxiety, and despair. For as the philosopher Schelling says: "Only a person can heal a person."

> This is the reason that the symbol of the Personal God is indispensable for living religion. It is a symbol, not an object, and it never should be interpreted as an object. And it is one symbol besides others indicating that our personal center is grasped by the manifestation of the unaccessible ground and abyss of being.

Let us try putting Tillich's argument in another form. Human beings who are being forced to walk through the Dark Night of the Soul, are not being thrown into overpowering feelings of rage, self-pity, anxiety, and despair, because they do not understand a particular mathematical law of physics, or because they misunderstand the precise biological functioning of the gall bladder. They cannot be pulled back into the light by teaching them about physics or biology, or by giving them a mechanical view of the universe.

Instead they have to discover (or be taught) a new source of personal meaning, one to which they can be persuaded to give their total loyalty and commitment. They need to learn about love and compassion for other human beings. They will have to allow themselves to feel all their sorrow for everything in the past which has now been destroyed, and weep tears if necessary, before they will ever discover true acceptance. They will need to come to terms with their own deep inner feelings of guilt, shame, and failure over the things which they did or did not do when their personal worlds were crumbling into ruins, both real guilt and also imaginary guilt (which can be even harder to overcome). They must learn how to find a core of true peace and calm inside, and then discover where to find it outside their minds as well. All of these things have to do with personal values and require us to drive down far below the surface intellectual level into the deeper levels of feeling and imagery which we call the realm of the heart. When we are caught in the Dark Night of the Soul, we are "heart-sick," to use a traditional English-language metaphor, and (continuing that metaphor), we must recognize that mechanical, sub-personal, intellectual theories will not heal "a broken heart." Nor will theories of that sort turn those who are cowering in fear, into people of courage, nor give them the impetus to jump once more into the fray, and take on the struggles that will be required to climb out of the dark pit in which we see only night all around us.

Can we remake our lives at the personal level without using personal language to talk about our relationship to the ground of all being and meaning? In practice, it does not work very well, if at all. It can at best achieve only a partial healing of the inner wounds which are crippling the soul. We cannot truly relate what are deeply personal problems to a purported source of help which is viewed as sub-personal.

And on the other side, because the ground of being is a source of personal healing for the injured soul, we must regard it as supra-personal because it is not only the ground of being from which physical objects and the mechanical forces of nature emerged, but the ground of meaning from which personal healing can emerge. The ground is not in itself a natural object, but is supra-natural in its role as the cause of the world of nature. In similar manner the ground is not itself a person but is supra-personal in its role as the cause of personal change.

Other than that, however, Tillich cautions us that symbolic language using the metaphor of a personal God is only one among many different kinds of religious symbols, and that we should not literalize it or (in Tillich's understanding of things) we will necessarily end up turning God into an object which we will then begin trying to "figure out" and manipulate to our own advantage. Or if not that, we will begin complaining about this over-literalized God-figure whom we have imagined and viewing him as a cruel tyrant or our worst enemy, simply because he does not run the universe in the way we would like to see it run.

The common ground between Einstein and Tillich: cosmic religious feeling

The most interesting thing however about the debate between these two great thinkers, was the area of common ground which in fact lay between them. Einstein laid out similar arguments in another place, in an article which he wrote in 1930, where he said that there were three kinds of religion: there was a religion of fear, a moral religion based on belief in a God who gave rewards and punishments, and a third kind of religion, which he called "cosmic religious feeling."[86] Einstein rejected all fear-based religion, and said that morality was important to human life but had nothing to do with God, and was best dealt with on totally humanistic grounds. The only valid aspect of religion lay in the third kind of religious impulse. This was a kind of "cosmic consciousness," although without the kind of personalistic element which appeared in Richard Maurice Bucke's influential book on that topic.[87]

Einstein attempted to describe this cosmic religious feeling in his article, which he said had been a part of religion at all periods of history, although it was rarely found in a pure form:

> It is very difficult to elucidate this feeling to anyone who is entirely without it, especially as there is no anthropomorphic conception of God corresponding to it. The individual feels the futility of human desires and aims and the sublimity and marvelous order which reveal themselves both in nature and in the world of thought. Individual existence impresses him as a sort of prison and he wants to experience the universe as a single significant whole. The beginnings of cosmic religious feeling already appear at an early stage of development, e.g., in many of the Psalms of David and in some of the Prophets. Buddhism ... contains a much stronger element of this.
>
> The religious geniuses of all ages have been distinguished by this kind of religious feeling, which knows no dogma and no God conceived in man's image; so that there can be no church whose central teachings are based on it. Hence it is precisely among the heretics of every age that we find men who were filled with this highest kind of religious feeling and were in many cases regarded by their contemporaries as atheists, sometimes also as saints. Looked at in this light, men like Democritus, Francis of Assisi, and Spinoza are closely akin to one another.
>
> How can cosmic religious feeling be communicated from one person to another, if it can give rise to no definite notion of a God and no theology? In my view, it is the most important function of art and science to awaken this feeling and keep it alive in those who are receptive to it.

The infinite and holy

Tillich preferred to use a slightly different terminology for referring to what Einstein called "cosmic religious feeling," but he was talking about the same kind of experience. In his *Systematic Theology*, for example, he stressed the importance of the awareness of the infinite. It arose, he said, from our human recognition of our own finitude, which simultaneously disclosed, over against us and limiting us, that which was not finite.[88] This was an integral and necessary part of the existentialist base which lay under much of his philosophical system.

In a little autobiographical essay which Tillich wrote at one point,[89] he also explained how important the idea of the holy was in his theology. He talks about how he lived in Schönfliess when he was a small child, a town of three thousand, which was still surrounded by its medieval wall and towered gates, and governed from the old medieval Rathaus or town hall. He remembered how they lived in the parish house,

> ... with a confessional Lutheran school on the one side and on the other a beautiful Gothic church in which Father was a successful pastor. It is the experience of the "holy" which was given to me at that time as an indestructible good and as the foundation of all my religious and theological work.

He knew at first hand what it was like to live with the sacred presence of the numinous surrounding him on all sides, which enabled him to understand the enormous importance of Otto's famous book the moment he began reading in it.

> When I first read Rudolf Otto's *Idea of the Holy* I understood it immediately in the light of these early experiences and took it into my thinking as a constitutive element. It determined my method in the philosophy of religion, wherein I started with the experiences of the holy and advanced to the idea of God and not the reverse way. Equally important existentially as well as theologically were the mystical, sac-

ramental, and aesthetic implications of the idea of the holy, whereby the ethical and logical elements of religion were derived from the experience of the presence of the divine and not conversely.

Tillich was around thirty and serving as a military chaplain in the German army at the time Otto's book was published. He apparently used what Otto taught him as the basic tool for getting himself spiritually back on his feet. His war experiences left him in grave doubt about whether there was a God, and whether attempts to act morally meant anything at all, and even whether the universe was a rational place.

But Otto's book told him where to start. He had to go back to the primordial awareness of the numinous, and then build some new idea of God on that base. He had to go to the same source, the fundamental feeling of the holy, and build some new kind of moral and ethical code for himself. How must he act in his life, so as not to betray the vision of the holy, the beautiful, and the good? And in a strange sort of way, even rebuilding his sense that the universe was rational required him to go first to the pre-rational experience of the holy, so that the foundations of his intellectual beliefs could be built on something which he knew with certainty was really there and could not be yanked away. No matter what kind of horrors we are in the midst of, and no matter how much of our lives and our futures have been destroyed, the holy is still there, and gives us something which is oddly totally comforting at the deepest level, as long as we cling to it closely enough.

The sacredness of nature
and "nature mysticism"

In his little autobiography, Tillich explains how he always rebelled against the theology of Albrecht Ritschl (1822-1889), which had dominated much of Protestant liberal thought during the nineteenth century. Ritschl had sketched a view of a two-layer universe, with an infinite and uncrossable gap separating them: Nature vs. Morality, the realm of scientific investigation vs. the realm of value judgments (*Werturtheile*). When he came to America, he found that many American Protestants were deeply dyed with a kind of Puritan and Calvinist perspective which was very similar:

> Nature is something to be controlled morally and technically, and only subjective feelings of a more or less sentimental character toward nature are admitted. There is no mystical participation in nature, no understanding that nature is the finite expression of the infinite ground of all things, no vision of the divine-demonic conflict in nature.

Tillich never found this viewpoint compatible to his own nature, he says. First, he had always, from the time he was a child, enjoyed communing with nature. We have an interesting report about him from a Duke University website:

> The theologian Paul Tillich first visited Duke when the Sarah P. Duke Gardens were taking on their present shape in the late 1930s. He was taken to see them as was common for any visitor of the time. But he strongly identified with the Gardens in being himself uprooted and planted in a new land and culture. Every time he returned to Duke through the years he asked to have time to revisit the gardens, visits reported by Tommy Langford, former Dean of the Divinity School and University Provost, that seemed to be an almost mystical experience. Tillich seemed to be lost in thought remembering his past and identifying with the growth and maturing of the landscape as it changed through the years. One almost felt like an intruder accompanying him on his visits, says Langford.

Tillich's final resting place, as we noted in the previous chapter, is in the middle of a tiny but beautiful garden enclosed by evergreen trees in New Harmony, Indiana, at a site which he had visited and approved before his death.

A second factor in his own attitude toward nature, Tillich says, arose from his love of poetry. He cites German literature, but a similar series could be assembled of American, English, and Canadian authors from the eighteenth, nineteenth, and early twentieth centuries, including not only poets like Tennyson ("Speak to Him thou, for He heareth, / And spirit with spirit doth meet, / For nearer is He than breathing, / And closer than hands and feet"), but also the New England Transcendentalists like Thoreau and Emerson, as well as Richard Maurice Bucke's book *Cosmic Consciousness* (which we mentioned several pages back). But in Tillich's case, it was the traditional German poets who taught him how to look at nature this way:

> German poetic literature, even aside from the romantic school, is full of expressions of nature mysticism. There are verses of Goethe, Holderlin, Novalis, Eichendorff, Nietzsche, George, and Rilke which never have ceased to move me as deeply as they did when I first heard them.

But there was also an important theological reason for his position, Tillich says. By the end of the Protestant Reformation, Continental European Protestants had divided into two major groups, the *Lutherans* (who followed Martin Luther up in northern Germany and Scandinavia) and the *Reformed* (to the south and west, in the Netherlands, Switzerland, and parts of southern and middle Germany) who followed the different kind of approach seen in the theologians Zwingli and Calvin. And Tillich was brought up as a Lutheran:

> A third cause of this attitude toward nature came out of my Lutheran background. Theologians know that one of the points of disagreement between the two wings of the Continental Reformation, the Lutheran and the Reformed, was the so-called "Extra Calvinisticum," the doctrine that the finite is not capable of the infinite (*non capax infiniti*) and that consequently in Christ the two natures, the divine

218

and the human, remained outside each other. Against this doctrine the Lutherans asserted the "Infra Lutheranum"—namely, the view that the finite is capable of the infinite and consequently that in Christ there is a mutual in-dwelling of the two natures. This difference means that on Lutheran ground the vision of the presence of the infinite in everything finite is theologically affirmed, that nature mysticism is possible and real, whereas on Calvinistic ground such an attitude is suspect of pantheism and the divine transcendence is understood in a way which for a Lutheran is suspect of deism.

The sacramental view of the universe

To put this in another way, the Lutheran position (and Tillich's position) was closely similar to what Roman Catholics call "the sacramental view of the universe." God communicates himself to us via the material world. The divine grace is given to us in the sacraments of the church only in and through material substances like bread, wine, and water. The same is true of all of nature, where we can apprehend a sunset, a small Spring flower, or a quietly flowing river as alive with the divine presence.

Tillich in Dallas

When I was a seminary student at Perkins School of Theology at Southern Methodist University in Dallas, Texas, Tillich came to give a lecture. It has to have been at some time in the early 1960's, not long before his death. He was given an honorarium for speaking, but he made it clear that his salary and the royalties from his books gave him ample to live on, and explained that he gave away all his honorarium money in the form of scholarships to needy seminary students.

I can still remember what I experienced when he began to speak. He had a slight bit of what the Vietnam veterans of later years called the thousand-yard-stare. His experiences among the wounded in the

First World War, and what he had heard from the hundreds of Jewish refugees whom he helped resettle in America during the period of the Second World War, had left their permanent mark on his soul. Some of the seminary students who had attended Union where he taught in the later 1940's had been World War II combat veterans, and they had responded to him enthusiastically, because they knew that he knew what they had experienced.

But in addition to this, there was an almost visible glow around the man. It startled me, and I realized for the first time what medieval artists were trying to depict, however inadequately, when they painted a halo of light surrounding one of the great religious figures. He was not a saint in the conventional sense, not by any means. His many affairs with women over the years were well known among the professional theologians. He made his own code to live by and made his own decisions. He was in that way like a medieval Jewish *Lamed Vaver*,[90] or one of the great Native American shamans, or one of the early Christian desert saints, or one of the deeply spiritual A.A. good old timers like Ernie G. the second of Toledo or Raymond I. in South Bend. There was an overwhelming power and sense of presence, and an aura of danger too. This was someone who was close to God in a way which allowed him to make up his own rules.

He had allowed the sacred to penetrate his own heart and soul to such a degree, that his entire being had been rendered a vehicle of the numinous presence. He was a God-bearer. And you knew beyond a doubt that it was real.

Can one create a spirituality based on the awareness of the infinite and the holy, based on contact with a ground of being which is not in itself describable as a personal God? Tillich was living proof that this was possible, and that such a spirituality was a tool of enormous spiritual power, which could lead human beings through the Dark Night of the Soul and bring them up to the mountain top where the sunlight of the spirit perpetually shines, and the words of healing and salvation are whispered in our ears.

Chapter 12

The God-Bearers
and the Analogy of Being

In the way that God actually encounters me, there will always be another human being involved, who serves as a messenger, a teacher, or someone who at least points towards some particular manifestation of God's power and holiness and says "Look at that, hear that, notice that." Since the messenger is personal, the message will be couched in personal terms, and it will be directed towards me in my own personal situation.

The nature of real personal problems

People are not thrown into heart-breaking and soul-shattering problems by puzzling over the correct mathematical equation to use in solving a problem in physics. Or at least not by that in itself: for if I am going to flunk out of college if I do not figure out the answer to the test problem, or if I am going to fail to get tenure in my university position, or otherwise fall short of my career goals, this is the actual problem that is the cause of my anxiety, not the problem in mathematical physics.

Personal problems have to do with matters like being rejected by someone with whom I had fallen in love, having a close family member die, being left jobless and with no way to earn a living, being caught in a bad marriage, having an illness which leaves me barely able to function physically, being caught in a situation where someone else is continually attacking me and belittling me, being robbed or raped and beaten by my assailant, being arrested by the police, being caught in a war or in a gun battle between rival gangs.

We are not helped in dealing with real personal problems by being taught a chemical formula, a biological observation, or a sociological or political or economic theory. We are not helped either by being taught a psychological theory. If that were so, all of our personal problems could be solved by three or four sessions with a psychologist who would give us an explanation of the psychological factors involved, and with this new intellectual understanding, we would walk away happy and free. Alcoholics could read several books giving a scientific account of how alcoholism develops and how it should be treated, and be able to stop drinking right on the spot. We would not send criminals to prison, but give them a short list of books to read, explaining the theoretical reasons for their criminal behavior. Rapists and murderers and wife beaters and bank robbers and teenagers who stick up convenience stores would immediately reform their ways, and learn to live productive lives where they loved other people and began to display positive accomplishments which helped to make the world a better place. The wife who had just buried her husband of forty years would be able to wipe all the tears off her face by reading a book with the correct intellectual theories about the grieving process.

Reality comes in layers: the realm of nuclear particles, the level studied by the chemists, the more complex level studied by the biologists, the areas studied by the social scientists (psychologists, sociologists, economists, and political scientists), and the realm of meaning and personal value. All are equally "real," and to obtain useful information, we have to turn to people who have done research at the particular level we are concerned with and have real knowledge and experience in that field.

If I need to have my appendix removed, or have a broken leg set, do not take me to a nuclear physicist! If I have a real personal problem, I need to go to people who have skill and experience (and a proven track record) in helping other people with these problems.

The God-bearers

Let us say that I have been forced by circumstances to enter the Dark Night of the Soul, where the ground of being, the infinite, and the river of time all appear to me as hateful and destructive things, opening up an abyss of non-being which threatens to swallow up and annihilate all that I value and wish for myself. These are personal problems, and they can only be resolved (a good deal of the time) if I can encounter another human being who can personally reintroduce me to some new and saving aspect of the universal ground, or some new and saving way of finding meaning and personal value for my life. All parts of the process are personal to the core.

I refer to these people who serve as representatives of new being as the God-bearers. Because God comes to us mediated through the material world, through the sacredness of nature and through good people who "bear God" to us, who *carry* and *convey* God to us.

Therefore, much of the time (and usually in the most important ways) God comes to us in acutely personal form. His love and care are the love and care of his personal agents.

Christianity

The enormous spread and success of the Christian religion has surely been in part due to the skill with which it has made use of the God-bearers—the human beings who are the carriers and agents of saving grace—to make God personal to those to whom it has carried its message. Their divine representative *par excellence* was of course the figure of Jesus, who especially illustrated an important part of what we mean by the role of the God-bearers. It was not just what Jesus said when he stood up to preach, but also what he did—the actions which he took in his dealings with other people—which were the bearers of the divine grace which he transmitted. The fullness of a human being's existential reality is displayed, not just in the words that person speaks, but in the way that person behaves in life, and the inner values and purposes which are revealed in that man or woman's actions.

Let us take one of the famous stories about Jesus to illustrate this point, a story contained in Luke 7:36-50. To explain some of the terminology, the Pharisees were various small fundamentalist Jewish sects in first-century Palestine. The word "Pharisee" means the Separated Ones, for they regarded most Palestinian Jews as not real Jews at all. They were like some of the Puritans in England and the Thirteen Colonies during the seventeenth and eighteenth centuries (the kind who were nonconformists and separatists), because the Pharisees formed their own little puritanical groups following their own ultra-rigid interpretation of the Jewish law, and believed that the members of their little group were the only ones who were going to be saved.

When it says that the woman was a "sinner," it means that she had been a prostitute. In that part of the eastern end of the Mediterranean world it was believed (just as it still is in many Muslim countries of that region to this day) that it was very lewd and shameful for a woman to allow anyone to see her hair when she was out in public. Proper women had to wear a veil or shawl completely covering their heads so that no hair was showing at all. Only prostitutes went out with no hair coverings. So when the poor woman, who knows nothing about polite society, starts wiping Jesus' feet with her hair, it was roughly the equivalent of a woman in modern American society taking off one of her private undergarments at a proper dinner party, and wiping lipstick off a man's face, where she had kissed him too enthusiastically. It was not just shocking—Jesus allowing the woman to have intimate personal contact with him must have made the Pharisee's skin crawl, as he thought about the kinds of diseases the woman might have been carrying.

To his surprise, Jesus not only defends the woman, but attacks him. The woman, in her own way, tried her best to show real love for Jesus and act with grace towards him, even if she did not know how to do it "right" by the standards of the higher levels of society. And that kind of love and gratitude and spontaneous graciousness comes only from people who have been touched by the divine grace. The Apostle

Paul said explicitly in 1 Corinthians 13, that the recovery of the ability to show *agapê* love was the highest gift of God's grace, given only to the saved. So we know for certain that, whatever kinds of sins she might have committed earlier in her life, and no matter how degrading or nasty they may have seemed to a man like the Pharisee, she is one of God's blessed children now, and Jesus and the God whom he represents will not condemn her. No, we can say even more strongly, it is clear that Jesus will not only welcome her into his heart but defend her against anyone who attacks her.

So when we see the face of God in the person of Jesus, we see a personal God of grace and compassion and all-forgiving love, who will welcome us home again, no matter how depraved or degraded our past lives have been.

> One of the Pharisees asked him to eat with him, and he went into the Pharisee's house, and took his place at table. And behold, a woman of the city, who was a sinner, when she learned that he was at table in the Pharisee's house, brought an alabaster flask of ointment, and standing behind him at his feet, weeping, she began to wet his feet with her tears, and wiped them with the hair of her head, and kissed his feet, and anointed them with the ointment.
>
> Now when the Pharisee who had invited him saw it, he said to himself, "If this man were a prophet, he would have known who and what sort of woman this is who is touching him, for she is a sinner."
>
> And Jesus answering said to him, "Simon, I have something to say to you."
>
> And he answered, "What is it, Teacher?""
>
> "A certain creditor had two debtors; one owed five hundred denarii, and the other fifty. When they could not pay, he forgave them both. Now which of them will love him more?"
>
> Simon answered, "The one, I suppose, to whom he forgave more."
>
> And he said to him, "You have judged rightly."
>
> Then turning toward the woman he said to Simon, "Do you see this woman? I entered your house, you gave me no water

for my feet, but she has wet my feet with her tears and wiped them with her hair. You gave me no kiss, but from the time I came in she has not ceased to kiss my feet. You did not anoint my head with oil, but she has anointed my feet with ointment. *Listen to me, the fact that she has shown gracious-ness and has loved so much, proves that her many sins have been forgiven.*[91] The person who is forgiven little, loves little."

And he said to her, "Your sins are forgiven."

Then those who were at table with him began to say among themselves, "Who is this, who even forgives sins?"

And he said to the woman, "Your faith has saved you; go in peace." (Luke 7:36-50)

In early Christianity, the saving work of Christ was summed up by St. Irenaeus in the second century in the phrase, "he became like us, that we might become like him." This was put in even stronger form by St. Athanasius in the fourth century: "God was humanized that we might be divinized." In Jesus and the saints, the impersonal ground of being is humanized, in such a way that, by allowing ourselves to be touched by the divine grace of which they were the bearers, our own lives in turn may take on some of the numinous character of the sacred.

During the Middle Ages, Christianity continued to add other human figures, the whole calendar of the saints, so that if one entered an old-fashioned Roman Catholic or Eastern Orthodox church, one was confronted with dozens of images of the divine power and grace, each one different but acutely personal. Protestantism, when it appeared in the sixteenth century, removed the statues and icons of the saints, but continued to preach a message which was centered on human beings who represented the power and goodness of God's grace by being personal heroes in one way or another. They preached sermons on biblical figures like Abraham, Joseph, Deborah, Ruth, David, and Elijah from the Old Testament, and Jesus, Peter, Paul, and Stephen from the New Testament. And they had their own denominational heroes, like Martin Luther for the Lutherans and John Wesley for the Methodists, as well as encouraging their congregations to read the biographies of famous missionaries and preachers. Great Protestant preachers can still travel around and draw enormous crowds of people, because they give the message of salvation their own personal touch.

Judaism and other religions

In Judaism, the great philosopher and theologian Philo (20 B.C. - 40 A.D.) believed that God in his essential reality was the unknowable ground of being. There was little or no way to directly personify that bottomless and infinite abyss which lay prior to everything else in the universe. But spirituality could be rendered personal in two important ways. In the same way that the laws of nature which the scientists study came out of the ground of being, and tell us how to make television sets and airplanes and medicines for curing all sorts of physical ailments, so likewise in the sphere of human personal relationships, the Torah (the Jewish Law) informs us how the law of creation works at that level of reality, and tells us how best to live in harmony with other human beings, and how to heal our personal and spiritual problems.

And Philo also wrote a series of short biographies of various figures from the Hebrew Bible (what the Christians call the Old Testament), in which he talked about the *theios anêr*, the "divine man," and showed how figures like Moses and Joseph illustrated in their lives various of the personal qualities which we had to embody in our own behavior, in order to live lives which were filled with the sacred and divine presence.[92]

Good rabbis were also used as Jewish religious heroes, and their sayings and stories lovingly preserved and discussed as part of higher Jewish spiritual training. One variety of Judaism, the Kabbalah, teaches that the goal of the spiritual life is to become divinized. Beginners who wish to follow that path seek out those who have progressed deeply into the Kabbalistic vision of the divine and the ground of being, and ask them to become their instructors, for this sort of spirituality can only be truly learned by finding a human teacher to serve as our guide.

We must also not neglect to mention that in the middle ages and early modern period, the Lamed Vavers were strange and scary Jewish holy men who demonstrated the divine power in their personal lives in various powerful ways.[93] We can only humanize God so far without totally falsifying him. As it says in Hosea 11:9, "For I am God and not man, the Holy One in the midst of you."[94] Those men and women who have been deeply penetrated by the divine power and grace can have a frightening quality to them in certain ways, for there is something far greater than the merely human running like a current through their lives.

In the Hindu tradition, one searches for a wise man or woman to serve as one's guru or spiritual guide. The saving power of the ground of being becomes especially embodied in certain human lives, "avatars" of God as they are termed. In the vision of the Godhead in the Bhagavad-Gita, we see the impersonal ground appearing to us in the form of hundreds and thousands of different faces. We can never comprehend the ground of being as it is in itself. But when we see the millions of stars and galaxies shining overhead in the night sky, we can sense its infinite power, and when we look at the human faces of God down through history—all the great God-bearers who have taught mercy, compassion, honesty, and love—we can see this aspect of the creative power of the ground of being. The thousands and thousands of God-bearers who have taught us how to emerge from the Dark Night of the Soul are just as real as the stars and galaxies which the physicists and astronomers study. The Bhagavad-Gita teaches that the inner core of God may be suprapersonal, but that he appears to us through the masks of thousands of human and divine faces who present to us all the variety of the manifestations of the divine saving grace down through human history. The inner core of the Godhead may be nonpersonal, but the acts of God's grace are always personal.

In Buddhism, even in the nontheistic varieties, the personal always appears in the quest for spiritual healing and salvation. One might search for a great Zen Master and join that person's monastery in order to receive individual tutelage, or study the lives of the great Masters of the past, in order to learn the path to satori. Or in other forms of

Buddhism, one might pray to bodhisattvas, human beings from the past who, out of compassion, refused to enter nirvana themselves in order to help other human beings achieve nirvana.

To gain healing for myself through the rituals of Native American shamanism, I must find a shaman who knows the rituals, and if I want to become a competent shaman myself and obtain the greatest and highest visions, I must find a great shaman and become his student.

In all spiritual traditions, the quest is always a personal quest, and it always requires a source of personal grace.

The twelve step program

When the Alcoholics Anonymous program first started, it was noted from the beginning that one alcoholic could talk to another alcoholic with an effectiveness which no non-alcoholic could ever have. When someone who had never had a drinking problem tried lecturing alcoholics about their excessive drinking, they typically responded with lies, alibis, excuses, anger, rebellion, and at best a kind of outward compliance which contained no inner commitment. On the other hand, two or three alcoholics who were staying sober could tell their story to an alcoholic who was still drinking, and there was an appreciable chance that the drinker would actually listen. This principle became enshrined in the last of the twelve steps, where those whose lives had been saved by A.A. were instructed to go pass that message to others. The other twelve step programs followed the same rule: it took a compulsive gambler to reach out to another compulsive gambler, someone with a severe eating disorder to make personal contact with someone else suffering from the same problem, an Al-Anon to pass the saving message in a way which would make sense to another person in need of Al-Anon, and so on.

One of the most important discoveries was that the bearer of the saving message did not have to be a saint or a great guru or spiritual master. One could become a God-bearer and a channel of the divine grace just by telling one's own story with deep honesty and humility.

The more we get our own pride and egos and control issues out of the way, the more transparent our lives and stories can become to the power of God's grace.

The higher power of the twelve step program is always revealed as a personal God, in the sense that it will be the higher power whom I discovered when I listened to some twelve step speaker or sponsor: Submarine Bill, Grateful Deb, Big Book Agnes, Goshen Bill, Brooklyn Bob, or whoever it was. This higher power will speak to me in personal terms, for the rest of my life, in those people's voices, and in the memory of crucial events where they played critical roles.

The analogy of being

St. Thomas Aquinas (c. 1225-1274), the greatest theologian of the High Middle Ages, did not think of God in his own essential being as highly personal. He did not believe that God felt emotions like anger, for example, and regarded biblical passages describing that sort of emotional reaction on God's part as purely metaphorical. But he did believe that God could be described as personal in meaningful fashion by means of what he called the analogy of being.

Aquinas described three different kinds of statements we can make, where we are using what appears to be the same word in two different sentences. If I say that "the Apostle Peter is a man" and "the Apostle Paul is also a man," these are *univocal* statements. The word "man" means exactly the same thing in both statements.

If I say that "the Apostle Peter is a man," but then (while playing chess or checkers) tell the other person "you need to move your man," this is an *equivocal* use of the word "man." Referring to a game piece on a playing board as a "man" involves some sort of vaguely metaphorical or extended sense of the word.

But it is the third type of statement which is important here. If I put my hand in front of a fire in a fireplace and say "my hand is hot," and then say "the fire is hot," I am using the word "hot" *analogically* in the second statement. In the first case, I feel my hand getting hotter and hotter, and eventually feel pain. If someone is holding my hand to the fire where I cannot get it away, I will feel human emotions like anger and fear and desperation. When I say "the fire is hot" however, the fire feels nothing. Is this a misuse of the word "hot"? No, Aquinas says, this is one kind of perfectly proper usage. The fire is hot because it can serve as the cause of what a human being will feel as heat.

The term "the analogy of being" refers to situations where God, as the ground of being, creates certain effects in the universe, which is his creation. If I say in one statement that "all true salvation is *personal* salvation, and we receive this in a necessarily *personal* way, via a long chain of messengers, each person acting as a vehicle of God's grace to the next person," and then say in another statement that "God as the source of saving grace is *personal*," this latter statement is using the word personal analogically, but is also completely true.

I say that "the fire is hot" because when I hold my hand up to it "my hand is hot." The God-bearers who bring me the saving message are highly personal figures, who nevertheless do not save me by their own human power, but by the power of God's grace, for which they serve as channels. The grace is personal in its impact on me, which means that, by analogy, the God who sends me this grace is also personal, embodied in (or incarnate in) the agents of his grace.

God coming to birth

Aquinas was also trying to come up with a way of talking philosophically about another ancient and very important idea in western spirituality, the idea of God "coming to birth" here on earth in acts which bridged the gap between heaven and earth (the sacred realm and the everyday realm). Heaven was brought down to earth and earth was lifted up to heaven.

The Irish theologian John Scotus Erigena (c. 810-c. 877) introduced this way of speaking to western European spirituality at the beginning of the Middle Ages. It became a standard theme in western Christian religious thought, and was represented during Thomas Aquinas's time in the kind of Dominican spirituality which we see in the Dominican preacher Meister Eckhart (c. 1260-1327). We need to remember that, as a Dominican monk, Aquinas attended the seven daily offices and the night office every day, singing hymns with his fellow monks and listening to Dominican preachers deliver sermons on the spiritual life. Aquinas's theology was simply an attempt to give greater formal structure to the living and real spiritual life which flourished in the medieval European monasteries.

In Erigena and Eckhart, God "comes to birth" whenever human beings consciously sense the presence of God in the world around them. It is also the case that human beings only attain their full personhood as this awareness of God is born in them. When I suddenly become aware of the holiness of the numinous in a little green caterpillar crawling down a twig, Eckhart preaches, and I then marvel in awe, God comes to birth here on earth. God comes to birth over and over again, in a constant stream of revelations of his presence. God took on material form when he created the stars and galaxies; in similar fashion he takes on personal consciousness when a human being becomes conscious of the universe filled with God.

Emmet Fox and New Thought

In the kind of theology which we see in Erigena and Eckhart, how does the personal element fit into the system at the deeper metaphysical level? One of the best passages I have ever read explaining this kind of vision of the divine is found in one of the books written by the great New Thought teacher Emmet Fox (1886-1951). Fox's God is an essentially impersonal absolute which imposes laws on the universe, not only physical laws but also spiritual laws.[95] The most important spiritual law is that the way I think about the universe will determine the way my universe will become. If I think angry thoughts, I will eventually find myself surrounded by anger and anger-producing circumstances on all sides. If I think loving thoughts, I will eventually find myself surrounded by love on all sides. If I think healing thoughts, I will find not only my soul and body being healed, but also the torn relationships around me.

God is Mind, but only in the sense that God is a being which "thinks" a set of abstract ideas, general concepts, and universal laws which govern all of the universe. The basic argument here is that if we have a coherent and well-organized set of universal ideas ruling everything, then there must be something in some sense "thinking" these ideas, that is, holding them in existence. Even if one rejects the idea of calling this a "Mind" which is "thinking ideas," it is nevertheless obvious that the laws of nature are ideas (not material things) which subsist over and above the material universe to which they give direction. The important thing here, however, is that in Emmet Fox's version of New Thought spirituality, even if he refers to God as Mind or Spirit (*Geist*), he means this only in the almost completely impersonal, intellectual sense found in Aristotle's God, in later pagan Greek Neo-Platonism, and in some forms of nineteenth-century German Idealism.

God is simply a set of abstract ideas. Man's task is then "to express, in concrete, definite form, the abstract ideas with which God furnishes him." He must do this, not as an automaton, but as "an individualized consciousness" possessing the power of real creativity.

> God individualizes Himself in an infinite number of distinct focal points of consciousness, each one quite different; and therefore each one is a distinct way of knowing the universe, each a distinct experience .... If God did not individualize Himself, there would be only one experience; as it is, there are as many universes as there are individuals to form them through thinking.[96]

Or as the early Christian patristic tradition put it, each of us human beings is an individual hypostasis (personification) arising within God's creative energy as it is expressed in the world which it brings into being.

Emmet Fox was part of a modern tradition which has developed many versions, including the teachings of such groups as Unity Church, the Divine Science church, the Religious Science church, and ACIM (A Course in Miracles). It is true that in the strict philosophical sense, Emmet Fox's God was a set of scientific laws and abstract ideas, and that personhood in the fully human sense only appeared in *individual human beings*, as they attempted to apply these laws and ideas creatively to their lives. But the people whom I know who follow the New Thought spiritual path with true commitment, and read Emmet Fox with deep respect, are some of the most loving and compassionate men and women whom I have ever known, people who are deeply aware and sensitive to the feelings of the other persons around them. It is a spiritual tradition which in fact leads to a truly good life.

The Theotokos

When we see Mary the Mother of Jesus portrayed on medieval Byzantine icons, we will often see the title *Theotokos* placed beside her figure. This ancient theological term is sometimes translated into modern English as Mother of God, but this is a very poor and misleading translation. The Greek verb *tekô* (or *tiktô*) meant to bring forth, bear, give birth to. *Tokos*, the noun derived from it, did not mean the one who gave birth, but the actual act of giving birth. In medieval Christian theology, both Roman Catholic and Eastern Orthodox, there were two different theories about the theological significance of Jesus's mother Mary. One was that she played the role of divine Intercessor. We could pray to her, and she would then intercede with her son Jesus and convince him to help us.

But in the other theory, Mary was the *Theotokos*, the act in which God gives birth and comes to birth, the iconic figure who represented that stroke of grace in which God brings human beings to consciousness of the divine reality. When we begin thinking in terms of God giving birth, we are using feminine imagery for God: Mary as the *Theotokos* was one of the most important traditional images for the feminine aspects of the deity. In this role, she was described in the Byzantine liturgy as the Bridge between Heaven and Earth, and the Gateway between Heaven and Earth. In Dante's *Paradiso*, when he finally ascends to the Seventh Heaven, he sees a vision of the Mystic Rose with Mary seated at its center. It is only by passing through this, the archetypal symbol of the femininity of God, that he will be allowed to receive the final vision—the full vision of the Divine Light and the Human Being of Light superimposed upon one another in such a way that it is difficult to tell one from the other.

In order to open up the mind fully to the awareness of the divine ground, we have to "go back in time" so to speak, to something similar to the way we apprehended the world during the pre-Freudian period of early infancy, before we had made the split with our mothers, and begun to see ourselves as independent and autonomous individuals. When we get in trouble in our lives, it is often because we and our mothers failed to make this split cleanly and properly. We emerge carrying fragments of our mothers with us, and leaving fragments of ourselves behind. We oscillate between trying to be too autonomous (where we are trying to play God and over-control everything around us) and trying to be too infantile and dependent (demanding that the world take care of us magically and totally, with no need for any responsibility on our part). If our mothers suffered from panic attacks, a fragment of that breaks off in our souls, and we too suffer from similar panic attacks. If our mothers suffered from crippling depression, a fragment of that becomes lodged in our souls, and we find ourselves also suffering from inexplicable chronic depression over and over again in our lives. In order to be healed, we have to enter into a meditative state where we can return to that primordial awareness, and then make the split in the right kind of way as we emerge back out into the world again, so that we will be able to preserve the right kind of balance between taking personal responsibility and acknowledging our dependence, and learn how to leave the bad fragments behind.

Dante's vision

At the end of the *Divine Comedy*, the great Italian poet Dante (1265-1321) described his vision of God as one of supernatural light. But the light had a structure, and this structure is important. He first describes the three hypostases within the divine essence:

> In the profound and clear subsistence
> Of that lofty light appeared to me three circles,
> Of three colors but enclosing the same area:
>
> The second from the first appeared reflected,
> Like rainbow from rainbow, while the third seemed fire
> Breathed back and forth by the other two.[97]

But as he continued to gaze upon the divine light, the second circle suddenly

> Appeared to me painted in our image
> Within itself, of its same color.[98]

"Our image"—the human image, the personal in fully human form—suddenly shines within the divine light as an intrinsic part of its radiance. The Human Being of Light who thus appeared was the God-bearer; it could also be Dante's own human life if he permitted it to be filled with the luminosity of the numinous and the divine grace (which was the gift that he was being offered at the end of the story as a reward for his long journey through hell and purgatory); but most importantly of all, the essence of personhood—in a form which we human beings could instantly recognize as like our own—was therefore also *an intrinsic part of God* by participation.

Dante tried to bequeath to the modern world the medieval vision of God. As the ground of being, we might well view God as an impersonal abyss of mystery. But within that primordial abyss lay the sacred and the power of the numinous. The goal of the good spiritual life was to let the light of the sacred so permeate our lives and hearts, that we became filled with the divine. As we entered the divine presence more and more fully, we did not lose our humanity or our individuality, but found a kind of personhood that was filled with light and joy and indomitable courage.

There are spiritual systems which not only teach a totally impersonal absolute, but also assert that the only way of entering into unity with such a God must of necessity be through the destruction and complete elimination of our own individuality and personhood. But this was not the kind of God which Dante was teaching. Our human personalities in all their unique individualities were not destroyed but perfected by attaining union with the divine.

The God of the medieval Christian theologians often became fully personal only in and through human beings. But it was also believed that human beings likewise only became fully personal, in all their individuality, by fully entering the divine presence and allowing God to bring out all that was best in their own personalities. It was not an either-or, a struggle of human beings and humanistic values vs. an impersonal universe. There was a reciprocity, a dynamic which ran both ways, between the human and the divine in the best medieval teaching about God.

A spirituality of this sort should surely be the minimum goal for modern men and women who wish to pursue the spiritual life, even if they still balk at the idea of a fully personal God.

Chapter 13

Modern Personalist
Philosophies of God

In ancient and medieval philosophy and theology, as was discussed in the preceding chapters, the ground of being was often described in impersonal terms—totally, or at least almost totally. The God of the philosophers tended to be described as an impersonal absolute, perfect and unchanging, which was completely transcendent and far removed from the things of this universe, where we human beings lived our lives. In some of these systems—such as medieval Arabic Neo-Platonism—the ground of being was simply the impersonal base of a universe which operated, out of blind necessity, as a system of mechanical natural processes. That medieval Arabic God could not be said to know of the existence of human beings as individuals.

And most of the medieval philosophies (including the Christian ones) had great difficulty devising an adequate answer to the problem of how an eternal and unchanging ground of being could know of the existence of a universe moving through time, particularly if there were, in that universe, creatures like human beings who were exercising genuine free will. The tendency often was to try to solve that problem by denying human freedom, and attempting to describe human mental processes in deterministic and mechanical terms, where our belief that we were thinking through our decisions and making choices about how we would act, was simply an illusion. This tendency continued into the early modern period in one especially striking version, the Calvinist doctrine of predestination, which we can see still being defended in the eighteenth century by Jonathan Edwards in his book *On the Freedom of the Will.* The only way philosophers of this persuasion could see to put human beings into direct contact with an absolute, eternal, impersonal, and unchanging God was by effectually denying any real human freedom, and hence (in most thoughtful people's eyes) human moral responsibility. How could I be praised or condemned, either one, for doing that which I could not help doing, in a universe where everything operated mechanically and impersonally, and I was no more than a cog in that machine? Philosophers who begin by assuming that God could not possibly be a personal being, seem to find themselves also having major difficulties explaining how humans can be personal beings.

In reaction to this centuries old tendency in western thought, in the late nineteenth and early twentieth century there were a number of philosophical systems devised which attempted to show that God was a totally personal being at an intrinsic and necessary level. Ultimate reality was a conscious person or self, the new philosophers insisted, who was aware of us as individuals. In some of these systems, it was also possible for human beings to enter into a personal relationship with God, as for example in the kind of personal idealism developed by Mary Whiton Calkins (1863-1930), who was one of the three most important early women philosophers in America.[99] And there were many other philosophers and theologians during that same period who developed versions of these same kinds of ideas.

In particular, two of these ways of speaking about a God who was intrinsically personal to the core of his essential being, managed to develop into distinct schools of philosophy which, though small, managed to flourish and produce a series of competent thinkers lasting for at least three or more generations: the *Boston Personalists* and the *process philosophers.*

The Boston Personalists

The Boston Personalists were closely connected to Boston University and to Boston School of Theology, which was linked to the university, and was one of the two major Methodist graduate theological institutions during the late nineteenth and early twentieth century. Since the Methodists were the second largest Protestant group in the United States during that period (exceeded in number only by the Baptists), and since a majority of the Methodist bishops of that time had received their early training at Boston School of Theology (or if not there, at a Methodist seminary which had close ties with the Boston faculty), the Boston Personalists had an impact at the popular level, all across the United States, far greater than was normally associated with an abstract philosophical theory. These ideas ending up being embodied not only in numerous sermons in parish churches, but in the Methodist Sunday School literature and—most importantly of all—in the daily devotional work called *The Upper Room*, which the Southern Methodists began publishing in 1935. These little pamphlets spoke so well to the spiritual life, that Americans of many other denominations began using *The Upper Room* for their morning prayers, including Roman Catholics.

This Methodist meditational book, which was strongly influenced by the ideas of the Boston Personalists, was also the most popular meditational book during the first thirteen years of the Alcoholics Anonymous movement (1935-1948), so that we can see its influence coming out in a number of the fundamental ideas and perspectives contained in the A.A. Big Book. Anyone who wants to make a serious study of the concept of God which is taught in the Big Book, and even more importantly the inner dynamic of the tension between divine grace and human freedom which runs through every page of the Big Book, needs to be thoroughly acquainted with Boston Personalism, for although it was not the only source of ideas in these areas, it was one of the major and most important sources.

And later on in that century, the black civil rights leader Dr. Martin Luther King, Jr., received his Ph.D. in systematic theology from Boston University in 1955, with a thesis on Paul Tillich, to whom two earlier chapters of this study were devoted. This was the same year that a young black woman named Rosa Parks refused to give up her seat on a Montgomery, Alabama, bus to a white person, a small symbolic protest against the injustice of the racist world in which she lived, which sparked off the great mid-twentieth century American civil rights movement. King, who had become pastor of the Dexter Avenue Baptist Church in Montgomery, became one of the key leaders of the Montgomery Bus Boycott which followed. And King's movement, in turn, spurred other people into action, in a series of successful attacks on the old racist way of doing things (conducting voter registration campaigns, forcing an end to segregated schools, and so on), which did more to help African-Americans in concrete ways than anything else in the whole course of the twentieth century. The Boston Personalists had taught King about the fatherhood of God and the infinite worth of the human personality, and King took them seriously and acted on it.

Rudolf Herman Lotze

The Boston Personalists borrowed some of their key ideas and perspectives from a German philosopher named Rudolf Herman Lotze (1817-1881), a fascinating figure who combined deep philosophical interests with the study of medicine. He believed that the study of physics and particularly biology could be pursued with full scientific responsibility, without sacrificing belief in either a personal God or in human personhood. We study scientific *facts* in the context of scientific *laws*, which provide us the *means* to obtain the higher *moral and aesthetic values* which we desire. We can only make sense of that process however, in a world which we see as under the governance of a personal Deity who has voluntarily chosen those laws of nature, through whose natural operations he will ultimately gain his purposes.

That is because at the highest level, nothing is real except the living spirit of God and the world of living spirits which he has created, who are in continuous personal relationship to him as well as to each other.

But this did not require us to deny any of the major findings of modern science. As one of the Boston Personalists put it, God did indeed create all the species of living creatures which have ever lived on the face of the earth, but the way God created them was through the natural workings of the laws of evolution—including not only the evolutionary successes, but also the evolutionary failures and mistakes—because as any competent biologist will explain, there have been at least a thousand evolutionary experiments that failed for every one that succeeded. Evolution has never in any way been a process which was magically guided so that each step automatically was a smooth and workable step forwards. The fossil record is littered with the bones and shells of countless species which flourished for a brief period but then went extinct. Or in other words, neither Lotze nor the Boston Personalists wrote anything which would give aid or comfort to the modern anti-evolutionary figures who have attempted to teach "Creation Science" or "Intelligent Design." This is an important point to make. Lotze and the Boston Personalists accepted the findings of good modern science, and were in no way hostile to modern scientific methodology.

But if the laws of science and the ordinary workings of natural process are real and their existence unarguable, we must also say that human persons are real too, as well as the human perception of goodness and beauty, and this, Lotze and the Boston Personalists argued, can only be made sense of in a universe presided over by a fully personal God.

Borden Parker Bowne

The Boston Personalist movement was founded by Borden Parker Bowne (1847-1910). Brought up in a devout Methodist home, he did his undergraduate degree at New York University, followed by a masters degree, and then went over to Europe to study for two years in France and Germany. This was when he discovered the philosophy of Lotze. Shortly after his return to the United States, he accepted a position teaching philosophy at Boston University in 1876, where he continued to teach and eventually serve as Dean of the Graduate School, down to his death in 1910.[100]

His book *The Immanence of God*, which came out in 1905, was the classic statement of the Boston Personalist position.[101] Philosophically, it was a *personal idealism* which stressed personality as the fundamental reality, both at the natural level and at the level of the divine. God is revealed (through the human beings who act as channels of his grace) as an infinite Person, whose will directs the purpose of the world and whose grace is expressed in both creation and redemption.

> This doctrine we call the divine immanence; by which we mean that God is the omnipresent ground of all finite existence and activity. The world, alike of things and of spirits, is nothing existing and acting on its own account, while God is away in some extra-sidereal region, but it continually depends upon and is ever upheld by the ever-living, ever-present, ever-working God.[102]

Edgar Sheffield Brightman

Bowne's successor as leader of the Boston Personalists was Edgar Sheffield Brightman (1884-1953).[103] Brightman was an ordained Methodist minister, as his father had also been before him. He did his B.A. and M.A. degrees at Brown University, but then went to Boston

University and Boston School of Theology where he earned a Bachelor of Sacred Theology in 1910, followed by a Ph.D. in 1912. Like Bowne, he also spent two years studying in Europe, in Brightman's case at the University of Berlin and the University of Marburg. After teaching philosophy at Nebraska Wesleyan University and religion and ethics at Wesleyan University in Connecticut, he came back to Boston University and taught philosophy there from 1919 until his death in 1953.

The entire universe is personal, Brightman insisted. It is made up of minds and their consciousnesses. God presides over all as the Supreme Person.

> To deny that God is conscious is to assign to him a state of unconsciousness; it is to deny that he can love or know or will or purpose, for all of these are conscious processes. If there is a God at all, a being worthy of our worship, he must be conscious. A blind force might be feared, but could not be worshiped; an unconscious spirit might be pitied, but could not be adored. To be a God is to be conscious.[104]

This vision of a loving and compassionate God—a God with whom we could have a two-way personal relationship, talking to him just as we would to a good friend, and being aware of his response—flourished in Methodist circles through the whole first half of the twentieth century. And it also made its influence felt outside Methodist circles, including its profound influence on the Alcoholics Anonymous movement during its formative period in the 1930's and 40's.

The Boston Personalist school nevertheless began to gradually lose influence in Methodist circles in the 1960's, under the impact of Neo-Orthodox theology and existentialist theology (among other forces), along with the rise of process philosophy and process theology. During the 1980's I spent a year in Boston, serving as Visiting Professor of Ancient History at Boston University and Visiting Professor of Theology at Boston School of Theology. Boston Personalist ideas were still being taught, but the movement had lost most of the enormous power which it had wielded over the American Methodists during the first half of the century.

Process philosophy:
Alfred North Whitehead

As a result of this, at the Methodist seminary where I did my B.D. degree in theology in the 1960's,[105] process philosophy had already taken the place of the older Boston Personalist system. This was a philosophy linked closely to the writings of an Englishman named Alfred North Whitehead (1861-1947). Whitehead came from a staunch Church of England background: his father and uncles were all Anglican pastors, and his brother was a bishop. He started out as a mathematician, and taught that subject for thirty years at Trinity College, at Cambridge University. But he became interested in the philosophical foundations of mathematics when he collaborated with the philosopher Bertrand Russell in writing the *Principia Mathematica* (1910-13), a seminal work in which the two of them attempted to show that all of arithmetic could be deduced from a restricted set of logical axioms. He nevertheless continued to make his living teaching mathematics, and became Professor of Applied Mathematics at the Imperial College of Science and Technology in London in 1914.

But then in 1924, when Whitehead was sixty-three years old, he was invited over to the United States to teach philosophy at Harvard University, where he lectured on that subject until his retirement at the age of seventy-six. His two most important philosophical works were written during these later years: *Process and Reality* (1929) when he was sixty-eight, and *The Adventures of Ideas* (1933) when he was seventy-two.

In "process philosophy," as Whitehead's system was referred to, God and the universe formed a single evolving organism, in which all the other things in the universe were constituent parts of this cosmic process. Since all the individual pieces were involved in constant flow and change, God—one of whose main roles was to continually integrate everything else that was happening into an organized whole—of necessity likewise had to be involved in growth and change.

Whitehead's God stood in stark contrast to the God of the Western European Middle Ages, whose major traditional attributes were to be completely eternal and unchanging. The word "eternal" in medieval Latin philosophy and theology usually meant *static*, that is, not altering in any kind of way at all.[106] One can immediately see the philosophical difficulty that would arise from taking a God who was completely static and unchanging, and then trying to make sense of any claim that he was a warmly personal being who knew us human beings as individuals, and related to us with love and compassion in our ongoing daily problems.[107]

Charles Hartshorne

The spread and influence of process philosophy was however probably due more to the work of an American philosopher, Charles Hartshorne, 1897-2000 (these dates are correct, by the way, he lived to the age of 103, and was still writing when he was in his nineties). Like Whitehead, he came from an Anglican background—his father was an Episcopal priest in Pennsylvania, and his maternal grandfather had also been an Episcopal priest—but he eventually became more closely attached to the Unitarian Universalist Church, in which his wife Dorothy had been raised. He volunteered for the U.S. Army during the First World War, to serve as a hospital orderly.[108] He spent twenty-three months in the Army Medical Corps in France.

At all points in his philosophical development, he took for granted the terrible reality of pain, suffering, and tragedy, as a counterpoint to the goodness, love, and beauty in the universe. During those war years, he could see the victims of war lying in their beds, but almost simultaneously look out at the beauties of the French landscape. Both were a real part of life and the universe. Most importantly, however, he became convinced that a world of purely material things, devoid of all emotion and feeling, could not be claimed as the first and immediate datum of experience. All our sense impressions, even our awareness of particular colors, *were* feelings—feelings of joy, pleasure, and attraction, or distaste, unpleasantness, and repulsion. Pure materialism was a pale abstraction created in the mind, drawn from what we actually prehended and perceived, and what was really there.[109]

When he returned home to the United States, he went to Harvard, and finished three degrees in four years, a B.A., an M.A., and a Ph.D. After traveling abroad for two years, listening to the lectures of the great philosophers of Europe, he was made a research fellow at Harvard, and spent one semester grading papers for Alfred North Whitehead.

It would nevertheless be a mistake to regard him simply as Whitehead's disciple. Hartshorne had already come to many of the same conclusions on his own, well before he met the English philosopher. And in particular, Hartshorne had, at the heart of his own system, a basic image of God as the World Soul, a view of the divine which Whitehead always soundly rejected. Hartshorne spoke of his own system as a kind of "neoclassical theism," in which God was to the universe as the human consciousness was to the human body, a way of looking at the divine that went back two millennia to the ancient Stoics and Neo-Platonists.

Hartshorne's prolific writings gained him a large number of followers. Among the Methodist theologians, this included John B. Cobb, Jr., and my own seminary teacher, Schubert Ogden. But his ideas have had a far wider impact than that, influencing Christian theologians from a number of other denominations, and certain important Jewish thinkers as well, along with some of the current New Thought authors. Process thought remains one of the vital themes within American philosophy and theology, with a large number of devoted followers: the journal of *Process Studies*, for example, which began being published in 1971, is still going strong.

Process philosophy and Boston
Personalism: limitations on God

There were in fact many similarities, and even links between the process philosophers and the Boston Personalists. There was a period in Boston when many students were shuttling back and forth to hear E. S. Brightman lecture on personalism at Boston University and Alfred North Whitehead lecture on process philosophy at Harvard. Brightman and Hartshorne carried on a correspondence for many years, which has recently been made available in a volume published by Vanderbilt University Press.[110] There were many important places where the two of them held identical or at least closely similar philosophical positions. In particular, Brightman and Hartshorne both agreed that there were necessary limitations as to what God could and could not do.

Actual religious experience, Brightman argued, required us to hold to a kind of "finite theism," in which God's freedom to act was always to some degree opposed by "The Given" (as he called it) within God's own nature:[111]

> There is within [God], in addition to his reason and his active creative will, a passive element which enters into every one of his conscious states ... and constitutes a problem for him. This element we call The Given. The evils of life and the delays in the attainment of value, in so far as they come from God and not from human freedom, are thus due to his nature, yet not wholly to his deliberate choice. His will and reason acting on The Given produce the world and achieve value in it.

Hartshorne pushed this idea much further, and gave careful philosophical explanations of why it was necessary to include, within God's being, what many traditional theologians would regard as strong limitations. The clearest and simplest account of this was given in the introduction and conclusion to a book called *Philosophers Speak of God*, which he and W. L. Reese put together in 1953.[112]

When I began seminary in 1961, I was at first filled with great foreboding. I had done both a B.S. and half of the course work for a Ph.D. in physical chemistry and nuclear physics, and based on this training as a scientist, I could see no way that a theological education could go much further than some sort of glorified Sunday School classes. Three books totally changed my mind: Paul Tillich's *Dynamics of Faith* and *Courage to Be*, and this book by Charles Hartshorne, *Philosophers Speak of God.* Hartshorne's book contained numerous excerpts from a long string of philosophers and theologians from all eras of history and a vast number of different religious traditions, including not only pagan Greek and medieval Christian authors, but also Muslim, Jewish, and ancient Egyptian authors, along with a host of modern thinkers. In addition, at the beginning and the end, Hartshorne explained what the real philosophical and metaphysical issues were, and why they were so important. But beyond that, he also showed me that the most significant questions of philosophical theology could be explored at the highest levels of intellectual inquiry, and with the same degree of scientific precision with which one would pursue the fundamental questions in philosophy of science. In fact, the two areas are closely connected and interrelated.

One way perhaps to explain what Hartshorne saw was at stake, is to repeat the old conundrum raised by people who are attacking the concept of a loving and compassionate God. The underlying argument goes back to the Epicurean philosophers of ancient Greece, but the clearest and best statement of the argument which I have ever read, is that given in David Hume's skeptical work entitled *Dialogues Concerning Natural Religion* (1779). This was another work which I read during my first year in seminary. I think that every philosopher or theologian who wants to write about this issue should be compelled to first read and make a careful study of Hume's book. It is one of the most powerful collections of skeptical and atheistic arguments ever assembled. But if you cannot get past his arguments, there is no point in trying to write a defense of theism at all.

This particular part of Hume's attack on the concept of God is put in the form of a set of statements, followed by a question:

1. If God is omniscient (all knowing)
2. and omnipotent (all powerful)
3. and God is also loving and compassionate,
4. then where do evil and suffering come from?

Charles Hartshorne dealt with that argument by seizing the horns of the dilemma, and qualifying *both* of the first two claims: (1) If the universe is constructed in such a way that genuine novelty appears, so that the future is never completely knowable in advance, then a God who knows *everything that it is possible to know*, will of necessity know the still uncertain future only as "still uncertain." He will NOT know everything about every single future event with absolute certainty. (2) And a God who rules over a universe in which real change and novelty can occur, and in which human beings are granted some degree of free will and choice, will have additional limitations on his power, because he will find things happening in the universe which are not his doing—things which he could not step in and arbitrarily make come out different, without removing the possibility of real novelty and true human free will.

Meaningless statements and
logical incompatibilities

In the medieval universities, students were regularly presented with the paradoxical sounding statement that "not even God can make a square circle," and asked to explain why that statement was true. To understand why it is necessarily true, we need to pose the statement in two other equivalent forms, where the difficulty can perhaps be more easily seen:

"God can make a square circle."
"God made a square circle."

The basic problem is that neither of these two statements mean anything. They are quite literally nonsense statements. That is because the words "square circle" do not mean anything intelligible in English. If I said "God can make a goobah woobah," this would likewise be a nonsense statement, because the words "goobah woobah" do not mean anything intelligible in proper modern English.

Now it is true that the words "square" and "circle" both mean something in English, but it is still nevertheless true that if something can be described in English as a square it cannot simultaneously be described in English as a circle, and vice versa. So of the following three statements:

> (1) God can make a square.
>
> (2) God can make a circle.
>
> (3) God can make a square circle.

The first two statements are both possible statements, but the third one has no meaning, and could not describe any intelligible state of affairs.

What Hartshorne does in *Philosophers Speak of God* (and elsewhere) is to point out other sets of statements, which he likewise believes are incompatible. In both of the following sets of statements, he argues, we must choose either number one or number two, but we cannot have both being true simultaneously.

> (1) Genuine novelty and real creativity occur at various times and places during the course of history.
>
> (2) God foresees (and hence controls) every last detail of everything that is going to happen, through the entire infinite future, so that nothing ever happens or will happen which was not absolutely predetermined in advance.

> (1) Human beings have free will. On those occasions when human beings think at a fundamental level about the kind

of basic moral principles and values they are going to live their lives by, these are genuine choices which they make, and at least part of their decision for the good or for the evil is not controlled or determined by anyone or anything except the individual human who makes that decision.

(2) Human beings have no free will at the ultimate level. God foresees (and hence controls) every last detail of the infinite future, so that nothing ever happens which was not absolutely predetermined in advance. This means that human beings move and act in fact like puppets on strings, and it means that when we spend hours thinking that we are weighing our moral options, our belief that we actually have the power to decide anything is all an illusion.

The limitations placed upon a loving personal God

If a personal God, out of love, chose to create a universe in which real novelty would occur, and in which real creativity could take place—and if such a personal God, out of love, also chose to create a universe in which beings would evolve who could make real choices about values and moral issues—and if such a personal God, out of love, also chose to create a universe in which the flow of time would occur, where new things came into being as old things passed away—then this God would have to self-limit his own power and allow numerous things to happen which involved his creatures in pain, evil, and destruction, and would also find that even he would not know in advance all the future events which were going to occur.

Can the universe we actually live in, be construed as the creation of a personal God who in fact is loving and good? It depends on what we decide demonstrates the greatest amount of true love and goodness. If we think that real love and goodness means that no human being would ever be allowed to make any choice except the absolutely correct one, and if we think that real love and goodness means that nothing which exists can ever be allowed to die, be destroyed, pass away, or disappear, and if we think that real love and goodness means that nothing genuinely new or creative or unpredictable is ever allowed to happen, then I suppose one could argue that the God who rules over the universe we actually live in, is neither good nor loving. But if we decide that a truly loving God would therefore have to give his creatures the ability on occasion to think and choose for themselves and pick their own values, and the ability to engage in real creativity and innovation and scientific discovery, then the kind of universe which God has in fact given us is one of the greatest gifts which one loving personal being could give to another.

The important issue that Hartshorne raises is that we have to make a choice as to what we are going to regard as the most loving kind of behavior. We cannot have it both ways. We can have (A) a universe in which we have human free will, the flow of time, and the possibility of novelty and creativity, or we can have (B) a universe in which God absolutely controls every single thing that happens. But we cannot have both simultaneously. If statement B accurately describes the real universe, then it is difficult, given the presence of evil and pain and suffering, to describe God as loving and compassionate. But if statement A is the correct one, we can describe the evil, pain, and suffering as the necessary concomitants of a universe in which free will, time, and real novelty occur.

Good, evil, freedom, and a universe composed of more than one person

When I was a seminary student, I had the privilege to hear Charles Hartshorne speak. He was in his late sixties by then. He came up to Dallas from Austin, where he spent his retirement years as Ashbel Smith Professor of Philosophy Emeritus at the University of Texas. Like Tillich—perhaps not as strongly but still distinctly present—there was an almost visible aura around the man. Again, I saw what medieval artists were trying to convey when they painted halos on the holy men and women who had been in such an intimate connection with the divine. Somehow or other, the eternal numinous power had entered their hearts and souls and dwelt in them in a special way. Tillich had been a chaplain riding on the ambulances in the First World War on the German side. Hartshorne had been an orderly in a military hospital in back of the lines on the U.S. side. Both had been involved in a world filled with enormous horror and suffering, but both had learned how to turn to God and rise above it, and lead lives afterwards where they did good for other people.

I remember that in the question and answer period after Hartshorne's lecture, someone in the audience told him about a friend who had died horribly of some disease at a very young age, and asked Hartshorne how he made sense of that. With sadness and compassion, Hartshorne said simply, "He was unlucky."

Does this seem cold and hard, and lacking in love and compassion? In the twelve step groups, it is not uncommon for situations to develop where, for example, a member might tell the others at a meeting about some great tragedy that has just struck—perhaps a medical diagnosis that the person has some painful and fatal disease, and that there is almost nothing that the doctors can do for him or her—and one can hear statements like the following: "I turned to God and I screamed, 'Why me?' And then I remembered my program, and I thought to myself, 'Why not me?'"

When Hartshorne was ninety-three, he published his autobiography, with the very interesting title, *The Darkness and the Light: A Philosopher Reflects Upon His Fortunate Career and Those Who Made it Possible*.[113] In the preface, he calls his book "a celebration of life." But sometimes we manage things badly instead of well, and sometimes we have bad luck instead of good. That too is part of life.

> The root of evil, suffering, misfortune, wickedness, is the same as the root of all good, joy, happiness, and that is free-dom, decision making. If, by a combination of good man-agement and good luck, X and Y harmonize in their deci-sions, the AB they bring about may be good and happy; if not, not. To attribute all good to good luck, or all to good management, is equally erroneous. Life is not and cannot

be other than a mixture of the two. God's good management is the explanation of there being a cosmic order that limits the scope of freedom and hence of chance—limits, but does not reduce to zero. With too much freedom, with nothing like laws of nature (which, some of us believe, are divinely decided and sustained), there could be only meaningless chaos; with too little, there could be only such good as there may be in atoms and molecules by themselves, apart from all higher forms. With no creaturely freedom at all, there could not even be that, but at most God alone, making divine decisions—about what? It is the existence of many decision makers that produces everything, whether good or ill. It is the existence of God that makes it possible for the innumerable decisions to add up to a coherent and basically good world where opportunities justify the risks. Without freedom, no risks—and no opportunities.[114]

Freedom is the root of all evil, but also the root of all good. Is this in itself a great evil? Hartshorne says not at all, that we live in a fundamentally *good universe*, where "the opportunities justify the risks." But poor decisions are made by human beings, chance and randomness are real, and we live in a universe where there is not only a personal God presiding over all, but also countless human beings who are persons too, and—as Hartshorne would argue strongly—animals and birds and other creatures which are also to varying degrees personal beings. (Dogs, for example, feel love and hate and all the other emotions, and in their own way make choices and decisions. Hartshorne believed deeply that philosophers who had no love and respect for animals and birds as living and feeling creatures could never, in the long run, understand the highest and noblest part of what made human beings fully human.)

[The universe is not] the expression of a single will only ... it is a community of countless wills, whose supreme Will is not a tyrant, however benevolent or otherwise, nor yet the contriver of an all-inclusive machine, but the supreme inspiring genius of the Great Community of partly self-determining creatures. How this could be without risk of incompatibility and hence suffering in the innumerable decisions out of which existence is woven I at least cannot see. But I can see, I think, how sublime beauty and pervasive zest can and do result.[115]

For Hartshorne, the price of the "sublime beauty and pervasive zest" which we experienced in this universe, was the risk at all times of also having to undergo pain and suffering. Was this risk the greatest of all evils?—remembering that I could avoid that risk only by sacrificing all my own freedom, as well as everyone else's, so that I would become nothing other than an unfeeling puppet on a string, a machine programmed by an internal computer. Even as an old man in his nineties, Hartshorne proclaimed that the beauty and the joy of life were entirely worth the necessity of also experiencing dangers and hardships. As long as he could hear the music of the birds singing—his other great love in addition to philosophy—he knew that the universe was good, and he quietly rejoiced in it.

The Great Adventure

A fool demands a universe in which no one else has any freedom except me, a world in which people in foreign countries never do terrible things, a world in which the people in authority are always wise and honest, and no one in my family ever dies. And if I am a fool of that sort, I then proclaim myself as an atheist, denying that God exists, because God refuses to dance instantly at my bidding and make the rest of the universe obey me. Of all the beings in the universe, only I am to be allowed to do ignorant or cruel or uncaring things.

A coward whimpers for a universe in which there will never be any pain or discomfort or blighted hopes, for me at any rate, at whatever the cost. If I am a coward of this sort, I would in fact be willing to sacrifice all my own freedom in order to obtain it, and would willingly throw myself into the oblivion of all thought and feeling. Many men and women of that sort become alcoholics or drug addicts, while others commit suicide, or otherwise flee from reality and from having to feel their own feelings and emotions.

But heroes instead display the courage to live life as an adventure, *the great adventure* that we read about over and over again throughout the history of the world: Moses leading his people through the trackless desert, King David struggling for his throne, the prophet Elijah confronting Queen Jezebel and the prophets of Ba'al, the apostle Paul undergoing savage beatings and rejection in city after city, the brave death of the noble Socrates, and so on. In the field of science, think of Galileo fighting the ignorant opponents of the new science in seventeenth-century Italy, and twenty-two-year-old Charles Darwin signing on for the five-year-long voyage (1831-36) in which the sailing ship HMS Beagle, a three-masted barque only ninety feet (27 meters) long, ended up sailing entirely around the world. This trip was one of extraordinary danger, both at sea and in some of the places where they landed. Scientists have to show courage too, in order to carry out the great adventure of life.

At the level of popular culture, the American cowboy in the old-time movies and novels held his head high and rode the trail unflinchingly all the way to the finish, just like the knights of old. Real cowboys and real knights always knew that the trail eventually came to an end. In James Earle Fraser's famous sculpture, "The End of the Trail" (1894), the Native American's horse has his head bowed with fatigue, but he is still on his feet, and his rider is slumped but is still hanging on. The end of the trail is hard—no matter who you are, you finally get to the point where you are weary to the bone and have no more strength left in you—but even then you try your best to go down, if you can, with the same bravery with which you rode the rest of the trail.

What both the Boston Personalists and the process philosophers emphasized was that, at every step of the trail, our song can be *Immanu'el,* "God is with us," for the Divine Person is both our lord and our ever loyal companion on this adventure.

Chapter 14

The Three Primal Hypostases

The problem with Boston Personalism
and process philosophy

I have emphasized how important both Boston Personalism and process philosophy were in twentieth century theology. Nevertheless, neither system ever rose to the sort of all-dominating philosophical position which one saw, for example, in the case of Aristotle's philosophy during the High Middle Ages. This has been in spite of the extreme devotion and commitment which a large number of excellent young philosophers and theologians still give today to the ideas of that wonderful old man Hartshorne. As one young philosopher put it, once you have read Hartshorne, he changes your view of God and the world forever. Philosophy will never look the same to you again.

Both Boston Personalism and process philosophy were well-organized and well-argued positions. Alfred North Whitehead's philosophy was arguably *the* great architectonic system of the twentieth century. So why did not one or another of these systems take the entire theological world by storm? The problem, I believe, has arisen from the fact that both Boston Personalism and process philosophy force us to view God as completely personal. That is built into both systems at a necessary level. People are given no choice on that matter. But in fact, as we have seen from our survey of western history, many even of the most devoutly religious philosophers and theologians of the past have preferred to view God in impersonal or almost completely impersonal terms.

I believe that, to provide a widely acceptable basic philosophical metaphysics for the modern period, we must create one which gives philosophers a choice—one in which the ground of being can be regarded as either an impersonal absolute or a totally personal God and anything in between, without having to redo the whole basic foundations of the philosophical system.

Also, I believe that the question of whether the ground of being is or is not a personal God cannot be proved by wholly abstract philosophical argumentation. I believe that this issue has to be decided on what one might call pragmatic or existential grounds, by an individual judgment which each of us must make, based upon his or her own personal experience.

Reviving the idea of the three hypostases

My suggestion is that we go back and revitalize a philosophical position which served as the basis of most western philosophy for almost two thousand years. Although in most ways, we cannot analyze the ground of being and fit it into our science, it is nevertheless true that we can discern a three-fold quality to its being. The Greek word *hypostasis* in this context meant substratum, so this philosophy started with the position that the ground of being, in effect, contained three very different levels of reality.

This idea of the three primal hypostases (or layers or levels within the divine reality) went back to the world of Middle Platonic thought which began developing in the ancient Mediterranean world in the second century B.C., along with the Neo-Platonic systems which began further elaborating on some of those ideas in the third century A.D. Although referred to as Platonic systems, they in fact eventually incorporated many of the best ideas from a number of other Greek philosophical systems, including both the Stoics and Aristotelians. This was part of what gave it its enormous flexibility and universal appeal.

This provided a kind of lingua franca in which St. Augustine could teach about a highly personal God in the early fifth century A.D., St. Denis could argue for a totally impersonal absolute at the end of that century, and St. Thomas Aquinas in the thirteenth century could attempt to adjudicate between the two. It allowed one to read any philosopher from any place within that long period and make immediate sense of that thinker's arguments. And this was so, whether they were pagan Greek philosophers, Christian philosophers, Jewish philosophers, or even medieval Arab philosophers (with their impersonal scientific view of the universe, where the ground of being was regarded as simply part of the natural processes of the universe).

But in order to adapt and re-use this kind of approach, we need to deal with the problems raised by Locke in the seventeenth century and Kant in the eighteenth century, and in particular, we need to take into account the radically different picture of the universe which emerged out of the discoveries of modern science during the course of the twentieth century. Some of these discoveries showed how naive Locke's and Kant's ideas were, while others force us to make fundamental alterations in our characterization of at least two of the three hypostases.

There were various names given to the three primal hypostases during the ancient and medieval period, but for my purposes, I would like to use the following names, because they will enable us to focus on what I think are the most important features of each level, in ways that make sense in terms of modern scientific knowledge, without forcing us in advance into taking any position on whether the ground of being is or is not a personal God:

FIRST HYPOSTASIS: THE ARBITRARIUM
SECOND HYPOSTASIS: THE LOGOS OR SOPHIA
THIRD HYPOSTASIS: THE ENERGETIKOS

But whatever names we choose—the ones our ancestors used or these slightly modernized variants—they will allow us to rejoin once again that ancient and hallowed tradition in which, for century after century, men and women sang the Trishagion, the Thrice Holy Anthem, to the ground of being, and bowed down to do honor to its numinous glory: "Holy God, Holy Strong One, Holy Immortal One, have mercy upon us."

A brief review of the three basic
cosmological possibilities

Before investigating the three primal hypostases however, it would be helpful to make a brief review of the three basic cosmological possibilities: a universe that was created at a certain point in time, or a universe that has always existed, or a universe which is alternately created and destroyed over and over again for all eternity. During the intellectual ferment of the mid-twentieth century, for example, all three of these different cosmological models were in competition for a while.

(1) In the Big Bang theory, this universe had a beginning in time 13.7 billion years ago, when all of its mass-energy appeared, apparently out of nothing, in violation of the first law of thermodynamics, the principle of conservation of energy. For a discussion of modern attempts to get around this problem, one may see the appendix to this chapter, but to sum up what is said there, none of these attempts have been very convincing. It is necessary to presuppose that the big bang emerged out of something that was already there, even though that has

to have been a very strange kind of something, in order to make good sense out of this theory.

(2) In the oscillatory universe developed by Richard Tolman in 1934, the universe expands after a big bang, until it reaches its ultimate expansion point. At that time, it begins contracting instead, until finally all the mass of the universe implodes together in a "big crunch." But this then explodes in another big bang, so that the universe goes on forever, in a series of alternate expansions and contractions. This however would ultimately violate the second law of thermodynamics, the principle of entropy. Again, there would have to be something behind and underneath the known physical universe to empower its continued existence.

(3) In the steady state theory developed in 1948 by Fred Hoyle and others, the universe has always existed and will always exist, in a continual state of expansion, with the mass-energy required to maintain its functioning being provided by the continual spontaneous appearance of new mass, out of nothing, in empty space. This of course would violate the first law of entropy, in its attempt to get past the second law of entropy. To explain where the new matter was coming from, Hoyle finally began to acknowledge (by the end of his life) that there was the necessity for some sort of eternal "creative ground."

These form the three basic logical possibilities. In the ancient world, there were likewise philosophies representing all three models. (1) Nearly all Jewish and Christian philosophers argued that the physical universe we live in had a beginning in time, and would have an end in time. It was created by the ground of being, whom they called God. (2) The pagan Stoic philosophers argued in favor of an oscillatory universe with an eternally-recurring cycle of destruction and re-creation. It was true that our present physical universe had a beginning in time, as the Jews and Christians said, and would end at a specific moment in time (in a giant world conflagration called the *ekpyrosis*). But after each world conflagration, as the flames cooled and died, a new physical universe would be born, exactly like the preceding one. So the chain of universes extended to infinity. The Stoics did recognize however that such a chain of destruction and re-creation could only be maintained if there were an underlying ground of being, whom they identified with the god Zeus or Jupiter. (3) Aristotle and the pagan Neo-Platonists (as well as the medieval Muslim Neo-Platonists) defended the idea of a steady-state universe which had existed (and would continue to exist) for all eternity, with no beginning or end. The Neo-Platonists realized that such a steady-state universe could only continue in existence if there were a perpetual "fountain" or source of continually appearing new being, which they called the One, and identified as the ultimate ground of being.

The discovery in 1965, of the cosmic background radiation which fills the entire universe, convinced most modern physicists that the Big Bang model was the correct one. But the idea of the three primal hypostases is not necessarily tied to the Big Bang model alone. I want to stress this very strongly. Even if scientific discoveries made after this book is written make it seem more likely that the steady-state universe or the oscillating model describes the scientific evidence better than the Big Bang model, all three models violate one or more of the laws of thermodynamics, and all three models require the concept of a ground of being, which can in turn be analyzed in terms of the three primal hypostases.

In the rest of this book, I am speaking in terms of the Big Bang model because it is the currently accepted theory, and also because it is simpler and allows one to describe the fundamental issues more clearly. But I have read books by physicists who seemed to believe that defending the steady-state or oscillating model would allow them to create a universe without a God, so it is important to state clearly and unequivocally that some sort of God or transcendent ground of being, even if totally impersonal, is necessary in any coherent and honest cosmological model developed by the human race over the past two thousand years.

The Third Hypostasis: the Energetikos

Since, as Einstein showed, mass can be converted into energy (and vice versa) according to the formula $E = mc^2$, mass and energy are linked together, so that we must posit a single source for both. The ancient world was not aware of this, so the question of where matter came from, and where the energy in the universe came from, were apt to be treated as widely different questions. This is one of many cases in which the discoveries of modern science, particularly those of the twentieth century, force us to make extensive modifications in ancient philosophical ideas before we can take them over into the modern world. The Neo-Platonists, for example, whose ideas dominated the late ancient and early medieval world, regarded the third hypostasis as the source of the energy, change, and motion in the physical universe, but regarded the problem of matter as a totally separate issue. On this point—the role of matter in the fundamental makeup of the universe—we must therefore totally disagree with them. The matter and energy in the universe both emerge into being out of the ground of being in the same cosmic event.

For all of the three basic cosmological models, in fact, one is forced to say that the energy (or mass-energy) which allows the continued existence of our present physical universe comes into being out of a transcendent ground. We can call this "the ground of being," "God," "the One," "Zeus," or whatever we wish, but it serves as *in effect* an apparently unlimited source of new energy. This means that the transcendent ground is able to violate both the first and second laws of thermodynamics.

So one basic property of the ground of being is that it is what I have termed the Energetikos. It is the source of all the mass-energy in the directly observable universe. But the ground of being cannot contain "energy" in the sense in which we speak of energy in the directly observable universe, because if it did, it would be constrained by the same laws of physics which govern the directly observable universe, and would be bound by the laws of thermodynamics. This is why I have instead chosen to refer to this aspect of the ground as the "Energetikos," as that which is capable of producing all the mass-energy in the universe, of "energizing" the universe, while itself being something fundamentally different in kind.

Logos vs. Nomos

The Greek word *logos*, in ancient philosophy, was a rich and complex concept, referring to a number of different kinds of ideas and things. But let us at least start off with a simplified explanation of what the word often meant to them. In modern English, we get the word "logical" from that ancient Greek root. So we can say that when we use the word *logos*, we are talking about the realm of the rational and logical. We also get the English names of most of our sciences from that same root. *Zôê* in Greek meant life, so the science of zoo-*logy* studies the rational and logical structure of living creatures. The word *gê* meant earth, so the science of geo-*logy* deals with what we can say logically and rationally about why the earth behaves the way it does (the formation of rocks and mountains, earthquakes, volcanoes, and so on).

So in ancient Greek thought, the cosmic Logos was sometimes thought of (among other things) as the set of all the laws of nature. But this is not a way that we can go in building a philosophy in the modern world, or at least not simply and directly. Things are more complicated than that. These complications were produced by some of the philosophical issues raised by the philosopher Kant in the eighteenth century, when combined with the revisions in Kant's ideas which we must now make as a result of the discoveries of twentieth-century science, which tossed so many of his favorite ideas topsy turvy.

In order to make better sense of the issues here, I would like to introduce another ancient Greek word and use it to make an important distinction. This is the word *nomos*, which is usually rendered as "law" when translating ancient Greek documents. I would like to make an arbitrary definition, and use the word in this present book in the following way: in my definition (which I will be using in the rest of this book) the Nomos is made up of all of the laws of Nature, along with all of the other fundamental principles which make the observable physical universe behave the way it does.[116] The Nomos is that which provides the fundamental structure or framework within which the physical universe is constrained to act.

Locke and Kant deny our
ability to know the Nomos

In the early modern period, philosophers became quite skeptical about our ability to know anything important about the Nomos-structure of the universe. John Locke, in his formative work *An Essay Concerning Human Understanding*, published in 1689, insisted that we could never know the "real essences" of things. He believed that the human mind could know only the surface appearance of reality (as it directly appeared to us through the five senses), along with perhaps a few pragmatic observations about how certain things in the world around us always seemed to happen in pretty much the same kind of way. The latter he believed we learned through what he called the association of ideas, i.e., through our minds seeing certain things happening repeatedly and then becoming conditioned to expect the same things to happen in the future—but without ever knowing why, which is what is important to note. He used the examples of swans, which in England always looked a good deal alike (large water birds with white plumage, and so on) and gold, where any sample of that metal which one examined seemed always to be shiny and yellow and have the property that it could be dissolved in no acid other than aqua regia. But the reason why all swans looked so much alike, and the reason why all samples of gold behaved in such a similar fashion—the "real essence" of these two kinds of things—could never possibly be fathomed by the human mind. And Locke was convinced that he had conclusively *proved* this philosophically!

Why did philosophers of that period take him seriously? Because the nature of scientific knowledge at that time was still so primitive, that no one could even remotely imagine that techniques could ever be worked out for understanding that sort of thing. And even a century later, when Immanuel Kant wrote his *Critique of Pure Reason* in 1781, modern science had still not progressed enough to answer either of these apparently simple questions: why did all swans look so much alike, and why did all samples of gold behave so much alike?

In terms of swans, Gregor Mendel did not discover the genetic basis of inheritance until 1865, and it was not until the twentieth century (during the 1950's) that the structure and role of DNA was discovered. During Kant's time, the first experiments were performed which began to show that the ancient and medieval theory of the elements—namely that there were only four elements, earth, air, fire, and water—could not possibly be true. It was demonstrated that water was composed of something yet simpler, namely that it was a compound made up from what we would today call hydrogen and oxygen. It was also shown by another experimenter that air was not a simple substance, but was a mixture of what we would today call nitrogen, oxygen, and carbon dioxide. But it is doubtful that Kant would have known of these experiments—I see no signs in his writings that he did much of any reading in the natural sciences—and even then, in terms of understanding why gold had its specific properties, the first modern periodic table of the elements did not appear until the work of Dmitri Ivanovich Mendeleev in 1869, it was not until 1897 that J. J. Thomson discovered that the electron was a subatomic particle, and it was not until the twentieth century that chemists and physicists discovered that gold had its peculiar properties because of the nature of the outer electron shell about its nucleus.

So Kant simply assumed that the "real essence" of swans—or as he thought of it, the *noêton* or intelligible Platonic idea of the swan (that is, what made a swan a swan, instead of, let us say, a duck or a chicken)—was totally unknowable. And the same thing applied, he believed, to the *noêton* or intelligible idea of gold, and the Platonic ideas lying behind all the other phenomena of nature that the human mind encountered via the five senses. This was the unknowable realm of the *noumenon*, as Kant called it in Greek, using the passive participle of the root of the word *noêton*.

Just like Locke, Kant also believed that the grossness of the five physical senses allowed us to contact only the surface of reality. The Greek verb *phainô* meant "to appear," in the sense of sensing the mere surface appearance of a thing. So using the passive participle of that word, Kant referred to this surface appearance as the *phenomenon*. Our human minds could know the phenomenon, he argued, but they could never know the noumenon, and just like Locke, he was convinced that he had *proved* this philosophically.

Why did philosophers take Kant seriously for so long? Mostly, I believe, because his claims were believable in terms of the crude state of scientific knowledge at that time. In fact, it was not until the latter part of the twentieth century that scientific knowledge had built up to the point where it became clear and obvious, to anyone who thought about it seriously, that Kant could not possibly have been right.

The Kantian subjectivity imposed by our cognitive blinders

Kant did have one valid point. When we try to sort out our sense impressions and attempt to come up with a coherent account of why things happened in a certain way, the preexisting cognitive structure of our minds (our presuppositions and biases and what we think we already know in other areas) can in fact distort our findings. I think I already know what the questions are which I ought to be asking, so I never think to ask the question that would in fact solve the problem. My mind has no preexisting "slots" into which it could fit certain kinds of data, so it literally cannot even be aware of the existence of that kind of data. It is as though blinders were put over my eyes in certain areas. This difficulty applies to all domains of human thought, from the natural sciences to literary interpretation to historiography. Our presuppositions blind us to what is really going on, or at least seriously distort our processing of what we think our five senses are telling us.

Perhaps the most influential—or at least most controversial— philosopher and historian of science of the twentieth century, Thomas S. Kuhn, argued this sort of Kantian position in his major work, *The Structure of Scientific Revolutions* (1962).[117] In that book, he used the development of modern astronomy for some of his most basic examples. The commonly accepted medieval paradigm for astronomy, the Ptolemaic system, taught that the sun, moon, and planets revolved in circular orbits around the earth. The experimental data did not exactly match this model. The use of epicycles in the mathematical calculations could account in part for the retrograde motion of the planets, but centuries of tinkering with these calculations had never produced a perfect fit. Nevertheless, during this entire period, no scientists seem to have challenged the basic framework of the Ptolemaic theory. This was one of Kuhn's most important points. When working scientists find data that contradicts their theories, they do not by any means toss out the theories on the spot. The contradictory data is regarded at first as a "puzzle," and years of work will then be spent trying to figure out how to fit the apparently anomalous data into the accepted theory.

In fact, in this case, Ptolemy devised the basic paradigm in the second century A.D., and it took fourteen hundred years of scientists batting their heads against the puzzles created by the paradigm, before the time became ripe for someone to challenge it with a basically different paradigm. That finally happened in the sixteenth century. A Polish scientist named Copernicus devised a totally different model, one in which the earth and planets were seen as rotating in orbits around the sun. But even then, it took the work of several more generations (including the contributions of Tycho Brahe and Galileo) to assemble enough in the way of good data and observations to demonstrate the superiority of the sun-centered paradigm.

So it is in fact true that our presuppositions can not only block us from asking the right questions, and cause us to distort what we think we do see, but can also cause us to systematically discard all the counter evidence which keeps on appearing, and demonstrating that our presuppositions are incorrect.

In the field of psychology and psychotherapy, what is called cognitive therapy has had great successes in dealing with depression, and also with certain other psychological problems, such as phobias and anxiety attacks. Cognitive therapy takes what one might call a Kantian position, working on the principle that the cognitive framework of the mind, if distorted in the wrong kind of ways, can cause patients to incorrectly interpret all sorts of things which happen to them during their everyday lives, in ways which will trigger a depressive response (or phobic or anxiety-ridden response). Training the patients to reframe the cognitive framework of their minds—that is to change their assumptions about "what it means when someone else says such-and-such to me" or "what will happen to me if I fall into this particular kind of situation" or "who I am as a person"—will enable them to get through the ordinary stresses and strains of life without becoming completely psychologically incapacitated.

The reality of scientific progress

Both Kuhn and the cognitive therapists teach us that there was a point to what Kant was saying. But both of them also teach us what was wrong about the drastically overdrawn conclusions which Kant drew from discovering the potentially distorting power of human subjectivism. In Kuhn's work, we can see that science, given enough time, will get past the blockage of a false or distorted paradigm. In the numerous clinical successes of the cognitive therapists, we can see that depressives can in fact be taught to look at the world through a more accurate cognitive framework.

Since in Locke's time, it was believed that there were only four elements—earth, air, fire, and water—it was in fact the case that no one had the slightest idea why gold had its particular properties. But today we know that earth, air, fire, and water are not elements at all. The real elements are hydrogen, helium, lithium, beryllium, boron, carbon, nitrogen, oxygen, and so on. Today we know that gold is one of the basic elements, and we also know how the outer electron shell of its atom is constructed, which in turn allows us to explain why it is a metal, why it conducts heat and electricity so well, why it is shiny, and why it appears yellow in color, in addition to explaining why gold is so chemically inert in the presence of acids and other corrosive substances (its outer electron shell is so stable that it is difficult to ionize gold by adding or subtracting one of these electrons).

Genuine scientific progress is possible, and in fact the history of the last 3,000 years makes it amply evident how much progress has occurred. We need to remember the basic structure of the argument set out in the fourth of St. Thomas Aquinas' five proofs for the existence of God, the argument from gradations in truth and value. As he says in his *Summa Theologica* I, q. 2, art. 3:

> The fourth way is from the degrees that occur in things, which are found to be more or less good, true, noble, and so on. Things are said to be more or less because they approximate in different degrees to that which is greatest. A thing is the more hot the more it approximates to that which is hottest. There is therefore something which is the truest, the best, and the noblest, and which is consequently greatest in being, since that which has the greatest truth is also greatest in being.

Transferring Aquinas' argument over into the present context, we can then make this important and decisive statement: If we are forced to acknowledge, for example, *(a) that it is more correct to say* that the chemical elements are hydrogen, helium, lithium, beryllium, boron, carbon, nitrogen, oxygen, and so on—*(b) than it is to say* that there were only four elements (earth, air, fire, and water), and that all other material objects were made up of atoms of these four irreducible basic elements—*(c) then we are forced to admit* that the human mind can in fact make authentic progress in gaining knowledge of the Nomos (the basic laws and principles of science).

The famous twentieth-century learning psychologist Jean Piaget, who was also a highly skilled philosopher, put Kant's theory of knowledge to the test by observing how small children actually learned about the world. What he discovered was that, although what Kant called the fundamental categories of the human reason did not basically change, the *schemas*—the connecting links which Kant indicated were necessary to apply the categories to the phenomena—became more and more sophisticated as the child grew and developed a richer and richer knowledge of the world.[118] The fact of real, demonstrable gains in knowledge shows that we have some meaningful contact with the noumenon, even if we do not know it perfectly.

Therefore the claim made by Locke that we cannot know the real essences of things, along with Kant's later reworking of this into the claim that the human mind cannot know the noumenon *at all*, must be rejected. Modern science has worked out a vast body of useful and valid information about the Nomos (the basic laws and principles of science) which simply cannot be written off as pure subjectivism and illusion and relativism.

Modern scientists—the actual working scientists who are carrying out genuinely productive research in their laboratories—detest Kantians and the kind of philosophers who try to use the argument from Kantian subjectivity to denigrate the possibility of useful knowledge. To say that science knows nothing at all about what is really there in the external world, because science does not know everything about everything perfectly, is a hopelessly silly and unworkable position.

The Second Hypostasis: the Logos

Having therefore established the principle that science has over the centuries gained us more and more real knowledge about the universe, we must still say that even perfect knowledge of the Nomos would not be knowledge *per se* of the second primal hypostasis. That is why I have made this distinction between Nomos and Logos. Put in terms of ancient Christian philosophy, the Nomos is part of the created world, while the Logos is an intrinsic part of the Godhead.

The Logos is that aspect of the ground of being which produces the Nomos (the basic laws and principles of science) and imposes these laws and principles on the observable physical universe.

In spite of the fact that things pertaining to the ground of being lie almost totally out of our sphere of possible knowledge, we nevertheless can say just a little bit about the nature of the Logos. At the practical level, one cannot produce a long term, consistent pattern of order from an unordered first cause. I may see a cloud in the sky which temporarily takes the form of a rabbit's head, or of Abraham Lincoln's profile, but there is no way to set up a real predictive science of these kinds of pictures in the clouds. This means that just as the Nomos is rational and logical, so likewise its source, the Logos, must be equally highly ordered.

There are physicists today who believe that it might be possible, using even more powerful particle accelerators, to get at least a glimpse "in back of" the Big Bang. If this is ever accomplished, it would be information about the inner workings of the Logos. There is no way that one could say in advance whether a scientific experiment could or could not ever penetrate into that strange realm.

But it would be a strange realm indeed. The Logos cannot be the same as the Nomos, for if it were, the ground of being would be governed by the same laws of nature which shape the workings of the observable physical universe. And this would be an impossibility, for then the Logos and the ground of being would be forced to obey the first and second laws of thermodynamics as well as many other scientific laws and principles which would prevent it from being the eternal preexistent ground of everything else.

The important thing to note here however, is that a universe which came out of nothing in a big bang, could not itself be the source of the laws of nature which govern it. Physical scientists sometimes allow themselves to fall into the extraordinarily naive presupposition that the laws of nature are "just there," and would somehow or other just *have* to be there, so that no explanation has to be given for why there are laws of nature. And yet the laws of nature are not simply derivable from the principles of mathematical logic, or any other set of principles (such as the fundamental axioms of Euclidean geometry[119]) where one could perhaps argue that they are "just there" because there was really no logical way that they could not be true.

The source of the laws of nature has to have existed before the big bang occurred, and the power that still continually forces natural processes to obey these rules has to be something outside the natural order. That source and power—which lies within the ground of being—we are calling (along with two thousand years of philosophical tradition) "the Logos."

The First Hypostasis: the Arbitrarium

In our discussion of the First Hypostasis, we will need to begin by talking about some truths about the universe that eighteenth and nineteenth century thinkers wanted to avoid looking at. Let us start with the role played in nature by the fortuitous and the accidental. In the twentieth century, it was discovered that some things in the universe take place by chance, ruled by purely random factors in such a way that we can calculate probabilities at best, never certainties.

The eighteenth and nineteenth centuries would have been appalled by our modern recognition that chance and randomness rule much of nature. Such an idea would violate to the core their belief that human reason and the new science were going to make human beings the unchallenged masters of the universe. Even at the beginning of the twentieth century, there were numerous conservative thinkers (including Albert Einstein as one famous example) who wished to defend the old eighteenth and nineteenth century certainties; who tried to argue that events only *appeared* to be the result of chance in certain situations because we did not know all of the data required to predict with exactitude what was going to happen. What appeared to be chance was in fact merely human ignorance, they insisted.[120] "God does not play dice with nature" was Einstein's famous dictum on that subject.

Those who argued that chance did not really exist might point, for example, to the experience of flipping a coin. People often did this when they wished to obtain a random yes or no answer, because at the practical level, it was impossible to predict in advance whether the coin would land with its head or its tail on top. And over a long enough number of coin tosses, even this would average out to around 50% heads and 50% tails, so it was not as though this phenomenon was totally unpredictable—it was predictable statistically, if not in individual cases. But more importantly, the only reason the outcome of an individual coin toss appeared to be a matter of chance was because of human ignorance. If one built a machine where the coin was flipped into the air in such a way that one knew the exact magnitude and angle of the force, along with all of the other variables (mass of the coin, distance to the ground, the density of the air, the presence of any slight breezes or drafts, and so on) it ought in principle to be possible to predict in advance whether the coin was going to land heads or tails with 100% certainty.

But in many domains of nature, chance is real, and is not just an appearance of randomness arising from human ignorance. Let us take the field of thermodynamics. The fundamental laws of thermodynamics were first worked out during the time when the modern steam engine and internal combustion engine were first being developed, as a severely practical study on the part of the experimenters who were building these engines. They built pistons and cylinders, and then compressed gases inside these cylinders at different temperatures, keeping careful records of the pressures, volumes, and temperature changes which they observed. Their discoveries allowed them to design far more efficient steam engines—which allowed for the development of the steam-powered railway locomotive and steam ship—and then prompted them to invent the first internal combustion engines, which in turn allowed for the development of airplanes and automobiles running on gasoline engines, and so on.

Much later on, what was called statistical mechanics was developed, which looked at the problem of describing a gas confined in a cylinder from an entirely different direction, viewing it purely as an intellectual exercise in calculating the totally random motions of the molecules of that gas, as they bounced off of one another and off of the walls of the confining cylinder. What classical thermodynamics had called the temperature of the gas was now represented as the kinetic energy of the moving molecules, while what had formerly been called the pressure of the gas was now calculated in terms of the force and momentum of the gas molecules striking the sides of the container.

Statistical mechanics came out with exactly the same results as classical thermodynamics. All the same laws appeared, along with all the same predictions of the same experimental results, which could all be easily verified in the laboratory.

Now what this means is that the reason why the molecules of a gas appear to be in totally random motion is NOT because of our ignorance of all the data governing the position and momentum of each individual molecule. No, their motion appears to be totally random because it actually IS completely random. If that were not so, then statistical mechanics (which is a way of studying that which is totally a matter of chance) would come out with different laws and different predictions of the experimental results.

The Heisenberg uncertainty principle

Where are the purely random factors coming in? This is partly due to the Heisenberg uncertainty principle, which has a measurable and quite noticeable effect at atomic distances, such as when we are attempting to describe the collision between two tiny gas molecules. Werner Heisenberg (1901-1976), a German physicist, discovered this fundamental principle while at the University Copenhagen in Denmark in 1927 doing work on the mathematical foundations of quantum mechanics. It was one of the major discoveries which produced the great twentieth-century shift in our understanding of the universe. This principle states that the degree of accuracy with which we can know the position of a particle, let us say, multiplied by the degree of accuracy with which we can know its momentum (and hence its velocity), can never be less than a fixed fraction of Planck's constant, which is 6.626×10^{-34} joule seconds. This means that the more accurately we attempt to discover the location of a particle, the less accurately we will be able to tell its velocity, and vice versa.

When the Heisenberg uncertainty principle was first discovered, attempts were made at first to interpret it as being caused by the "observer effect," referring to the way in which an observer, by the very act of observation, will be interacting with the object and thereby changing its position and/or velocity and momentum. That is, the attempt was made to once again interpret chance and randomness and uncertainty in nature as only due to human ignorance or human meddling.

But that is not what the mathematical equations actually say. The mathematical foundation of the Heisenberg uncertainty principle makes it clear that in the known physical universe, there are intrinsic limits to our ability to know certain kinds of things simultaneously, which arise from the fundamental nature of things themselves. This uncertainty applies, not just to our subjective human knowledge, but to the nature of things themselves in their mutual interactions. The molecules of gas in a confined cylinder *also* do not "know" the precise position and momentum of the other molecules past the level of exactitude allowed by the Heisenberg uncertainty principle. Neither Nature itself or even God himself knows exactitudes past the limits set by that principle.

Chaos theory

Now there were those in the earlier parts of the twentieth century who attempted to get around the problems which the uncertainty principle raised for human knowledge, by asserting that, even though we could not know the details of many kinds of natural processes at an atom-by-atom and molecule-by-molecule level, nevertheless Nature operated in terms of such large numbers that we could still make confident predictions of the future by simply calculating probabilities. They pointed to the successes of statistical mechanics as one excellent example of how well this could work.

The problem is that some kinds of natural process cannot be predicted by standard probabilistic calculations, because they are chaotic processes. Let us give some examples of such processes. If I stand at the top of a mountain and toss several large rocks down the mountain, they will end up at different places at the bottom of the mountain. This is a chaotic process, because the precise angle at which the rock hits the mountain each time it bounces on its way down, together with the precise configuration of the ground at each of those points, will make it impossible (at the practical level) to predict in advance where the rock is going to end up. And yet this is not the kind of problem where calculating odds and probabilities can give any useful help.

The movement of the air over the wing of an airplane will produce places where the flow is turbulent instead of smooth. Since the airfoil surface provides no lift in the turbulent sections, these need to be eliminated as much as possible, in order to produce the most efficient airplane wing design. But these turbulent areas are chaotic domains, where there are no mathematical formulas in aeronautical engineering which can be applied to calculate how to smooth out and remove the turbulence.

In the early stages of the universe, according to the Big Bang theory, the matter and energy which made up the universe were still in an almost totally chaotic state. Since the interactions which were taking place were almost all at the level where the Heisenberg uncertainty principle had a measurable and significant effect, this meant that an omniscient mind which possessed all the knowable data about all of the particles in the universe at any given moment, would still have been unable to predict the exact position and velocity which all these particles would have arrived at, one second later. Although some of the wildly different possible results undoubtedly would have been cancelled out by the way in which large numbers can sometimes allow us to predict overall end results by the laws of probability, it is nevertheless the case that many of the details of our present universe might have been very different from what we actually observe today. Even an omniscient mind (that is, one which knew everything which it was *possible* to know) could not have predicted, shortly after the Big Bang, that this particular planet Earth was going to be formed around the particular star which we call our Sun. Why did the details of the universe come out the way they actually did, instead of some other way? This was simply a matter of chance in an often very chaotic universe.

The arbitrary nature of "what is there"

I have termed the first hypostasis the Arbitrarium, because it points to the purely arbitrary nature of "what is there" in many parts of the natural process. Why did chance produce this result instead of that result? There is no answer to that question. What happened is what happened, and we simply have to accept that. Why did a certain chaotic process end up producing this consequence instead of a different consequence? Again, there is no logical answer. What happened is what in fact happened.

But there are even deeper levels of arbitrariness to the universe. Why do certain mathematical constants which are used in physics equations have the numerical value which they do? The values which exist for the most basic of these constants seem to be totally arbitrary. There is no known logical reason why they could not have been different. But that is the value which they have in our present universe, and so these are the numbers which we have to use.

In addition to Euclidean geometry, there are also two other non-Euclidean geometries which would be equally possible, just in terms of pure mathematical logic. At the time I am writing this book, the experimental evidence has still not been good enough to determine which of these three possible geometric systems actually describes our universe. But it seems as though it would have to be one of the three.

Would there be any particular reason why it might be one instead of another? That too seems to be completely arbitrary.

The particular set of laws of nature which governs our universe likewise seems to be arbitrary. Yes, the laws of nature as we presently understand them all fit together logically, but scientists have over the centuries tried out many other different laws which also were internally coherent and logically organized. The Ptolemaic system which put the earth at the center of the universe was completely logical, as was the phlogiston theory of combustion, and the theory that the four elements were earth, air, fire, and water.

Or at an even deeper level, let us take the following little thought problem as being at least suggestive. We are taking a beginning physics course, in which the professor teaches us about Newton's laws of motion. One of Newton's key formulas, we are told, says that $F = ma$. That is a logical statement—force equals mass times acceleration—which is part of a completely logical set of physical theories. That corresponds to the Logos dimension of reality. But for anything to actually follow that law—for anything to actually happen in the physical world—we must have some portion of matter which has mass, and also some energy applied in the form of a force. That corresponds to the dimension of reality which we have termed the Energetikos, the source of all the mass-energy in the universe.

But we still cannot calculate anything using that $F = ma$ equation, until the professor tells us to take out our pencils and papers and calculate what force will need to be applied to accelerate a mass of so many grams by so many centimeters per second per second. That is, until the professor tells us the specific numbers, we have nothing which is actually useful. But those numbers which the professor supplies us are totally arbitrary. And at the ultimate level, that will also be true in any kind of practical situation in which we try to calculate what is going to happen in the actual physical universe using that formula. The specific numbers which we will have to plug into that equation will be arbitrary to the actual situation which we are trying to predict and describe.

This inescapable element of "thereness" which is an intrinsic part of the physical universe at all its levels—the fact that certain things, which logically could have been different, are nevertheless there and the way they are—is what is supplied by that aspect of the ground of being which we have referred to as the Arbitrarium.

The Arbitrarium, the Logos, and the Energetikos

The physical universe, as we have come to know it as the result of the discoveries of twentieth century science, is an eminently logical place. It is also bursting with energy, an internal power which is continuously driving natural processes ranging all the way from the subatomic to the galactic level. But not all of the universe is intelligible, in the sense of being able to give logical reasons for why it is this way instead of some other way. There are elements of chance, uncertainty, chaos, and the purely arbitrary which affect all things.

If the physical universe which we study in our sciences came into being out of some pre-existent ground of being—which seems in fact to be the case—then that transcendent ground would of necessity have to be supplying all three of these factors: the logic, the energy, and the arbitrary nature of many things.

The traditional doctrine of the three primal hypostases allows us to speak of all three factors, and demonstrates that it is possible to say a few things, at least, about the mysterious reality which existed before the Big Bang occurred, without necessarily having to invoke any idea of a personal God. That is why it served as such a useful base for western philosophy for so many centuries.

But it has the virtue that it also allows those who wish to, to speak of a God who is either fully or at least partially personal, without having to lapse into special pleading and fuzzy thinking of the sort which is destructive to good science. In the next chapter, we will need to look at some of the ways that this can be done.

Chapter 15

A Personal God: Love and Energy

A metaphysical system built around the three primal hypostases—that is, a system of the type which was assumed by most western thinkers (pagan, Jewish, Christian, or Muslim) for over two thousand years—allows philosophers who wish to view the ultimate ground of reality in totally impersonal terms to do so. The three hypostases were in fact all identified and delineated at the most basic level in non-personal terms:

The Threefold Structure within
the Ground of Being

1. Arbitrarium: ground of chance and arbitrariness
2. Logos: logical ground of the universe
3. Energetikos: ground of the universe's mass-energy

But the three hypostases also allow those philosophers and theologians who wish to do so, to speak of a warmly personal God and fit the personal attributes of God into the basic metaphysical system without doing injury to its basic underlying structure. They also allow this to be done—if it is done properly—in ways that do no injury to the spirit and practice of good scientific inquiry.

I want to begin to do that in this chapter by investigating the link between love and energy. The third hypostasis, the Energetikos, allows us not only to say something about where all the mass-energy in the universe came from; it also allows us to speak about what human beings call "love"—love seen as a special kind of energy operating at some of the higher levels of reality.

Panpsychism is not the answer

In this regard however, I should begin by saying that I do not believe that the philosophical position known as panpsychism is a useful way of trying to bring the force of love into the fabric of the universe. In ancient Greek, the word for soul was *psychê*, so "panpsychism" in the literal sense would be the belief that everything real in the universe had a soul: not just human beings, and not just birds and animals, but also things like electrons and white blood cells. Philosophers who have taken up this position have been apt to argue, for example, that the attraction which draws a negatively charged electron towards a positively charged proton, is simply a kind of "love"—not as multifaceted and rich as the love which draws one human being towards another, to be true—but a kind of love nevertheless. Philosophers who uphold this position can then argue that love is the basic power which drives the whole universe; the basic force which holds the entire cosmos together.

The problem with this position is that if we define the word "love" in such a weak and vague way that it can refer even to things like the blind attraction of positive and negative electrical charges towards one another, then we are using the word love in such a fuzzy and cloudy way that we have not in fact said much of anything at all. Even as a poetic metaphor, it is so overdrawn that it would be difficult to work into most really good poems. Electrons do not "feel love" towards protons in anything remotely like the way that human beings feel love towards one another. They do not have souls or psyches in that sense. Electrons are not conscious beings. And likewise, white blood cells do not use "free will" to "make the decision" to attack disease microorganisms which they encounter within the human bloodstream—this is nothing at all like conscious human decision making.

The layers of reality

Love does not operate at all levels of reality. Love is not a vague term for any kind of energy or attractive force in the universe. Love is a special kind of energy operating at some of the higher levels of reality.

Reality comes in layers. Just as the ground of being is divided into three *hypostaseis* (which should be translated as "layers" or "substrata" in this kind of context), so likewise the created universe is made up of various layers of reality.

At the lowest layer of which we know at present, we deal with the world of the nuclear physicists, a realm made up of electrons, protons, neutrons, and various kinds of small nuclear particles called quarks, gluons, neutrinos, muons, and so on.

At the next major level up, we encounter the world of the chemists. In principle, when a chemist mixes a solution of sodium chloride with a solution of silver nitrate, and a white precipitate of insoluble silver chloride falls to the bottom, a physicist could describe the entire process mathematically in terms of the interactions of all the electrons and atomic nuclei involved. These two layers are therefore related by *interdependence*, where one causal system can be reduced to another, more general and elementary one. But what the chemists study is real, and in practice, chemists spend most of their time learning about the behavior of molecules (where each molecule is an often fairly large assemblage of atoms and subatomic particles) without going into great detail on the behavior of all of the subatomic particles.

It should also be said—and this is extremely important—that no one can in fact work out what happens when a large beaker containing a solution of sodium chloride is mixed with the contents of a large beaker containing a solution of silver nitrate, by using physics to calculate the changing positions of every electron in those two solutions. This is not just because of the vast amount of data that would have to be assembled—far more than the largest present-day computer could contain and process—but due to the fact that physics has never truly solved the three-body problem, let alone the problem of setting up equations which could calculate the movements of (let us say) 6.023×10^{23} electrons simultaneously, which is the rough order of magnitude where chemists perform most of their experiments. Chemistry is not only a field of science which is separate from the study of physics, it has to be studied in and of itself. And it deals with real things, which actually happen.

The next layer is the one studied by biologists and physicians. Various kinds of cells and bodily fluids are made up of chemicals, and biological processes are made up of chemical changes and changing electrical potentials, so that biology is related to the two lower layers (chemistry and physics) by *interdependence*. In principle, all biological processes could be reduced to the more general and elementary levels described by the chemists and physicists. But again, biology and medicine form their own separate fields of study, and physicists and chemists are not able, simply on the basis of their knowledge of their own fields, to explain the hormone system of the trout or the proper medication to use for lowering blood cholesterol level in human beings. If I need my appendix removed or have a broken leg, do not send me to a nuclear physicist!

The fourth major layer is the one studied by the social scientists: psychologists, sociologists, economists, and political scientists. These also are real scientific fields, where researchers gather objective data and formulate verifiable theories. They are also talking about things that are completely real. There is nothing imaginary or subjective about people who are afflicted with schizophrenia or with obsessive-compulsive disorder. Human societies are made up of real, flesh-and-blood human beings who engage in totally real processes, involving the trading and bartering of material goods, struggles for power over other people, making group decisions, and so on. And political entities like the United States, Sweden, Brazil, the state of Indiana or California, the city of Chicago or Paris, and so on, are all perfectly real entities.

Some scholars argue that the social sciences are totally *interdependent* on the lower layers (biology, chemistry, and physics). This is however less obvious than the completely interdependent relationship between the three lower levels. Some of the factors involved in the study of the social scientists may also be linked to the lower layers by *correspondence* instead, about which we will explain in the next section. This is not the place however to engage in that particular debate, which often deeply divides scholars in those fields, particularly in the study of psychology, psychiatry, and psychotherapy.

The topmost major layers are formed by the realm of mathematics, logic, and *meaning*. It is here that we encounter not only the truths of mathematics and the basic principles of logical thinking, but also spirituality, the realm of goals and values, human individuality, and the purely personal dimension, along with certain important philosophical concepts. This level is related to the lower levels by *correspondence* rather than interdependence.

The layers of analysis in the
mind's investigation of reality

1. Meaning and value (at the highest level)
2. Logic
3. Mathematics
4. Social sciences
5. Biology
6. Chemistry
7. Physics (at the most basic level)

Jean Piaget: correspondence
vs. interdependence

When making the distinction between correspondence and interdependence, I am using the technical vocabulary of Jean Piaget (1896-1980).[121] This brilliant experimenter and observer was famous as a learning psychologist who discovered many valuable things about early childhood cognitive development, but he was also one of the most skilled philosophers of the twentieth century, who developed what is sometimes called a constructivist theory of knowledge. Insofar as one of the themes of this book is a sort of *contra Kantum* (an attempt to undo and redo Kant's philosophy in order to make theology possible again), Piaget is especially important because he investigated all of the major Kantian philosophical principles, not by sitting in an arm chair and musing upon them, but by actually observing babies and children to see how they actually gained their knowledge about the world.

Piaget pointed out that physics is related to chemistry by *interdependence*, but logic/mathematics is related to physics/chemistry by *correspondence*. One can set up a series of logical statements and mathematical equations which are *isomorphic* to a particular experimental situation in physics or chemistry, but one cannot derive the laws of physics or the research findings of the chemists from a study of pure mathematical logic alone. Physics and chemistry therefore cannot be *reduced to* the study of logic and mathematics.

The dangers of reductionistic systems

Most of the atheistic systems of the modern period are, at their base, illegitimate exercises in reductionism. Karl Marx tried to reduce all other knowledge to economic theory and Sigmund Freud tried to reduce all other knowledge to psychological theory, while others tried to reduce all other knowledge to the study of nuclear physics or genetics. Each group of partisans tried to claim that all other claims to genuine knowledge were illusory, for "if you study our field, we can give you the *real* answers to why everything in the universe happens." There is an extraordinary kind of arrogance among reductionists of that sort! And it always turns out to be, at heart, the arrogance of the fool.

Even in the case of two fields which are related by *interdependence* (like physics and chemistry), there is no way that universities can dispense with having departments of chemistry as well as departments of physics. There is no way that even the most brilliant university students can, on the basis of ten or twelve courses in physics, "work out for themselves" the chemistry of compounds based on the benzene ring, or synthesize chemicals that will serve as diuretics for treating problems like high blood pressure and glaucoma. The knowledge that one is taught in university chemistry courses is *also* valid knowledge.

And this is even more the case, when we are discussing two fields which are related only by *correspondence*. Physics cannot be reduced to the study of logic. The laws of physics cannot be derived by a process of deduction from the basic principles of logic. The concept of "mass" can be fit into a logical system, but it is not itself one of the principles of logic. Likewise, the concept of "kinetic energy" can be worked logically into the theoretical structures of mathematical physics, but the concept of kinetic energy plays no role in the theory and philosophy of logic, studied in and of itself.

In the same way, the word "love" refers to a valid and completely meaningful concept when we are talking within the realms of meaning, value, human relationships, and human motivation. These are the layers of reality "up at the top" of our list of layers. These realms are related by correspondence to, not interdependence on, the lower levels of reality, such as physics, chemistry, biology, economics, and (at least in part) sociology and psychology. The idea of love cannot be "explained away" by trying to reduce it to a statement in Marxist economic theory, or Freudian psychological theory, or the biochemistry of genetic change, or—in particular—a statement within nuclear physics about interactions among subnuclear particles.

So the concept of love has to be taken seriously. It refers to something real. It cannot be mechanically reduced to something simpler down at one of the lower levels of reality, although actions taken out of love may sometimes be in either tight or loose correspondence with processes going on at one of the lower levels. Love (at the higher level) may sometimes be in close correspondence with the biological processes, for example, which produce sexual activity and the propagation of children. Love at the higher level may sometimes be in positive and helpful correspondence with the sociological structures that keep a particular society running smoothly. But that is totally different from saying that love can be reduced to a set of mechanical biological urges and sociological forces.

Double determination and
multiple determination

Sigmund Freud made the interesting discovery that human beings almost never make a decision to take any significant action on the basis of one reason alone. They almost always have at least two reasons for acting, one conscious and one subconscious. He referred to this as "double determination." Actually the term multiple determination would be more accurate, because even in classical Freudian theory, what keeps a neurosis being played out over and over in a person's mind, or makes a destructive psychological game work so effectively, is a set of payoffs at several different levels.

The psychiatrist Eric Berne wrote a fascinating book in 1964 called *Games People Play*, in which he described a number of common psychological con games that people play on one another.[122] They were con games, in that the game-player was saying one kind of thing (and acting one way) on the surface, while in reality setting up the victim to be taken advantage of, as soon as the victim had been thoroughly seduced into playing the game. The archetypal example, Berne said, was the old traditional kind of con game played along the Ohio and Mississippi rivers in the nineteenth century by professional river boat gamblers. The con man would get into a poker game with strangers, and would pretend to be very bad at playing cards. He would spot his victim, called the mark, and then lose relatively small hands to that person repeatedly, until the mark believed (falsely) that he had found a really stupid person whom he could take advantage of. Finally, on a hand in which the professional gambler had his winning cards well hidden, he would push the mark into betting an extraordinarily large amount of money. Then he would turn over his cards, show his real hand, and smilingly scoop all the mark's money off the table.

Berne gave amusing colloquial names to a number of standard psychological games which human beings played on one another— Let's You and Him Fight, See What You Made Me Do, Wooden Leg, Peasant, I'm Only Trying to Help You, and so on—and his book became a great popular success. One of my friends, a good clinical psychologist, said he found these humorous names to be very useful however, for example, in teaching people to be union arbitrators, and in a number of other contexts, because they were not only easy to remember, they really did express the fundamental nature of the con game being played, in a way that was far clearer than a lot of the more traditional psychological terminology.

However, Berne was more than capable of describing each of these psychological games in classical Freudian technical language, and it is by looking at the more technical analysis that we can see the intricacy of each of these games, and some of the true complexity of the multiple factors and layers which are involved in real human decision making. Let us take one common psychological game as an example, one which Berne called Look How Hard I've Tried.[123] This is a con game of course, because although the ones who are playing this game are trying to appear on the surface as compliant, cooperative, and doing their best to make things work—saying to their victims over and over again, in one form or another, "Look how hard I'm trying"—in reality they are working underneath as hard as they can to completely sabotage any possible chance of success.

A husband and wife come for marriage counseling, for example, and the wife (let us say) tries to give the surface appearance, during the counseling sessions, of being cooperative with the therapist, and she talks continually about how much she wants to make the marriage work. But once they are back at home, she continues to do all of the things which she knows are driving her husband to desperation. Or she stops doing X (which the counselor has called her hand on) and shifts instead to doing Y (which she knows puts her helpless husband in an equally nasty double bind). After a suitable number of counseling sessions, she can then file for divorce, saying triumphantly, "Look how hard I tried."

Children will sometimes play this game on their parents, where the parents ask the child to do X, and the children put up a big show of attempting to carry out the task, while in fact making sure that it is going to be bungled, or that it will take so long that the parents will finally step in and do it for them, or something else of that sort.

Berne, in his book, analyzed this game in more detail for us so that we could see more clearly all of the complex factors involved in this psychological game:

> *The real aim of the game:* Vindication.
>
> *The real thesis being maintained by the game-player:* They can't push me around.
>
> *Internal psychological advantage:* freedom from guilt for aggression.
>
> *External psychological advantage:* evades external responsibilities towards others.
>
> *Internal and external social advantage:* being able to say triumphantly, "Look how hard I've tried," and appear vindicated in the eyes of the world.
>
> *Biological advantage:* opportunity to engage in belligerent exchanges, grow red in the face, scream, cry, and so on.
>
> *Existential advantage:* being able to play either "helpless" or "blameless" (depending on how the game is played) and thereby avoid falling into one or another specific type of existential anxiety.

The role of multiple determination in other kinds of human decision making

The concept of multiple determination has a far broader application however than Freud ever dreamed of. In terms of the levels of reality of which we are speaking here, human beings evaluate their options, when they are making decisions, with the aim of discovering solutions which will maximize the positive payoffs and satisfactions at as many different levels of reality as possible. At a trivial level, for example, a man needs to eat food for the sake of his biological survival. But there are many different things that he can eat, and places to go where he can eat them, which will all satisfy that basic need. Which of these will give him the most additional payoffs and satisfactions? Perhaps he decides to go to a fancy restaurant with his wife for dinner. That satisfies the basic need—something to eat simply for his biological survival—but it will also serve other purposes. It will also do things such as contribute positively to bonding with his wife, perhaps, and demonstrate his status in society, along with being able to experience the aesthetic enjoyments of food that tastes extremely good. It could also be a way of assuaging subconscious guilt feelings over various childhood issues, and so on and so forth.

To say that "he made the decision for such-and-such a reason" at one level, does not at all mean that he did not make the very same decision for an additional reason at one of the other levels. Both of those reasons for making that decision were equally real.

A couple buying a house will make the decision to purchase a particular property on the basis of a number of criteria: price, size, style, neighborhood, travel time to work, schools (if they have school-aged children) and so on. The house they actually select will be the best compromise candidate. Each factor which they weighed in their minds before making that decision would have been a genuine influence. Price would have to have been considered, and size would have to have been considered too. But I do not believe that anyone ever buys a house on the grounds of one single factor alone.

A place where thinkers get into trouble every time, is when they start writing books based on some theory that all important human decisions are based on one and only one determinative factor. One author tries to argue that all human decisions can be explained in terms of a particular economic theory, while another tries to argue instead that all these decisions are based on a single psychological need, and so on and so forth. That involves a kind of naive psychological reductionism which is totally false to the complexity of real human decision making. And yet the libraries are full of books written by "one theory" political thinkers, sociologists, psychologists, economists, philosophers, and theologians! All you can do is shake your head in dismay at the silliness of it.

Plato's theory of love

With all these things in mind, then, let us explore the way in which love functions as a real force—a real energy—at some of the higher levels of reality. Anyone who wishes to explore this topic seriously needs to begin by reading Plato, particularly the part of the *Symposium* where Socrates gave his discourse on the nature of love (although valuable information about the topic of love comes up in others of Plato's dialogues also).

When human beings first start feeling love towards other things, Plato notes that it is particular material things that they love. The Greek word he used for love was *Erôs*. I love another human being because of that particular man or woman's body. I love a particular horse, and delight in riding it around the countryside.

Just as Freud was to note again many centuries later, there was also often a strong psychosexual component in this most primitive kind of love. We need to remember at all times, that just as the Romans spoke of the goddess Venus and her son Cupid (the Latin word for "desire"), so the ancient Greeks spoke of the goddess Aphrodite (the personification of the numinous quality of sexual desire, as it appeared in both humans and animals) and her son Eros. The Greek word Eros, Plato's word for love, means—95% to 98% of the time in ancient Greek texts—simply the power of raw sexual lust.

But we could learn, Plato said, about higher levels of reality and higher kinds of love. As a beginning, we could learn to appreciate the beauty of material things in general. Instead of loving just one particular horse, I could learn how to go to a horse race and admire the beauty and goodness of all the swift and powerful horses on the field. I could learn to admire natural beauty in general—the beauty of the purple mountains and the rolling prairies, the wildflowers and the trees, the deer browsing in the undergrowth and the birds flying overhead.

The major breakthrough however, in Plato's theory of love, came when I first began to recognize the beauty and goodness of some particular field of skill and knowledge, and "fell in love with it." Plato was one of the truly great philosophers of education, of *paideia* as the Greeks called it. No one learns any art or craft truly well, no one learns any field of knowledge with impressive expertise, until that person first falls in love with it. No one becomes a truly brilliant violinist who did not, as a child, first fall in love with the violin—and that had to take place before the child was able to do anything but squeak and scratch on the instrument. No one becomes a world class football player who does not love playing football with an overpowering zeal. You are not going to do all the hard practice that is necessary unless you love it so much that your love will overcome your normal desire to avoid the long and sometimes painful hours of effort.

The same thing applies to being a good scientist. People who become truly outstanding physicists *love* the study of physics with a deep passion. They live for it, and devote their lives to it. Why? Because they regard it as good and, yes, *beautiful*—because they admire not just its usefulness, but also the pure elegance of the mathematical equations and brilliant explanations which it gives of the "why" of natural processes.

The next stage in our growth, Plato said, came when we learned how to love learning new things simply for the sake of learning itself. We fell in love with the creative process itself, and learned to feel a rich and deep joy at making new discoveries and devising new inventions and developing novel and better ways of understanding things and doing things.

I spent most of my adult life teaching at Indiana University, at the South Bend campus. During the early years in particular (the 1970's and early 1980's) a good many of the students were so-called nontraditional students. Most of these were the sons and daughters of factory workers and skilled craftsmen, where no one in their family had ever gone to university before. Instead of going to university right after they graduated from high school at age eighteen, they went out and got jobs just like their parents had done. But at some point in their twenties or thirties, they would decide to see if they could earn a college degree. These were such marvelous students, because they were coming to classes, not because their parents were forcing them to do it, or to avoid having to go out and get a job, but because they had developed a real thirst for learning. They were far brighter and more capable than most of the eighteen-year-olds, because of their fierce *love* for what they were doing.

Now the subjects I taught (such as ancient Greek and Roman history) were not normally regarded as interesting by Americans of that era. In fact, most Americans of that time would have regarded the study of ancient history as one of the most deadly boring things they could ever imagine. So I understood that my first task, when I began a new course each semester, was *to make the students fall in love with the subject.* If I could awaken that passion—that desire to know, and know more, built upon a sheer delight in the kind of things that were being learnt—then the students would do prodigious amounts of work, and rise to enormous levels of creativity and insight. I must have been fairly successful at that: the word out among the student body was that my courses involved three times as much work as any other courses taught at that campus, and yet my classes were always full. Other professors would attend one of my lectures on occasion and come away saying, "But you're not teaching at the level of an undergraduate course, you're teaching the kind of material that only comes up in advanced graduate courses .... although I will admit that they were nodding their heads at all the right times, and seemed to be understanding everything you were saying." And I would shrug, because what the students were writing on their exams showed that they were in fact understanding what I had been lecturing on. It was the power of love at work, which could empower people to do extraordinary things. If anything unusual was being accomplished, it was because my love for the subject was kindling a similar love for the subject in the students.

Intelligence and love

In the study of the evolution of species, it is clear that developing greater intelligence can confer certain kinds of evolutionary advantage. Let us not (as human beings) arrogantly speak as though intelligence was the only thing that could be useful. Sharper teeth or longer claws can sometimes also convey an evolutionary advantage, or simply the extraordinary survivability of cockroaches, which have been around almost since the first living creatures crawled out onto dry land. Nevertheless, fish are more intelligent than flatworms. Mammals (even small mammals like mice) are much more intelligent than reptiles. Chimpanzees and gorillas are more intelligent than mice or dogs or cats or horses. Human beings are more intelligent than chimpanzees and gorillas. It seems to be one way of sometimes improving your chances of surviving and having offspring.

Nevertheless, the standard biology textbooks used in schools and colleges, during all my lifetime, were very poorly and misleadingly written on the topic of the evolution of species, because although they acknowledged that having greater intelligence and intellectual ability could convey an evolutionary advantage in many kinds of environment, they invariably treated intelligence as only a tool for manipulating and controlling the environment. "Your teeth are longer and sharper than mine, Mr. Tiger, but I can still beat you, because I can use my human intelligence to trick you and fool you and take advantage of you, and thereby kill you before you can kill me." That is a rather grim view of reality, to say the least!

What the biology textbooks totally fail to note, is that greater intelligence can also (in addition) convey a greater ability to love. I have known people who kept pet reptiles (snakes or iguanas or something like that), and although reptiles will sometimes become used to you, where they come to regard you as something harmless (and warm to the touch) which is a regular source of food, and lie peacefully on your arm or coil themselves around your body, it would take a real stretch of the imagination to call this love. On the other hand, cats and horses and dogs, which are mammals, and are far more intelligent, are in fact capable of showing real love. This is particularly so in the case of dogs. The biological reductionists who are reading this book will immediately at this point begin angrily rejecting my statement, snorting and saying, "It's nothing more than the herd instinct, the pack instinct." But remember what we discussed two sections back—in the section on double determination and multiple determination—sometimes things are both/and instead of either/or. When dogs live in the same houses with human beings, we can indeed see the dogs interpreting numerous things in terms of the hierarchies of the pack. But when one particular human being and one particular dog become really close—and this may even be true more for some dogs than for others—there is a real mutual love that goes far beyond any mere "pack instinct."

Art and creativity

The kind of ability to love which comes with higher intelligence is not necessarily directed towards narrow physical survival in the immediate sense. The higher levels of love involve an ability to appreciate pure beauty and goodness in general, simply for the sake of the joy that is felt.

Chimpanzees have sometimes been observed beating on logs with sticks and jumping around. The observers who recorded those findings believed that this was, in a certain sense, a kind of primitive form of music and dance. Whether that is so or not, it is only human beings who are—because of their intellectual ability—able to devise and perform truly complex pieces of music, and dancing involving intricate choreography.

When chimpanzees are given paper and crayons, on rare occasions one of them will draw a primitive mandala: a crude circle with an X drawn inside it. This is the first complex figure which a small human child will learn how to draw, but human children rapidly advance beyond that point. The circle becomes a human head, with stick-like arms and legs attached directly to the head. And so on, developing more and more complexity and skill with time.

None of the ancestors of modern human beings left any surviving decorative arts. Even our relatives the Neanderthals left only a few pieces of mostly fairly crude artwork here and there. But the earliest true human beings of whom we know, were from the beginning drawing extraordinarily beautiful cave paintings and carving delicate little statuettes. The minute pottery was invented, human beings began decorating each piece of pottery with artistic designs.

This is one of the two major things which distinguishes true human remains from the remains of any of the other hominids who formed their ancestors and cousins: the presence of so much decorative art, done for the sheer love of its beauty. The other major distinguishing factor is the presence of creativity and the desire for continual novelty. Even the Neanderthals, having once worked out how to chip a particular kind of flint tool, would use exactly the same design for thousands of years. In the case of true human beings however, no one was ever happy chipping an ax head or knife in exactly the same way for more than a few decades. True human beings want continual novelty and innovation. Sometimes the new product is better (in the sense of working better for its established purpose), but most of the time it is simply different. Once human beings learned how to make pottery, one can see the shapes and decorations changing every few decades. Change just for the sake of something new and different, which in and of itself gives human beings joy. In the modern world, we can see this same need for continual creativity and novelty affecting clothing styles, popular slang, and everything else in everyday life.

The love for art and music, creativity and novelty, is the great distinguishing feature of truly human intelligence. This is why I find it so dismaying when biological reductionists and other kinds of reductionists try to "explain away" our human love for art and music, and the joy we feel at creativity and novelty. These reductionists like to think that their approach is "more scientific," when in fact they are undermining and trying to destroy the very heart of human intelligence. If it were in fact possible to have a human world without art or music or literature (which I doubt would in fact be possible, for most human beings would refuse to put up with that), we would ultimately produce a human world without any real scientific or technological creativity either.

Agapê love for other human beings

In the third to first centuries B.C., Jewish scholars translated the Hebrew Bible into Greek. On many occasions in that work, which was called the Septuagint, these rabbis used an obscure classical Greek verb *agapaô* to translate the common Hebrew word for love. Early Christianity picked up on this and coined a new Greek word from this root, the noun *agapê*, to describe a kind of love—loving other human beings in the sense of showing them kindness and mercy, and doing concrete helpful things for other people who were in need—which the ancient pagan world never truly talked about fully in their discussions on the nature of love.

The best of the ancient pagan Greek authors were aware to some degree of a kind of love for other human beings which was non-sexual, non-materialistic, and non-possessive. Plato, for example, at one point spoke of a higher Eros, a divine power of love which served as an intermediary between human beings and God. We could speak to God and God could speak to us through this higher love. And Plato also described a kind of love between two human beings which was based on an admiration of the inner spiritual qualities of the other person, and of a responsibility which human beings had toward the other members of the human community in which they lived. The ancient pagan Stoics touched on one aspect of this kind of loving care for our fellow human beings when they discussed the subject of duty. And going even beyond this, the Stoic philosopher Epictetus displayed in his *Discourses*, in the story of the man whose little daughter was dying, a deep knowledge of what the truly loving treatment of other human beings would require us to do. But the pagan Greek world never fully developed an understanding of the kind of love which Jews and Christians referred to by the words *agapaô* and *agapê*.

Agape love is close to being a unique part of human experience—something that can only be understood by creatures possessing a human level of intelligence, because it requires a level of abstraction and the ability to look on other human beings "from the outside," where we ignore our own selfish interests and desires and attempt to see what these other human beings need in and for themselves. A chimpanzee living in the jungles is not often apt to receive any kind of Agape love from his or her fellow chimpanzees, nor will a wolf living in the wild be very apt to receive a great deal of Agape love from the other members of the pack. Chimpanzees and wolves tend to be very ruthless in most of those kinds of situations.

In the atheistic reductionistic philosophies of the past century and a half, there has often tended to be a naive glorification of a return to the ruthlessness of the wolf pack, with the presupposition somehow that the human race would increase its own chances of evolutionary survival by cultivating ruthlessness and heartless savagery. The problem is, that is not what has actually happened over the course of evolution. Alligators are models of blind ruthlessness and savagery, but they are also not very intelligent. Wolves are more intelligent than alligators, and also kinder creatures—talk to people who have kept wolves as household pets if you do not believe me. Human beings, who are capable of functioning at an intellectual ability far surpassing any other creatures presently living on this planet, are the ones who have done the most (at least among the best and wisest human beings) to cultivate the ability to show Agape love. That is because truly showing Agape love requires the ability to perceive other human beings as complex and multidimensional beings, with complicated emotions and feelings, and goals and plans which may be quite different from our own.

The more intelligent and wiser a human being is, for the most part, the better able that person will be at showing the deepest and best kind of Agape love. I am talking about real thinking ability and understanding here, which does not necessarily mean the same as book learning and university degrees. But real intelligence and Agape love go hand in hand. They have to be both/and, not either/or.

The ground of being as the creator of love and the possibility of love

When we talked about the ground of being as the Energetikos, we began by showing how this transcendent ground was necessarily the source of all of the mass-energy in the observable universe. This was adequate for making sense out of the universe at its lower levels, where physics and chemistry and the other natural sciences dealt with the world.

At the highest level of reality however—the level of meaning and value—we meet a different kind of energy, the power of love. This highest level is in *correspondence* with the lower physical and biological levels, but is not *interdependent* with those lower levels. That is, we cannot reduce and totally explain away

> (1) Agape love and love for obtaining compassion and justice for all human beings,

> (2) the love of art, music, literature, theater, the dance, architecture, interior design, landscaping, the development of parklands and nature preserves, and so on,

> (3) and also the love of scientific knowledge and the scientist's delight in creativity and discovery,

by trying to portray love as the blind movement of subatomic particles and biochemical processes *and nothing more*. If love were not a real force and a real power, all those generations of scientists would never have devoted their lives to discovering these subatomic particles and biochemical processes.

Glenn F. Chesnut

We must therefore regard the ground of being as the creator of love and the possibility of love in the rest of the universe. This too is part of what we are talking about when we speak of the ground, at its third level or hypostasis, as being the Energetikos, *that which gives energy and vitality and the power to be creative and do productive work* to everything else which exists.

The third hypostasis as the divine love itself

When we are speaking of the kind of energy which appears in the formulas of the physicists (like Einstein's famous $E = mc^2$ equation), we know that this kind of physical energy cannot be part of the ground of being. Because otherwise, the ground of being would be subject to the second law of thermodynamics, the principle of entropy, and would have long ago run out of usable energy, at some time back in an infinite past. This present universe could never have been created in the Big Bang 13.7 billion years ago, because the ground of being would already have been dead at an infinite time before that. Therefore, to avoid confusion, we have been careful to call the third hypostasis *not* Energeia, the divine energy itself, but the Energetikos, the source and creator of mass-energy in Einstein's sense.

But when we begin speaking of love as a kind of energy (operating at the highest level of reality, at the level of meaning and value) we have a different kind of situation. Love is not subject to the laws of thermodynamics. If I have a supply of physical energy (say a box containing one hundred flashlight batteries, or a drum containing fifty gallons of gasoline) and I begin giving this away to other people and letting them use it, eventually all my supply of energy will run out. But love is a kind of energy where I have to give it away to keep it! If I give my love to other people, projects, and things in the right kind of way, I will find that my own inner supply of love will in fact grow larger and stronger.

And there is an additional truth, spoken with great clarity in the First Letter of John in the New Testament (4:10 and 19):

302

In this is love, not that we loved God but that he loved us.

We love because he first loved us.

The only way to teach someone else to love, is to love that person oneself. Parents teach their children to love by loving their children. Teachers teach their students to love physics by loving physics themselves, and by loving and caring enough for their students to patiently teach them how to love physics too (or playing the violin or basketball or mathematics or what have you).

How could God create a universe in which some of his creatures were able to love with a truly deep and powerful love, unless God too felt love, and could show love to his creatures in innumerable kinds of ways? As it also says in the First Letter of John (4:7-8),

> Love is from God; everyone who loves is born of God and knows God. Whoever does not love does not know God, for *God is love.*

It was St. Augustine, at the end of the Late Roman period, who first identified Plato's higher Eros (the divine power of the love which connects us to God) with the third divine hypostasis. Love is part of the godhead itself, Augustine said, the creative power which gives life and motion and continued being to everything else in the universe. That was one of his most important contributions to western theology.

A thousand years later, at the beginning of the Renaissance, the Italian poet Dante was still teaching that same great traditional truth. In his vision of God at the end of the *Divine Comedy,* Dante described in poetic imagery the three hypostases which make up the ground of being, the eternal Godhead:[124]

> In the profound and clear subsistence
> Of that lofty light appeared to me three circles,
> Of three colors but enclosing the same area:

The second from the first appeared reflected,
Like rainbow from rainbow, while the third seemed fire
Breathed back and forth by the other two.

The holy fire which was the third hypostasis, the divine Love, was not only the power leaping back and forth within the godhead itself, but also shone forth its light and heat and energized all the rest of the universe—the sun, the stars, and likewise Dante's own mind and heart, which was suddenly given a new energy and power to go back into the world and deal with life on life's terms:

> *Ma già volgeva il mio disio e'l velle,*
> *sì come rota ch'igualmente è mossa,*
> *l'amor che move il sole e l'altre stelle.*

> But already it turned my desire and
>   my freely given will,
> like a wheel evenly put in motion:
> the Love which moves the sun and other stars.

For Dante had begun writing the *Divine Comedy* at a time in his life when he was plunged into enormous bitterness and despair. Because of internal political machinations in Florence, he had been exiled from his native city-state for no fault of his own, and was forced to wander around Italy in exile for the remainder of his life (his tomb is located in Ravenna, on the other side of the Italian peninsula up in the north, far from his beloved home). The *Divine Comedy* was the symbolic three-part tale of his own descent into a hell of anger and resentment and bitterness (in the first part, the *Inferno*), his painful recovery through working stepwise on the Seven Deadly Sins as they had permeated his own soul (in the middle part, the *Purgatorio*), and his final triumphal return (in the last part, the *Paradiso*) to the light of God's love.

Likewise let us remember that St. Augustine was writing at the time when the German barbarians were invading the western half of the

Roman empire and destroying civilization as he knew it. All of western Europe was already plunging into the long Dark Ages by the end of his life. As he lay on his deathbed, the little Roman city in which he lived was under siege by one of these savage tribes, and eventually fell into their hands. The foundation stones of the church where he presided as bishop can still be seen lying in the sands of the North African desert, but that is about all that remains of Augustine's world.

When Augustine and Dante wrote about the saving power which a loving and compassionate God gives to our souls, they most certainly did not mean that believing the right things and murmuring the right religious phrases would guarantee us that nothing bad would ever happen to us, nor did they think that we could necessarily keep bad things from happening in the world around us just by having faith in a loving personal God.

In my own reading, it has seemed to me that God always loved the real fighters, the people who did not give up when the going got tough: Paul Tillich confronting the Nazis, John Wesley riding horseback on dirt roads thousands of miles a year through every kind of weather and facing down angry English mobs, David the great king, the Israelite war leader Deborah, the prophets Elijah and Elisha, the Apostle Paul being beaten up over and over again but continuing to go from town to town preaching the gospel, the emperor Constantine attacking the armies of the idol-worshipers and bringing an end to the Great Persecution.

What God's love gives us is the restoration of our own ability to love, the renewal of our courage so that we can jump once more into the struggle and fight the good fight, and the restoration of our ability to be aware of all the goodness and beauty and love which still surrounds us. There is more goodness than evil in the universe. Our job as human beings is to help keep it that way (starting with our own personal behavior). To return once more to the First Letter of John,

> In this we may have boldness on the day of judgment. Perfect love casts out fear.

God as the Great Ocean of Love

For myself, one of the most memorable ways I have ever run across for talking about the divine Love was a phrase I ran across in one of the writings of John Wesley, the eighteenth-century theologian who was one of the founders of the modern evangelical movement. Wesley spoke of God as "the Great Ocean of Love" in which we lived and moved and had our being.

We may think of an enormous energy field of love spreading over the entire universe and beyond. As an individual human, the higher part of my being (the part that loves) is like a tiny subcurrent or rivulet within the sweeping larger currents of this huge ocean of love, deriving all of its power and motion from its inclusion within the ceaselessly flowing divine love. If I try to separate myself from this surrounding field of infinite and eternal love—Dante's *amor che move il sole e l'altre stelle*, the "love which moves the sun and all the other stars"—my own power to love will begin to ebb and die away.

But when I allow myself to just sit quietly and feel the presence of this great ocean of love surrounding me on all sides, and allow myself to feel its mighty power running through my own being, I will find myself being restored and renewed.

Discovering a personal God

Is this a philosophical proof that the ground of being is a personal God? I would prefer to describe it as a set of good reasons why belief in a personal God of a certain sort would make good philosophical sense as part of a rich and coherent view of reality. Or perhaps one could regard this chapter as a set of suggestions about ways we could conduct our own private experiments in thinking and acting. When I think and act this way over an extended period of time, and then consider my life from a pragmatic or existential level, has my life gotten better or worse? Have I coped better with my problems and had some triumphs over shortcomings that used to have a very destructive effect on my life? Or has my life instead fallen into greater and greater resentment and self-pity and anxiety and fear?

American philosophers traditionally have called this the pragmatic test. European philosophers would call it an existential test. This is the only way that I know, however, for deciding whether (and how far) one wishes to conceive of God as personal.

The friends of God and the
spiritual marriage

The Protestant theologian John Wesley in the eighteenth century said that one of the principal goals of the spiritual life was to become one of the friends of God, like Moses, who used to talk with God every day "as a man talks with his friend."[125] Some of the early Christians during the patristic period, like Eusebius of Caesarea in the fourth century A.D.,[126] had portrayed "the friends of God" in the Old Testament as the greatest exemplars of the true spiritual life, and I believe that this was where Wesley (an excellent patristics scholar) came upon that motif.

In her book *The Interior Castle*,[127] St. Teresa of Avila in the sixteenth century described the last and highest stage in the development of the spiritual life as what she called "the spiritual marriage." I believe that she and John Wesley were talking about very much the same kind of thing, for as I read St. Teresa's description, I get the impression that she is not talking in this context about the passions and ecstasies of a young, newly-married couple going on their honeymoon. She talks about ecstasies and raptures of emotion aplenty in that book, but always in the context of the early middle stages of the spiritual life—at a point when the spiritual seeker has first begun to have some firsthand experience with the power of God's grace, but at a stage where the seeker has not yet begun the slow assimilation of a deeper wisdom. But growth in the spiritual life was spoken of by St. Teresa as a long process, in which she described the consciousness progressively exploring the various parts of its own soul, as though the human soul were a castle composed of seven interior courts or chambers or "Mansions."

Teresa's spiritual marriage comes in the Seventh Mansion, after years of continuous prayer and devotion and growth, and so seems to me to be a metaphor reflecting the everyday experience of an old married couple who love one another deeply. The wife is perhaps working at something on the kitchen counter, while the husband is sitting at the kitchen table quietly doing something else. And they are filled with a deep peace and happiness, just at being quietly together in one another's warm and reassuring presence. They do not have to chatter to one another continually, but when they do speak, they understand one another instantly and intuitively. Each one knows that he or she can depend on the other one absolutely.[128]

It is important to remember, that when we speak about discovering a personal God by learning how to immerse ourselves in the Great Ocean of Love which fills the entire cosmos, we are not necessarily talking about experiencing enormous religious ecstasies. This is a standard beginner's error. But an important and crucial part of the spiritual life means learning eventually that God simply wants to be friends with me, and then deciding on my side that I want to be friends with him. I am not sure anyone has said it more beautifully or evocatively than Richmond Walker (a recovered alcoholic from Boston who was one of the two most important spiritual authors in the twelve step program) in the reading for February 6 in the little book of meditations Rich wrote in 1948, entitled *Twenty-Four Hours a Day*:

> God finds, amid the crowd,
> a few people who follow Him,
> just to be near Him,
> just to dwell in His presence.
> A longing in the Eternal Heart
> may be satisfied by these few people.
> I will let God know that I seek
> just to dwell in His presence,
> to be near Him, not so much for teaching
> or a message, as just for Him.

It may be that the longing of the human heart
  to be loved for itself
is something caught from the
  great Divine Heart.

Chapter 16

A Personal God:
Meaning and Logos

The second of the three primal hypostases was most often referred to in the ancient and medieval world as the *Logos* (the logical substratum) or *Nous* (the intellectual substratum) within the primordial ground of being. I chose the former word for this book (the word Logos) because it ties in so nicely with the names of so many of our sciences: bio-logy, geo-logy, psycho-logy, socio-logy, paleonto-logy, zoo-logy, anthropo-logy, meteoro-logy, and so on. The reason why it is possible to have sciences like these, is because the ground of being is of such a nature, that it gave birth in the Big Bang to a universe which can be the subject of rational investigation and logical explanation.

So one of the key connotations of the word *logos* in ancient Greek was its reference to the kind of *logical* and *rational* analysis and explanation which we see used in all of our modern sciences. But the word *logos* could also be used in a different way: it not only could be translated as "logic" or "reason," but could also be used to refer to what we would call (in English) the realm of *meaning*.

Meaning

What is the difference between the logic of a statement and the meaning of a statement? Let me give a simple and homely example, as a kind of beginning explanation. We told this story earlier, in the chapter on "The Taste of Pineapple," but it bears repeating here, because it makes certain parts of the problem of meaning so clear. The Registrar's Office at Indiana University where I taught for most of my academic career, apparently got its address somehow or other on a computerized mailing list being used by a women's magazine which was selling a special selection of women's cosmetics. The advertising flyers which the company mailed out were in the form of a letter printed out by a computer using that mailing list, following a formula which had been programmed into the computer. The computer programer had assumed a mailing list composed of entries like "Jane Smith, 214 Mill Street, Middlebury, Indiana." The form letter which the Registrar's Office received started out with their mailing address, given quite correctly:

Registrar's Office
Indiana University South Bend
P.O. Box 7111
South Bend, Indiana 46634

The form letter then moved on to give what the computer program regarded as the logical opening salutation to use with such an address: "Dear Ms. Office." Everyone in the university who saw the letter burst out laughing the minute they saw it. The computer was correctly carrying out the *logic* of the program which it had been instructed to follow. If a letter to "Jane Smith" should open with the salutation "Dear Ms. Smith," then a letter to the Indiana University Registrar's Office should logically begin with the salutation "Dear Ms. Office." Or so the computer's logic told it. And unlike a human being, unfortunately, the computer understood the logic but nothing about the *meaning* of what it was printing in the letter.

Or let us take another simple and homely example. During my teaching years, students would sometimes come up to me complaining that they had tried to look up a word which they did not understand in a standard English dictionary. The dictionary definition defined it in terms of another word, which they also did not understand. When they looked up the definition of that unknown word, it explained it using yet a third word which they also did not understand. On looking up that definition, they were then referred back to the first unknown word.

All English dictionaries which define (in English) various other words in the English language will by necessity always ultimately give circular definitions. And the same will be true of a dictionary of definitions written totally in French or totally in German, or any other language. People who do not already know the meanings of a fair number of words in that language will be given no useful information.

There are those who argue that a big enough computer, which could hold a large enough list containing lengthy enough definitions (along with rules for using those definitions) could solve that problem. They miss the real crux of the problem. The very nature of the defining process itself requires either that (a) the linkages ultimately be circular, because otherwise it would not be a coherent language, or that (b) the linkages will go back in a never ending infinite regress.

They also miss an even more basic point. The twentieth-century philosopher Wittgenstein once said to his students, pointing out the window at the lawn of the college quad, "Are you going to tell me that I do not know what the word grass means, because I cannot give you a definition?"

Good English dictionaries are put together by gathering together a number of writers, college professors, radio and television people, editors, and others who have shown great competence in writing and speaking clear and meaningful English. This committee already understands what the words *mean*; its job is to put together formal definitions which might help someone else, who already has a fairly good grasp of how to say lots of things in English meaningfully, to understand more precisely what a word like "pellucid" means, or "limpid," or some other word unfamiliar to him or her.

We talked about the problem of meaning at the very beginning of this book, because it is so important to understanding the key theological issues when we try to talk about any kind of knowledge of God. In the chapter on "The X-factor in Conversion," we looked at people who had heard the words of the saving message many times before, and who understood the internal logic of the saving message at a kind of abstract intellectual level. But as we saw, no conversion experience actually occurred until these people suddenly, in a moment of insight, grasped the *meaning* of those words for their lives.

Then in the next chapter, we looked at the story of Moses and the Burning Bush. Moses asked God what his name was, because he wanted a logical and rational *theory about* God. What God told him instead was simply, "I am what I am." What will save us is not a *theory about* God, but meeting God and recognizing that he-whom-we-confront "right in front of us" (so to speak) is the one whom we call God. Or in other words, learning what the word God *means*, refers to learning how to recognize those events and circumstances where we can see and feel and hear God immediately present and acting in our lives.

In the next chapter, the one on "The Taste of Pineapple," we talked about situations where we can grasp the meaning of a word or phrase, without being able to explain its meaning to someone else who has never experienced what we are talking about. And we also talked there about the philosophical contributions of Michael Polanyi, who pointed out the importance of "tacit knowledge." The connoisseur of French wines can take a single sip from a glass, and can frequently tell exactly what part of France the grapes came from, and even the year that the wine was bottled, although the taster cannot explain to other people, if these people have never tasted any of the wines in question, how to recognize which wine is which. This expert knows what words like Mâcon, Beaujolais, Côte de Beaune, and Côte d'Or *mean*—in terms of how a glass of Burgundy wine from each of those geographical regions will actually *taste*—as a living experience, not just a theory in a book or a definition in a dictionary.

St. Justin Martyr

The first real philosophical theologian during the early Christian period was St. Justin Martyr, so called because he was denounced to the authorities as a Christian, and died as a martyr in the city of Rome around 165 A.D.[129] Justin had been born a pagan, and spent many years searching for some sort of meaningful spiritual way of life among the various kinds of pagan philosophy current at that period. He tried Stoicism, Aristotelianism, and finally Platonism, all without finding the kind of answer he was seeking. Finally he met a stranger on a beach—we are never told the man's name, so we have to refer to him as simply the Old Man by the Sea—who laughed at all of his philosophical ideas and tore them to pieces logically. And he asked Justin how many of these teachers of philosophy had ever truly found God themselves, and how far he himself had gotten in meeting God, in spite of all of his years of study. And Justin had to admit that, in spite of years of reading books and attending lectures, he felt as though he had gotten nowhere really in his spiritual quest, and that he did not in fact have any real respect any more for all of these teachers of philosophy with whom he had spent so many years studying.

The old man had a strange serenity and power to him, and Justin finally asked him where he had gained his spirituality. The old man simply said that he was a Christian, and Justin began exploring that route to God, and found his eyes opened to what he had been searching for all his life. Pagan philosophy had not worked, but this strange new religious system (only a little over a century old) had in fact led him to God, and done it in a very short time.

Justin used an interesting little trick to try to explain why the Old Man by the Sea's method worked, whereas the methods used by the philosophers had not, and it hinged upon the difference between logic and meaning. He used the Greek word *logos* without the definite article "the" to refer to the general human ability to use reason and logic. The theories of the ancient Greek philosophers, just like the theories of the modern scientist, were based upon *logos* in this sense.[130] But he said that in his experience, rarely if ever did any student grasp the real *meaning* of who God was, in such a way as to be empowered to actually live the spiritual life with serenity and power, without confronting *ho Logos* (THE Logos with the definite article), that is, the living God who spoke to us and revealed himself to us in both the Old and New Testaments.

LOGIC

logos = logic and reason = science and philosophy, and the realm of definitions and theories

MEANING

ho Logos = THE Logos = revelation as opposed to reason, the I AM whom Moses encountered in the Burning Bush, the Word of God who speaks to us in the language of the heart, speaking directly to our hearts, or through the words of scripture, or through the incarnate Christ, or through the prophets and preachers and apostles, and others who carry the message

It is not words-about-God, no matter how well spoken, which save us, but the-Word-of-God spoken to us by the living God himself. The speaking-of-the-Word-of-God is an event in which one person (God) speaks to another person (me) and reveals himself, and says to me in effect, "This is who I am."

Meaning and value

At a higher level, the problem of meaning can often be linked to the topic of value. The psychiatrist Viktor Frankl was thrown into a concentration camp by the German Nazis during the Second World War because he was Jewish. He somehow managed to survive, and after the war devised a kind of psychiatric methodology which he called Logotherapy, which was designed to take people who were caught in situations which seemed to have destroyed any possible meaning in life, and help them find a new kind of meaning to use as the basis of their lives.[131] One of the simplest examples in his book was that of a patient who was an older man whose only son had recently died. The son was all he had, and the light of his life. Dr. Frankl helped the man devise a way that he could devote the rest of his own life to helping a cause which had been vital to his son. By helping accomplish something which he knew his son had wanted to do above everything else, he could restore a focus of meaning to his own life.

Can we see the difference here between what Justin Martyr called *logos* (bare bones logic) and *ho Logos* (meaning and value)? The Nazis who imprisoned Viktor Frankl and many other Jews during the first half of the twentieth century and killed six million of them with cyanide gas and other methods, regarded their actions as perfectly logical. And they were right to the extent that, in its own sick and perverted way, this was one "logical" way of carrying out their goal of getting rid of all the Jews on the continent of Europe.

But Frankl insisted that Logotherapy, as a higher psychiatric and spiritual discipline, had to move beyond the mere consideration of what was a logical way of accomplishing some particular goal, and look instead for goals which had a kind of value or meaning which could make life worthwhile.

People who are sane will find that the struggle of life will eventually become unbearable, unless they have something to do which is meaningful to them. It need not be complicated or sophisticated. It does not have to involve "saving the world." In the United States today, people who are dying who go to hospices, are told to concentrate on living one day at a time. By doing that, there will be things which will happen every day which will make that day worth having lived. For someone who only has a few days left to live, seeing the sun come up in the morning is of infinite value. Talking with one of your children for a few minutes is of infinite value. Smiling and thanking a nurse who is helping you is a deed of infinite worth.

Saint Thérèse de Lisieux (1873-1897), called the Little Flower, was a young French girl who died of tuberculosis at the age of twenty-four, after a long period of illness, but quickly became regarded after her death as one of the greatest saints of the modern period. Her youth and her ill health had condemned her to live out her life in total obscurity. There were no great deeds which she could see that she could possibly have carried out. Her health was too poor to be a missionary to foreign lands, and she was no scholar who could write great books solving all the logical puzzles of theology. So she said that she was forced to follow, instead, what she called "the Little Way."

> Love proves itself by deeds, so how am I to show my love? Great deeds are forbidden me. The only way I can prove my love is by scattering flowers and these flowers are every little sacrifice, every glance and word, and the doing of the least actions for love.

If I cannot give meaning to my life by performing great deeds, then I can give meaning to my life by performing little deeds, but doing them with great love.

The atheistic attack on meaning and value

It is strange—no, it is far more than that, it is grotesque and astonishing—that the great attacks made by modern atheism upon the concept of God have been so often accompanied by equally bitter attacks upon the concepts of any kind of higher meaning and value. What will such people say at the end of their lives? Will they say, "I have sacrificed my entire life to prove that life has no meaning"? What was the purpose of writing all the books, and engaging in so many political campaigns, and attacking everyone around you for all your lives?

Sometimes they try to smuggle in meaning and value, even while denying that it exists. There is no other way of making sense of the old-fashioned twentieth century Communists, for example, who denied all higher concepts of meaning and value, but who often showed great heroism and bravery in their compassion and care for the poor factory workers and oppressed peasants of the world. Like Saint Thérèse, they embraced love, but unlike her, they tried to deny that their enormous love for these people gave meaning to their lives in a way that had nothing to do with their economic theories.

What is the point of studying nuclear physics unless it gives some worthwhile sense of meaning and purpose to your life? What is the sense of becoming a psychotherapist unless it gives a sense of meaning and value to your life? And why, in the ultimate scheme of things, do you believe that understanding the theory of the atom will really produce a more satisfying life, than being able to bake a really delicious chocolate cake? Those who know how to bake truly good cakes will make a good many more people happy, over the course of their lives, than people who only know how to explain the mathematical calculations for the Bohr model of the atom!

The ground of being as personal

When we speak of the second hypostasis in the ground of being as the Logos, we are asserting that the ground of being not only gave rise (in the Big Bang) to a universe which was highly logical, but that it also gave rise to a universe in which human beings could discover meaning in moments of insight, and in which human beings could find things of value which would give meaning to their lives and make living worthwhile.

But in this created world, the only kinds of beings which are able to recognize meaning and value in the higher sense, are beings which have personal being. And the only kinds of beings which are able to create meaning and value in the higher sense, are also personal beings.

Beings which have personal being can devise logical systems which embody meaning, which in turn enables other personal beings to decipher that meaning. An ancient Egyptian priest can devise a system of hieroglyphics for writing about his beliefs about life and death, because the priest is a person. A modern Egyptologist can learn how to decipher that ancient system of writing and translate that ancient priest's ideas into some modern language (like French or English) because this modern scholar is also a person.

But if human beings, who are persons, can devise languages filled with meaning for talking about the universe, how could this be done if the universe did not already have meaning built into it at some level by a personal creator?

Beings which have personal being can create things of value and meaning (goodness, beauty, and so on), which other personal beings can then appreciate. Michelangelo carved his extraordinary statue of David five hundred years ago, as an expression of his own love for beauty. Modern tourists who go to Florence can marvel at this statue today, if they too have the capacity as persons to understand and delight in beauty.

How could the universe have natural beauty and goodness in it, which we humans as personal beings can see and feel and hear and touch and taste, if the creator of this universe was not, like Michelangelo, a personal being?

Not a proof but a suggestion

Is all this a logically compelling and irrefutable proof that God is personal? Probably not. There are any number of ways that a philosopher could wiggle around these facts, if this philosopher were bound and determined to reduce the ground of being to an impersonal absolute. On the other hand, all of these observations make it clear that regarding the ground of being as a personal God is not ignorant foolishness or childish superstition. You can produce a very coherent view of the universe if you conceive of it as presided over by a personal God, and a good many things become a good deal simpler to explain. In fact, I would definitely be tempted to argue that Occam's razor is on the side of those who believe that God is personal. You actually have to hypothesize a whole lot more unprovable things to argue against the idea of a personal God.

But the purpose of this book is not to develop philosophical proofs that God is personal. I'm not sure that can be done. I believe that the decision as to whether God is personal is one which each of us has to make as a kind of pragmatic or existential decision. I as a person, based on my own personal life experiences, have to decide for myself whether I believe the ground of being to be a personal God.

The primary purpose of this book is to show that a spirituality can be built upon either basis—personal God or impersonal absolute—but that either way, God is most assuredly real, and it is time for the modern world to give up the kind of naive and very destructive atheism which began to appear during the 1840's. And the secondary purpose for this book, here in its closing chapters, is to try to show that belief in a personal God is not silly, but in fact has a good many things that can be said in defense of it.

Chapter 17

A Personal God:
Will and the Arbitrary

In a previous chapter we referred to the first of the three primal hypostases as the Arbitrarium. That word was chosen, in part, because the Latin adjective *arbitrarius,* among its various meanings, referred to that which was either *uncertain* or *arbitrary.* Both of these meanings pointed to important aspects of the first hypostasis.

If we regarded the ground of being as merely an impersonal absolute, this meant that we were simply pointing towards the way in which the transcendent was the ground of everything in the universe that was *uncertain,* including everything that could not be predicted in advance, because it was *random* and *accidental.* This embraced all those things which took place by *pure chance,* as well as all those processes in the universe which were *chaotic.* In addition, everything going on in the universe which was affected by the Heisenberg uncertainty principle had to be included here—which meant a wide variety of things taking place at the subatomic level—for that principle introduced *an inescapable indeterminate element* into our attempts to describe natural processes at the atomic and subatomic level, and made our picture of the universe turn arbitrarily "fuzzy" if we attempted absolute precision at the smallest levels.

The first hypostasis, the Arbitrarium, was also that which determined all the *purely arbitrary factors* in the universe. Why did we have this particular set of scientific laws instead of some different set? Why were the constants which we employed in our equations in mathematical physics set at those precise values instead of different ones? We have purely mathematical constants (I am rounding off all of the numbers in this paragraph, of course, because they have all been calculated to far higher degrees of precision): pi is 3.1416 and e (the base of the natural logarithms) is 2.7183. The numerical values of constants of this sort seem totally arbitrary. And we also have a wide variety of physical constants: the speed of light in a vacuum, for example, is 299,792,458 meters per second. The elementary charge—which is the electric charge carried by a single proton, or equivalently, the negative of the electric charge carried by a single electron—is 1.602 X 10^{-19} coulomb. Planck's constant, which plays such an important role in quantum mechanics, is 6.626 X 10^{-34} joule-seconds, and so on. When we determine the numerical values of these kinds of constants by experimental measurement, they seem just as arbitrary as the values of pi and e.

Experimentally, we find that the course of the physical universe is determined by a large number of perfectly arbitrary numbers and laws. But this means that there must be something equally arbitrary in the nature of the ground of being itself which is responsible for them being the way they are, instead of some other way.

Arbiter, witness of all things, and He Who Sits in Judgment over the universe

The first hypostasis, the Arbitrarium, therefore plays an important role in determining the nature of our physical universe, even if the ground of being is only an "It is," that is, some sort of totally impersonal ultimate. But what does the first hypostasis *also* become, if we suppose that the ground of being is not an "It is," but instead is an "I am," a deeply personal God?

In Latin, the word *arbiter,* which comes from the same root as the word Arbitrarium, means a witness or spectator, who knows and sees all things, and who then acts as arbiter and judge of all things. And the closely allied Latin word *arbitrium* refers to an act of will in which a decision or judgment or choice is made. So the Latin phrase *liberum arbitrium,* for example, in both Roman Catholic and Protestant theology, refers to our human capacity of free will or free choice.[132]

So when we refer to the first hypostasis as the Arbitrarium, if the ground of being is in fact a personal God, then this refers to that level within the divine reality where God sees and hears and acts as witness of all things, and then not only sits upon the throne of judgment and serves as judge and arbiter of all things, but also, in an act of will, can take action—whenever he so chooses—in order to change the course of events.

A personal God vs. an impersonal ground in early Christian spirituality

If we look at the patristic period in Christian thought (the era that ran from the second century down to somewhere around the fifth, or perhaps the seventh or eighth century), there were a few theologians and writers on spirituality who spoke of God in deeply personal terms. Two of the most influential figures in the history of Christian spirituality in fact fell into that camp.

St. Augustine (354-430), who was the most influential figure outside the Bible in western Christian thought (both Roman Catholic and Protestant) was the one who developed some of the most vivid and memorable imagery within the patristic and medieval Christian tradition for interpreting the three primal hypostases in personalistic terms. We can think of the relationship between the three divine hypostases, Augustine said, as partly analogous to the interconnection between (1) a lover, (2) that person's beloved, and (3) the love which mutually joins them. The western world was fascinated by that particular image, which portrayed God in strongly personal language, and used it throughout the middle ages. We see it still being used by Dante for example, a thousand years later, in his metaphor of the three circles of light in his description of the vision of God at the end of the *Divine Comedy.* Augustine said however that an even closer analogy could be seen in the kind of internal threefold structures which we found in various aspects of the inner workings of the human mind. A personal God should have something at least partly analogous to the kinds of personal characteristics which humans have. For example, we could look at the interrelationship between (1) memory, (2) understanding, and (3) will or intentionality in a human mind, and see many parallels to the relationship between the three hypostases in the Godhead.

In Eastern Orthodox Christianity, one of the most important early formative spiritual authors was St. Macarius, the head of a small monastery in eastern Syria or western Mesopotamia, whose sermons and instructions to his monks were set down in a work called the *Fifty Spiritual Homilies* at some point during the latter fourth or early fifth century.[133] He taught the religion of the heart, and explained how to develop a deeply personal relationship with God in which we learned to depend on God with every aspect of our being. He founded one of the most important spiritual traditions within Eastern Orthodox spirituality, the tradition which later included St. John Climacus's *Ladder of Divine Ascent* (a thirty-step spiritual program from around 600 A.D.), along with the teachings of figures like St. Symeon the New Theologian (949-1022), St. Gregory Palamas (1296-1359), and others who were associated with the Hesychast movement. In western Christianity, Macarius was admired by some of the Lutheran pietists, and had a major influence on John Wesley, the founder of the Methodist and Wesleyan tradition, whose emphasis upon personal religion, the development of the inner life of the soul, and the religion of the heart gave him an especially profound respect for St. Macarius. Wesley translated Macarius's homilies into English for his Methodists, and incorporated into the core of his own theology the basic principles of this tradition of early orthodox spirituality.[134]

St. Augustine and St. Macarius therefore—two of the most important theologians from the formative period of Christian theology—both taught a deeply personal view of God. But if we look at a number of other Christian theologians from that same era, what we often see instead is a kind of philosophical theology which totally (or almost totally) removes the sense of a highly personal God and replaces it with some sort of abstract philosophical absolute. God tends to be described as Being Itself or something of that sort, and as the Being from which all other beings derive their being, knowledge of which is mediated to the world through a metaphysical principle called the Logos, which is the Platonic philosophical Idea of the ideas and the supreme principle of pure reason itself.[135] Or God gets pushed back even further into the philosophical depths, and becomes described as that unknowable reality which is beyond both being and essence. Everything personal tends to get lost in abstract philosophical principles, and the vision of God tends to be reduced to the terrifying view into the bottomless abyss of nonbeing.

And this tendency towards the depersonalization of God continued in the middle ages which followed, particularly among the theologians who taught at the great medieval European universities of the twelfth and thirteenth century and afterwards.

How would one describe a "personal being" or "personal consciousness" in Greek?

We have been talking (in English) with no difficulty about the difference between a "personal" God and an "impersonal" absolute, and about "personal consciousness," and so on. But if we go back to the patristic period—the formative period in Christian thought—and try to ask what various theologians like St. Augustine and St. Gregory of Nyssa believed on this issue, we find to our surprise that—at least at first glance—it seems that no word even existed in ancient Greek to describe "personal consciousness" in that sense.

It is true that the word *syneidêsis* could sometimes mean "consciousness" in ancient Greek, in the sense of one person being aware of something that someone else knew, but that Greek word could not have been used to translate the word consciousness in an English sentence like "human beings are creatures who have consciousness, as opposed to rocks and potatoes, which do not have consciousness." And the word *syneidêsis* was normally used in Christian Greek to refer to something different from that anyway, the faculty of "conscience," that is, our inner knowledge of the difference between right and wrong, which is something totally different.[136]

The Greek word *prosôpon* is sometimes translated as "person," but that word basically referred to a person's face, or the expression on that person's face, or an actor's mask used in Greek drama. By extension it could therefore mean the role someone played (either in a theatrical performance or in real life) or the personal façade created to indicate one's role (as in the way a soldier puts on a uniform to show that he is in the army). It could also mean the legal right to act in another person's name, in the sense in which the king's ambassador could make statements and enter agreements in behalf of the monarch who sent him.[137] In the orthodox Christian doctrine of Christ's person and work as it was worked out during the patristic period, it was correct to say that Jesus and God the Father were united in a single *prosôpon* or "person" in this sort of sense. But none of these meanings would accurately translate the English word personal when we were trying to distinguish between beings which had personal consciousness (like human beings) and inanimate objects like chairs and turnips.

The Greek word *hypostasis,* which we have been using quite freely in this book, is also sometimes translated as "person" in theological writings, but this is such a misleading translation, that I prefer to keep that word in the Greek and not translate it at all. As we have noted, hypostasis basically meant substratum or layer. In classical Greek it could mean the sediment which settled out at the bottom of a container of wine, or the foundation stones upon which a wall was constructed.[138] Over the course of the fourth century, the Christian church (after long argument) finally agreed that this was the proper technical term to use to describe the three primal layers or substrata within the Godhead. By the fifth century, the word hypostasis could also be used to refer to the substratum of defining characteristics which enabled us to distinguish one human being (like James) from another human being (such as Paul), so it might be used to translate the word person in a phrase in which we said that "Paul was one person of importance in early Christianity, who fought for the principle that we were saved by faith and not by works of the law, whereas James was a quite different person, who taught that faith without works was dead."[139] But that was simply talking about what made them two different people, not the faculty of personal consciousness in itself. So again, the word hypostasis could not have been used in ancient Greek to speak of a *personal* God as opposed to an *impersonal* philosophical absolute.

And in fact, none of these three words—*syneidêsis, prosôpon,* or *hypostasis*—ever were used in ancient Greek, either pagan or Christian, to the best of my knowledge, to describe the idea of a personal God.

Personal consciousness: power to think and make choices

This did not mean that the ancient Greeks were unaware of the difference between personal beings and inanimate objects. What it did mean was that it normally took the combination of *two* Greek words to express the idea of what we call personal consciousness in modern English. In ancient Greek, what philosophers said was, that beings who possessed personal consciousness (like human beings) had both "will" (*thelêma*) and "reason" (*logos*), while things like rocks and turnips did not.

So we can look at Aristotle, for example, who began by making a distinction between *ta empsycha* (living things) and *ta apsycha* (inanimate things like rocks), and then went on to divide living beings into three varieties: vegetative life (by which he meant plants), the kind of animal life which could respond to sense stimuli but was incapable of reasoning, and intelligent life. The last group was made up of living beings who were rational (*logikoi*) and who had the power of *proairesis* or "forechoice": in his *Nicomachean Ethics* (3.1.1112a) he defined this as "voluntary action preceded by deliberation."[140]

And in fact, the two linked concepts—will and reason—always went together in the Greek mind: in Thucydides' history of the Peloponnesian war, for example, the leaders and representatives of different Greek city-states who were present in Sparta, at the point where the Spartans were debating whether they should join in with Corinth in declaring war on Athens, rationally explored the possibilities and consequences of taking different courses of action, and then the Spartan warriors voted on which choice they wanted to take.[141]

In fact, for the Greeks it was impossible to have a being which possessed reason but *not* will, and the reverse was also impossible. Being able to *reason* meant seeing that in many situations I had a choice of responses I could make, and vice versa, a genuine act of *will* meant that I had rationally explored the possible responses before choosing the one I thought was best.

So saying in Greek that a being had both reason (*logos*) and will (*thelêma*) was a very good translation of what we mean in English by saying that a being has full personal consciousness.

A God who possesses a will

This is why in all the previous chapters, I have been careful to put in the guarding word "almost" when talking about the highly impersonal nature of a good many of the patristic and medieval Christian theological descriptions of God. I have said that "the language that these theologians employed when speaking about God was often totally impersonal or *almost totally impersonal*," and used other qualifying phrases of that sort.

I think it would be fair to say that some of these theologians—St. Denis for example—spoke of a God who was for all practical purposes totally impersonal. But if we look at a figure like St. Gregory of Nyssa, we have to be more careful how we phrase things. We see Gregory regularly describing the vision of God as the view into an impersonal and formless abyss of apparent nothingness. Yet Gregory and the other Cappadocian fathers built the concept of *the will of God* into the very heart of their philosophical theology, and in particular, went into great detail in discussing the relationship between God's will and his operations. And if God has a will, and the second hypostasis is the divine Logos itself, then Gregory of Nyssa's God has both will and *logos*, and is by definition a personal being.

When I said therefore that many patristic and medieval Christian theologians presented a view of God which was *almost* totally impersonal, I was referring to authors like Gregory of Nyssa. In his spirituality, the emphasis tends to be placed on the way that the material world begins to fragment and lose its solidity and permanence and reality after long meditation, and on the overwhelming sense of the alienness and total otherness of the divine which then confronts us, and on the way our minds reel at the vision of the infinite abyss of nothingness, and at the total disorientation which this realization produces. But to understand Gregory's metaphysics, we also need to note that he explains the relationship between God in his essence (which is eternal) and the created world (which exists in chronological time), by describing creation as a temporal operation (*energeia*) of the eternal Godhead, where this temporal operation and the act of the divine will which directs it, link the three hypostases into a single divine creative force. And at this level, we have to say that Gregory of Nyssa's God was a personal being.

This idea of a God who *willed* to create the world was crucial to the Christian reaction to the Arabic Aristotelian philosophy which began coming into western Europe in the twelfth century A.D. Some of these Arab systems spoke of a "God" or higher power *who had no will*: the rest of the universe came forth out of this highest power by a purely mechanical, natural process as a matter of physical necessity. What these particular Arab philosophers were doing, was combining their Aristotle with a good many Neo-Platonic motifs. They had imported the Neo-Platonic concept of *emanationism*, where the highest level of reality, the One (the first hypostasis), continuously overflowed with Being, thus giving rise by a natural process to all the lower levels of reality. The material realm had therefore existed from all eternity along with all of the divine levels.

Against this, thirteenth-century medieval Christian theologians like St. Albertus Magnus, St. Thomas Aquinas, and St. Bonaventure argued that God had *created* the universe by a deliberate act of will and choice. Or in other words, these Christian theologians responded by asserting, in classical language, that God is a being who has a will, and created the physical universe because he chose to do so.[142]

Or to put the central issue in yet other terms, those medieval Arab philosophers were portraying God as some sort of cold, mechanically impersonal natural force, whereas the thirteenth-century Christian theologians who opposed them proclaimed a personal God who had conscious awareness and was at some ultimate level a personal being.

The decay of the concept of the will of God in the early modern period

By the time we get to the seventeenth and eighteenth centuries however, as part of the rise of the modern scientific view of the world with its emphasis upon immutable natural law and automatic natural processes, a good many European philosophers (like Leibniz and Kant for example) had forgotten what the middle ages understood about this, and had largely turned God into a distant philosophical absolute, who for all practical purposes was not viewed as a conscious being any longer, or who at the very least was certainly not regarded as a being with whom one could have any kind of intimate personal relationship.[143]

"I am who I am"

At the beginning of this book, we read the story of Moses and the Burning Bush. We need to remember what the Heavenly Voice actually said, because the precise words are very important. The voice from the Burning Bush did *not* say, "It is what it is." The voice said, "I am who I am." As the great Thomistic scholar Etienne Gilson remarked on many occasions, this simple phrase—I AM—is the foundation of all Catholic teaching about God.[144] I would only add to his statement, that it is the foundation also of all good Protestant and Jewish teaching about God.

Atheists are frightened of the concept of God, because they want an impersonal reality which they can manipulate and control, and not a living person who knows who they are and will make his own decisions about what he wants to do. Unfortunately, there are also many religious people who talk on the surface about believing in a personal God, but who also want a set of mechanical rules to follow and rituals to perform and words to say, which will enable them to manipulate and control God. They are equally frightened of a God who is a living person who knows who we really are and will make his own decisions about what he wants to do.

Almost twenty years ago, I had the opportunity to eat lunch with one of the A.A. good old timers named Tex Brown, who had been sober for forty-four years at that time, and was one of the great figures from Chicago A.A. I asked Tex about how we could find God, and Tex said, "Well, there's just two things you need to remember. He's not you. And he's not stupid. Once people get that straight, they always end up working it out."

This is saying the same thing as "I am who I am," only even more strongly. God is not someone whom I can predict in advance, and hence manipulate and control. God makes his own decisions. He says "yes" where he wishes to say yes, and "no" where he wishes to say no, and he wills to happen whatever he wishes to happen.

I am not in charge, God is. That is the most frightening statement in the world to a certain kind of atheist, and also to certain kinds of pseudo-religious and pseudo-spiritual people. But to those who have truly beheld the love of God and the glory of God and the majesty of God, these are the most comforting words in the entire world, the ones which will restore my soul to peace and send the demons of fear and despair back down into hell, no matter what kind of catastrophic circumstances have encompassed me in the external world: *I am not in charge, God is.*

Chapter 18

The Turing Test

Turing the code-breaker

Alan Turing (1912-1954) was an English mathematician, logician, and computer scientist who played a major role in establishing some of the most important underlying principles of modern computer science.[145] In 1936, in a famous paper, he applied the underlying principles of Gödel's proof to show that there would always be possible questions which one could ask of any possible computer program, for which the computer would run infinitely without ever coming to the end of its computations. Or in other words, on fundamental mathematical and logical grounds, he showed that no computer, no matter how large or sophisticated, would ever be able to come up with all the answers to all the possible questions.[146]

Advanced computer theory still makes frequent use of the concept of a "Turing machine," as it is now called, which he also developed in that article (an extremely simple device which one could even construct by using a strip of paper and an ordinary pencil with an eraser on the end). He demonstrated how this device could solve any conceivable mathematical problem as long as it could be represented as an algorithm. And even more important, he showed that any kind of ordinary computer or programming language we could devise, no matter how complex and sophisticated on the surface, was either the equivalent of, or a subset of, the capabilities of a Turing machine.

At the beginning of the Second World War, he was assigned by the British government to help decipher the German military and naval codes. He made major contributions to the British code-breaking work in 1939-42, which allowed the British to read coded messages which the German command sent on Enigma machines to their U-boats, which in turn has been described as a deciding factor in allowing the Allies to win the battle of the Atlantic. The Germans eventually switched to using stream cipher teleprinter systems for their most important coded messages, but one of these systems, which the British code-named TUNNY, was broken by Turing's group with the use of a device which they called "Colossus," which was one of the forerunners of the modern programable electronic digital computer. It has been estimated that the successes in reading German codes carried out by the group Turing was working with, brought the Second World War to a successful conclusion for the British two years sooner than otherwise would have happened.

This is important, because in addition to all of his knowledge about mathematics and logic and computer science, Alan Turing was also a code-breaker, a man who had spent years deciphering some of the most sophisticated military codes devised up to that point, and had in fact, over and over again, managed to read German messages sent on their complicated encryption devices.

When most modern human beings are asked to start paying attention to messages from a personal God, this often seems to them like being confronted with an impenetrable secret code, where no one would ever be able to figure out how to actually read any message being sent. So what better way to approach this problem than to go to a real expert who was a specialist in reading secret codes!

The Turing test: can one build computers that think?

And in particular, one part of Turing's theoretical studies was especially relevant to the issue of whether God was a personal being, because one of the questions he asked represented the same underlying issue: how can I tell the difference between a real person and what is only a machine? This was because people at that time were already beginning to ask the question, could we build computers that could think? Could we create an artificial intelligence? In popular fiction and Hollywood movies, computers began to appear, sometimes made small enough to reside in the heads of mechanical man-like robots, which reacted in human fashion to the world around them.

So in a famous paper which he published in 1950, Alan Turing asked the real question in a way that got right to the heart of the matter.[147] If a device could perform arithmetical operations such as adding two plus two to get four, then at that level, there were already electronic computers by that time which could "think." But that was not what people were actually asking. They were asking whether a truly advanced computer could become a *personal being*.

When Turing and his companions were deciphering German codes, with a war going on around them, no one had the time to bother with complex philosophical problems and elegant mathematical solutions. The rule they had to operate on was, whatever works, works. If a German operating a code machine began doing careless work, they capitalized on that. If they recovered decoded messages (or one of the Enigma machines themselves) from a captured German ship, they used that to help them.

Perhaps one of the biggest problems in philosophy is the tendency of philosophers, on many occasions, to over-complicate issues. One might almost call it "the philosophers disease." Turing refused to be drawn into all the complex philosophical debates going on about "what thinking was" and "the nature of thought," and instead he focused on the truly central question, and the simplest possible way of solving it.

He asked us to imagine a situation like the following. I am in one room with a computer terminal and a keyboard. My computer is connected to a computer in another room. In that other room, there is either another human being sitting at a keyboard, or the computer itself contains a program that will allow it to simulate a human response. My task is to type messages on my computer and read the answers that come up, and then try to figure out whether it is a human being or just a machine in the other room. This is the *Turing test*. If a computer and a computer program could be built which would fool human observers all of the time into thinking that there is another human being at the other end of the line, even after days and weeks of passing messages back and forth, then Turing said, we would have to say that we had created, for all practical purposes, *a computer which was a person*.[148]

Is God personal?

In the twelve step program, the early members of Alcoholics Anonymous found that a large number of alcoholics were atheists or agnostics, and that the overwhelming majority of alcoholics who came into the A.A. program were totally hostile to organized religion.[149] They found that the best way of dealing with these newcomers was to ask them not to prejudge the issue, but to pray anyway, and to begin living their lives seriously on a spiritual basis, just as an experiment, and then to pay attention to what happened. Within a year or two, and often much sooner, most of them were discovering to their surprise that the only way they could make sense of their experience, was to regard God as a personal being who loved and cared for them, and would help them in countless ways. They would often say that the kind of God they discovered was very different from the God-figure they had been taught about as children by their pastors, priest, and rabbis, but that this higher power whom they had now found was a God who loved, who grieved, and who even—to their delighted amazement—was capable of playing little jokes on them and then doing the divine equivalent of laughing at them heartily. He did not get upset if they got angry at him and swore at him in situations that were deeply frustrating. He was always there, and always on their side.[150]

I do not believe that we can prove that God is personal by complex philosophical argumentation, and I believe that it is a mistake to try to build the concept of a highly personal God into the bedrock of our metaphysical system. We learn that God is personal by actually forming a personal relationship with God.

The pragmatic test

If we wish to put this kind of approach into philosophical language however, the best way to describe it would be to say that we have to put the issue of a personal God to the pragmatic test. By that I mean that the most strenuous and exacting way of determining if God is personal is to simply take that idea and *field test* it in actual practice for a sufficient length of time.

Let us say that two engineers independently design bridges, working on different theories. We field test the two designs by building some bridges according to the first engineer's theories, and some bridges according to the second engineer's theories. If the first engineer's bridges keep on falling down and killing numbers of people, while the second engineer's bridges remain standing, no matter how fast the current of the river is flowing, and no matter what the weather is, and no matter what kind of traffic drives across the bridge, then we are justified in saying that the second engineer's design has been proven to be the correct one to use.

Those who have served in the United States military are well aware of designs for airplanes, weapons, and armored vehicles which were devised by engineers sitting at desks, tested in the laboratory and in mock field exercises to see how well they did at dealing with all of the issues which the engineers' minds could hypothesize might be relevant, and then mass produced and handed out to soldiers, sailors, and air force personnel for use in real battlefield conditions. There have been total catastrophes produced that way, and numerous other cases where the new design did not work even half as well as the engineers claimed it was supposed to work. Not just theoretical arguments, no matter how brilliant and logical they may sound, but genuine field testing in real battlefield conditions is necessary, in order to see how well a given device or strategy will actually perform.

I prefer the word pragmatic to the word empirical, because the latter term tends to suggest a series of rigidly controlled experiments in a laboratory-type setting. We see with military weaponry, the kinds of catastrophes that can happen that way. And God does not usually show up at all in that kind of experiment, because of an interesting circumstance that Kant in fact first noticed. The presuppositions we bring to an inquiry can prevent us from even sensing the presence of phenomena which do not fit into the set of presuppositions we brought to the experiment.

We become tempted to explain away what is going on as "merely coincidence," or the most important things appear only as idiosyncratic and inexplicable "blips" in the data (in the way that we discussed in the first chapter of this book, on what we called "the x-factor in conversion"). The temptation in the latter case, you see, is to assume that since we cannot explain one thing that happened in one of our experiments in terms of our preexisting naturalistic theories, that we must have done that particular experiment wrong, so we need to redo the experiment until we get results which we can explain. This is like the story of Procrustes' bed in ancient Greek mythology, where the murderous innkeeper insisted that every traveler who stopped for the night would perfectly fit his iron bed. If they were too tall, he cut parts of them off, and if they were too short, he stretched them to fit. They always fit! But not a single traveler who came into his inn at nightfall and asked to spend the night, ever emerged alive the next morning.

There are other problems too with empirical testing in the way it is usually done in laboratory experiments. We cannot write down data in numerical fashion when the experiences are like the ones we discussed in chapter three, where we talked about what John Locke called "the taste of pineapple" and what Michael Polanyi called the dimension of "tacit knowledge" that enters into all of our knowledge about the world—a kind of real knowledge which can rise to the level of real expertise, without the experts being able to explain in words why it is that they know what they demonstrably know.

But there is an even deeper level to this problem. In the twentieth century, work on the electron eventually started producing quite puzzling and paradoxical results. When we perform a laboratory experiment on electrons, setting up the apparatus on the assumption that electrons are particles, they will in fact appear and act as particles.

But when we perform a laboratory experiment on the assumption that electrons are waves, they will instead appear and act as waves. Which are they "really," particles or waves? It depends totally on how the experiment is set up.

In the case of trying to set up experiments to try to find a personal God, if I set up controlled empirical experiments using the normal assumptions of the present day natural sciences or social sciences, the experiments will actually *make* the phenomena follow the reductionistic rules of atheism. The most I will be able to discover is an impersonal ground of being.

The great advantage of talking instead about putting the question of a personal God to the pragmatic test, and "field testing" the idea under "actual field conditions," is that we can then ask people to carry out this test over a period of many months (and even years), where the chances will become much higher that most people will, in the press of real events, stop over-intellectualizing everything in a reductionist kind of way, and start noticing what really happens when they just relax and go with the idea that there is a personal God watching out over them. And also, they will end up having to deal with *real world problems*, instead of just carefully selected kinds of controlled problems which were dreamt up by the researchers at their desks.

The existential test

The word "pragmatic" has been a favorite one among American philosophers over the years, but is neither familiar nor congenial to philosophers from many other languages and cultures, particularly the continental European philosophers. So let us use a term which is more familiar to Europeans, which can get us to very much the same kind of conclusion, albeit by a different kind of route.

Using terminology borrowed from the existentialist philosopher Martin Heidegger (1889-1976),[151] we could take a hammer lying on a table and describe it in scientific language as something *vorhanden* (present-at-hand). We could write down its weight in grams and its length in centimeters. We could determine the chemical composition of the metal in its head, its specific gravity, its conductivity to electricity, and so on. We could write down mathematical equations which we could use to calculate the force with which it would strike something if it were swung at such-and-such a velocity. The hammer would be turned into a pale and intellectualized object, about which we could theorize and reason and calculate. But that is a higher level abstraction, and is not the way in which objects appear immediately to human consciousness, in the form in which our senses first perceive them.

The idea of a hammer is initially formed in our minds as something *zuhanden* (ready-to-hand) which fits into a context of human care and concern (*Sorge*). It has its meaning only within a set of purposes, emotions, and what we perceive as our primary wants and needs. To the carpenter it is something which can be used to strike nails. To the sculptor it is something which can be used with a chisel to carve a marble statue. To a young person who has had no experience with tools and who is attempting to hang a picture on a wall for the first time, it may be an object of at least mild fear—"How do I use this now? How hard do I hit? What if I get it wrong?" To a crazed murderer looking around for a weapon, it could represent a handy object with which to bludgeon someone to death. And for each of these four people, the hammer would also be part of a wider net of cares and concerns. The first may be concerned principally with the everyday job of earning a living, the second attempting to become a great artist, the third wanting to display proper taste in order to maintain social status, and the fourth living in a world of monumental grievances and resentments and frustrations.

We can go further. The real world in which we live is much more than just a set of scientific concepts and theoretical explanations. I could never find words to adequately explain the quality of the green in the trees and grass in Indiana on a summer's day. It can sometimes seem to almost glow with its own inner light, and particularly when walking by a grove of trees, the chiaroscuro effect of the dark shadows contrasting with the different luminous greens in the leaves on the different kinds of trees and the grass beneath, is something of extraordinary beauty.

I found during my year at the American Academy in Rome that it was in fact true that no photograph or painting could do justice to the experience of walking into the Pantheon in Rome and looking up at that lofty ancient dome. And this would be even more true if I attempted to picture or describe what it felt like to walk through the Monastery of Chora in Istanbul (the monastery of the Sleepless Ones, called by the modern Turks the Kariye Camii), where the tiny gold tesserae forming the background in the mosaics on the walls spark and glisten with every movement of one's head, and one seems surrounded on every side by flashing light. Or how could one truly describe standing in the middle of an ancient Roman ruin and breathing in the fragrance of all the wild flowers growing between the fallen stones which was richer than the finest honey I have ever known?

My friend Frank Nyikos was talking just yesterday evening about "the little things," and his discovery that if one got down and looked closely, the ground outside his home was filled with thousands of tiny little flowers just growing wild, each of them as beautiful, in spite of their smallness, as the huge blossoms of the roses and chrysanthemums and peonies which gardeners worked so hard to cultivate. And in the early morning, each blade of grass was covered with tiny drops of dew, each of them glistening with a different color: red, blue, yellow, clear. Of course, as Frank said, one could explain all of that scientifically in terms of the laws of refraction and all of that sort of thing, but that would be missing the whole point.

At the most basic level, Heidegger said, you and I are *Dasein*, being-here-and-now, in a world in which everything is alive with our cares and concerns, our needs and wants, our joys and delights, our ability to appreciate beauty and our disgust at evil and ugliness, and so on. When we begin turning everything around us into scientific theories and objects, we quit living in the here-and-now and go off into an abstract world which has no direct immediate existence in reality.

And even more important, as the existentialist theologian Martin Buber pointed out in his beautiful little book *I and Thou*,[152] I must learn to see all persons as genuine persons in all aspects of my life if I wish to live fully, which means in terms of my relationships with all the other human beings around me as well as in my relationship to God. From the existentialist philosopher Kierkegaard and from Feuerbach's concept of ego, Buber realized that we must stop turning persons into It's and start responding to them as Thou's. The full richness and depth of human existence can only become illuminated when I apprehend the personal dimension within the other as well as within myself.

So how do we put the question of whether God is personal to the existential test? I must learn to pay attention to the full range of my experience in the world as *Dasein*, as being-here-and-now. I must stop trying to turn God into a *Begriff* (an intellectualized concept) and instead start learning how to *fühlen* (feel) God as a person. It is at the level of *Gefühl*—in the search for the only kind of ultimate concern (*Sorge*) which I can build my life upon which will give me the fullness of authentic existence—that I will find the God who encounters me as a person.

Personal communication between two vastly different kinds of being

Now it must be remembered that if we ask whether God is an *independent personal being*, we are not asking whether God processes information in a way which exactly parallels the cell structure of our human brains with their interconnected neurons and axons. Computers, to draw a comparison, can be constructed in any number of different ways and still carry out the same computations.

The English mathematician Charles Babbage (1791-1871), for example, designed programmable computers in the nineteenth century, built out of iron gears and escapement mechanisms, which would have been capable of calculating complex mathematical computations to 31 digits of accuracy. The principle problem raised by Babbage machines was their sheer size. The first one he designed (whose construction was begun but never completed) would have weighed fifteen tons (13,600 kilograms), and stood 8 feet (2.4 meters) high. A computer which is considered by some to be the first modern electronic computer was built at Iowa State University during the Second World War for use in solving differential equations. The heart of that computer was a hollow cylinder many feet long, covered with capacitors which could either be charged (representing a 1) or discharged (representing a 0). By the time that I was doing my graduate work in physical chemistry and nuclear physics at that university, only fifteen or so years later, we were using far more powerful computers built out of vacuum tubes. Even that kind of construction was going to be quickly outmoded however, since the first small integrated circuits composed of transistors were already being invented in 1959-1961. These microchips as they are now called can contain the equivalent of several hundred million transistors at the time I am writing. This allows fairly small computers (like the one on my desktop on which I am writing this book) to contain an extremely large amount of computational capacity in a very small unit. And there are already experiments being made at constructing computers using fiber optic cables which will use light instead of electricity to achieve even higher computational speed. So in other words the mechanical substrate and the precise mechanisms by which computers carry out the logic of their programming can be extremely variable, and yet the basic underlying logical processes which are being carried out will remain the same.

So we could say that God could "think" without having to know the internal mechanics of how such a personal God would carry out that process. In fact, to pretend to know how God would carry out his thinking processes would probably be quite insane. We also do not mean to claim that God thinks exactly like us or has anything quite like a human consciousness. Surely God thinks even more differently from us than we do from dolphins or eagles or (if such exist) sentient beings living on another planet in another galaxy. What we are asserting is that we do clearly encounter (in prayer and meditation and through what happens to us in this world while we are attempting to live the spiritual life) a higher power who loves, forgives, delights, and makes personal choices.

Human beings and dogs

We might find a useful parallel, I believe, in observing the way human beings interact with house pets like the family dog. You do not have to live in the same house for very long with dogs before you notice that they are independent personal beings. To those who are sensitive and observant, they have very distinct personalities. Even more interestingly, communication back and forth between human beings and their dogs takes place continuously. Dogs themselves care a good deal about such communication.[153] To a certain extent, they learn to understand spoken human language. They can learn to follow simple commands. Beyond that, we had one family dog which could identify the word "bath" in the midst of even a complex human sentence with such precision, that the only way to keep her from running and hiding was to speak of giving her a bath with a good deal of circumlocution, spelling words, and so on. Another family dog could identify a vast number of English phrases having to do with "going out."

Dogs can also read tone of voice with great ease (like small children, who cannot be fooled by the actual words you use, but read the feeling tone of the way you are speaking directly), and they can interpret human body language quite effectively, even though the signals are sometimes quite different from those which dogs use with one another. In fact, it should be noted carefully that dogs and human beings can communicate *basic emotions and feelings* with far greater accuracy than they can abstract ideas. I think people have gotten into trouble repeatedly down through the centuries by pretending that they had received some doctrine or dogma (essentially an abstract idea) straight from God by direct divine revelation. The truth is that it would seem far likelier that I could somehow "feel" that God loved me at some deep and basic level with far higher accuracy than I could ever work out what God actually thought about the doctrine of geminal supralapsarian predestination, or the doctrine of *perichôrêsis* (which allows one to ascribe properties of one of the three primal hypostases to either of the others), or premillennialist vs. postmillennialist interpretations of the thousand year reign of Christ, or any other of the literally thousands of complex dogmas which various human theologians have devised over the centuries—claiming in every case that their ideas were based infallibly upon divine revelation.

But simple ideas can be communicated to dogs, sometimes by signs and gestures and tone of voice as much as by spoken words. And in terms of communicating back the other way, dogs can learn various nonverbal ways of making their ideas known to human beings, starting with such simple things as whining or looking up into your eyes pleadingly, or wagging their tails, or pacing nervously, but also more complex messages such as scratching at a door ("please open this door for me") or coming up with a leash in their mouths ("would you take me for a walk?"). In fact, most of the communication between dogs and their owners does not involve understanding the dictionary meanings in the vocabulary of a human language at all.

Philosophically, real communication between two beings involves the problem of *meaning*. In translating from one human language to another, accurately carrying over the true *meaning* of a word or phrase in one language into another language can be difficult enough—try to translate the Hebrew word *shalom* into English, for example, or the German word *Gemütlichkeit*, or the Italian word *simpatico*, or the Yiddish word *chutzpah*—but it can be done after a fashion. Translating meaning from one species to another (say dogs to human beings or vice versa) appears harder at one level, but in actual practice can sometimes be even easier.

A dog cannot understand the more complex levels of human thought at all. I am not sure that a dog ever truly understands why the human being whom it loves takes it to a veterinarian's office for something very painful, even though the human being knows that the procedure will keep the animal from getting very sick indeed, and perhaps even dying. Likewise, we as human beings are never able to understand the reason why God makes many decisions. Like the family dog, we must simply continue to love God and trust him and not hold grudges afterwards—as far as I can see, God does not hold it against us in these situations if we yelp and whimper, any more than a dog owner feels anything but sympathy for a pet who has to undergo something extremely painful.

Discovering the God who loves and cares for me: the knowledge of long term personal encounter

The way dogs and human beings learn to understand one another at the level of real *meaning* is by living with one another for an extended period of time. In the same way, a human being who wishes to learn to understand God better at a deeply personal level needs *to live with God on a daily basis for an extended period of time.* The problem seems to be, not God understanding us (which he does even before we speak), but vice versa, because the conveyers of meaning in this kind of communication can often be very subtle.

That is why I like to use the phrase, *the knowledge of personal encounter,* when referring to the way we human beings can come to know a personal God. This spiritual equivalent of the Turing test requires time and effort. It is a *pragmatic* knowledge or *existential* knowledge which we are attempting to gain, which must be based on our actual personal experience in order to be meaningful. That is why it is useless to sit in an armchair and carry out endless intellectual speculation on the proofs for the existence of God and supposedly logical demonstrations of God's true nature, and that sort of thing.

One of the problems which we face at the practical level, here at the beginning of the twenty-first century, is that most of us human beings (at least in the industrialized parts of the globe) no longer know how to listen for God. If I am a raw beginner, I will probably therefore need to join a group of people, some of whom at least know more about listening for God than I do, in order to even learn what to listen for. They will show me how some of this listening is done by paying more attention to the complex interactions between the events of my daily life. Some of this is also done by learning how to engage in a kind of prayer and meditation that involves serious listening on my part, instead of just the endless recitation of words to God. A good teacher who is more advanced than you are in the spiritual life can help you understand better how to do this.

It has also been discovered frequently over the course of human history—which is quite interesting—that when a group of human beings get together, and begin with a prayer and a dedication of themselves to doing God's will, and proceed to talk with full honesty and caring and compassion, something often happens which transmutes the group into something far greater than simply the sum of its individual members. In the twelve step groups it is called "the spirit of the tables." In traditional Christianity it is similarly called "the presence of the Spirit." (I am not referring here to the flamboyant speaking in tongues and prophesying at a charismatic or Pentecostal meeting, which is a separate issue, but the quiet work of the Spirit, such as one might find especially in such groups as the Methodists, pietistic Lutherans, Mennonites, and so on.)

When I am in a group where the spirit of the tables is present (the quiet work of the Spirit), if I learn to truly listen, I will discover that almost always at least once in that meeting, one of the other people speaking will become not just an ordinary human being speaking purely human wisdom to me, but will somehow or other become transparent to God, and communicate to me (in human language I can understand more easily) what it is that God wants me to know. When they say a certain phrase, I will suddenly realize that this is the Word of God being spoken to me. A good pastor can sometimes do that in a sermon. I do not pretend to know how God does this—to speak of the human unconscious being the medium through which God communicates with human beings, as William James did for example, may indicate a possible mechanism for part of the process, but still begs the basic question of how it would be possible for God to send us messages.

It seems to be in fact the case that most human beings who attempt to remain in close prayerful contact with God over a long enough period of time—and who are looking for this possibility—will come to the inescapable conclusion at some point that the higher power they are contacting is an *independent personal being.* They finally decide that what they are dealing with could not possibly be the result of some abstract principle or unconscious natural force—nor could it be the kind of relapse into the infantile personification of inanimate objects that causes grown adults to curse and shout threats at a soft drink machine which ate their quarter but did not give them their beverage, or kick the tire of an automobile that will not start. They discover (often to their enormous surprise) that God reacts to them in ways that show that he thinks in a truly independent fashion, has feelings (love, compassion, joy, delight in humor, and so on), and makes choices. This (a kind of spiritual equivalent of the Turing test in the study of artificial intelligence) is what it would mean in that context to say that God was a person rather than a thing.

The important thing is that it seems to happen. If I work at this over a long enough period of time, I will find that the complex of the events of my everyday life, what I am intuiting in my daily prayer and meditation, and what I am hearing from the mouths of other human beings who are deeply involved in the spiritual life, will all start to come together and make sense. It will make sense out of who God is as a person, and it will make sense out of my own life, in a way so remarkable that a person who has never engaged in this process could never even begin to appreciate it. I find my soul being healed, my life being transformed, and my behavior being totally changed, while at the same time I find myself developing a warm and immediate awareness of God's presence with me at all times in a strengthening, comforting, and life-giving manner.

As we have seen, there have been some truly fine spiritual authors down through history who have steered away from regarding God as personal. But I still believe that some of the most precious fruits of the spiritual life can only be received after I have entered into a relationship with God where his heart can speak directly to my heart and vice versa. And I believe devoutly that the deepest spiritual healing can only come from truly hearing and understanding the simple words of 1 John 4:7-8.

Love is of God, and he who loves is born of God and knows God. He who does not love does not know God; for *God is love.*

And especially 1 John 4:10

In this is love, not that we loved God but that he loved us.

God is the one who loves us until we learn how to love ourselves. This is the true and eternal gospel. It is the "pearl of great value" (Matthew 13:45-46) for which wise men and women will sell everything else which they possess, if necessary, in order to hold it in their hands and rejoice in its overwhelming beauty and goodness.

Chapter 19

The Nature of Grace

The early Christian belief in free will

In the early patristic period, during the first four centuries A.D., practically all Christian authors agreed that it was the power of the divine grace which saved us. We could not save ourselves until we turned to something external to ourselves and sought help from that source. It required the intrusion of some outside divine power, coming from God, to lift us out of our compulsive self-destructiveness and put us on the path which led to the healing of the soul and a good life. But these early Christian writers also believed equally strongly in human free will. We had to rely on God's grace, but we also had to make decisions and conscious choices if we wished to be saved.

The only exceptions to this belief in human free will in the early Christian world came in some of the unorthodox gnostic sects of the second and third century. Some of these taught that this fallen world was dominated by astrological fatalism (presided over by the seven planetary archons or rulers), where not only external events, but also our inner emotions and feelings and attitudes towards the world were controlled by the positions of the planets in the zodiac. There was also one kind of gnostic belief which taught a system of predestination, in which human beings were born as either *somatic* (tied to the body, Greek *sôma*), *psychic* (tied to the *psychê*, the seat of the emotions and passions), or *pneumatic* (deeply in touch with the *pneuma*, the indwelling spirit of light, in an automatic and natural way). It was impossible for the first group to be saved, and the second group could be saved only by great effort on their part, for the deep spiritual truths of gnosticism could be grasped by them only with great difficulty. Only the third group of people found the path to salvation easy and immediately intuitive.

Orthodox Christianity however rejected this kind of gnostic belief. God predestined no one to damnation, and all human beings were offered the gift of God's grace repeatedly over the course of their lives. Why was it that not all human beings found the spiritual path? We were saved *sola gratia*, by grace alone, but because we have free will, our own wills also play a small but necessary role in our salvation. This is called a doctrine of synergism, from the Greek word *synergeô*. The verb *ergô* means "to work" in Greek, so synergism refers to two things working together, co-operating in conjunction with one another, to accomplish some goal.

The great Aristotle scholar Werner Jaeger wrote the best description I have ever read of this aspect of early Christian belief, and in particular, shows how it liberated the ancient world from the conviction, found in so much of the pagan philosophy of the period, that all change was bad, and that salvation was to be found in attaining complete changelessness. True salvation, these early Christian thinkers proclaimed, was to be found, not in trying to block change and achieve a static changelessness, but in delighting in a life of continual spiritual progress, meeting new challenges with yet deeper spiritual growth, and going on "from glory to glory"[154] in a life of ever new discoveries and adventures. Change did not necessarily have to mean "decay," the corrupting second half of the Aristotelian philosophical understanding of "the coming to be and the passing away." It did not have to mean *degradation*, because it could also mean *progress* and *transformation*, God and a human being working together to bring that man or woman to the mastery of a new and enhanced kind of life.[155]

John Wesley, one of the two cofounders of the modern evangelical movement during the 1730's and 40's, taught patristics at Oxford University, and bequeathed this early Christian doctrine of free will and synergism to the Methodist, Wesleyan, and holiness churches which have made up one of the two major strands of the modern evangelical tradition.[156] In the twentieth century, in the early Alcoholics Anonymous movement (from its founding in 1935 down to 1948, when Richmond Walker published *Twenty-Four Hours a Day*), the most commonly used meditational book in A.A. was *The Upper Room*, published by the Southern Methodists, so the Big Book of Alcoholics Anonymous (published in 1939) and all of the early A.A. literature which I have read, simply assumes that kind of early Christian/ Wesleyan combination of a belief in salvation *sola gratia* (by grace alone) with a weakly synergistic doctrine of human free will. One will still hear A.A. members make statements in meetings like "sober today by the grace of God, the help of you people, and a little bit of footwork on my part."[157]

Predestination and fatalism in St. Augustine

Christianity in most of its western versions (both Catholic and Protestant) underwent a sharp mutation however in the late fourth and early fifth centuries, under the influence of Augustine (354-430), the great African saint. During his youth in Africa, Augustine had no firsthand access to either the world of Greek philosophy or to the great theologians of the early Christian period (who had almost all written in Greek). There were no books of that sort available in that entire part of Africa. He did pick up some of the fatalistic teachings of the Greek Stoic philosophers at second hand from Latin literary authors like Cicero and the essayist Seneca. And he also belonged for a while to a gnostic sect called the Manichaeans, which meant that he was definitely exposed to the gnostic belief in astrological fatalism, and may also have known about some of the gnostic predestinarian systems.[158]

It was only when Augustine finally got out of Africa in 383, and eventually ended up in Milan in 384-386, teaching university and serving as the Roman emperor's public spokesman, that he got his first exposure to real Greek philosophy. In his *Confessions*, he says that someone in Milan allowed him to read copies of "the books of the *platonici*," as he called them, the works of the Platonists.[159] After his conversion to Christianity, which occurred at the end of this period, in 386, Augustine began writing a series of works on philosophical theology which dominated the western world during the entire Middle Ages and down into the period of the Protestant Reformation. Unfortunately, he had never read any of the sophisticated early Christian theology written by the great eastern teachers like St. Athanasius, St. Basil the Great, St. Gregory of Nyssa, and so on, and his knowledge of Greek philosophy had large gaps. Being an extraordinary genius, however, Augustine took the bits and scraps of theology and philosophy which he had managed to pick up, and created a philosophical theology of incredible breadth and depth. But it was very different in many ways from anything written by a Christian theologian before.

In particular, by the time he was around half way through writing his *City of God*, he declared that the Roman Stoic author Seneca had been correct in saying that God ruled the universe through the power of Fate (*fatum*). Everything that happened in the universe, down to the smallest detail, was determined by God's decree. He said in the *City of God* that he usually tried to avoid using the actual word *fatum*, because the common people thought that this meant astrological fatalism, and he felt that trying to predict the future by astrology and calculating people's horoscopes and the positions of the planets, was silly and ridiculous, and simply did not work. But if by Fate one meant what the Stoics had taught—and they were totally rigid fatalists—then he believed exactly what the Stoics had believed. God had an absolute and fatalistic control over every aspect of the universe and human life.

We could only be saved by means of God's grace, and only God had the power to decide whom to send his grace to. Furthermore, since God was all-powerful, those human beings to whom he sent his grace had no choice but to accept it. The question of which human beings were going to be saved, and which were going to be damned, was therefore completely predestined. We human beings had no free will or choice on the matter.[160] And in particular, Augustine's views on the nature of history as an unending conflict between the City of God and the Earthly City, completely determined by the unseen power of hidden divine grace and control, cast its shadow over western theories about the nature of history for many centuries to follow.

Eusebius of Caesarea and human free will

Augustine's opposite number in the pages of early Christian theology was Eusebius of Caesarea (c. 260 - c. 340), archbishop of the capital city of Roman Palestine, and the greatest Christian scholar of the fourth century.[161] His *Ecclesiastical History*, which told the story of the first three centuries of the Christian religion, along with his other historical writings, almost completely dominated the way history was written in the western world for over a thousand years to follow. His *Chronicle* was still our major source for most of the dates of historical events and people's lives in the study of ancient history in general (including Greek, Roman, and ancient near eastern history) until past the middle of the twentieth century.

Eusebius was a librarian in the great library in Caesarea, one of the two or three most important libraries in the ancient world, when the Great Persecution was begun by the Roman emperor Diocletian in 303. The bishop of Caesarea, where Eusebius lived, was arrested and, under torture, denied the faith. Eusebius himself eventually fled north to the city of Tyre in Lebanon, where he remained until the persecution ended in 313. At that point, the bishop of Tyre consecrated Eusebius as a bishop and sent him back to Caesarea to rebuild the shattered Christian flock in that city.

Eusebius's various writings give us an alternative to the starkly fatalistic doctrines of predestination and foreordination which we find in Augustine's theory of history. He follows the general Christian tradition of the first three centuries by teaching a doctrine of salvation *sola gratia* (by grace alone) which nevertheless allowed a necessary role for human free will.

The laws of nature

Arising from the rational character of the Logos (the second level within the ground of being), the universe as it came into being out of that creative ground was structured by natural laws (*nomoi*): rules that determined such things as the position of the earth in the universe, the regularly changing pattern of day and night, the regular motion of the sun, moon, and planets, the yearly cycle of the seasons, the geological structures that caused the continental masses to remain pushed up above the level of the water that fills the ocean basins, and the meteorological structures that provided for transfer of moisture through evaporation and precipitation.[162] These laws (*nomoi*) not only specified the nature (*physis*) of each kind of living creature, they also determined its natural physical limitations (*horoi*). That was important to Eusebius's understanding of nature. All creatures had limitations; there were things they could not do. Fish could not live on the dry land because of their natural limitations, while the laws of nature likewise prevented land creatures from living permanently beneath the surface of the water. In the same way, a limitation that was part of their nature prevented human beings from soaring aloft on wings like the eagle.[163]

Miracles and the accidents of history

God was capable of working miracles, where instead of events taking place as they would have according to nature (*kata physin*), he acted to make something else happen instead.[164] He would make human beings hear his voice talking inside their heads. He could show them a vision of the divine light shining all around them, something which was beyond our normal human limitations.

The commonest way however in which God made special interventions in the course of history was not through performing miracles, but through arranging *ta symbebêkota*, the "accidents" of history, as Eusebius called them. He got this technical term from the philosopher Aristotle, who had used it in his *Physics* in his analysis of the role of chance in nature. Aristotle had said that, in the analysis of cause and effect in natural processes, "Fortune is an accidental cause," *hê tychê aitia kata symbebêkos.*[165]

The cosmos as a whole was made up of countless natural entities, each one attempting to carry out its own natural processes: acorns growing into oaks, fish swimming under the water, land animals breathing air, planets moving through the heavens. Insofar as each entity was following its own laws (*nomoi*), the laws of nature formed a structure of universal specifications that unified the whole cosmos at an abstract level.[166] But the impingement of the concrete natural activity of one concrete natural entity on the concrete natural activity of another concrete natural entity was "accidental." If a squirrel came upon an acorn and ate it, this was an "accident," from the acorn's point of view at any rate. Since the cosmos was made up of countless natural entities of this sort, each struggling to go its own way according to its own natural behavioral patterns and sequences, the progress through time of the cosmos as a whole was constituted of the accidental *conjunctures* of these countless individual natural processes.[167]

A squirrel happens upon an acorn and eats it. A giant meteorite collides with earth and the resultant dust clouds cause a global chilling which kills off millions of species of plants and animals. In East Asia about 15,000 years ago, human beings domesticated some of the local wolves, and modern domesticated dogs (in all parts of the world) are descended from those first dogs. The flap of a butterfly's wings in Brazil sets off a tornado in Texas, or at least a famous meteorologist once calculated that this was theoretically possible.[168] Had Mark Antony and Queen Cleopatra of Egypt not fallen in love with one another, the history of the entire Mediterranean world in the first century B.C. would have been quite different. These conjunctures or accidents or synchronicities—call them what we will—can shape the course both of the physical universe and of human history in amazing ways.

Eusebius's technical term, *ta symbebêkota*, meant "chance events" or "accidents" of this sort. But what made the term particularly useful was that it was the perfect participle of the verb *symbainô*, "to happen," which meant that the participle could also be translated literally as "those things that have happened." So the *symbebêkota* were, to Eusebius, those aspects of the historical context in which a person found himself or herself at any given moment, *as that historical situation had been created by the sum of all the things that had happened in the past.*[169]

This meant that, in existentialist language, the *symbebêkota* furnished the basis of our fundamental existence itself as that-into-which-we-had-been-thrown. None of us ever had the freedom to project our future onto just any kind of ultimate-for-the-sake-of-which that might pop into our heads. It was in the context of our *thrownness* at any given time that each one of us—if we wished to live authentically in that moment—had to devise and live out a *destiny* which was the organic working out of that specific and unique life situation.

General providence and the general graciousness of the universe

Eusebius used this kind of analysis to make a distinction much like the one made by later theologians between "general" and "special" providence: (1) By means of the laws of nature, God exercised a general provision for what took place in the universe. (2) Through miracles and through his control of the accidents of history, God dealt with specific individuals in specific situations in acts of special providence.

Those who believe in a God who is only an impersonal absolute can speak in terms of a general providence, but of course have to deny any kind of special providence. Nevertheless, even then, those who regard God as only an impersonal (or largely impersonal) absolute can use the concept of a general providence carried out through the workings of the laws of nature, to speak of a kind of divine grace which is a sort of "general graciousness" operating through the general workings of the universe.

Emmet Fox and New Thought:
a universal power of grace

We can use the kind of theology which is called New Thought to give good examples of the way in which the universal laws of nature can be regarded as powerful vehicles of grace and healing. Emmet Fox (1886-1951), who was a pastor in the Divine Science Church, was one of the most famous teachers of New Thought during the first part of the twentieth century. His book on Jesus' Sermon on the Mount—a spiritual classic that had an enormous influence on the early Alcoholics Anonymous and twelve step movement—is still widely read today.[170] *As a Man Thinketh* by James Allen (1864-1912) was another much read New Thought book which took the same basic position.[171] *A Course in Miracles*, as developed by psychologists Helen Schucman and William Thetford during the 1960's and 70's, was a later development within that same basic tradition, although this teaching is often described as New Age rather than New Thought.

But let us stick to Emmet Fox's teaching. If I might explain his position in my own words, he argues that just as the physical world has its unbreakable laws of cause and consequence, so too does the spiritual dimension. If we want to lead a good spiritual life, we have to learn how to live in harmony with the laws of that realm, which also are in fact scientific laws—the denomination to which he belonged called itself quite deliberately the Divine *Science* Church—and these laws can be scientifically *demonstrated* in the same way as the laws of physics.

Now if I break my arm, the laws of nature provide for the healing of that broken bone as part of a natural healing process. I may need to put a splint or cast on that arm to hold the broken ends together for several weeks, in order to allow for the natural healing process to occur. But it is important to note that physicians do not heal broken arms, they merely help the natural healing process go as smoothly as possible. The same observation applies if I cut my arm. If the cut is extremely deep, it might be helpful to have a physician put stitches in it, but even then, it is the natural healing processes of nature which are going to heal that cut.

In the same way, there is a universal healing power which can heal a wounded spirit. But I have to quit doing things which keep the spiritual wound open. Rehearsing my anger and resentment over and over in my mind prevents spiritual healing, for example, and has much the same effect as continually wiggling a broken arm so the two halves of the broken bone can never heal back together. Refusal to forgive the other human being who wounded me will also keep the spiritual wound pulled open where it cannot heal properly.

Thinking the right thoughts inside my head will not only promote healing, but can also bring me peace and prosperity. Thinking the wrong kind of thoughts however will bring misery and catastrophe down on my head. If I think continual thoughts of anger towards other people, I will find myself increasingly cast into situations in which more and more things are being done to me which make me angry. If I think continual thoughts of love towards other people, I will find my life increasingly filled with loving people all around me. If I think continual thoughts of being ground down in poverty, I will bring even worse poverty down on my head. If I think thoughts of prosperity and gratitude for all the good things I am going to receive from the universe, I will find my life filled with an overflowing material prosperity.

There is nothing truly "supernatural" about this law of spiritual cause and consequence in New Thought, not really, because we can see that these effects are not violating natural law, once we realize that spiritual laws are just as real as the kind of laws of nature which physicists study.

There are many other ways also in which we can encourage people to turn to a kind of universal power of grace, which is built into the laws of nature and the very structure of the universe itself. Every good physician whom I have ever asked has given me their observations on the profound effect which their patients' mental states have on their recovery rates. They tell me how they have had patients die whom modern medical science could otherwise have healed, because these patients gave up their will to live. And contrariwise, patients who were willing to fight to live could often pull through when all the normal medical odds seemed against them. What are apparently very simple things can sometimes have major effects: important studies, for example, have shown that patients who have just undergone surgery and are put into a recovery room with a window where they can see the world outside the hospital, have a higher survival rate and a more rapid recovery than those who are put in windowless rooms.

In the early twentieth century, not just the Alcoholics Anonymous movement, but also the Emmanuel Movement and the Jacoby Club,[172] showed that bringing alcoholics together into fellowship groups, and encouraging them to give psychological and emotional aid and support to one another, could by that means alone enable alcoholics to carry out a much more successful struggle against their desire to drink.

So there are a lot of things that we can do to help people which do not involve any real notions of miracles (where the laws of nature are broken) or any special acts of divine grace where a personal God decides to intervene actively in the course of an individual human being's life at a particular time and place.

The power of coincidence:
Carl Jung's concept of synchronicity

The Swiss psychiatrist Carl Jung (1875-1961) wrote a paper in 1952 entitled "Synchronicity—An Acausal Connecting Principle," in which he discussed experiences in which we observe two events taking place simultaneously, which are related to one another conceptually in a deeply meaningful manner, yet which appear to be totally unconnected causally. At the level of normal cause and effect, we would be forced to say that these two things happening simultaneously was merely coincidence, yet Jung insisted that their synchronous appearance was in fact the bearer of a healing and life-giving message from the divine realm of the archetypes and the collective unconsciousness. The example of synchronicity which he gave in this article involved a patient's dream about one of the scarab beetles made out of gold which the ancient Egyptians used as amulets and placed in their tombs:

> A young woman I was treating had, at a critical moment, a dream in which she was given a golden scarab. While she was telling me this dream I sat with my back to the closed window. Suddenly I heard a noise behind me, like a gentle tapping. I turned round and saw a flying insect knocking against the window-pane from outside. I opened the window and caught the creature in the air as it flew in.

It was a large European beetle, not a scarab, but belonging to the same family. Now up to that point, Jung had been having difficulty in working with the young woman because she was such a total rationalist. She had been steadfastly denying the reality of symbolic meanings and irrational urges and unconscious forces operating within the mind. He had been trying to explain to her that the scarab in Egyptian mythology was one of the classic symbols of rebirth, where new life comes out of death and decay, and what we have been rejecting as "excrement" in our lives.

But suddenly Jung was able to thrust into her sight this large insect with its iridescent metallic shell: the symbol within her dream suddenly appearing in real life. The shock effect of this suddenly made her realize that the realm of feelings, emotions, and the kinds of knowledge which could only be represented in symbols and archetypes, was completely real. From that point on, she was able to start coming into contact with her own unconscious, and raising to the level of consciousness those pieces of knowledge which she had to have in order to heal and find a happy life.

When Jung spoke of synchronicity, it is important to note that he was not talking about just any kind of odd coincidence, but something that he had observed happening when patients were involved in productive therapy, and when people living the spiritual life were deeply engaged in a program of continuous spiritual growth. Synchronicity was one of the ways, in that kind of context, that reality gave us "messages." That is, it was one of the ways that the transcendent world attempted to communicate with us in ways that would heal our souls if we were willing to heed the content of these messages.

"Coincidence" and divine grace in the twelve step program: Father Ralph Pfau

In the twelve step program, people find that what Eusebius of Caesarea called *ta symbebêkota* (the accidents of history) are deeply interwoven into the fabric of the spiritual life. One vivid example of this comes from the story of the way that Ralph Pfau came into the Alcoholics Anonymous program. Father Ralph, the first Roman Catholic priest to get sober in A.A., was a priest in southern Indiana, and one of the four most published early A.A. authors.[173]

The year was 1943, and Ralph, who was thirty-eight, had been getting in trouble because of his drinking ever since he was ordained to the priesthood.[174] From May to October of that year, he had been sent to a sanitarium in Wisconsin to see if the psychiatrists there could help him. After giving him a series of shock treatments by running 1,000 milliamps of 110-volt AC current through his brain (enough to light up a one hundred watt incandescent light bulb) they had released him, saying that they had done all that they knew how to do.

The bishop of Indianapolis had now sent Father Ralph to be one of the assistant pastors at St. Joan of Arc parish in Indianapolis. He had only been in his new post for a week or two, when a friend offered him a drink, and he accepted. He was a full-fledged alcoholic by now, and that one drink was all that was required to send him off on the kind of nonstop extended binge drinking where he drank himself into a total blackout. When he finally came to, unable to account for where he had been or what he had done during that period of time, he became truly frightened.

He went to see one doctor who gave him such a large dose of Benzedrine, that he was out of his mind for two hours. Then he went to another doctor, who gave him barbital instead, which made him see brightly colored pictures of imaginary scenes, much like the hallucinations produced by LSD (lysergic acid diethylamide), the illegal drug which was used by hippies of the 1960's. Somehow or other Ralph managed to avoid drinking, because he was even more frightened of going into another alcoholic blackout than he was of the effects of these drugs. But the craving for a drink was still obsessing him, and he had still never found any way of defeating the desire for alcohol except by turning to drugs instead.

Then something very odd occurred. We could call it coincidence, or an accident, or an example of what Carl Jung called synchronicity. Ralph was called at two o'clock one morning to give the last rites to a man who was supposed to be dying. It turned out the man was not dying, but had just passed out from combining alcohol with barbitals. This was an ominous message to Ralph, who had been playing with doing exactly the same thing—drinking while also taking the barbitals that his physician had prescribed for him to "calm him down." And then as he was leaving the man's home, he saw a book on the mantel in the living room with the curious title *Alcoholics Anonymous*. This was the so-called Big Book, which described the A.A. way of dealing with alcoholism, which had only been published four years earlier in 1939, and was still not widely known. When he picked it up to look at it, the man's family told him to go ahead and take the book with him if he was interested, so he carried it back to the rectory, and there at three o'clock in the morning started reading it. He could not put it down until he had finished the whole book.

For the next three or four weeks, Ralph read the Big Book through at least once a day, sometimes twice. And he didn't drink. Something very strange was happening. He also noticed that there were A.A. pamphlets set out on a side table in the vestibule of the rectory. When he inquired, he was told that they had been left there by a good Irish Catholic named Doherty Sheerin, who was a wonderfully fine man, the other priests all said, a retired manufacturer. Ralph started reading these pamphlets too, and they gripped him the same way the Big Book had: "They told stark, simple stories of despair and hopelessness and terror and defeat," but also—even more importantly—announced a way out of the horror. So finally on November 10, 1943 (the evening of his thirty-ninth birthday) Ralph phoned Dohr, who came over to the rectory, and talked the priest into going to an A.A. meeting. The next one would be on Thursday night, at 8 p.m., at a small branch library called the Rauh Library. A.A. in Indianapolis was still small and struggling; there were only seven people at the meeting.

But Ralph was now on the path which God had intended for him. He never drank again, and died sober twenty-four years later on February 19, 1967, after helping A.A. to spread and grow from that tiny handful of groups that had been formed by 1943. He ended up aiding thousands and thousands of alcoholics, not just in Indiana, but all over the United States and Canada, and ultimately all over the world.

It was the pure coincidence, if that is the way that you would like to view it, of visiting the home of a man who almost died from mixing alcohol with the same kind of drugs that he was taking, a man who just accidently happened to have a copy of the A.A. Big Book sitting on his mantel. Or you can read it as a healing and life-giving message having been sent from God and the divine realm. Father Ralph heard the message, took it seriously, and it saved his life.

The understanding of apparent coincidence in the twelve step program

A.A. people, and people in other twelve step programs like Al-Anon, talk about the role of these synchronicities and accidents on a regular basis. The oldtimers, for example, may point to something which just happened in a newcomer's life, and then say with a big smile, "Coincidence?" And if the newcomer wishes to argue that this was all it was, just a coincidence, the oldtimers simply smile again, and shrug, and refuse to argue, and just walk away still smiling. Taken one at a time, there is no way that one could "prove" scientifically that a particular synchronicity was anything other than pure coincidence.

The problem with that approach however, is that among those who are truly working the twelve step program with real dedication, there are entirely too many of these coincidences for them to be coincidences. It is not just Father Ralph Pfau's story of how he came into the twelve step program where this sort of thing happened. If one goes to twelve step meetings for a long enough time, one will hear hundreds and hundreds of people tell how they too came into the twelve step program under circumstances where there were also some quite extraordinary coincidences.

People who are newcomers to the program regularly experience the phenomenon where they go to three or four meetings in a row, attending different groups in different parts of town, but find that the topic to be discussed is exactly the same in each of these meetings. Perhaps the topic which keeps on being repeated is tolerance for other people's opinions, or learning how to quit exploding with rage when I do not receive instant gratification for one of my desires, or doing the fourth step (which is always painful, but necessary for continuance and growth in recovery). When a newcomer comments on this, the oldtimers will smile and comment, "Perhaps God is trying to send you a message?"

Newcomers to A.A. and Al-Anon are told, "When the student is ready, the teacher will appear." And I may need to spend two years, five years, or ten years working the program before I become ready to deal with one of the aspects of my life. If I feel like I am spinning my wheels in one particular area, it may be that it is simply not time yet for me to deal with that issue. But in a strange fashion, at precisely the right moment, when I finally reach that point of readiness, someone new will appear who knows exactly how to teach me what I need to learn next. The important thing to remember is, that this will be the time when I will need to throw myself wholeheartedly and without reservation into that next major learning experience of my life.

The people who come into the twelve step program, and hear these messages, and act on them, stay in recovery and keep on growing into greater and greater amounts of joy and happiness and serenity. The people who scoff at these things as meaningless coincidence, go around congratulating themselves on being hardheaded rationalists, but their lives seem to invariably just keep getting worse and worse. They end up going back to alcohol or drugs or whatever, filled with greater and greater rage at the world and feelings of self-pity and futile despair. So who in fact is the more intelligent?

These coincidences appear in many other kinds of contexts as well, among people who truly dedicate themselves to the twelve step program. A woman named Sue C. was in charge of a project being carried out by the city government in the Indiana town in which she lived, where a huge abandoned factory building was cleaned up and fixed up and subdivided into smaller rooms, and turned into a place where dozens of smaller businesses could be set up. Sue had a number of years in Al-Anon, and was deeply devoted to the program. Her second-in-command was a man named Lee B., a former officer in the Los Angeles Police Department, who was an equally devoted member of Narcotics Anonymous and Alcoholics Anonymous. After successfully completing their task, some sort of political machination going on in the city government (which was totally outside their knowledge and control), got them both removed from their jobs with only twelve hours notice.

Two days before this unexpected event, Lee had received a job offer from another business which was so attractive that he had already decided that he was going to have to take it. One day after this event, Sue then received a job offer from the city's largest and most prestigious real estate company.

What would the good oldtimers in the twelve step program say? Coincidence?

God is more than simply some kind of general graciousness to the universe, although he is that too. God is more than simply some universally accessible healing power in the universe, although he is that too. For sake of those whom he loves, he can and will control these conspicuous accidents of history, whatever we may choose to call them—coincidence, synchronicity, acts of chance—to send them saving grace, communicate vital messages, and provide them all the help they need along the way. God is a personal being. He has free will, and makes these decisions to send his gifts of special providence to whomever he chooses, whenever and wherever he wishes.

Random distribution and patterns of meaning: correspondence vs. interdependence

The pages of this book were run off (in its first edition) by a laser printer which printed at 600 dots per inch. That meant that each square inch of the page was subdivided by the computer which governed the press's operation into 600 times 600 = 360,000 pixels. Each individual pixel was designated by the computer program as either black or white in color. If one looked at a portion of the printed page under high magnification, each letter on the page (a, b, c, d, e ... A, B, C, D, E ...) would be seen to be made up of hundreds of tiny little black dots.

Now if one analyzed the distribution of the black dots on any given page of this book simply in terms of the probability of any given pixel being black as opposed to white, the distribution of dots on the page would be, in terms of a first-order application of the laws of probability, totally random. The dark areas would appear to be just as random as those which would appear from bird droppings if the piece of paper had been used to line the bottom of a canary's cage for a suitable length of time. That is because, at that initial level of analysis, one must calculate the probability of each event or thing in complete isolation from the probability of preceding or succeeding events. The odds of flipping a coin, and having it come up heads instead of tails the first time one flips the coin, is 50%. But regardless of whether it came up heads or tails the first time, the odds of flipping the coin a second time and having it come up heads instead of tails is still 50%. That is, as long as we are operating at that level of analysis, looking at the page pixel by pixel, and calculating only the probabilities that that particular pixel would be black instead of white.

If one did a little more complicated analysis of the distribution of black dots on any given page of this book, looking for patterns this time, one would soon discover that certain patterns of dots appeared with great regularity, forming the various letters of the alphabet and marks of punctuation. In the English language, the marks "e" and "t" would be found to occur with greater frequency than any other little patterns. But past that point, the marks and patterns would still appear to be fairly randomly distributed, as long as we went no further than that level of analysis.

The fact that the black dots on the pages of the book are not random at all, only appears when we start fitting the letters of the alphabet into words, and turning the words into meaningful statements. *It is only when we start looking for messages,* in other words, that we realize that someone is trying to use the pages of that book to communicate with us.

We talked in Chapter 15 (and will speak further in Chapter 21) about the learning psychologist Jean Piaget and the distinction he made between correspondence and interdependence.[175] It may be simplest to explain the difference by giving an example: physics is related to chemistry by *interdependence,* but logic/mathematics is related to physics/chemistry by *correspondence.* The physicists' description and the chemists' description are interdependent because one can set up a series of logical statements and mathematical equations describing a particular experimental situation using the terminology of the physicists, which are *isomorphic* to the description of that very same experimental situation using the terminology of the chemists.

But one cannot derive the laws of physics or the research findings of the chemists from a study of pure mathematical logic alone. There is a *correspondence,* because in physics and chemistry both, we have to put all our statements in language which is mathematically and logically correct. But physics and chemistry cannot be *reduced to* the study of logic and mathematics. We cannot prove on the grounds of pure logic alone that a molecule of water is made up of two hydrogen atoms and one oxygen atom. Physics and chemistry add additional information about the world that is not present in pure mathematics and logic, but requires mathematical and logical statements as a vehicle for presenting that additional information.

In the spiritual life, at one level of analysis, some events in the world appear to be random accidents and pure coincidences. But at another level of analysis, these events can be seen to convey messages filled with meaning. There is a correspondence between the two levels of analysis, but they are not interdependent.

We remember in the first chapter of this book, we talked about the x-factor in conversion. The stories at the end of the Big Book talked about men and women who were destroying themselves with their out-of-control drinking, but whose lives suddenly turned around in dramatic fashion at a certain point, in spite of the fact that no immediate logical cause was given, at least at the level which a psychologist or sociologist or professor of English literature or secular historian would wish to see. From their critical and hostile point of view, the kinds of patterns and messages and synchronicities which we saw when we were studying the spiritual life were no more than random events and sheer coincidences. What we saw as the periodic appearance of some inexplicable x-factor which momentarily disturbed and disrupted the smooth flow of the this-worldly events, their critical eyes saw as only places where we were still ignorant of some of the things that had been happening in those people's lives.

In the face of that kind of criticism, how could we say that we were talking about anything real when we claimed that God and his grace were acting at those specific places in individual human lives? Well, if one looks at the pages of this book, not as a purely random distribution of black dots on a white sheet of paper, but as a set of messages and meaningful statements, there is a lot of meaning being conveyed in and through the words of this book. We can also note that people traveled from all over the world to undergo psychoanalysis with Carl Jung, because it was discovered that those who learned from him how to read the healing messages of synchronicities and archetypal images, often underwent spectacular recoveries from their psychological problems. Likewise, people who enter a twelve step fellowship and begin working the steps and learning how to read the coincidences in their lives as messages and gifts of grace from a loving personal higher power, make equally spectacular recoveries from alcoholism, narcotics addiction, gambling addictions, eating disorders, and a host of other extraordinarily destructive problems.

How does one prove that a particular method of reading messages works? The proof lies in the fact that it works.

The two planes of existence

My dear friend and teacher, Professor Jean Laporte, once commented to me, that in the ancient world it was believed that human beings had the souls of angels in the bodies of monkeys. Ernest Kurtz, the outstanding thinker of the second generation within the A.A. tradition, made a closely similar statement in his little book on *Shame & Guilt*.[176]

> Man, located on the scale of reality between "beast" and "angel," contains within himself both "beast" and "angel." To be human, then, is to experience from within the contradictory pulls to be both angel and beast, both more and less than merely human. Because of these contradictory pulls, to be human is to live in a tension: because one is pulled to both, one can exclusively attain neither.

We therefore are compelled to live on two planes of existence simultaneously. This was at the heart of Eusebius of Caesarea's understanding of the accidents of history. To him, certain kinds of events, that seemed to be accidents when one looked only at proximate causes, in fact fell into empirically observable patterns when one looked at the overall course of history over the centuries. Eusebius therefore postulated a second network of empirically observable cause-effect relationships, separate from yet involving the same objects as the network of ordinary cause-effect relationships. There were two interpenetrating networks of cause-effect relationships—the network of cause-effect chains exposed by ordinary historical analysis, in which human beings contended with each other and with the elements, and a second, separate network of interrelationships in which a human being stood before a personal deity as a free and morally responsible agent. Within each network it was possible to give a complete (but different) explanation of why the same particular event had occurred: the same event that appeared as a clear-cut instance of a divine message or warning or gift of grace within the "theological" cause-effect network appeared as an "accident" within the cause-effect networks explored by the causal analysis of naturalistic empiricism. The same event was therefore "doubly determined" in Eusebius's understanding of how God works in history—determined by a set of naturalistic causes, but also determined by a set of theological causes.[177]

Miracles and the supernatural

As we mentioned at the beginning of this chapter, Eusebius of Caesarea saw God shaping the course of human lives in three different ways. (1) There was a kind of general providence, where the laws of nature provided universal mechanisms for supplying grace and healing to human beings who learned how to use them. This sort of grace did not necessarily require belief in a personal God, because even though these were principles of love, forgiveness, healing, and positive thinking, they nevertheless operated just like any other laws of nature, without regard to individuals or persons. (2) Eusebius however believed in a personal God, who could control the accidents of history in such a way as to send messages and gifts of grace to specific human beings in specific ways, tailored to each individual person, at times and places which God chose. (3) And he also believed that this personal God had the power, whenever he chose, to change events in ways which violated the laws of nature.

When I was a very young man, I was completely skeptical about reports of people seeing visions and hearing heavenly voices and being prompted by direct acts of God's grace. But over the past forty-six years, I have had a few direct experiences of such things myself, and I have talked with so many other people who have experienced such things, that I now believe that these events are real, and must be taken with total seriousness.

Let us give a famous example from the twelve-step tradition. Marty Mann was one of the first women to gain long term sobriety in A.A. (she eventually founded the National Council on Alcoholism and played a major role in revising the whole attitude toward alcoholism in the United States). But she had to hit bottom before she could start her spiritual journey towards sobriety, and the place where she hit her bottom was at a psychiatric center called Blythewood Sanitarium in Greenwich, Connecticut, at the very beginning of 1939. She had developed a massive resentment at Blythewood's business manager, and stormed into her room, literally seeing red. She decided that she was going to sneak out of the psychiatric center, buy two big bottles of whiskey, get totally drunk, and then kill the business manager. But then she saw, lying open on her bed, one of the multilithed copies of the prepublication draft of *Alcoholics Anonymous* that was being circulated for people's comments and suggestions.[178]

> In the middle of the page was a line that stood out as if carved in raised block letters, black, high, sharp—"**We cannot live with anger.**" That did it. Somehow those words were the battering ram that knocked down my resistance.

Marty fell to her knees beside the bed, and began weeping on the bed's coverlet, while praying for the first time in years. She felt that the room was alive with light and beauty and the sense of the divine presence of God. Now the interesting thing is that even the words she saw on the page were a divine vision, not anything natural that she was seeing with her physical eyes, because the closest one can find to that particular line in the multilithed draft of the Big Book is one that reads "If we are to live, we must be free of anger."[179]

To give another example, a man I knew who went by the nickname Fod, was a Methodist minister who told about how he received his call to preach. He was a young man working at an atomic energy facility, he said, when—on a hot August afternoon—he suddenly found himself standing in front of the judgment bench of God. "I did not see any image in front of my eyes," he told me, "but I knew somehow that this was where I was standing. And I did not hear any heavenly voice speaking words. But I knew somehow that I was being told, that although there was nothing evil about the life I had been living, nevertheless if I continued along that route, I would be separated from God forever. If I wished to continue to live in God's presence, I was going to have to totally change my career, and begin working full time for God. I gave up the career I had been pursuing in science, and enrolled in seminary. And strange to say, although this was probably the single most important decision I ever made in my life, it was the only major decision I think I have ever made, where I never once questioned it or had second thoughts later on. I heard what God was telling me, and I made the right decision, and I will be grateful until my dying day that I did so."

In the twelve step program, I have talked with people who saw angels, had visions of heavenly light, or suddenly heard a voice from heaven speaking to them. At the moment when God's grace touched him for the first time, Brooklyn Bob (one of the South Bend A.A. old timers) says that he felt a feeling of incredible warmth sweeping through his entire body.

But particular acts of God's grace may come in subtler form, by way of an insistent, inexplicable prodding coming into my mind somehow, where something is poking at me and compelling me to do something for no reason that I can understand. Chic L., in Goshen, Indiana, regularly told the story of how he came into A.A. He was working at his job, when he suddenly decided that he had to do something about his out-of-control drinking, and got in his car to return home. Just after he had gone into his house, he saw another automobile drive up. A man who was no more than a casual acquaintance got out, and came up his front walk and knocked on his door. He told Chic that he did not know why he had decided to pay this visit, but that some inexplicable urge had seized him. But at any rate, he had had a drinking problem, and had recently joined Alcoholics Anonymous. He did not know whether Chic would be interested or not, but just wanted to let him know, that if he ever wanted to know more about A.A., he would be glad to talk about his own experiences in the program.

Another man tells about something that happened to him a couple of weeks before he came into A.A. He was at the supermarket when he saw a stack of free magazines sitting over against the wall. "For some reason," he said, "I felt compelled to go over and pick one of the magazines up. It was a magazine for young singles, and I was happily married, but in spite of that, I felt this irresistible compulsion to take one of them and start reading in it. I began reading an article written by a psychotherapist which was describing the way she treated patients who were suffering from emotional problems that sounded a whole lot like what I was experiencing. And then she mentioned two books on the subject. Well, again I cannot make any sense out of my own behavior. I have never done anything like this before, but I felt an irresistible compulsion to drop everything else and go to the nearest mall and check the bookstores there. One of the books was written by an A.A. member, and the other was written by an Al-Anon member. I bought the two books and, oblivious to everything going on around me, I felt irresistibly compelled to sit down on a bench in front of the bookstore and start reading in them. This was God's way of 'priming the pump,' I later realized, before setting the wheels in motion to sweep me into my first A.A. meeting a couple of weeks later."

Salvation by grace alone

There is no version of the Protestant tradition which is even remotely orthodox, that does not teach a doctrine of salvation *sola gratia*, by grace alone. Lutherans and Calvinists believe that no human beings can be saved who are not touched by particular acts of God's grace which irresistibly compel them and prod them into accepting God's gift of salvation; our human wills are so deeply in bondage to evil, death, and self-destruction that they can play no effective role in bringing about our salvation. Methodists and other Wesleyans, on the other hand, believe that human beings can reject that prodding of grace, and turn a blind eye and a deaf ear to God, if they are determined enough to turn down God's offer of salvation. But they believe just as strongly as the Lutherans and Calvinists that no human beings turn to God of their own accord. There is always first God reaching out to each of us, at particular times and places, in ways which God precisely tailors to each of our idiosyncrasies as individuals.

That means a personal God, one who makes personal decisions, and acts towards each of us human beings in a deeply personal way.

The Protestants have thought more deeply about this issue than the Roman Catholic or Eastern Orthodox traditions, but in the case of these traditions too, how can we read the spiritual teaching of St. Teresa of Avila's *Interior Castle* or St. Macarius's *Fifty Spiritual Homilies*, to give two good examples, without seeing the principle of *sola gratia* being proclaimed here too? Both St. Teresa and St. Macarius teach a personal God who wills to send particular acts of grace to aid and guide individual human beings at particular times and places, matching each divine action to where that individual human being is at that precise point in his or her spiritual life.

We are not talking here about stories of people walking on water, or the Red Sea being parted in two, or tales like the one about Balaam's talking donkey in Numbers 22:28-30, or biblical references to a giant sea serpent called Leviathan living beneath the earth and shaking its tail (which was what the ancient Israelites believed caused earthquakes). If modern people want to reject these sorts of thing as unbelievable ancient myths and legends, I would have no problem with that. This is not what is at stake here.

We are talking here about a different kind of supernatural. We are talking here about a God who reaches out to each one of us, as one person touching another, and prods us and cajoles us and arranges the coincidences of our lives, in order to lead us—if we will allow this—to the fullness of happiness and serenity. Most grace is supernatural. We cannot explain how the synchronicities are produced, or how God can reach into our minds and souls and hearts.

But look seriously at this extraordinary universe. How can we "explain" any of it? The thousands and thousands of galaxies spreading through space for countless light years. The marvels of all the animals and plants that live on the earth, from the largest to the smallest. The beauty of the sunsets, and the mountain ranges. The incredible mathematical intricacy of the laws of nature. All is unexplainable grace.

The highest and best response to the world is one of overpowering wonder and gratitude. What we are asked to do is to enjoy the extraordinary beauty and magnificence and opportunities for joy which this universe gives us, and not to hurt others.

Choose life and not death. All is grace. All is God's gift.

Chapter 20

Why the Future Cannot
Be Totally Predicted

Scientific determinism vs.
human moral responsibility

From the beginnings of the rise of modern science in the seventeenth century, the problem of determinism has been one of the central worries within western thought. If modern science were to eventually give us all the answers to all the possible questions, and explain exactly why everything happened the way it happened, wouldn't this put us in total control of the world, and turn us into the masters of the universe? And wouldn't this totally remove the need for God? Many of those who were the friends and defenders of modern science proclaimed that this was so, and looked forward with pleasure to being able to destroy the power of the ignorant, hypocritical priests and nuns, and pastors and rabbis, who had scolded and frightened them and made their lives so miserable during their childhoods. "Down with religion and up with science!" became their battle cry.

But a nagging doubt tended to creep into this atmosphere of congratulation. Wouldn't this also remove all human free will and moral responsibility? "I killed the eighteen-year-old convenience store clerk after robbing her of $13.53 from the cash register, because of my early childhood upbringing. You can't punish me because it wasn't my fault. It was my mother's fault, society's fault, the fault of the laws of nature." Scientific determinism seemed to take away all our power of self-determination at the same time that it held out the hope of us becoming the masters of the universe.

We can see the first statements of the idea of scientific determinism being expressed as early as the time of the philosopher Leibniz (1646-1716). What he called in his philosophical system the *principle of sufficient reason* basically required us to embrace a theory of total causal determinism. "Nothing takes place without a sufficient reason," he said. "Nothing occurs for which it would be impossible for someone who has enough knowledge of things to give a reason adequate to determine why the thing is as it is and not otherwise." And it seemed impossible to deny that this was the basic working principle of the modern scientific method.

If we note the sun and moon and planets moving across the background of the fixed stars, for example, we can ask why this happens the way it does. We can carry out careful research and try out hypotheses until finally we successfully discover *the reason why* this happens. This was of course exactly what was done by Sir Isaac Newton (1643-1727) during Leibniz's own lifetime, and the result was Newton's explication of the three laws of motion which lay at the heart of classical physics.

Leibniz vs. Kant

It was the philosopher Kant (1724-1804) who became the most important spokesman from that general period for those who were concerned about the other side of the issue. He saw Leibniz's philosophical position as the destruction of any notion of real moral responsibility. It was that—not God—which was the central problem in his eyes. In fact, Kant was not concerned at all about belief in God. In a footnote to one of his books, he stated that he sort of believed that there probably was, or might be, a God of some sort, but he added that he certainly did not believe that he could prove that. And other than that, Kant's Critical Philosophy was basically an unrelenting attack on traditional belief in God.

But Kant believed that he had at all costs to figure out a way of defeating the idea of total causal determinism and providing for some kind of human free will somewhere, even if only in certain limited kinds of situations, or human moral responsibility would be totally destroyed, and with that, the concept of humanity itself, and what the Boston Personalists would later on describe as the fundamental concept of human personality and personhood.

Scientific determinism and
Laplace's Demon

It was not until the beginning of the next century that the French mathematician and physicist Pierre-Simon de Laplace gave in the introduction to his *Essai philosophique sur les probabilitéés* in 1814 what is still regarded as one of the simplest and clearest descriptions of the theory of scientific determinism:

> We may regard the present state of the universe as the effect of its past and the cause of its future. An intellect which at a certain moment would know all forces that set nature in motion, and all positions of all items of which nature is composed, if this intellect were also vast enough to submit these data to analysis, it would embrace in a single formula the movements of the greatest bodies of the universe and those of the tiniest atom; for such an intellect nothing would be uncertain and the future just like the past would be present before its eyes.

I am going to take Laplace's formulation as my basic statement of the principle of total scientific determinism in the discussion which follows. This basic idea has been regarded as an article of faith by an enormous number of modern philosophers and thinkers ever since. What it stated was that a sufficiently intelligent and knowledgeable observer (sometimes referred to by modern philosophers as "Laplace's

Demon") who knew all of the scientific laws which govern the world of nature, and all of the principles of mathematics and logic which underlay these laws, together with all the data, would be able *in principle* to completely predict the future course of the universe down to the last detail.

Now that little phrase "in principle" is an important one to notice. Because we do not in fact know all of the laws of nature, and we also do not in fact have all of the data explaining the location, energy, and so on, of every nuclear particle and bundle of energy in the universe. But philosophers who argue that the universe is totally determined by the laws of science brush this aside, by agreeing that this is so, but then saying that this is irrelevant, because *in principle* it is so clear and obvious that we could predict the future with this kind of unfailing accuracy once we had obtained all these laws and data.

I remember when I won the *Prix de Rome* in 1978 for my work on ancient Roman history and was able to spend a delightful year at the American Academy in Rome, that there was a wonderful Italian phrase which I often ran into in going about Italy. Some American would be explaining to an Italian how the rules said that it was possible to do such-and-such in such-and-such a way, and the Italian would smile broadly and say, "*Sì, sì, in principio, ma* .... " "Yes, yes, in principle, BUT ...." and then explain how things were actually done, which was usually quite a bit differently!

So my answer to Laplace's Demon and his claims is to say, "*Signor Demonio, sì sì, in principio, ma* ...." It is a good theory, but reality does not work that way, for many fundamental mathematical, scientific, and philosophical reasons. In this chapter I want to begin exploring why total scientific determinism does not in fact work, and in particular does not work the way Laplace and his defenders have claimed, without falling into the traps that were laid in Kant's attempts to defeat the idea of determinism. Or in other words, I want to explain how we can defend human free will and moral responsibility without destroying the idea of God in the process.

Defending human free will
against the clockwork universe

The philosopher Kant agreed with my basic claim here: he insisted that the idea of a universal causal determinism was an illusion, an artifact produced by the way that our minds attempted to create a phenomenal world—a statement which I believe is completely true. But in his *Critique of Pure Reason* (1787), he gave no real reasons for why this was so, other than the bald statement that it was impossible in practice to carry out all of the causal analysis to its conclusion.

A more important problem, however, was that the only situation in which Kant was able to argue for any kind of genuine human free will was when our minds rose up into the realm of the pure ideas, and there chose appropriate categorical moral imperatives by which to live our lives—general principles arrived at (and adhered to) without reference at all to any specific moral cases within the material world of space and time.

I want to begin showing in this chapter that there are in fact basic principles of logic and mathematics and science and information theory which make a total causal determinism impossible in terms of basic theory itself. We must go beyond Kant. It is not just that it is impossible at the practical level to work out a total solution for why all things happen exactly the way they happen, down to the finest details. It is impossible in terms of basic principles. And I want to show later on that human free will is much more extensive than Kant ever acknowledged, because that is equally important.

But most of all, I want to demonstrate by the end of this book that Charles Hartshorne and the process philosophers were basically right, in that human personality and the personhood of a real God, who knows us and loves us, and whose influence is felt in every aspect of our lives, is necessary for understanding how the enormous fruits of modern science can be best appropriated by removing the idea of an implacable universal determinism, and replacing it with a vision of a universe in which real creativity and real novelty can occur. What is the point of modern science, if it does not produce acts of genuine creativity and genius, and if it does not allow us to shape a world in which human beings will be able to obtain greater happiness, and in which love and kindness and true compassion can abound?

Or to put it another way, Laplace's Demon produces a deterministic universe in which we see human shapes moving mechanically like the figures on one of those old ornate clock towers found in Central Europe, where whenever the clock strikes the hour, a doll-figure shaped like a man with a hammer comes out of a little door in the front of the clock and circles around, hitting a bell to tell what hour it is, or performs other mechanical actions, and then returns (on its gears and cogs) back inside the clock through another little door. Or a cuckoo comes out a door above the dial of one of those marvelous clocks built in Germany in the Black Forest, and cuckoos however many times to indicate what hour it is, and then is pulled back inside the clock again by the clockwork mechanism. Laplace's Demon turns us into mechanical men and women and cuckoos who go through life cuckooing and hitting bells simply because that it is the way the gears and cogs make us move and cry out, with no ability to act in any way other than the ways the laws of nature compel us to move and cry out.

That is not only a grim view indeed of the nature of human life and the universe, it also flies in the face of what our own common sense tells us. Sometimes, even though everything in the underlying mechanism is trying to make me cry "Cuckoo," I decide to say something else instead. The history of real scientific progress, and real individual spiritual growth, is a history of brave and insightful individuals deciding that there is something which would be better— or at least more fun, or more creative and delightful—than shouting "Cuckoo" in the way that the mechanisms of the past were trying to get me to shout.

In the history of evolution, until we arrive at true *Homo sapiens*, we discover that our ancestors (even our close cousins the Neanderthals) had great problems in doing things in any way different from the ways they had been programmed to do them. Neanderthals kept on chipping out the same ax heads in the same ways for thousands of years. They rarely put fully human artistic decorations on any of the things which they constructed. But then the first true *Homo sapiens* appeared, and instantly we have this fierce joy in figuring out ways to chip an ax head in a little bit different way—maybe better, but at least different from the ways our grandparents chipped them—and sheer delight in discovering the bow and arrow, and how to make pottery, and weave cloth, and above all, in finding new ways to decorate our homes and the objects we used with artistic motifs which had no necessary practical utility, but made things beautiful and gave us joy and pleasure. Novelty, creativity, discovery, and free will are of the very essence of true humanity. If we successfully argued ourselves into believing that we were no more than clockwork figures moving mechanically, the best we would be able to accomplish would be to send ourselves back to the cave again, living like *Homo habilis* and *Homo erectus* and *Homo neanderthalensis*, and the other species of ape people who lived before modern human beings came along.

The twentieth century

I should also say, before going any further in this chapter, that it is the discoveries made in physics, mathematics, and logic which were made during the course of the twentieth century—during my own lifetime in fact, or just before I was born—which force us to totally revise the picture of implacable causal determinism portrayed in the notion of Laplace's Demon. I have had the privilege of living in very exciting times, to say the least, an era which has changed the fundamental presuppositions of human thought in a massive way seen only once before in human history, during the period of the Classical Greeks.

Or to put it another way, the Greeks showed us that it was not helpful to recite ancient near eastern myths and say that gods caused earthquakes, epilepsy, and the other phenomena of nature. And likewise, the great scientists and thinkers of the twentieth century, working in Europe and North America—the new "classical period" if we chose to so designate it—showed why and how Laplace's Demon was not helpful either, and liberated us to achieve a new vision of the infinite worth of the human personality, and a new vision of the divine world, centering on a loving personal God, who can and will save our souls and lives when we are hellbent on the road to destruction.

The ancient Greeks, in their tragic drama, showed with beautiful clarity how we place ourselves on the road to tragic doom by our own wills and decisions and obstinate actions, but they devised no ways to stop these tragic heroes and heroines once they were embarked upon this destructive road. In the twentieth century however we discovered ways of halting that plunge to tragic doom. Alcoholics Anonymous and the twelve step movement which followed it was, in my view, the twentieth-century group *par excellence* which understood the genius of the new view of the universe and of spirituality which was emerging, because the Big Book of Alcoholics Anonymous (as well as the writings of the other early A.A. authors like Richmond Walker, Ralph Pfau, Ed Webster, and so on) were able to separate spirituality so decisively from outmoded pre-twentieth century modes of thought without losing any of the ancient power of divine grace and the experience of the holy, and because they demonstrated in literally millions of changed lives that they could reverse the horrifying descent into tragic doom.

And these new ways of looking at ourselves and the universe will literally save our planet, and the human race itself, from destruction at the hands of some of the other developments of the new science which were also unleashed. We will learn this, or we will die, from drugs and nuclear bombs and global climactic changes and the creation of totalitarian dictatorships—both secular dictatorships based on crazed pseudo-scientific notions, and dictatorships based on blindly authoritarian religious principles grounded in a world long vanished, which have no solutions to our modern problems—for these destructive forces too were part of what the twentieth century bequeathed us.

"Choose this day whom you will serve," as Joshua once said to the Israelites (Joshua 24:15). Will we attempt to solve the problems of the present by trying to live in the past? The consequences will be incredibly destructive if we try to go back to the nineteenth century and the grandiose proclamations of some of the would-be scientific philosophers of that age of secular atheism. But the consequences will be equally destructive if we try to go back to an even earlier century, and join hands with those religious fundamentalists who want us to live by the authoritarian moral codes of the dark ages. Will we continue to try to live in the past, or will we try to create a decent future for those who today are hurting and helpless, and those who are going to be hurt in generations to come if we obstinately and fearfully and blindly continue in the old ways?

The two body problem

But let us move on to a more careful philosophical analysis of the problem of determinism, beginning our attack on Laplace's vision of a totally deterministic universe by looking at something extremely simple and obvious, which for some reason seems to have been completely overlooked by most people talking about this issue.

Modern mathematical physics is based upon the mathematical techniques devised by thinkers like Descartes (and the Cartesian coordinate system which he devised in 1637) and Sir Isaac Newton (who published his *Philosophiae Naturalis Principia Mathematica* in 1687 and gave us the foundations of classical physics).

Newton showed that he could calculate the motion of a planet (like the planet Mars) around the sun by placing the sun at the center of his coordinate system, and then working out equations to describe how the force of the sun's gravity compelled the planet to move around it in an elliptical orbit, speeding up in the part of its orbit which was closest to the sun (which was at one focus of the ellipse) and slowing down as it plunged into the further reaches of its orbit. This is the classic two body problem.

The foundations of modern quantum physics were laid by the Danish physicist Niels Bohr (1885-1962) who published his work on what is called the Bohr model of the hydrogen atom in 1913. This too was a version of the classic two body problem. Bohr placed the positively charged proton which formed the nucleus of the hydrogen atom at the center of his mathematical coordinate system, and then calculated the position of the negatively charged electron which moved in an orbit about this center. Just as the sun's gravitational pull tended to pull the planet Mars towards it in Newton's model of the solar system, so the electrical attraction between positive and negative charges tended to pull the electron towards the proton.

In this case however, Bohr discovered that the electron could only occupy certain orbits at narrowly specified energy levels. They were "quantized." If one bombarded the hydrogen atom with energy, and the electron absorbed some of this energy, it could not move smoothly up to a higher energy level, but had to move up stepwise, jumping from one specific quantum level to the next. Bohr's calculation of these quantum levels matched up with the spectrum of hydrogen as observed, not only in the laboratory, but also in the sun and other stars. When the electron in a hydrogen atom jumped down to a lower quantum level, it emitted electromagnetic radiation (some of it at the level of visible light) at the precise energy levels (wavelengths) which separated the quantum levels of the possible orbits.

The insolubility of the three body problem

What is not realized by most people who are not mathematical physicists, is that although the two body problem is something that can be handled—indeed is at the heart of many of the formative discoveries in physics in the modern period—the three body problem is *not* solvable, except in certain odd kinds of circumstances.[180] So if we took three molecules of oxygen, for example, and placed them in a cylinder and then tried to calculate their simultaneous interactions, it would be impossible, because there is no known kind of mathematics which can set up a coordinate system and mathematical equations which will deal with the generalized case of three bodies.

What do scientists actually do when they have to cope with more than two bodies? Newton calculated the orbit of each planet individually, looking only at that planet and the sun. Using what is called perturbation theory, it is possible to do certain mathematical calculations in which we can measure, to some degree of accuracy, the disturbance in the orbit of Mars, for example, when it comes too close to Jupiter, whose gravitational pull is not nearly as great as that of the sun's, but does have a measurable effect.

One can only go so far with this kind of calculation, and the fact that it can be carried out at all is based upon the fact that calculating the interaction between Mars and the sun will give one a very accurate first order approximation, whereas the influence of Jupiter on the orbit of Mars will only be very tiny. And calculations of this sort ultimately become approximations rather than mathematically exact.

There is no known system of mathematics which will enable one to calculate the interactions of all the molecules in the human body, let alone the interactions of all the subatomic particles which make up the molecules in the human body. It is not a matter of not having a big enough computer or enough time to do all the calculations. It is just purely and simply impossible to do so, on the ground of basic mathematical theory. And yet I have read the works of hundreds of philosophers of science blithely going on about how we could carry out these calculations and *prove* that everything that human beings say and do is predictable by the iron law of determinism, moving implacably according to the laws of modern physics.

Philosophers who try to defend that kind of determinism usually at this point say, "Ah yes, but in principle it could be done." No, *in principle* it cannot possibly be done. That is the point: the basic principles of mathematics themselves render this kind of all-inclusive explanation totally impossible. Laplace's Demon is not science, but myth—and wishful thinking and fuzzy logic and evasive game playing—invoked by people who in their hearts do not want to give up the fantasy of someday being able to become masters of the universe.

Situations in which we can totally and exhaustively predict the outcome of natural events occur only in certain kinds of carefully controlled situations, where the number of variables can be artificially constrained and thereby rigorously pruned down. And this applies not only to physics, but to all the other natural sciences, and to the social sciences like psychology and sociology as well.

The Heisenberg uncertainty principle

In 1927, the German physicist Werner Heisenberg (1901-1976) discovered the uncertainty principle. Attempting to determine simultaneously certain kinds of paired quantities, such as for example both the position and momentum of a particle, results in an unavoidable uncertainty. This can be derived directly from the axioms of quantum mechanics, where the uncertainties are a necessary consequence of the way the mathematical quantities themselves have to be defined.

I mention this, because popular interpretations of the Heisenberg uncertainty principle still sometimes confuse this with what is called the observer effect. This latter refers to situations in which the very act of observing a phenomenon will change the nature of the phenomenon being observed. So for example, if we attempted to see an electron, a photon would have to strike the electron, which would change the path and energy level of the electron. So the electron that we thought we "saw" would not be the electron that was there before we altered the situation.

The uncertainty principle could not be gotten around, however, by attempts to observe a situation by even the most subtle means. No matter what pains we went to in our effort to avoid disturbing the phenomenon in the process of observing it, the uncertainty principle would still block us from exact knowledge of many quantities at the atomic and subatomic level.

Chaos and the butterfly effect

In the eighteenth and early nineteenth century, the kind of physics that Newton and Laplace developed focused itself on deterministic situations in which the laws of science could precisely predict the course of events, such as calculating the orbit of the planet Mars around the Sun, or the trajectory of a cannonball fired from a cannon. In the later nineteenth century, statistical thermodynamics was developed, which allowed scientists to describe systems such as the molecules of a gas in a closed container, working on the assumption that the bouncing of the molecules off one another (and the walls of the vessel) were purely random, and followed the normal laws of chance. But there are physical phenomena which are neither rigidly determined nor purely controlled by chance, at least in any way where we can deal statistically with large numbers of events in situations where all we are interested in is the cumulative effect of all the incidents.

These are called chaotic situations. One example would be the places where the smooth flow of air over an airplane's wing is thrown into turbulence at one or more points, as a consequence of some factor in the shape of the airfoil. This can seriously affect the lift and performance of the wing, so aeronautical engineers have to determine in wind tunnels where excessive turbulence appears with their most recent airfoil design, and then they have to figure out how to modify its shape to remove as much of the turbulence as possible. The problem they face is that neither deterministic equations nor statistical analyses will help them.

Another example would be a man who stands on top of a mountain, and takes a large stone and starts it rolling down the mountain. Even very tiny differences between how the man pushes the two different stones, and the exact places at which each stone hits as it bounces down the uneven surface of the mountain, can cause the two stones to end up at the bottom of the mountain in completely different places.

Chaotic processes are those in which tiny differences early in the process can have major effects by the end of the process, effects which are all out of proportion to the initiating cause.

This is sometimes referred to as the butterfly effect, because of the speeches and articles of an American mathematician and meteorologist named Edward Lorenz who showed the power of this effect. Lorenz was going to make another trial run of a computer model which he had developed for predicting the weather, and since all he wanted at that point was a rough calculation, instead of entering the precise figure of 0.506127 at one place, he just typed in 0.506 and left it at that. To his surprise, the kind of weather that it predicted was totally different from what it had predicted when the exact figure had been used, even though the two figures only differed by 0.025 percent. When he published his discovery in a paper for the New York Academy of Sciences in 1963, he commented that one of his fellow meteorologists had remarked to him that, "if the theory were correct, one flap of a seagull's wings could change the course of weather forever." In later years, Lorenz changed the metaphor slightly, and began speaking of butterflies instead of seagulls. When he gave a talk at the meeting of the American Association for the Advancement of Science in 1972, it was given the title, "Does the flap of a butterfly's wings in Brazil set off a tornado in Texas?"

How does this apply to the topic we are pursuing in this chapter? If Laplace's Demon were to try to describe the future course of the universe down to the tiniest detail, once he got down to the atomic and subatomic level, he would be confronted with Heisenberg's uncertainty principle, and would find himself unable to predict exactly how the atoms and subatomic particles were going to interact with one another, and what their paths were going to be. And if Laplace's Demon had attempted, shortly after the Big Bang, to predict all the details of the universe which was going to emerge, this was a chaotic situation through and through. A single collision between two particles at that point—a collision whose outcome could never be precisely predicted on the grounds of the uncertainty principle—could at times have put one of the galaxies which developed later on in a totally different part of the universe.

Gödel's proof

There is another reason why Laplace's Demon cannot predict future states of the universe, which links with the very foundations of mathematics, and does so at the most fundamental level. This is based on what is called Gödel's proof.

Kurt Gödel (1906-1978) was an Austrian mathematician who published his famous theorems (there were actually two of them) in 1931, when he was only twenty-five years old. In 1940 he came to the Institute for Advanced Study in Princeton, New Jersey, where he and Albert Einstein became close friends, walking to and from the Institute every day until Einstein's death in 1955. Gödel seems to have been one of the few people whose mind and brilliance awed even Einstein.

Gödel's *first incompleteness theorem* has become one of the most famous statements within the field of modern mathematical logic:

> For any consistent formal, computably enumerable theory that proves basic arithmetical truths, an arithmetical statement that is true, but not provable in the theory, can be constructed. That is, any effectively generated theory capable of expressing elementary arithmetic cannot be both consistent and complete.

The kind of theory which Gödel was talking about was constructed by taking a set of starting axioms, which were assumed to be true, and then using those to derive any required number of theorems using standard first-order logic. A theory is consistent if no contradictions can be proven. Gödel confined his theorem to what he called elementary arithmetic, which meant adding and multiplying the natural numbers.

But his proof showed that there *are* no formal systems of the sort he was describing which are both *consistent* (involving no internal contradictions) and *complete* (allowing one to derive all possible true statements from the starting axioms in mechanical fashion).

Gödel's *second theorem* stated in effect that any axiomatic system which can be proven to be consistent and complete from within itself, can be shown on those very grounds to be inconsistent.

Why is this so important? In order for Laplace's Demon to predict the entire future of the universe exhaustively, its vast intellect has to have a formula into which it can place all of the data about the present state of the universe, and this formal theory which the Demon uses in turn has to be used for mathematical calculations, using fundamental mathematical principles which are—so Gödel's proof shows—by necessity neither consistent nor complete.

If the basic math itself is neither consistent nor complete, the Demon's calculations using it can be neither consistent nor complete. Ergo, there can be no exhaustive prediction of the entire future of the universe using elementary arithmetic (adding and multiplying the natural numbers). All mathematical formulas used in physics require the use of elementary arithmetic (and much more besides) to make their calculations.

Stephen Hawking

Now Gödel's proof was, in itself, only applicable to the narrowly defined area of elementary arithmetic. But as other researchers began to think about the full implications of Gödel's proof, they began to realize that his basic conclusions could be extended to many different kinds of formal systems in addition to elementary arithmetic.

One of the most famous living theoretical physicists, Stephen Hawking, has written on these implications. Hawking (who was born in 1942) was educated at Oxford University and, in spite of being almost totally physically disabled by amyotrophic lateral sclerosis (Lou Gehrig's Disease), is now Lucasian Professor of Mathematics at the University of Cambridge. He is one of the great heroes of the ability of the determined mind to triumph over the infirmities of the body. In his lecture "Gödel and the End of Physics,"[181] he begins by describing the fundamental idea of scientific determinism which the theory of Laplace's Demon expressed:

> If at one time, one knew the positions and velocities of all the particles in the universe, the laws of science should enable us to calculate their positions and velocities, at any other time, past or future. The laws may or may not have been ordained by God, but scientific determinism asserts that he does not intervene, to break them.

But the problem, as Hawking indicates, lies in the simple question, "will we ever find a complete form of the laws of nature?" Because otherwise Laplace's Demon cannot carry out the necessary calculations. And not only do we have to find the ultimate overarching law of physics, this law has to give precise and unambiguous mathematical answers. And already by the beginning of the twentieth century, some of the most important discoveries of modern physics had begun to cast doubt upon our ability to even devise laws which would give specific answers instead of mere probabilities and ranges of possible answers:

> At first, it seemed that these hopes for a complete determinism would be dashed, by the discovery early in the 20th century, that events like the decay of radio active atoms, seemed to take place at random. It was as if God was playing dice, in Einstein's phrase.

Although many philosophers still seem unaware of this, the physicists simply abandoned the claim, at that point in the early twentieth century, that the laws of nature necessarily gave precise and unambiguous predictions of the future. Or as Hawking put it:

> Science snatched victory from the jaws of defeat, by moving the goal posts, and redefining what is meant by a complete knowledge of the universe.

Quantum theory, as developed by Paul Dirac (1902-1984), no longer attempted to describe a particle by its position and velocity in the primary equations which the physicist used, but instead characterized it as a wave function. Dirac, whom Hawking greatly admired, was one of his predecessors as Lucasian Professor of Mathematics at the University of Cambridge, although as Hawking quipped in his lecture, Dirac's professorial chair was not motorized like his!

Now if Dirac's wave function sharply peaked at one point, one could at least state that there was little uncertainty as to its position. But if the wave function was varying rapidly, one was still left with a good deal of uncertainty as to its velocity. So at one level, one could say that physics still provided for a deterministic picture of the universe. We knew with absolute certainty the wave equation which was describing an individual particle. But once one attempted to ask the practical question once again, as to exactly where the particle was at this moment, and how fast it was moving, the uncertainty principle blocked us from knowing both (in particular) with any kind of absolute certitude.

Nevertheless, modern physics has advanced so far, that we can perhaps say that Maxwell's equations describing the nature of light, and the Dirac equation (the relativistic wave equation) "govern most of physics, and all of chemistry and biology."

> So in principle, we ought to be able to predict human be-
> havior, though I can't say I have had much success myself.
> The trouble is that the human brain contains far too many
> particles, for us to be able to solve the equations. But it is
> comforting to think we might be able to predict the nema-
> tode worm, even if we can't quite figure out humans.

And as an outstanding issue, there are still important areas of physics which we cannot integrate into our knowledge of other areas of physics. The weak nuclear forces have been unified with the Maxwell equations by the electroweak theory, but the strong nuclear forces can still not be brought into a single unified theory with the other fundamental forces which describe the interactions between subatomic particles. And the force of gravity still has to be described by physicists using Einstein's general theory of relativity, which is not a quantum theory. Nevertheless, Hawking said,

> Up to now, most people have implicitly assumed that there is an ultimate theory, that we will eventually discover. Indeed, I myself have suggested we might find it quite soon. However, M-theory has made me wonder if this is true. Maybe it is not possible to formulate the theory of the universe in a finite number of statements. This is very reminiscent of Gödel's theorem. This says that any finite system of axioms, is not sufficient to prove every result in mathematics.

And even if we could in fact come up with some sort of unified field theory or force theory which would give us a single fundamental formula which would unify all the other laws of physics—which physicists have still not accomplished—with the idea that this might allow Laplace's Demon to totally predict the future in completely deterministic manner, we would still be confronted with the underlying problem raised by Gödel's proof:

> According to the positivist philosophy of science, a physical theory, is a mathematical model. So if there are mathematical results that cannot be proved, there are physical problems that cannot be predicted.

But even beyond that point, as Hawking pointed out, the basic principles behind Gödel's proof would seem to be potentially applicable to any kind of sufficiently complicated formal system, and not just elementary arithmetic alone. There is a good deal of evidence pointing to the possibility that an ultimate theory of science that could be formulated in a finite number of principles—the central goal of modern theoretical physics—might well be subject to the same limitations that Gödel proved applied to the foundations of mathematics. That is, it is entirely possible that *there can be no set of laws of physics* which will be both *consistent* (involving no internal contradictions) and *complete* (allowing one to derive all possible true statements from the starting axioms in mechanical fashion).

The Cretan paradox and
self-referential statements

As Hawking point out, Gödel's theorem is proved using statements which refer to themselves. Self-referential statements can easily become insoluble paradoxes. Hawking gave the example of the simple phrase, "this statement is false." If it is true it is false, and vice versa. Another example Hawking gave was what philosophers call the barber paradox. Suppose we claim:

> "The barber of Corfu shaves every man who does not shave himself." Who shaves the barber? If he shaves himself, then he doesn't, and if he doesn't, then he does.

One could argue in fact that Gödel's proof was in many ways simply a more sophisticated version of one especially important ancient Greek paradox, called the Epimenides paradox or Cretan paradox, whose author was a philosopher who lived on the island of Crete somewhere around 600 B.C. This philosopher, Epimenides, made a reference at one point to "the Cretans, always liars." The logical problem with that statement was that Epimenides himself was a Cretan, so that if the Cretans always lied, this statement was also a lie, which meant that the Cretans were not in fact always liars.

The problem for theories of physics, as Hawking pointed out, was that the physicists who devised them were part of the universe they were attempting to describe, which meant that all of the truly basic laws of physics were self-referential statements. As Hawking put it:

In the standard positivist approach to the philosophy of science, physical theories live rent free in a Platonic heaven of ideal mathematical models. That is, a model can be arbitrarily detailed, and can contain an arbitrary amount of information, without affecting the universes they describe. But we are not angels, who view the universe from the outside. Instead, we and our models, are both part of the universe we are describing. Thus a physical theory is self referencing like in Gödel's theorem. One might therefore expect it to be either inconsistent, or incomplete. The theories we have so far, are —both inconsistent, and incomplete!

Faced with this possibility, Hawking's reaction was, interestingly enough, not despair. Instead he chose to embrace the point of view we saw in Charles Hartshorne's philosophy. A universe which, instead of being rigidly deterministic, provides for novelty and unpredictability can actually be a good deal more interesting kind of universe to live in, because it allows the adventure of our lives and our intellectual pursuits to go on without bounds or limit:

> Some people will be very disappointed if there is not an ultimate theory, that can be formulated as a finite number of principles. I used to belong to that camp, but I have changed my mind. I'm now glad that our search for understanding will never come to an end, and that we will always have the challenge of new discovery. Without it, we would stagnate. Gödel's theorem ensured there would always be a job for mathematicians.

If modern physicists likewise, Hawking said, find themselves with the same kind of open-ended universe of continual new challenges and continual new discoveries, he thought that they would ultimately find it exciting and invigorating. And speaking particularly of the great mathematical physicists of the past, Hawking said, "I'm sure Dirac would have approved."

Gödel and the nature of intelligence itself

In the field of computer science and artificial intelligence, Douglas R. Hofstadter, in his book *Gödel, Escher, Bach*, which won the Pulitzer Prize in 1980, explored a variety of ways in which the Gödel paradox intruded itself into any kind of sequence of logical thought, once the thinker began asking self-referential questions.[182] Hofstadter made the same basic observation that Hawking made, that is, he pointed out how the basic principles inherent in Gödel's proof applied to much more than simply a few little odd philosophical paradoxes.

The human brain, and any kind of true artificial intelligence that the computer experts could build, would of necessity have to be capable of both asking and answering questions, not just about the external world, but also about itself. But the moment any kind of intelligence (whether human or artificial) begins asking self-referential questions—that is, asking questions about itself and the characteristics and logical framework of its own thought processes—the puzzles start to appear. As Hofstadter indicates in numerous examples in *Gödel, Escher, Bach*, the thinker becomes mired in questions to which the rules of his thought processes give "yes" and "no" as equally logical answers. He finds statements where he can correctly deduce from starting principles that they are either "true" or "false" with equal ease. Both can be proven true within that particular system of thought. Immanuel Kant discovered some of these, and called them the antinomies of the human reason and attempted to resolve them, but in fact if we apply the principles of Gödel's proof, we can discover antinomies that are unresolvable.

And as Hofstadter showed, when self-referential questions are not giving us self-contradictory answers, they all too often send us down a path of infinite regress. Each apparent answer to the question requires that I ask yet one more question before a conclusive answer can be given, in an unending process that will never find an end.

Or in other words, Laplace's Demon has more than one problem. First, he is confronted with a universe in which Gödel's proof prevents him from ever coming up with a fully consistent and complete set of all the laws of science. But second, the Demon's very own thought processes are also affected by Gödel's proof, in such a way that as he continues to calculate the future state of the universe, he will find his own thought processes either giving him contradictory answers or sending him down infinite regresses of questions upon questions, to which no final answer will ever be given.

Information theory

As long as we are discussing the matter of pseudo-infinite regresses, it would be useful here to explain yet another reason why Laplace's Demon can never finish his task, and can never give us a complete and consistent account of why all the things that exist in the universe are as they are and could be no other way.

Information theory was another of those marvelous sets of discoveries that took place during the twentieth century, which have so greatly changed our view of the world. It initially arose in the study of the engineering problem of the transmission of information over a noisy channel. Its origins lay in an article entitled "A Mathematical Theory of Communication," which was published in 1948 by an American electrical engineer and mathematician named Claude E. Shannon (1916-2001) who was working at the Bell Telephone Laboratories.[183]

Just like physical objects—where we can use numbers to specify the length and height and thickness of an object, and its mass—information also has a "size." Shannon used the word "bit" in his famous paper (a shortened form of the phrase "binary digit") to refer to the basic unit of information. The bit is the amount of information which we obtain when we learn which one of two equally probable alternatives is true. In binary computer language, the two alternatives are represented as either 0 or 1. So if we look at a computer calculation in the form in which it is actually computed within the processor, we will see a string of 1's and 0's (perhaps something like 00101110100010), where each 1 or 0 represents one bit of information.

A bit of information is so small, that in the development of modern computer terminology, a larger unit was eventually devised, called a Byte, which at present is usually equal to 8 bits (this is because at one point in twentieth century computer development it took roughly eight bits to encode a single letter of the alphabet). As computers got larger and larger, bigger units had to be devised, so at present a kiloByte is a thousand Bytes, a megaByte is a thousand kiloBytes, a gigaByte is a thousand megaBytes, and so on.

But to return to Laplace's Demon. Let us give the one who is doing this calculation every help that we possibly can, so let us imagine that it is a God who is attempting to predict the future. Being a God, he has no problem determining all of the necessary data about every single particle and wave and field in the entire universe external to himself, and also knows all of the laws of nature and the mathematical and logical theories required to apply these laws. This represents such an enormous amount of information, that we will have to devise an extremely large unit of measure to describe it in information theory. Let us measure God's knowledge of the universe in GodzillaBytes.

In the Western European Middle Ages, and particularly in the High Calvinism which developed in parts of Western Europe and North America during the Early Modern Period, it was believed that God had already foreseen everything that was going to happen before he even created the universe. God already knew that Adam and Eve were going to eat the forbidden fruit and that it was going to be necessary to send Christ to get the human race back on track. He knew in advance who would win every Indiana University basketball game and every University of Notre Dame football game for the entire course of the twentieth century and beyond. He also knew exactly what each human being who was ever going to live was going to do through the entire course of that person's life. Some human beings were going to be created for redemption, while others were going to be created for damnation. The question of whether any individual human being was going to be saved or damned was the result of an arbitrary divine decree, in such a way that human beings had no free will at all on that issue. (In High Calvinistic theology, that was called a doctrine of geminal supralapsarian predestination, and was believed to be the only orthodox position.)

But let us look a little more carefully, and see whether this would all be possible. In this kind of Calvinism, human beings may not have any real free will (or at least the way a good many of us would define that), but God has free will. So in between doing these calculations and actually creating the universe, God could change his mind about something. It might only be a small thing: letting the Indiana University basketball team win one game they had previously been foreordained to lose, or saving the soul of some poor man or woman instead of damning that person to eternal hell. Also, the Calvinist God is not only omniscient (all-knowing) but also omnipotent (all-powerful). So he could decide, if he wanted to, even after the universe had already been created, to alter the course of events. In fact this seems to be almost a necessary power to give him. What would be the point of praying to God, if it were not possible for him to change what was otherwise going to happen?

But this raises a major problem. This God cannot predict in advance exactly what is going to happen at all future stages of the universe, because he himself is an actor in that sequence of events. So we will need to come up with a meta-God to calculate what this God is going to do. Now if the amount of information needed to describe all the data in the universe is 10 GodzillaBytes, the Calvinist God will have to contain at least 10 GodzillaBytes of information just to store all that data in his divine memory. So our meta-God will need to have a memory capacity of at least twice that amount: 10 GodzillaBytes of information about the universe, plus an additional 10 GodzillaBytes of information about God, for a total of 20 GodzillaBytes of information at a bare minimum (actually much more, in order to carry out the processing of all this information).

I think the reader can see the next problem at this point. The meta-God is also part of the overall equation (this is what is called the observer effect, which we mentioned earlier, which is not the same as the Heisenberg uncertainty principle, but can introduce similar kinds of problems). So we will also need a meta-meta-God to tell us what the meta-God is going to do. And this meta-meta-God will need over 30 GodzillaBytes of memory simply to put all of the necessary data about the universe, God, and the meta-God into his information storage system.

But alas, this too will not give us our perfect prediction of the future, so that we will be driven into consulting next a meta-meta-meta-God, and then a meta-meta-meta-meta-God, and so on, in an infinite regress which would go on forever, but never give us the deterministic universe which the theory of Laplace's Demon seems to promise.

Total determinism is an illusion

The idea that one could in principle totally predict the future is an illusion. It is a harmless illusion when it drives scientists on to solve yet more problems and devise better and better theories. But it becomes a dangerous illusion when we begin believing that we live in what is only a mechanical, totally deterministic universe. The real universe is one in which human beings are oftentimes at the mercy of forces they cannot control, but they must never forget that they are also granted, here and there, moments of true freedom. That means that they are morally responsible for what they make of their lives.

And above all, the real universe is one where there is not only enormous goodness and beauty and holiness, but also real novelty and the opportunity for genuine creativity. Time is not the mechanical ticking and grinding of a clockwork mechanism, where I am forced to run along a predetermined track set for me by the blind forces of subhuman nature, but a journeying forth into a Great Adventure. And as we walk this path, fighting the good fight and seeking ever new horizons, we become true children of the great Alpha and Omega who eternally proclaims (Rev. 21:5-6), "Behold, I make all things new."

Chapter 21

Self-Transcendence

The gifts of modern science

What are the positive things which we gain by looking at the universe scientifically? It would take an entire book even to begin to list all of the marvelous and useful discoveries that have been made over the past three hundred years, which have made human life easier and more pleasant in countless ways. The development of the modern germ theory of disease (by scientists like Agostino Bassi, John Snow, and Louis Pasteur during the period 1835-75) has saved innumerable human lives, while the medical use of nitrous oxide ("laughing gas"), ether, and chloroform beginning in 1846-7 relieved the unbelievable horror of surgery without anesthesia which human beings had faced on most occasions throughout all of preceding history. The development of modern farming machinery and techniques has provided tables overflowing with food for much of the world. The invention of steam-powered railroad locomotives and steam boats was followed by the development of automobiles, trucks, and farm tractors powered by internal combustion engines, and the airplane. The invention of the telegraph was followed by that of the development of the telephone, radio, and finally television.

Who could deny that modern science works? We are surrounded on every side by its fruits. Only a romantic fool would attempt to challenge the basic presuppositions of modern scientific methodology. And one of the central articles of faith in modern science is that everything that happens has a cause, and that if scientists investigate for long enough, they can determine what that cause was.

The need to act as though
all events have causes

When I was a student at the University of Louisville, in 1959-60, I worked on a research team which was irradiating various simple amide compounds with high energy radiation from a cobalt 60 source, to see what chemical reactions were induced. The object was to learn more about what causes radiation sickness when human beings are exposed to an overdose of radiation. The proteins that make up such a large part of the human body are very complex molecules, but they are composed of chains of alpha-amino acids joined by amide linkages, so that the amide structure $(O = C - N)$ is an essential part of their makeup. By taking much simpler amide compounds, it was hoped that useful information could be learned about what causes radiation sickness, which in turn might be able to suggest better ways of treating it and healing the radiation damage. The team study, which was eventually published in the *Journal of Radiation Chemistry*, was in fact my first scholarly publication.

At any rate, when I took the simple amide compound which I had been assigned, and dissolved it in carbon tetrachloride and froze it and then sealed it under high vacuum in a glass ampoule and irradiated it, the liquid in the sealed glass container ended up filled with beautiful white crystals. None of the other experimenters were obtaining any kind of results like this, and the nature of the crystals was at first a total and quite puzzling mystery.

Now at that point, it would have been possible, I imagine, for me to have gone to the chairman of the chemistry department, and said, "I believe that we have an instance here where the laws of nature do not operate, so that we have an uncaused effect. Well, since there could be no answer to a situation of that sort, further investigation would clearly be futile here." At best, I would have been laughed out of his

403

office, and told to get back to work and figure out what the crystals were, and why they were being created.

In fact, I already knew that it was incumbent on me to solve that problem, which I eventually did. It took a lot of work to prove what the crystals were, and then even more work to make sure that they were not being produced by minute amounts of water vapor which might have entered as a contaminant at some point. I had to re-perform the experiment using a dry box with rubber gloves for handling the materials, and go to other extreme lengths to make sure that this was not happening.

The point of all this is, that the development of modern science would have been undercut at its very roots if scientists had allowed themselves to say that perhaps yellow fever had no cause, or that cancer had no cause, or that the strange behavior of static electricity had no rational causes and could not be explored by rigorous scientific experimentation.

So real scientists tend (understandably) to draw back in horror if a theologian begins talking about certain kinds of events which take place (he claims) without prior determining causes. To the scientist, this sounds like a retreat back into the Dark Ages, where fuzzy minded mythological thinking was allowed to rule human societies, and scientists who dared to ask about the real causes of things could be threatened with being burnt at the stake—or at the very least, could be told that the public schools in a certain district would no longer purchase and use the biology textbooks these good scientists had written, because these books said things about evolution based on copious fossil records[184] and the comparison of the DNA chains between different species,[185] which contradicted two primitive creation myths (one coming from a band of wandering nomads and the other from the cities of ancient Babylon)[186] which came from the pre-scientific world of the Ancient Near East in the second and third millennia B.C.

And there is also the severely practical question: would you rather believe in Laplace's Demon and the principle that all events have scientific causes, or live in a world without science where men would have to have legs amputated after industrial accidents and women would have to deliver babies by Caesarean section, all without anesthetics?

The deterministic paradox and self-referential questions

Phrased that way—either all events have scientific causes or we have to give up all the benefits of modern medicine and go back to a world where leprosy and epilepsy are believed to be caused by demons—it all appears to be so simple.

But the reality is more complicated than that, and contains a puzzling paradox. On the surface, it may appear that our ability to use scientific reasoning to work out sequences of cause and effect commits us to a world ruled by Laplace's Demon. And that in turn would seem to necessitate that human beings are no more than the kind of clockwork figures which come out to strike the hour on one of those marvelous Central European clock towers—or perhaps no more than cuckoos in the cosmic cuckoo clock! We stick our necks out, and do whatever we do, not because we truly decided to do so, but because the mechanism made us do so.

The reason why this is not so is that, at any given time, my human brain can ask the simple self-referential question, *"But how is the situation being affected by the way that I myself am thinking about it?"* The principle of scientific determinism, paradoxically, does not take away my human freedom, but is the real basis of that freedom.

Let me give a simple example. Somewhere in the 900's B.C. roughly, the city of Rome began when several early iron age villages were built on the tops of some of the hills on the banks of the Tiber river, at the place where the major north-south trade route had to cross that river as it ran along the west coast of Italy. The small island in the Tiber at that point produced two narrow channels instead of one wide channel, which allowed for the building of two short wooden bridges instead of one extremely long one—a crucial factor, given the primitive state of technology at that time.

What radically decreased the value of this real estate, was that the area between the hills, although higher in elevation than the nearby river, was nevertheless lower than the surrounding hills and completely surrounded by them, so that rainwater pooled up and turned it into a soggy marsh, which was an ideal breeding ground for mosquitoes. The villagers continually suffered from malaria. When the more civilized Etruscans to the north began to extend their sphere of influence to the Tiber river, they prompted the villagers to ask a self-referential question: "What would happen if, instead of just swatting at the mosquitoes and suffering from malaria, we drained the swamp?" The Etruscans helped show them how to do it, and around 600 B.C. a giant drainage ditch (later a covered tunnel) called the Cloaca Maxima was dug, which is still in operation to this day. The area between the hills which was drained was then turned into the Roman forum, the site of many of ancient Rome's governmental offices and some of its principal temples. If visitors to Rome visit the church of San Clemente today, they can go down into the excavations under the present building, and down at the lowest excavated level, hear the rush of the waters coursing through the Cloaca Maxima.

The early Romans made a primitive scientific observation, namely that "all over the Mediterranean world it is observed that people who live beside swamps suffer from malaria," and then asked themselves a simple self-referential question, "How would it change the situation if we ourselves did something different?"

The reason why some modern scientists (and a large number of modern philosophers) try so vigorously to defend the notion that everything that happens in the universe is governed by deterministic scientific laws, is because they are deathly afraid that, if it were not so, we would no longer be in control of our lives. What they do not seem to realize is, that if the kind of scientific determinism they are defending is the kind of rigid total determinism described in the theory of Laplace's Demon, we would in fact have no control at all.

We need to learn how to firmly embrace the Deterministic Paradox and turn it to our advantage. A certain kind of event may be rigidly determined by prior causes until we discover exactly how it is being determined. But that very discovery allows us to do something different ourselves, and this in turn allows us to change the course of events and assert control once more.

It is therefore necessary to assert both that *we can predict what the future would be* (if we allowed things to run their course) on the basis of a scientific investigation of how present causes would have certain future effects, and that *we can change what the future will bring* on the basis of what we learn. Scientific determinism and the exercise of human free will are not contradictory to one another, but simply two different phases of the same investigative intellectual process.

This, we remember, was one of the broader implications of Gödel's proof. Once we begin asking self-referential questions, the simple and mechanical way in which logical consequences could be derived within any given system of thought, can quickly start to break down.

The study of human beings
vs. the study of Nature

I think it might comfort the physicists (and chemists and biologists) to a certain degree, to agree with them that deterministic chains of cause and effect do in fact fairly rigidly determine the course of subhuman Nature most of the time. Not completely so—we have already discussed the effects of chance and probability, chaos theory, and the Heisenberg uncertainty principle, among other things—but even the exceptions to the rule of rigid determinism can themselves be described with precision in good mathematical formulas.

The place where rigid scientific determinism begins to work less well, is where human minds are concerned. This is because it takes something at the level of sophistication of human mental processes to ask the kind of self-referential questions (at a level of full conscious awareness) which are capable of breaking an existing cause-effect sequence by the entry of something completely new and different.

Many computer scientists believe that they will someday be able to create artificial intelligence which will be able to do the same thing. I can think of no philosophical reason why this should not be theoretically possible. But there are no computers at present which can truly understand meaning and perform acts of higher order self-transcendence, so for now we can draw a clear distinction, here on the planet Earth, between human beings (whose brains can ask self-referential questions and practice a little bit of real free will) and everything else in the universe which scientists are able to study.

And even then, the psychologists, sociologists, and political scientists have shown that if one engages in real scientific investigations of the way human beings think and behave, that one can come up with extremely valuable discoveries, because human beings still act in fairly deterministic fashion a good deal of the time. It is less often, comparatively speaking, that men and women produce real creativity and novelty.

The attempt to explain away
self-transcendence

There are modern philosophers who will try to argue that what I have just asserted is a fallacy. "Yes," they will say, "it is true that a scientist can discover the cause of something and then realize on that basis what can be done to change the course of events. But the scientist's discovery of that was also the result of education and influences from the environment, and that too—at least in principle—could be analyzed in such a way as to show that this discovery was completely determined by preexisting causes."

Let us first be wary of "in principle" arguments! Can Einstein's discoveries really be "explained" that way? Granted that the historical context supplied the impetus to solve those particular problems, were the solutions which he devised mechanically produced? Or any works of extraordinary genius? Every person I have seen who has claimed that he could explain great acts of human creativity and sudden insight has given such facile and trivial "explanations" that no intelligent person could ever take them seriously.

But rather than trying to argue out things of this sort on a case by case basis, let us instead acknowledge that there are "degrees of freedom," if we might put it that way. There are lower level decisions and insights where perhaps we can explain how and why the person made the discovery or decided to do things differently. But there is a higher kind of act of free will, where the human being engages in an act of true self-transcendence. If I ask, "how is the situation being affected by the way that I myself am thinking about it?" I can include in that act of self-analysis the question, "how are my own prior prejudices and assumptions, and the influences from the environment, trying to make me act?" and then I can see if there are ways that I can break free of all of those forces too.

Kant understood this apparent paradox at a certain level. As he put it, the acts of real freedom which we could carry out on certain occasions, came when we investigated the categorical imperatives which we were allowing to rule our lives. We could take rules of living (such as "always tell the truth") and examine in detail how these rules would require us to live and act. But we could not only analyze them, we could also decide to change them, and then freely commit ourselves to a new and different kind of life based on a different set of principles. The twentieth-century existentialists took Kant's idea and expanded it into even more powerful philosophies of freedom.

Good psychoanalysis and psychotherapy is designed to produce situations where that kind of self-transcendence can occur, and where, in a moment of insight, the patient can see how he or she could break free from all the psychological forces of the past, and all the attempts by family and friends and co-workers to keep the patient trapped in his or her old ways of thinking and behaving. There were attempts in the twentieth century to do therapy on the basis of deterministic theories of operant conditioning and producing conditioned reflexes, and none of them produced very good results, particularly if patients were evaluated three and five years later. The therapies that worked best were the ones which attempted to encourage patients to assert their true freedom and become self-initiating and self-actualizing. Seeing for myself exactly why a certain traumatic period in my childhood produced a pattern of behavior on my part which has now become destructive, is the key to releasing me from its power, and restoring my freedom—the freedom to choose whatever alternate way of living looks best to me.

The reason why there appears to be a paradox here is because there are in fact two infinite processes going on. (1) I can continue forever asking myself what the causes were which made me act in certain kinds of ways over and over, and what the causes were which made me think in certain kinds of ways. And then I can ask about the causes of those causes—psychological issues going back into my childhood, sociological issues arising from the pressures of the society around me, the improper functioning of my own brain chemistry (which might be potentially correctable with medication), the political events which created the war or the collapse of the stock market or whatever else affected my life so severely at one point, the negative effects of racism or sexism or religious prejudice, and so on—and I can then go on and investigate the causes in turn of those causes. (2) But I must simultaneously carry out the infinite process of figuring out, step by step, how to free myself as much as possible from the negative impact of some of these forces, because it is in this that I will find my freedom.

Self-transcendence in the
twelve step program

One of the best places to see how we can learn to practice self-transcendence and regain our freedom, is to look at the twelve step program, where the fourth of the twelve steps requires the participants to make a self-inventory. In that step they are asked to look introspectively at themselves, and work out—totally by themselves and for themselves—the factors in their own character which produce obsessive resentments and fears. It is vitally important to do this, and to carry it out thoroughly, because gaining an insight into a particular character defect brings with it the possibility of being freed from its effect. No one tells people in the twelve step program what their character defects are—each person has to work that out for himself or herself. No one tells them what kind of life they ought to live instead—there too each person is given total freedom. But it works. The results are incredible, where we see men and women undergoing total transformation over a period of only two or three years.

A woman in Al-Anon named Karen C. was told by her grown daughter (an alcoholic and addict) that she was that way because of her childhood upbringing, and the way her mother had behaved when she was a child. Karen, who had quite a few years in the twelve-step program, simply said, "Well, then, get over it!" A man in A.A. named Steve C. remembers how he was whining and complaining about his life in an A.A. meeting, and talking about his abusive father, and his traumatic experiences in the jungles of Viet-Nam. After the meeting his sponsor, a man named Fritz, pulled him aside and leaned into his face. Fritz chewed tobacco, was unshaven, and had taken out his false teeth. He leaned into Steve's face—and Steve could smell him breathing in his face—and snapped, "When are you going to grow up?" Steve walked away angrier than he had ever been in his life, but as he thought about it, he finally realized the gift that old Fritz was trying to give him. He could be freed from his past at any time he wanted, if he were only willing to seize his freedom.

That is the only way alcoholics and addicts and Al-Anon members ever get freed from the past: analyze it, work out what it has been making you do, and then quit doing it. The most important objective of the twelve step program is to push people into practicing self-transcendence, and exercising it in such a way that they are no longer at the mercy of other people, and influences from the environment, or even their own pasts.

Again, the central message of this chapter is that seeing how my past has been determined is not an imprisoning exercise which dooms me to act like a clockwork figure on a bell tower, repeating that same tired old chain of cause and effect over and over again. It is the key to the door which will allow me to walk away from my past, and assert my true freedom for the first time in my life. It is the cry to those who have been in slavery to the past, to cast off their chains and emerge from their prisons, and breathe once more the clean air of freedom.

The ghost in the machine

I am well aware that a ghost has been hovering in the background, so to speak, when looked at from the viewpoint of many of my readers. It is a famous ghost, which goes back to the time of the French philosopher and mathematician René Descartes (1596-1650).[187] In his dualistic philosophical system, Descartes acknowledged that the human body worked like a machine and followed the laws of chemistry and physics. But he argued that the human mind was immaterial and was therefore exempt from the deterministic laws of chemistry and physics. The problem was how to account for pure thoughts (which were immaterial) being able to influence the actions of material bodies (our arms and legs and so on as they were connected by the nervous system to the cells in the human brain). Descartes came up with the rather quaint idea that the soul was able to move the body through the intermediary of the pineal gland. But it is easy to see that even if this were so, the pineal gland is a collection of cells (and hence a material object), so the problem of how pure thought can move material objects is still not fundamentally resolved.

Phrased in this fashion, the idea that our thoughts could control the motions of our bodies does appear to be an absurd idea. Sitting here at my desk, I could think as hard as I wished, but I would be unable to make the cup sitting beside my computer keyboard rise through the air and move into the kitchen and refill itself with another serving of coffee, and then come back again (moved by my thoughts alone) and obediently place itself at my right hand. And so we are left with the image of the human brain as a piece of mechanical clockwork with gears and cogs meshing with one another, while a pale white ghost flits nervously through the spinning gear wheels attempting futilely to make the machinery do something different from what we all know it will invariably be forced to do. But since it is completely immaterial, when the poor ghost attempts to shove on one of the cogwheels, its hand simply passes right through the wheel.

Ideas (which are completely immaterial) cannot affect the course of physical bodies (which are material). We all know that—or think we do—here at the beginning of the twenty-first century, with all our modern knowledge. But is that in fact true?

The first step in exorcizing the image of the ghost in the machine is to realize that pure ideas can indeed shape the movements of physical bodies, and do so all the time. This is the fundamental basis of modern science. The laws of science are all cast in mathematical form as pure ideas. When an apple detaches from a tree, it falls to the ground because the law of gravity (an idea) compels it to do so. The law of gravity determines the course of a cannonball shot from a cannon, and the elliptical orbit of the earth about the sun. *Of course pure ideas can make physical objects move in specific paths!* It is sheer nonsense to try to argue otherwise.

Why can't I make the coffee cup move just by sitting absolutely still and thinking at it really hard? Thoughts going on in a human mind can control what is going on in the brain cells, because our thoughts take place *in correspondence with* the electrical processes and tiny biochemical changes taking place in our brain cells. There is no such direct one-to-one relationship taking place between the thoughts in my mind and the coffee cup sitting on my desk. So I have to do it a different way. My thoughts have to command my hand to pick up the cup, and my legs to carry my body out to kitchen, where I have to further command my hand to pick up the coffee pot and pour some of the coffee into my cup. That's the way life is, the coffee cup is not part of my brain.

Jean Piaget

In order to fully explain, however, why the figure of the ghost in the machine is an empty phantom, we need to talk more about the distinction between *correspondence* and *interdependence*. We already discussed this issue in part in Chapter 15, but we need to say more about it now, because it is so extremely important. And in this context, we need to explain who Piaget was, for he gave one of the best explanations ever given of that distinction.

Jean Piaget (1896-1980), a Swiss developmental psychologist, was one of the greatest philosophers of the twentieth century. He took the fundamental ideas of the great formative western philosophers, ranging from Plato to Immanuel Kant—their speculative theories about how the human mind learned about the world—and spent his life doing experimental work with infants and small children, to see what actually happened in reality. In the process, he wrote some sixty books, plus several hundred articles, describing his observations. A brilliant American named John H. Flavell, who is currently Professor Emeritus of Developmental Psychology at Stanford University, used Piaget's work to totally shift the direction of developmental psychology in the United States. The best systematic account of Piaget's discoveries which I have read, is Flavell's *The Developmental Psychology of Jean Piaget*, which came out in 1963.[188] If I were in charge of a doctoral program in philosophy, I would require that all of the graduate students study that book and be able to pass a detailed exam on its ideas.

What Piaget learned through his observations of infants and small children forms yet another of the marvelous sets of discoveries which turned the twentieth century—that remarkable century—into one of the two most formative periods in the development of western thought, paralleled only by the revolution in human thought which took place in classical Greece during the fifth and fourth centuries B.C. For literally thousands of years, philosophers had sat in their armchairs and speculated about how the human mind learns about the world, but until Piaget came along, no one ever carried out any detailed observations of infants and small children to see what actually happened. It was rather like the ancient Greek philosophers arguing interminably about whether atoms did or did not exist, but never attempting to carry out any scientific experiments to see what was true.

As I have mentioned before, this present book is in part my attempt to write a sort of *Contra Kantum*, a refutation of some of the key principles in Kant's philosophy. This is because in my perception, for over two centuries (Kant's *Critique of Pure Reason* was published in

1781) western theology has been going around in meaningless circles for a good deal of the time, and has become nearly paralyzed in terms of coming out with any kind of philosophical theology which would make sense in terms of modern science, but would also be genuinely helpful to ordinary people who wish to pursue the spiritual life.

In my reading, Piaget was fundamentally a Kantian, but a Kantian who explained how to get past the central problem raised for philosophy by the *Critique of Pure Reason*. In Kant's system, the fabric of time and three-dimensional space was simply directly intuited, and formed a kind of invariant and unchangeable straitjacket in which our minds were forced to create the phenomenal world. The fact that our souls were imprisoned in material bodies,[189] inside a box of space and time which we could not change or choose to intuit in any way other than a strict Euclidean geometry, blocked us off from ever being able to directly grasp the noumenon, the real world of ideas which actually structured the universe. And Kant came up with a list of the fundamental categories of the understanding, which he likewise assumed were invariant and unchangeable, which our minds had to schematize in order to turn the phenomena of sense perception into an intelligible universe.

Piaget showed that the schemas which connected the categories to the phenomena did in fact change, and change remarkably during our childhood—something that most Kantian philosophers either deny or largely ignore. So for example, Piaget demonstrated that infants and children did in fact change their understanding of space as they developed, through their interactions with the real world around them.

Now the reader should be warned that the Swiss children whom Piaget studied were quite bright, and were learning in a highly intellectual milieu, so the age ranges given below seem to have been correct for them. But at any rate, the four basic developmental stages which he discovered were as follows, where I am giving the age ranges at which his Swiss children made the transition from one level to the next:

Sensorimotor stage: birth to age 2 (children experience the world through movement, manipulation of objects, and sense perception, and learn object permanence)

Preoperational stage: ages 2 to 7 (acquisition of a sophisticated understanding of space and an elementary understanding of causality, but initially in a totally preverbal way, and throughout without any strong self-analytical capability)

Concrete operational stage: ages 7 to 11 (children learn to think more logically about concrete events, but still in an oversimplified way, where they have difficulty in analyzing situations in which two different causes or two different dimensions of the situation are affecting the outcome)

Formal operational stage: after age 11 (full development of abstract reasoning)

In terms of the age ranges given above, I and some of my fellow professors at Indiana University discovered to our dismay that some of our college students (who were 18 years or older) had not truly progressed to the full formal operational stage in terms of their ability to handle abstract reasoning, which Piaget's children had mastered by age 11. Their elementary school education (and their high school education as well) had been very poor compared to the Swiss institutions where Piaget's subjects had been educated. But this is not necessarily fatal. My colleague Eileen Bender in the English Department carried out some interesting experiments with small seminars, in which she was able to bring some of these college students with lesser reasoning ability to a fuller understanding of the schemas that adults use in carrying out abstract reasoning. And one of our mathematics professors likewise discovered that valuable remedial teaching techniques could be developed by applying Piaget's kind of analysis to the issue of understanding why some mathematics students got the same kind of wrong answers over and over to certain kinds of thought problems.

The main point however, is that Piaget demonstrated through thousands of experimental observations, that the human mind is not at all locked into a specific intuition of time and three-dimensional space, and that it is also not locked into any specific set of schemas for using the fundamental categories of the understanding to organize the world around us in rational and productive fashion. Will we ever perfectly know the fundamental ideas which structure the universe, or know exactly what the fabric of space-time is? Probably not, but the noumenon (the ideas which structure the universe) are hardly impenetrable mysteries, about which we can say nothing at all. Let us remember what we noted in an earlier chapter. Back in the period when Locke and Kant were writing their philosophies, in the late seventeenth and eighteenth centuries, it was in fact the case that no one knew why all swans looked so much alike, or why all samples of gold acted the same way chemically. Locke (with his theory of the unknowable real essences of things) and Kant (with his theory of the totally unknowable noumenon) were able to frighten their readers into believing that answers to scientific questions of that sort could never be worked out, because of the essential nature of human thought itself. And philosophers who were terrified by the bugbear which Locke and Kant created by those theories, drew the unfortunate conclusion that we could likewise know nothing at all about God, even if a God of some sort did exist. This was what has disrupted western theology for over two hundred years.

But it isn't so. Scientists can now talk intelligently about the genetics of swans, and the nature of the outer electron shell in the gold atom. And likewise, theologians can learn to say at least a few things about what God is, that are equally rational and logical, and grounded in what the universe external to our minds actually is.

Piaget on correspondence
vs. interdependence

As part of his analysis of how infants and children learn about the world—first at the purely operational level, without any ability to adequately verbalize or analyze their discoveries, but later with the ability to give carefully reasoned analyses of their observations about the world around them—Piaget found it useful to distinguish between layers of analysis which were *interdependent with* other layers of analysis, and those which were *in correspondence with* other layers. So he discovered, for example, that although the properties of space which children gradually discover are in correspondence with the principles of pure mathematics, one cannot derive the properties of space from elementary mathematical principles by a process of simple deduction. Mathematics gives us tools for talking about space at a higher analytical level, but physical space as it actually exists (along with many of its basic characteristics) cannot be mechanically deduced from the foundational mathematical theorems and axioms themselves.[190]

To draw a contrast, chemistry and physics are related by interdependence. In principle at least, all of the findings of modern chemistry could be explained in terms of the physical laws governing the atoms and molecules which the chemist investigates, and could be deduced from the basic laws of physics.

We can use Piaget's distinction to help make better sense of the mind-body problem. Every time a thought in my mind changes, there will be a *corresponding* change in the minute electrical impulses and tiny biochemical balances in my brain cells and their interconnections. But one cannot mechanically deduce higher human thought structures simply by detailing all the causal connections between the electrical and biochemical changes which occur as part of that process.

Let me give a simple example to illustrate this point. Douglas Hofstadter, the computer scientist at Indiana University's Bloomington campus, has recently published a book called *I Am a Strange Loop*, in which he describes a simple computer setup for determining whether a given integer is a prime number. I am going to modify his story a little bit, but I want to give credit to him for posing the issue in this interesting fashion.[191]

When I was in high school, I won a minor prize at a science fair with a small computer which I built, using mechanical electromagnetic relays salvaged from old pinball machines. Each relay consisted of a steel lever which would be pulled down to close a circuit if an electrical impulse traveled through an electromagnet made of coiled wire. A mechanical catch then held the lever down, so that the current continued to flow through the wire attached to it, even after the original electrical impulse was no longer being applied. But there was a second electromagnet which would, if an electrical impulse passed through it, pull the catch back so that the lever would flip up, at which point the relay would no longer be sending current down a wire to the next relay. So the relay basically consisted of an on-off switch, which would transmit a continuous electrical current if one magnet was activated even momentarily, but would turn that current off again if the other magnet was activated even for just a second or so.

Although the computer I built was designed to solve a different kind of problem (it was designed to carry out the basic computations involved in solving syllogisms in elementary Aristotelian logic), it could easily have been rebuilt to solve Hofstadter's prime number problem. It could have been set up so that when a number like 19 was entered, it would first divide the number by 2 to see if there was remainder. And in this case, 19 divided by 2 would give us 9 plus a remainder. The computer would then work its way down stepwise from 9, dividing 19 next by 8, then 7, then 6, and so on, all the way down to 3, checking each time to see whether there was a remainder, or whether 19 was evenly divisible by one of those numbers. By salvaging a few more parts from old pinball machines, the computer could have been constructed so that a red light would start blinking the first time the number which was input was evenly divisible by some smaller number (indicating that the number was *not* a prime number) and that a bell would start ringing if the process carried through to completion with no even divisor being found (which meant that we had successfully found a prime number).

No matter what number we entered—a prime number like 17, 19, or 23, or a non-prime number like 18, 20, 21, or 22—we could "explain" what happened by simply describing the way in which each electromagnetic relay was activated by its predecessor in the series, and then transmitted an impulse to its successor in the series. But would that in fact be a real explanation? No matter how the relays were connected to one another, one could "explain" which relays were triggered (or de-triggered) and how by this kind of explanation, but one would come nowhere near explaining what the idea of a prime number meant. The most important thing going on would be left totally unexplained by this kind of analysis.

The fundamental idea of what a prime number is, and the way we would have to structure our ideas and thought in order to determine whether a given number was a prime number, were *in correspondence with* but NOT *interdependent with* the clicking and clacking of the mechanical electromagnetic relays as they opened and closed.

The human brain as a computer which can creatively reprogram itself

To see more clearly what is at stake in this distinction, let us look at an important difference between that primitive little computer and the workings of the human brain. That computer made with parts from old pinball machines was programmed during its construction so that it could only function in that specific way. That is what can mislead us into believing that reciting the details of its construction gives a complete and totally adequate explanation of what was going on.

There are computers today which can, to a limited extent, rewrite parts of their own programming on the basis of patterns found in the mass of accumulated data in their memory banks, but the rewriting does not go very far. Could we one day build computers that could engage in more extensive rewriting of their own programs? I do not see any theoretical reason why it would be impossible, but it is sufficient to say here, that such computers do not exist at present. On the other hand, the human brain functions like a computer which can carry out massive rewriting of its own programs. That was in effect what Jean Piaget was studying, put in the language of computer science. As the children he was studying grew and learned, they totally rewrote their basic internal mental "programs" for interacting with objects in three-dimensional space and objects which were involved in causal connections.

That is what the capacity for self-transcendence means. By "reprogramming" the thought structures of our minds (that is, by "reframing" the cognitive framework of our minds as the cognitive behavioral therapists would say) we can put the thoughts themselves in the driver's seat, instead of functioning simply by mechanical reflex to whatever is presently programmed into the electrical and biochemical structure of our brains.

The pattern of our thoughts must always of necessity be *isomorphic with* the underlying electrical and biochemical changes going on in our brain cells and their interconnections. But that does not mean that our thoughts can be *reduced to* an account of what is going on at the electrical and biochemical level. This is simply another way of describing what is meant by *correspondence* rather than *interdependence*.

Human free will

So can human beings practice free will? Kant grasped the basic idea of how this can be done, at least at one level. He argued that we do have free will when we practice self-transcendence and begin examining the moral imperatives by which we have been governing our lives. We have the freedom to change them, and begin living our lives on a different set of moral principles. Some of the twentieth-century existentialist philosophers, like Martin Heidegger,[192] expanded on this idea and showed how we could reclaim our independence and autonomy as human beings. Heidegger showed that the way our minds actually perceived phenomena was determined in part by thought structures like the moral imperatives we live by and the goals we set for our lives. The being itself of these phenomena was ontologically constituted by the structuring of these thought patterns. When I change my basic thought structures, all of the beings in the external universe change at the deepest ontological level—insofar as I can perceive them as phenomena—and literally become a whole set of different objects. Objects from the past cannot determine the direction of major personal self-transformations (in the way in which they were supposed to control things according to the theory of Laplace's Demon), because those objects from the past literally no longer exist in the new and transformed thought world which is created. Oh, at one level, it may still be the same father and mother, and the same eighth grade teacher in high school, and so on, but when we undergo deep personal transformation, those images take on totally different characters and valuations in our new view of the world.

Perhaps it would be fairer to say that we have a certain degree of free will in certain kinds of situations. No one totally escapes the heritage of his or her own past. I am who I am today at least in part because of the world in which I was brought up, and the places where I received my education. But the story of my life also involves instances in which the plot suddenly changed in a surprising direction. We remember the first chapter in this book, about the mysterious "x-factor" that can show up in many people's life stories. Sometimes this is God's grace at work, sometimes it is us practicing free will and transcending our own pasts, but most of these instances I believe are a combination of those two things.

Can "the ghost in the machine" sometimes put itself in control of what the body is doing? Well, ideas aren't ghosts—the law of gravity is not a ghost although it controls the movements of physical objects—but in a sense, yes, when the x-factor shows up in someone's life story, one can pretty well be guaranteed that the thoughts and ideas in that person's brain were taking control of what was going on. Real free will can indeed exist on occasion, at least to a certain degree, and this is vitally important, because real spirituality at its best is directed at making the most productive use of this human ability.

God cannot know that 2 + 2 = 5

We need to think now about the implications of this—along with the things we discussed in the previous chapter, "Why the Future Cannot Be Totally Predicted," and see how this applies to God and the way an intelligent, personal God would know the world.

We already mentioned in an earlier chapter that the professors in the Catholic universities of medieval Europe would point out to their students that "Not even God can make a square circle." What they really meant was that the statement "God made a square circle" would be a meaningless statement, because the phrase "square circle" did not mean anything intelligible. Standing around delivering grandiose statements that were totally meaningless did not count as writing serious theology, no matter how piously one proclaimed these words.

I am now going to push this principle a couple of steps further. "God knows that 2 + 2 = 5" is likewise not a serious theological statement. "2 + 2 = 5" is a logical contradiction, which means that a statement involving that phrase means nothing intelligible. We are not trying to talk here about what God could or could not do—that is not the issue—but saying instead that any claims we make about things that God can do have to be put in the form of meaningful statements. And this in turn means that the claim that God can know the universe in ways that violate Gödel's proof is an unintelligible and hence meaningless proposition which would require logical impossibilities as great as the assertion that "God knows that 2 + 2 = 5."

And in addition, making statements such as "God knows that tigers have six legs and are blue with pink polka dots" would also lead us to a very peculiar kind of theology, because the person making that statement presumes that God is very ignorant and thinks he knows things about the world which are in fact false. Claiming that God "knows" something about the universe which is obviously and blatantly contrary to fact is either a nonsense statement, or even worse. For how could we be saved by a God who was more ignorant even than us? So the assertion that God "knows perfectly" things which are impossible to know with certainty according to the Heisenberg uncertainty principle, would in like manner involve either self-contradictory nonsense, or the claim that God thinks he knows facts about the universe which even our human minds can tell are factually untrue.

Trying to build a system on "2 + 2 = 5" statements, and propositions about blue tigers with six legs and pink polka dots, and similar kinds of assertions, is not a good way to try to write theology.

God knows the future as it actually is, as still partially undetermined

High Calvinism taught a doctrine of geminal supralapsarian predestination, along with a doctrine of total foreordination. By that they meant the claim that God knew, even before Adam and Eve ate the apple in the Garden of Eden (and in fact even before the world was created), everything that was going to happen in the universe, and that God had already decided and decreed which human beings were going to be saved and which human beings were going to be damned. But if you remember the things we discussed in the previous chapter, this is no more meaningful ultimately than saying "God makes square circles" or "God knows that 2 + 2 = 5." It also presupposes that God is so ignorant that he believes things that are empirically false.

Even shortly after the Big Bang, no one—not the Calvinist God nor Laplace's Demon nor the brightest scientist in the world—could have predicted the exact state of the universe today. It is not just a matter of chaos theory and the Heisenberg uncertainty principle and things of that sort, but far more basic issues raised by Gödel's proof and information theory, which strike to the heart of mathematics and logic itself, and the very nature of knowledge itself.

And in this chapter we see the most powerful reason of all why Alfred North Whitehead and Charles Hartshorne were correct, and why God cannot know the exact shape of the future. We must posit human free will as a necessary prerequisite for us being able to know the universe well enough for us even to be able to talk about God at all. If you removed human free will—that is, the ability to ask self-referential questions and engage in self-transcendence—then there would be no human beings of a sort who could make new discoveries and be involved in real creativity. Scientific progress and spiritual growth both require the same basic human ability: the ability to come to new and novel insights, make real discoveries, and act creatively to change the future.

Encountering a personal God

When I enter upon the path of the spiritual life, I begin what will become a dialogue between two persons, God and me. I am not going to be allowed to set myself up as my own God and take over the rulership of the universe. But God on his side respects my freedom, and will never force me to accept any of his gifts of grace. I can take everything God gives me and throw it away, if that is what I foolishly want to do, and he will not stop me.

As an encounter between two persons, there are no mechanical rules which can describe and predict what will happen. We can try to draw up a legalistic religious system involving hundreds of complicated rules, but all it will do is block us from receiving any real grace. God delights in doing the unexpected (and sometimes, I believe, laughs heartily at the expressions on our faces). But God also delights in us human beings when we are innovative and creative and come up with a completely new and novel way of doing something. If he enjoys completely surprising us, I believe that he also gains enormous pleasure from the situations in which we surprise him, and do something so noble, so good, so beautiful, so humorous, so courageous, that it makes all his work in creating the universe worth it.

We human beings are not clockwork mechanisms. It is at the level of pure thoughts and ideas—at the level, in other words, of meaning

425

and the pure life of the spirit—and not in the underlying electrical and biochemical substratum of the brain, that the creativity and the freedom occur. And along with that, it is also in our thoughts and ideas that we find both the joy and the tears, both the delight in beauty and goodness and the horror at evil.

It is an extraordinary universe in which we live. But we human beings are likewise truly extraordinary creatures. Let us not cheapen either the universe or ourselves, by trying to turn the universe into a machine grinding along mechanically, without the splendor or glory of a God whose divine light and love illuminates and fills all things, or the sheer delight of a great artist or scientist (or a true master of the spiritual life) who has just made a brilliant new discovery, or created something of extraordinary beauty and goodness.

Chapter 22

The Faith of a Nomad

The faith of a devil
will not save you

In the middle ages, the biblical word "faith" became misunderstood, even by very good theologians, as *intellectual belief* in the truth of a set of doctrines:[193] the concept of the Trinity, the divinity of Christ, his virgin birth, the resurrection of Christ on Easter morning, the substitutionary doctrine of the atonement (the eleventh-century theory that Christ's death on the cross had—as its central purpose—paying the penalty for our sins), and so on. But the epistle of James in the New Testament made it clear that a faith which was merely intellectual belief in correct doctrine could not save anyone:

> Someone may say, "You have faith and I have actions." Show me your faith-without-actions, and I will show you my faith BY my actions.

> You have a faith that God is one? You do well: even the demons have that faith and shudder .... Just as the body without a spirit is dead, so also faith without works is dead.[194]

When Archbishop Thomas Cranmer brought the Protestant reformation to the Church of England in the sixteenth century, he wrote a homily in which he used the phrase "the faith of a devil," borrowed from that passage in the letter of James, to describe those who believed all the correct church doctrines and dogmas, but did not have the faith that saves. John Wesley in the eighteenth century, one of the two great theologians at the founding of the modern evangelical tradition, picked up this phrase from Cranmer and loved to use it to describe the difference between formal, outward religiosity and the true religion of the heart and spirit.[195] You could go to church every Sunday and mouth all the right words—and even believe them, at a certain kind of intellectualized level—but still have no more than the faith of a devil.

Whenever I used to talk about this in a lecture to a class of university students, I would always get looks of real alarm and disbelief on the faces of some of the students. But the traditional Christian account of how Satan and his devils fell from heaven, implies exactly what the epistle of James was saying. According to the ancient story, the ruler of hell was once an angel of light named Lucifer, the highest in rank of all the angels. But since Christ was above even him in the heavenly hierarchy, Lucifer was still only in the number two place, not the number one place: this filled him with an insane envy and jealousy. Finally he talked some of the other angels into joining him in a rebellion against God. After a hard-fought heavenly battle, Satan and his fellow rebels were cast down into hell and changed into demons. But since all of them were once angels up in heaven, of course they knew all the right doctrines about God and Christ and the road to salvation—they knew the truth at the intellectual level, but they could not stand that truth, and rejected it in their hearts.

The same thing applies to human beings. You can know all the right theological answers and still be Satan's minions.

Martin Luther: faith is trust

The German priest and college professor Martin Luther, who started the Protestant reformation which spread across much of northern Europe in the sixteenth century, rediscovered the biblical truth that "faith" as mere intellectual belief could not save anyone, while he was giving lectures in 1515 at the University of Wittenberg on the Apostle Paul's letter to the Romans. This was in fact the key proclamation of the Protestant movement. The only kind of faith that could save was not a particular kind of intellectual theory, but a willingness to *trust*.[196]

In his lectures on Romans, Luther used the biblical metaphor of the good physician to illustrate his point. It would be absurd if I went to a doctor, and the doctor examined me and then drew back in horror and said, "Get out of my office! You're sick, and I don't allow sick people into my office. You're just nasty and disgusting. Now go get well, and don't come back to my office until you're well." And it would also do no good, if I refused to tell this doctor the truth. If the doctor asked me, "Now where does it hurt?" and I responded by shaking my head and saying, "Won't tell you," this would also hamper the doctor's ability to heal me.

If we could get well on our own, we would not need the doctor in the first place. The whole reason for having doctors, is to treat people who are extremely ill, and help them get well. And if we are so afraid (or are too embarrassed or ashamed) to even go to the doctor, or to tell the doctor what is really wrong with us, then even the best modern medical science will do us little or no good. *In the same way, I have to trust that the power of God will heal me, not condemn me, if I enter into the divine presence asking for help.*

And to grow into the fullness of the spiritual life, I have to learn to trust this divine power, not only as a source of healing, but also as a power which will guide and protect me, and hold me up, no matter what kind of difficulties I am going through in life.

Walking the tight wire over the abyss

Let us tell a modern story which may help illustrate the difference between believing and trusting. Once upon a time, so the story goes, the greatest circus tight-wire walker in the world had a wire stretched across Niagara Falls. A crowd gathered on one side to watch him. He had a wheelbarrow, and he asked the crowd, "Do you believe that I can push this wheelbarrow across the wire to the other side and back?" "Yes, we believe in you!" the crowd cheered, "We believe you can do it!" He slowly walked the wire, pushing the wheelbarrow to the other side, then turned around and came back across the slender, swaying wire. "Do you believe I can do it a second time?" he asked. "Yes," the crowd shouted, "we believe in you! We believe you can do it!" "All right," he said, and turned to the person closest to him, "climb in the wheelbarrow."

Having faith in this kind of way does NOT mean that I am not afraid. Being human means that I will sometimes find myself in extraordinary danger and pain and torment. Read the Bible—or today's newspaper. It sometimes means hearing the bullets and bombs all around me, and the screams of the dying. It can mean looking through the window and realizing that the airplane or automobile is crashing. It can mean hearing the doctor tell me that I have only days or months to live, or that I will have to live with enormous physical pain for the rest of my life. It can mean watching a parent, or my spouse, or my child die, where I am left totally helpless and unable to change what is going to happen.

What this kind of faith does mean however is that I can make myself climb in the wheelbarrow *in spite of my fear*.

In the A.A. Big Book, where it describes how to carry out a fourth step moral inventory on our lives, it explains how all the truly evil and destructive things that we do, arise from two sources—resentment and fear. It tells us that resentment is apt to lie on top, where it is easy to spot and identify. We are angry, enraged, embittered, and filled with self-pity and hurt feelings because of what we see as other people's wrongs. We then use that to justify our own selfishness, dishonesty, aggression, and refusal to show personal responsibility. We act in ways that do great harm to other people (and ultimately to ourselves as well) on the basis of the resentments which so obsess us.

But down underneath all of the surface resentment, the Big Book warns, after we continued this fourth step and carried out a deep enough analysis, we found something in addition to seething resentment. We found *fear* running through "every aspect of our lives [as] an evil and corroding thread; the fabric of our existence was shot through with it." We became convinced that "our self-esteem, our pocketbooks, our ambitions, our personal relationships (including sex) were hurt or threatened." We tried so hard to be in control of our own lives and to master all the threats around us, using our intelligence, our cleverness, our ability to manipulate other people, our aggressiveness, our strength of character, and (when necessary) our capacity for rage and violence. But in the long run, the fear simply grew greater and greater. "We began to see that the world and its people really dominated us. In that state, the wrong-doing of others, imagined or real, had power to actually kill." We tried to dominate and control the external world, but in the long run, it was the external world which totally dominated and controlled us.[197]

Only the kind of faith which was *trust in God* could free us from this all-dominating fear which lay underneath our greatest evil deeds. As the Big Book said in that section on the fourth step:

> Perhaps there is a better way [than fear]—we think so. For we are now on a different basis; the basis of trusting and relying upon God. We trust infinite God rather than our finite selves. We are in the world to play the role He assigns. Just to the extent that we do as we think He would have us, and humbly rely on Him, does He enable us to match calamity with serenity.[198]

The medieval Catholic tradition:
Meister Eckhart, Johann Tauler, and
the Theologia Germanica

The Protestant movement, when it first began, was very deeply linked to the preceding medieval Catholic spiritual tradition. In the fourteenth and fifteenth centuries, the Catholic universities of Europe had been largely taken over by the arid intellectualism of the nominalist movement in theology and philosophy. The early Protestant leaders were Catholic priests, bishops, and university professors who wanted to go back to what they believed was the true heart of the Catholic faith—to the spirituality of the medieval monasteries and convents, which was based on intuition and feeling, and what the spirit learned through prayer—and adapt this monastic spirituality to the life of ordinary men and women living in the world.[199]

In Luther's case, he was deeply influenced by the Dominican mystical tradition of Meister Eckhart (c. 1260-1327) and Johann Tauler (c. 1300-1361), a tradition which represented one of the more important strands of fourteenth-century Catholic thought, and in particular by an anonymous work (representing the same sort of spirituality) called the *Theologia Germanica*, which had been written by a priest living in Frankfurt in Germany in the mid fourteenth century. Luther himself supervised the production of the first printed edition of the *Theologia Germanica* in 1516 and 1518, and said that, "Next to the Bible and St. Augustine, no book has ever come into my hands from which I have learned more of God and Christ, and humanity and all things that are." This was right after he gave his lectures at Wittenberg on Paul's letter to the Romans (in 1515), when he had first begun to fully realize what Paul meant by faith, and the year before his Leipzig debate with Johann Eck which pushed him into a more radical position, and into open confrontation with Rome.

These works are very useful for understanding what Luther meant by trust, and abandoning oneself completely to God. His basic ideas (particularly in his earlier period) were not at all alien to the late medieval Catholic tradition.

But we must be careful when reading those medieval texts. The Protestant movement which developed in the sixteenth century tended to use the word *faith* to describe this kind of trust, because they based their vocabulary so much upon Paul's New Testament letters to the Romans and to the Galatians, where this was the operant technical word which the apostle used. The medieval Catholic tradition however tended to look more towards a different part of the New Testament, the gospel and letters of John, which meant that their writings tended to use a different word, the word *love*, as the key term. The bond of love, however—whether between two human beings or between God and a human being—implies a willingness to *trust* the other person (1 John 4:16-18):

> So we have known and trusted (*pepisteukamen*) the love that God has for us. God is love, and those who abide in love abide in God, and God abides in them. In this way the ability to love has been restored among us, so that we may have boldness on the day of judgment. Because as he is, so are we in this world. There is no fear in love; instead perfect love casts out fear. For fear has to do with punishment, and whoever fears has not been perfected in love.

Trust is in fact a key expression of a constantly abiding love. In the fullness of love, as even the Apostle Paul notes in his great Hymn to Love in 1 Corinthians 13:7, love "protects from all things, trusts (*pisteuei*) all things, hopes all things, endures all things." In the fullness of love, lovers abandon themselves and surrender themselves to their beloved in complete trust, holding nothing back.

In the A.A. Big Book, at the beginning of Chapter 5, "How It Works," it was made clear to the reader that twelve step spirituality would not work at all unless we committed ourselves to God with what

Luther called faith, and what the medieval Catholic spiritual tradition thought of as love-as-trust-in-the-beloved. The authors of the Big Book said that "if you have decided you want what we have," then you must become "willing to go to any length to get it." We found, they said, that "the result was nil until we let go absolutely." We discovered that "half measures availed us nothing," and that we had to turn to God and ask "His protection and care with complete abandon."

That is the ecstatic language of the great Catholic mystics, not only Eckhart, Tauler, and the *Theologia Germanica*, but also the entire tradition of medieval western European mysticism, continuing through its two great flowerings in the twelfth and fourteenth centuries and down into the early modern period, where we encounter figures like St. Teresa of Avila in the sixteenth century. As Evelyn Underhill explained in her famous book on mysticism,[200] this sort of spiritual life goes through five stages: awakening, purgation (i.e. moral cleansing), illumination, the dark night of the soul which eventually forces a final surrender to God, and finally union. This culminating stage is one in which our souls and hearts and spirits are finally united with the object of our love, that highest and ultimate reality which we call God. This ecstatic union with God happens when, as the A.A. Big Book says, we turn ourselves over to his "protection and care with complete abandon," tossing all of our inhibitions aside, holding nothing of ourselves back, and casting away all our cares about what the world thinks about our behavior.

John Wesley and the Upper Room: faith as the door and love as the goal

Medieval Catholic spirituality talked about love. Then the sixteenth-century Protestant Reformation came along and began talking about faith instead, even though there was some important overlap between what they and the Catholics were saying. In the eighteenth century John Wesley, one of the founders of the modern evangelical movement, decided that a good spirituality would need to do justice to what both sides had been trying to teach. It was time to stop seeing everything as an either/or battle—Catholic vs. Protestant—and start looking instead at ways we could talk about both/and—the best of Catholic spiritual teaching combined in a creative synthesis with the best of the early Protestant spiritual insights.

In the United States, the various Methodist and Wesleyan and holiness churches all based their teaching on John Wesley's theology, and in particular, the southern Methodists who began publishing *The Upper Room* in Nashville, Tennessee, in April 1935 were good Wesleyans to the core. *The Upper Room* was a little pamphlet with a different meditational reading for each day of the year. It is still being published today, and although a Methodist publication, is widely read by Christians from all sorts of different denominations, including a large number of Roman Catholic readers.

In the early Alcoholics Anonymous movement, from its beginning in the summer of 1935, down to the publication of Richmond Walker's *Twenty-Four Hours a Day* in 1948,[201] *The Upper Room* was the most commonly used A.A. meditational work. In the process, in a variety of important ways, it set its Methodist and Wesleyan stamp very distinctly upon Alcoholics Anonymous and the Big Book.

Wesley said that faith was the door opening the way into the spiritual path, and that continual growth in love was the goal of this journey.

When we begin the spiritual life, we are spiritual babies (1 Corinthians 3:1).[202] We scream and cry, and want everything instantly! As spiritual infants, we are filled with resentment and fear. We are almost totally incapable of loving either other human beings or ourselves, not in any sense of real *agapê* love. Even if it is true, after a fashion, that the ability to trust someone else even a tiny bit is a very primitive kind of love, these newcomers to the spiritual life would not be able to understand anything that subtle. At the practical level, the best way of getting through to them is to tell them that all they are asked to do is to show that little bit of trust. In A.A., newcomers are asked to get down on their knees in the morning and ask God for help, whether they believe in God or not. They are asked to come to meetings every week, even if they feel that they are getting nothing from these meetings. God is not going to reject them, in spite of some of the things they have done in the past, nor is he going to turn away from them because of all the anger and hatred and self-pity and selfishness and resentment and blind pride and egotism which are still seething in their hearts at this point.

At the beginning, all God asks us to do, is to trust him enough to try. That is why faith (in the sense of trust) is the doorway through which we have to pass, in order to enter upon the spiritual path.

What Evelyn Underhill said in her very Anglo-Catholic explanation of the spiritual life, about having to go through a series of stages first—awakening, purgation, illumination, and so on—before finally arriving at union with God in love, is all well and good. But we can achieve *a fundamental reunion with God* at the very beginning of the spiritual life, without the awakening or cleansing or achieving of dramatic spiritual insights which take years to carry out. And in fact we must have *this initial restoration of our union with God*, which is accomplished by clinging to him by faith alone, or we will never be able to carry through on the growth process which will have to follow.

Building on faith at every point, we must then walk the spiritual path, working to replace all of the resentment and fear in our hearts, as much as possible, with greater and greater love. The kind of ecstatic union with God of which Evelyn Underhill and the medieval Catholic mystics spoke, is the result of many years patiently living the life of faith (of trust) in the God who heals us and slowly fills our hearts with more and more of the divine love and light.

As John Wesley emphasized, we need to pay attention to what the Protestants say about faith, and to what the Catholics say about love. We need the Protestants to get us in the door, and we need the Catholics to tell us how to walk the path that lies beyond.

Being saved by faith alone: present tense (now), not future tense (after I die)

In the New Testament, the word *dikaioô*—being justified, being saved, being put right with God—is a verb which we see used over and over *in the present tense*, rather than in the future tense. We see this for example in the passages where the Apostle Paul proclaims the central gospel message of salvation by faith alone.

> For we know [*logizometha*, present tense] that a human being is justified [*dikaiousthai*] by faith, without works of the law. (Romans 3:28)

> Since we are justified [*dikaiôthentes*] by faith, we have [*echomen*, present tense] peace with God. (Romans 5:1)

> A human being is not justified [*dikaioutai*, present tense] by works of the law, but through faith. (Galatians 2:16)

In other words, "being saved" does not mean going to some heavenly realm at some future date, after I die.[203] "Being saved" means being saved *from* the compulsive need to act despicably and destructively. "Being saved" means being saved *from* continual thoughts of resentment or self-pity which intrude themselves into my mind and make my everyday life a living hell. "Being saved" means being saved *from* having to live perpetually racked with internal fear, worry, anxiety, shame, and guilt. The reason why the biblical verb is so frequently used in the present tense, is because the kind of being saved that is truly important is available here and now, today, to anyone who will simply trust God enough and turn this panicky anger over to him.

Abraham: the faith of a desert nomad

In the New Testament, when the Apostle Paul was looking about for an example of the kind of faith that saves, it is very interesting that he did not pick any Christian figure for his example, but turned back to the Old Testament, to the figure of Abraham.[204] The part of the story of Abraham which he cited came at the very beginning of the tale, long before the sacrifice of Isaac, and had nothing to do with that later story. Somewhere very roughly around 1800 B.C., Abraham and Sarah were with a nomadic Hebrew tribe which was living in tents and pasturing its sheep and goats in the semi-arid areas which stretched through parts of Iraq and over into Syria. They were in Syria when they were commanded by God to take their sheep and goats and head south, down into the hill country of Palestine, with a vague and general promise that they would be extraordinarily blessed if they did so.

This tale of a desert nomad may be one of the best descriptions of all, if we want to know what faith really means. Faith is a homeless nomad, wandering through the desert, who has been told the next step he must take, but none of the details about what will come after that. Real faith is always a journey into the uncharted and unknown frontier. Will he have to fight? There was one notable occasion when Abraham had to take up the sword and fight. Will the food start running out? Or will he discover a beautiful green oasis with date palms and pools of blue water just in the nick of time? But faithful to God, one day at a time, he is told what that day's journey will be, and goes where God points him. Faith means *committing* myself to try doing what God wants me to do. Faith means *the courage to venture into the unknown*. Faith means *trusting God enough* to do what he tells me to do today without worrying about what may happen tomorrow.

Hebrews 11:1 and John Calvin:
faith as a sense of truth or a kind
of higher knowledge

In spite of the importance of the word faith (*pistis*) in New Testament thought, there is only one real attempt in the Bible to give a definition of it, in a short passage in Hebrews 11:1.[205] But this is very important, because it introduces an additional dimension to the meaning of the word.

> *Pistis* is the underlying, supporting foundation-stone of hope; the sense of truth within the invisible realm of the spirit.

The word faith may refer to a kind of trust, but it is not a blind commitment made in total ignorance. It is a trust based on a special kind of knowledge or intuition. It is a kind of gut feeling that we get, for example, when we hear people talking about the spiritual life and we somehow sense that they know what they are talking about, and that what they say is true.

John Calvin (1509-1564), the most important Protestant reformer on the continent of Europe after Martin Luther, wrote about this in his *Institutes*, where he called faith a kind of "higher knowledge":[206]

> When we call faith "knowledge," we do not mean the sort of comprehension that concerns itself on the everyday level with those things which are objects of human sense perception. For faith is so far above sense that the human mind has to go beyond and rise above itself in order to attain it. Even where the mind has attained it, it does not intellectually comprehend what it is feeling. But as long as it is *persuaded* by that which it does not intellectually comprehend, it understands more than if it perceived any human thing by its own ability.

> *Even weak faith is real faith* . . . When even the least drop
> of faith is instilled into our minds, we begin to contemplate
> God's face, peaceful and calm and full of grace towards us.
> We see him from far off, but so clearly that we are not at
> all deceived. Then, the more we advance . . . with steady
> progress . . . the more we obtain a still closer and surer sight
> of him.
>
> The mind illuminated by this knowledge of God is at first
> wrapped up in a great deal of ignorance . . . . It is like a
> man who is shut up in a prison into which the sun's rays
> shine at an angle and half obscured through a very narrow
> window, who is indeed deprived of the full sight of the sun.
> Yet his eyes fix on its dependable brightness and receive its
> benefits.

Even "a small drop of faith," Calvin said, enables us to behold God's glory with such effect that we are transformed into his very likeness.[207] Nevertheless, since "our hearts by their own natural instincts tend vigorously toward unbelief," any small amount of genuine faith we have will inevitably be mixed with "the greatest doubts and fear."

This is extremely important. Even the hard-nosed, rigorous Calvin acknowledged that we will still be afraid to trust God completely and will still be beset by anxiety and doubt even when we also have enough genuine faith to be making real progress in the spiritual life. So even if I have to force myself to climb in the wheelbarrow (so to speak) quaking and trembling with fear, after delaying and putting it off for as long as I could, and even if I grip the sides with white-knuckled terror every time I look down and see how far I would fall if God dropped me, as long as I am ultimately willing to climb in the wheelbarrow, I have the kind of faith that saves.

John Calvin also said one other important thing, about the greatest fear which we are apt to have in those moments when we *have* to have faith. The forces of evil, he warned, direct their strongest attack toward making us feel like we are so evil and bad that not even God could love us. These forces of evil have one central lie, he said, that they are continually trying to dupe us into believing: "that we should imagine God to be against us and hostile to us, so that we could not hope for any help from him, and should fear him as if he were our deadly enemy."

Calvin and the medieval Catholic tradition:
St. Bernard of Clairvaux

Just as we could see the influence of Eckhart, Tauler, and the *Theologia Germanica* on the Protestant reformer Martin Luther, so we can see the effect of St. Bernard of Clairvaux (1090-1153) and his spiritual teaching on John Calvin. Dennis E. Tamburello has written a good book on this, called *Union with Christ: John Calvin and the Mysticism of St. Bernard.*[208]

St. Bernard was also the figure whom Dante regarded as the greatest spiritual teacher of the medieval church. In the *Paradiso*, it is St. Bernard whom Dante portrays sitting enthroned in the sphere of Saturn, the highest of the planetary spheres, and guiding the poet into his vision of the Mystic Rose, where Mary the *Theotokos* (the archetypal symbol of the feminine aspect of God) in turn takes Dante through the heart of the rose, and into the ultimate vision of the Godhead.

The great modern authors (like Evelyn Underhill and William James) who have written about the medieval mystical tradition have likewise tended to stress the fact that our faith in God and love of God is based upon a real contact with God, where there is some kind of real knowledge present, even though it is not the kind of knowledge that can be expressed in scientific terms, and seems to operate more at the level of feeling and intuition.

God communicating with us
via the material world

When we human beings are trying to communicate with one another, we normally use the material world as a medium for carrying messages and meaning back and forth. When I speak to another human being, I use waves in the air to carry vocal messages. I can also use facial expressions and gestures, which involve my material body, and which the other person can see by means of light waves. Books and letters put the message on pieces of paper. Through the sense of touch, I can communicate directly with another person by means of a comforting hand, a kiss, or a hug.

So likewise, God regularly uses the material world as a medium for communicating with us. Every particle of matter in the universe exploded out of the ground of being in the Big Bang, which was the opening event in God's great work of creation, and everything in the universe continues to derive its continuing existence from that ground of all being which continues to underlie everything else. So God can contact us through every piece of matter and bundle of energy in the universe, in whatever way he chooses: through the world of nature, through words in books and words spoken by other human beings, or through the cells of our own bodies.

These messages from God may sometimes involve knowledge that is very different from the kind of measurable data that the natural sciences like to collect and analyze. In chapter 3, for example, we talked about John Locke and his observations about the difficulty of describing in words the taste of pineapple. Locke used this example to give us warning that we can sometimes know things by personal experience that are perfectly real, even though we cannot put what we know into objective language, or explain what we know to other people who have never experienced it themselves. Michael Polanyi's book on tacit knowledge showed how we could have people who were in fact demonstrably experts, in some area like wine tasting for example, who clearly knew an extraordinary amount about their area of expertise, in spite of being unable to give any clear explanations for how they knew these things.

In chapters 4 and 5, we talked about the experience of the holy or sacred dimension of reality (the numinous) as a kind of love or Eros which could wash us clean and heal our souls. It was obviously real. It could be felt, and its effects on our lives could be dramatic. But this was an experience which could only be described in metaphors, analogies, and ideograms—not directly, as in the highly objective and measurable concepts used in the natural sciences.

In chapter 11, one of the chapters on Paul Tillich, we discussed the sacramental view of the universe, a very Catholic understanding of the way in which God can make his presence felt and bring his acts of grace to effect through the medium of material things like bread and wine and water, and holy buildings, and landscapes filled with the mystery of his presence.

We also talked in that chapter about how we can read scripture by means of the cataphatic-apophatic method. Using the cataphatic method, we read the scriptural passage and the images which it contains in the way that scientists observe the world, which is actually only taking a surface look at the passage. But then we must go past that kind of narrow analysis, and employ the apophatic method to look below the surface meaning, in such a way that we can penetrate down into the deeper truths which that scriptural passage contains. The cataphatic method describes the sign post; we then must use the apophatic method to look in the direction the sign post is pointing.

In chapter 15, where we looked at love as a kind of energy, we talked about the way that I, as a human being, can intuit or sense the love of someone else who loves me, and in chapter 19, we talked about learning to recognize synchronicities and higher patterns of meaning in the universe.

In all of these different ways of communication, we are dealing with a material substratum as the medium through which the communication is carried out. But the way in which the knowledge is perceived operates at the level of what we normally call intuition and feeling, and at a level which is difficult to translate into the objectifying language of the natural sciences. This does not mean that this is nonsense, or hopelessly subjective, or that we cannot communicate what we are sensing at all. It also does not mean that any supernatural powers are required on the human side of the occasion.

The supernatural dimension: God breaking through to us from outside

When we talked in chapter 19 about the nature of grace, however, we noted that any kind of reasonably orthodox traditional Catholic or Protestant teaching would insist that operant grace also has of necessity a supernatural element. Our human minds are locked inside what the philosopher Kant called the box of space and time. Divine grace has to come into our phenomenal world from the outside, at particular times and places, to act on our souls and minds in particular ways. It may be a subtle nudge that pushes our wills in the direction God wants us to go. It may be in the form of visions or heavenly voices or angelic visitations. But God has to reach out and touch us and push us in order to change the course of our lives.

The light motif occurs frequently in the great spiritual literature. Jonathan Edwards spoke of "a divine and supernatural light" shone by God on the world around us. Quakers referred to the teachings of the Inner Light. Hesychastic monks in the Eastern Orthodox tradition sought the vision of the Uncreated Light, as they called it. The early A.A. people talked about having the Sunlight of the Spirit shine upon them. To speak of being "enlightened" or "illuminated" in some fashion is one of the commonest recurring images in the history of spirituality.

Kant claimed that the human mind lacked the power to break out of the box of space and time which was held in place by our finite human thought processes. But even if true, that kind of restriction would not apply to God. Even if our human minds could not break through to God by their own unaided natural powers, God—who has supernatural powers—can break through back the other way. Some of the sixteenth-century Protestant theologians believed that this was the way it had to work. Faith could arise in the human heart only when God, by a supernatural act, crossed the infinite abyss which separates the Creator from the created, broke through into our finite human world, and there revealed to us who he was.

The heavenly dimension of the soul

On the other hand, in chapter 21, when we talked about self-transcendence, we discussed the strange way in which human beings were put together. What is the "soul" or "spirit" and how is it related to the physical body? Am I as a human being made up of the soul of an angel placed in the body of a monkey, as many in the ancient world believed? Or is it more complicated than that? My brain in fact seems to be divided up into many different levels, with the lowest level being formed by the so-called reptilian brain—the extremely primitive part of the human brain which works just like that of an alligator or crocodile or snapping turtle. On top of that we have the part of the brain which functions like that of higher mammals, but still has no concept of higher moral values. And there may be other levels too. But there is one level which stands above all the others, the level at which I can rise up into a transcendent world, and enter a realm of divine creativity and freedom and higher meaning.

This highest part of the human soul is not itself God of course. That would be an absurd thing to say. Our puny little human minds cannot create a universe of countless galaxies *ex nihilo!* Human beings, no matter how spiritually advanced, do not have that kind of godlike powers. But we must also say that the highest part of the human soul is not part of the phenomenal world either. The phenomenal world is a construct of my mind, which means that as the subjective human observer, I stand outside the phenomenal world which I perceive.

So in some way, I too (just like God) am part of the transcendent realm. There is a part of me which is a Being of Light, however pale and feeble this light is compared to the great Divine Light which is

God. St. Macarius said that he once saw the Man of Light which was his true divine self. Richmond Walker, the second most-published early A.A. author, spoke of the spark of the divine light within each human soul in his book *Twenty-Four Hours a Day*, in the reading for June 1:

> You were born with a spark of the Divine within you. It had been all but smothered by the life you were living. That celestial fire has to be tended and fed so that it will grow eventually into a real desire to live the right way. By trying to do the will of God, you grow more and more in the new way of life. By thinking of God, praying to Him, and having communion with Him, you gradually grow more like Him. The way of your transformation from the material to the spiritual is the way of Divine Companionship.[209]

So perhaps it is God reaching down to us and shining his light on us, but perhaps it is more a case of "like communing with like." Or perhaps it might even be that the human soul has "natural" supernatural powers, that is, that the soul was created by God with the ability to pierce through the veil which separates the phenomenal and material world from the divine world, if we abandon ourselves totally to that which lies beyond ourselves. These are questions which can be disputed without end.

But it is clear, from the experiences of people who progress far enough in the spiritual life, that contact of some sort can be made between us and the divine realm where God dwells. In the opening pages of the Big Book, Bill Wilson, the founder of A.A., describes the events which happened to him at the very end of 1934: the visit from Ebby where the scales fell from his eyes, the reconnection he made with the ability to perceive the numinous, and the vision of the heavenly light in Towns Hospital. As he puts it there, "I was ... catapulted into what I like to call the fourth dimension of existence." By the time the Big Book was written in 1939, he had taught many others how to use this strange inner ability of the human soul to come into contact with that supernatural realm which lies outside the narrow box of time and three-dimensional space: "We have found much of heaven and we have been rocketed into a fourth dimension of existence of which we had not even dreamed."[210]

There is part of the human soul which is able to sense and draw power from the eternal divine world which lies behind the physical and material world studied by the natural scientists. Is this because there is a part of us which is also divine in some sense? Or is this entirely a gift coming to us from the outside, coming down from God on high? Whether it is one or the other (or a little bit of both), we need to learn how to connect with God and learn who God is, if we wish to find the faith that saves.

Chapter 23

The Journey of Faith:
the Railroad Man

The story of Ed Pike

It is easy to become confused by complicated intellectual theories, and easy also to misunderstand the real meaning of some kinds of religious metaphors and symbols. The best antidote to this can often be simply telling the story of an individual human being where we can see what happens to that person in real life, in a way that we can relate more easily to our own personal experiences.

So let us take the story of an ordinary man who came to faith, a man who held a simple sort of everyday kind of job, living in a small midwestern city, far from the excitement and glamour of the world's great metropolises. The man was Ed Pike, a railroad conductor from Elkhart, Indiana, who explained in very simple language what the kind of faith was which a beginner to the spiritual life must learn to hang onto, in a tape recorded talk which he gave in 1980.[211]

Ed was one of the great A.A. oldtimers in northern Indiana. He first came in contact with A.A. in the first half of 1947, when he was around forty years old. At the time the tape recording was made, he had been, for most of the intervening thirty-three years, one of the mainstays in the A.A. program in north-central Indiana. His quiet wisdom, his knowledge of how to say the right simple thing to a person at a critical time, and above all the basic decency and love and kindness which one could instantly *sense* and *feel* in the man, made him one of

the most universally beloved A.A. figures in the entire region. Even
some years after his death, when his name was mentioned to oldtimers
who remembered him, their eyes instantly grew soft with reminiscence
as they recalled instances from the past where he had loved them when
they most needed loving.

The first step: becoming more and more frightened by our problem

Ed said in his talk that he first began to realize the seriousness of his
plight when he quit drinking for fifty-nine days but then, inexplicably
and compulsively, started up again and could not stop.

> And from then on, until I did come to A.A., life was very,
> very unhappy for me because I believed that since I *knew*
> how desperately I wanted never to drink again, and since
> I *did* drink again, that I must be hopelessly and helplessly
> *insane*. This is what I thought, this is what I believed, and
> I worried every day for fear that someone—the people next
> door, or on the job, or whatever—would discover that I am
> insane, and they would throw the net over me and take me
> away.
>
> And that, of course, to my way of teaching—I'm a
> Polack, and to us, the worst form of degradation was to be
> *insane*, to lose your mind. And at that time, there really
> wasn't the phrase "mental health" or "mental illness"—it
> hadn't come into much being then. In fact, it didn't come
> into being until the early 50's. *Then* you were *insane*, and
> they took you not to a mental hospital, but to an *insane
> asylum*, and you rarely came out. Well, I lived with this fear
> for the next seven or eight months—but still, I had to drink,
> I could not go without drinking. But when the day came
> that the first drink that I *had* to have in the morning wiped
> me out, made me drunk—there was a moment of decision
> there.
>
> [This was the work of] God—although I did not know
> him then, he apparently *knew me*—because he gave me the

grace to realize that I had reached a point where I had to make a decision. As I said, I was married, I had a beautiful young wife, and a three-year-old baby girl, and I was so proud. I was comparatively an old man—I was thirty-eight years old when Penny was born. And I thought I *invented* babies, I was so proud and all, and man oh man!—here I am, I can't *drink* anymore. If one drink makes me drunk?—I was given the *grace* to understand that I had to do *something*.

This was what John Wesley (following the Calvinist and Puritan doctrine) called the first gift of God's grace, which comes before the gift of saving faith, but which is the necessary precursor.[212] God must force us to "hit bottom" (as the A.A. people say) before we will ever turn to him for help, and to do that, he must make us progressively more and more aware of the seriousness of our problem. We have to become increasingly frightened and dismayed by the self-destructive compulsion that has taken over our lives, until we finally reach the point of total desperation. Although this slide downhill may seem cruel and unbelievably painful to us at the time, it is in fact a good gift of God, because he is the power of Truth Itself, and we cannot ever get well until we first face the agonizing truth of our sickness, so that we will seek treatment. With Ed Pike, the central problem was alcohol— for you, the reader, it may be something entirely different—but when you arrive at the point where you realize that your problem has put you in a position where *you know that you cannot make yourself go on any further*, you have hit *your* bottom.

We are then progressively driven further and further downward

Different people have different kinds of bottoms. Ed Pike was what the A.A. people call a high bottom drunk: he still had his job, his family, and his home when he finally got to his breaking point.

There are also low bottom drunks, and also, unfortunately, no bottom drunks: these are the people who die in a gutter on skid row some place, still insisting that their problems are caused by what other people did to them, or by the way the world is, or because God treated them cruelly and unfairly.

If you, the reader, are struggling with a personal problem of any sort which just keeps getting worse and worse, and getting you into more and more misery and trouble, you must decide if you want to be a high bottom person, or keep on pridefully trying to solve it all by yourself until you become a low bottom person. Or perhaps you are the saddest kind of all, the no bottom person, who will let this problem destroy you—railing against God and accusing him of being uncaring and cruel while you steadfastly continue to reject every offer of help he sends you.

Ed (and his wife Bobby, who was also an alcoholic) decided once again to stop drinking, but then a minor crisis caused all of Ed's resolve to vanish in a moment:[213]

> I got a letter from the Internal Revenue Department, and they told me that I owed 'em some money, and man, that really, you know, pulled my bobber under, because I didn't know, you know, what to do. I don't know why I got so excited over that letter, 'cause, hell, I'd had four or five just like it—you know, previously—and they hadn't bothered me.
>
> But this time, it really shook me, and being an alcoholic, the first thing I could think of was to go get a drink! Not that we alcoholics believe that a drink will remove the problem—no, we're not that stupid. But like Scarlett O'Hara ["Tomorrah is anothah day"] we'll think about it *tomorrow*!
>
> But I had a problem—I didn't know how I was gonna go get *me* a drink, and I didn't have enough money to bring *home* a bottle, and I was literally afraid to go get *me* a drink and not bring some home for Bobbie. Now, none of you here know her, of course, but she was about five foot one, and weighed about eighty-five pounds soaking wet, with her winter underwear on, but I was literally *afraid* of her.

And so, I'm trying to figure out how I'm going to go get this bottle, and I'm reading the newspaper, because, as I said, I *am* a reader. I'm a compulsive reader. And I was reading the Elkhart *Truth* (we had in the meantime moved to Elkhart) and I found this little story, way back on maybe page thirteen or fourteen, about Alcoholics Anonymous here in Elkhart—that A.A. had grown to such numbers that they had to have three closed meetings a week, in order that everyone would have the opportunity to get to a closed meeting.

At the very bottom: God's little nudge to push us onto the healing path

This story (with only slight variations) is commonplace in accounts by twelve step people of how they came to the final point of decision. After they hit bottom, God, in his grace, intruded something small into their vision, and gave them one last nudge. In this case, it was a small article in a newspaper that the person suddenly, through some interior divine prodding, unaccountably stopped and read slowly and carefully. But whatever the clue is which God throws out, he then seems often to add some strange internal urge (a compulsion that is not-me but is within-me) to actually take action on that inner feeling.

Whenever people are telling their own personal story of how they stopped hurting and destroying themselves, and got themselves started on the path that leads to God, we are apt to find inexplicable and unaccountable things that seemed to have happened at the moment of the crucial decision. For St. Augustine, it was the child's voice from the other side of the wall with the sing-song chant, "Pick it up and read it, pick it up and read it." For Ed Pike it was the little newspaper article.

This is grace at work, the mysterious x-factor referred to in the first chapter of this work. No one ever enters the true spiritual life because one fine day they decide (totally on their own initiative) that, although their lives are going just great, their way of living would possibly be even richer and fuller if they became more spiritual. People truly enter the spiritual life only when God has finally poked, prodded, and driven them so hard that they cannot stand their old way of life any more.

The appearance of
the messenger sent by God

As a result of reading the newspaper article, Ed Pike contacted the A.A. people in Elkhart, and went to his first meeting, an open meeting one Saturday night, where they had brought in an outside speaker—a comparatively young man who was a newspaper editor from Warsaw, Indiana, who also flew airplanes (this was Bill Mollenhour, the editor of the *Warsaw Times-Union*).

> He just inspired *confidence*: he made me *believe* what he said. And that was a new experience to me, because I never believed anybody—I thought everybody was as dishonest as I was. But I believed what Bill said that night. And it made me want to discover whatever else there was to it.

At this point in our transition from people who hate or totally ignore God into people who are willing to walk the spiritual path, God commonly begins speaking to us in more detail than he has up to that point, through some other human being whom he uses as his intermediary or messenger. He also commonly puts us in contact (directly or indirectly) with other human beings who can serve as living examples to us of what we will be able to achieve if we walk the spiritual path—for St. Augustine at this point it was the example of the lives of the desert monks, and for John Wesley it was the faith of the Moravian missionaries whom he had encountered.

Proto-faith or implicit faith

Ed Pike had been convinced enough by the speaker at the Saturday night open meeting to try going to a second meeting. This one was a closed meeting, which met once a week, on Wednesday evenings, in some member's home. Ed was thrown back into a panic again, almost from the time he entered the door. He had in fact discovered God the preceding Saturday night, and he had responded with the kind of proto-faith (if we may call it that)[214] which was willing to make the commitment to go where that strange power pointed him, but he was not yet aware at the conscious level that it was the power of God which he had felt and sensed so strongly.

> Now at the first closed meeting that I went to, the chairman, he spoke for about ten or fifteen minutes, and mostly on this *God* business, and it *scared* me. Not that I have ever been an atheist—I have *not*—but I never in my life ever felt a *moment's* feeling of any relationship with God— "higher power"—whatever you want to call him. I knew the answers in the catechism, because I was brought up in the Roman church, and I could probably answer most of the questions in the catechism tonight, and I haven't looked at it in sixty years or more.
>
> But there's a difference—I mean, I knew the [catechism] answer, but never in my life did I ever have a feeling of *faith in God*, and I didn't have when I came to A.A., and naturally, I thought, well, if you have to believe in God to get sober, well then, I'm doomed, I'm done, you know.

Ed was a very sharp man, so that within the first ten or fifteen minutes he was there, he caught the vital distinction between those two different meanings of the word faith. He already had faith at the level of intellectual belief, that is, faith as belief that a being called God exists, and faith as the ability to state, in the precise, officially correct words, the intellectualized and verbally conceptualized doctrines about God taught by his religious denomination. But what the people at this closed A.A. meeting were talking about was faith as awareness of a direct relationship with God at the feeling level, and faith as a confidence or trust in God based on things sensed or intuited at the pure feeling level.[215]

Ed did not think he had that second kind of faith at all, which was to some degree an exaggeration on his part. He did not realize yet that what he had experienced at the Saturday night open meeting at the feeling level—the spirit of love and total honesty, and the feeling of new hope and confidence which this inspired in him—was in fact the basic underlying substance of the living relationship with God's continuous presence which was faith in the second sense. Perhaps we could say that he had a "proto-faith" at this point, or a "tacit faith" as opposed to an explicit faith (to use Polanyi's terminology),[216] but just did not realize yet that this could be an authentic form of the faith that saves.

A physician at the meeting (it must have been either Jack Swihart or Art Kissner) saved the day by giving Ed an interim-position he could handle. If he had no living faith of the second sort, at least at the level of conscious awareness, then God would accept, in lieu of that, *a sincere and honest desire* for that kind of faith.

> Another fellow that was there, a doctor, made a statement that really saved me. He said that the next best thing to *having* faith was to have *a desire for faith*. Well, God must have known that I had a desire for whatever I needed in order to learn whether I could live and function, produce, without drinking. And so I just made a deal with myself, that I will do anything that they tell me they do—*anything*—and if I'm big enough, I'll do it.
>
> They said that, you know, you should ask God to help you. And I did that. And I felt foolish when I did it, because, you know, it didn't ring any bells or anything. They said, you know, read the Big Book. I personally didn't read the Big Book so much, but Bobbie did—she would read it, and we would talk about it. And I even started listening to her, you know—boy, there's a big change!

So Ed followed their instructions and consistently prayed to God and asked God for help even though he did not consciously feel anything special happening. This was important—the most significant work going on in the human psyche during this kind of spiritual transformation is usually taking place far below the level of normal conscious awareness.

This is why I believe that it is necessary to stress the importance of the kind of proto-faith or implicit faith that is indicated by willingness to make a commitment, willingness to start listening and become teachable instead of talking and arguing and blustering all the time, willingness to change, and the courage to plunge into the new and the unknown. The ground of faith is seen in the courage of a nomad leaving the part of the desert which he knows and heading southwards into a new and unknown sector of the wilderness, trusting one day at a time that God will continue to guide him tomorrow to his next night's encampment.

As John Calvin said, the tiniest drop of real faith, even if mixed with considerable fear and doubt, will start the spiritual process of restoring the image of God within our spirits. We will start to grow and change, in a continuous process that will lead us (if we stay on the spiritual path) "from glory to glory,"[217] as each new spiritual triumph and each new vision of God leads us into becoming ever better mirrors reflecting the love and compassion and honesty of God down into this world.

Unconscious change and growth gradually evolving into explicit faith

Ed Pike began to alter the way he thought and acted, at first without realizing it. Other people noticed it first, but finally even he began to get a glimmering that some major changes had come over him. He had always had a tendency, for example, to dally with the ladies, even though he was a married man, and had never felt any particular guilt or hesitation about these sporadic affairs. If the woman seemed willing, Ed was after her. But after a relatively short while walking the spiritual path, Ed had what for him was a totally strange experience:

> It wasn't too much later that I was furloughed from the railroad, and [had] one experience that I'll share with you: I took a job with the state, examining drivers for drivers licenses. And I went to Goshen—I went one day a week—I would go to Goshen and examine people there, give 'em the drive test. And I ran into an old girlfriend of mine. We'd had a beautiful romance, years ago, when I was single. I was single a long, long time . . . . I never got married until I was thirty-six, I think, something like that. Anyhow, here this gal came up there and we went to a restaurant for lunch and we talked, and we talked, and we talked. And I just *know*— I *know*—that, you know, she expected more than that. And when we went back to the office, she made the remark, she says, "Well, no girl ever got a *nicer* turndown."
>
> And I was mad at myself that whole afternoon! And then I remember when I walked in the door, there was another member of A.A. there, and I said to him, "I'm still mad—at *me*, you know." And I said, "Boy, don't you ask God to help you, if you don't want him to do it!" *[Laughter]* I'll never forget that, because that was a very vivid experience in my life. And so I still believe that, to this day. Don't ask him to help you, if you don't want him to!

Ed was developing a stronger and stronger faith down at the unconscious level, and it was beginning to affect his behavior in ways of which he was sometimes consciously aware. But it was not until he had been in the A.A. program for a whole year that he began to have a fully explicit faith in God in the sense of a conscious sense of *trust*, and an awareness of a direct relationship with God at the feeling level.

So he tried to warn his listeners about two things: First, it is not necessary to believe in the detailed doctrines of some particular religion in order to walk the spiritual path and find God. Even if you were to intellectually accept all of the dogmas taught by any particular religious group—any group in the world, no matter which one—that in itself would not produce a good relationship with God, nor would it give an alcoholic the power to stop drinking. Second—and perhaps even more important—at the beginning it is not even necessary to be consciously aware of having any particular trust in God or awareness of God at the feeling level. As Ed put it,

> The point that I'm trying to make here—and I'm wandering all over the place, because I sure as hell ain't no speaker—the point I'm trying to make is, you don't have to believe in God to get sober. On the other hand, if you *do* stay away from a drink for a reasonable length of time—with me it was a year (of course I'm pretty dumb)—but I was sober at least a year before I was given the gift of faith in God as *I* understand him. And so, that's the point that I was trying to make. Don't let that discourage you. If you don't have a faith in God today, don't let that discourage you from continuing one day at a time with your *sobriety*. And I do believe, since it was my experience, that faith will be given to you.
>
> And as I remember hearing someplace—and I'm quite sure it's in the Bible, although I'm not a Bible scholar—that faith is a *gift* from God. I didn't get it because I worked harder at it, or because I even had a greater desire for it. Certainly not because I was smarter, because I never even finished the tenth grade in school. So, you know, it is a gift. And today I do—*I do* have a very childlike faith in God as *I* understand him.
>
> Now I have many friends today who are members of the clergy, members of the cloth, and I would hesitate to describe to them *my* conception of God. I think most of 'em would be horrified if I did, but *I* am happy with it, *I* am contented with it. And that's what the Big Book says: "We came to believe in a power greater than ourselves." And whenever it refers to God anywhere in the Big Book, there's always that clause, "as we understand him."

Journeying into Abraham's desert: stubborn commitment, willingness to change, becoming teachable

If we have the kind of proto-faith that I have termed "implicit faith," that will be adequate to start us on the first steps down the spiritual path that leads to God. But how can we tell whether we have the kind of implicit faith which is necessary? There are some questions we can ask ourselves:

Are we willing to make a real commitment to following the disciplines of the particular spiritual path we have chosen to follow? Sometimes there is not a whole lot of difference between faith and pure stubbornness, that is, the kind of attitude that says "nobody and nothing is going to stop me from seeing this thing through to the end!" Are we willing to stop talking all the time, and start genuinely listening to other people instead? Are we willing to become teachable, and stop being know-it-alls who think we already have all the answers? Do we actually *want* to change, or would we rather stick with the endless futile misery we already know?

If we actually want to change, we must have the courage and the guts to roll up our tents and put them on our donkeys' backs and then head out across the sands and hills covered with little dried-up brown desert bushes, following Abraham's footsteps, and venturing boldly into a totally unknown world that we have never experienced before. But there is where the Promise lies situated. And the God who promises this to us, as well as the men and women who have been there and come back glowing within with a divine love and quiet serenity and irrepressible good humor, give us their guarantees that we too can travel to that blessed place and become one of its citizens.

"I know there is a God"

It is not all a matter of faith, either explicit or implicit. At an A.A. meeting several years ago when the topic of faith came up, an oldtimer named Rob G. said, "I don't believe that there is a God." Everyone looked a bit puzzled, because Rob was a very pious man. But then he went on to say, "I don't believe that there is a God; I *know* that there is a God. Otherwise, I wouldn't be alive here now. Everything I have, including my life itself, I owe to his grace." Rob had been a drug dealer, a pimp, and everything else under the sun, and as his life plummeted further and further downhill, he would pass out drunk on the side of the street and later wake up groggily to see the passersby looking down on him with pity and scorn and disgust as they walked past. He found himself going into dirty dope houses shaking with fear as he looked for his next fix and hoped he could get back out of that building with his life. But then A.A. turned his life around, and by the time he made this remark he had been (for a number of years) one of the most successful sponsors around for young people just entering the program.

And many other people who have been in twelve step programs for a while would say the same: "I do not just *believe* there is a God, I *know* from my own immediate experience that there is a God, and I *know* from firsthand knowledge the power of his grace."

Nevertheless, anyone who has walked the spiritual path for a few years, or even thirty or forty or fifty years, will tell you that no matter how many times you have seen God push the wheelbarrow across the tightwire stretched over the abyss, and no matter how many times you have ridden in the wheelbarrow yourself and had its total safety demonstrated to you, it is still not always easy to jump on board! Now certainly in a lot of kinds of situations, it gets much easier as you go along to make yourself climb in the wheelbarrow and hang on, but people with long experience will tell you that there are still times when you are scared to death every time you look down, and your hands have clenched the sides so tightly that they practically have to pry your fingers loose after you get to the other side.

Going on an adventure into a new land

What God is inviting you to do is go on an adventure with him. This is not sitting in a movie theater or in front of a television screen and watching other people experience what are only pretend adventures on the screen, or riding in a roller coaster that may seem frightening but is actually far safer than even a short trip in your family car. This is a real adventure that God is inviting you to take part in.

What God is saying is that he wants you to go on an adventure with him where you are going to see some incredible sights and do some amazing things and receive gifts so great that you cannot now even imagine how wonderful they will be. It is not a *safe* adventure at all, because it will be a real adventure. The one thing it is guaranteed to be is an infinitely *satisfying* adventure.

Do you have the faith and courage and pure ornery stubbornness to follow Abraham doggedly out into the desert wastes and see the marvelous grandeur of the sunlight of the spirit rising above the distant horizon at dawn and shining out in all its divine glory? If so, come join us as we journey along the path of eternal life.

Chapter 24

The Chariot of the Soul

Does God exist? The rise of modern atheism, which began to become increasingly more widespread in the 1840's and the decades which immediately followed, convinced many people that the word "God" described nothing at all, and that it referred to a totally imaginary concept. More and more people became afraid to have faith in God, afraid that this idea was nothing but a childish myth and a fantasy created inside their own minds. What could there possibly be in the real external world to which the word God could refer?

The Big Bang

And yet the first glimpses of the answer to this nineteenth-century problem began to appear early in the very next century. In 1915, Albert Einstein published his field equations (as part of his theory of general relativity) in which the force of gravitation was described as a curving of spacetime caused by the presence of matter and energy at certain locations. A young Russian mathematician and physicist named Alexander Friedman then discovered the expanding-universe solution to these field equations in 1922, which thereafter formed the basis of what came to be known as the Big Bang theory of the origin of the universe.

The Big Bang theory did not begin to be taken with real seriousness however until the American astronomer Edwin Hubble published his observations on the red shift in 1929, including a statement of what came to be known as Hubble's Law. He did his observational work at the Mount Wilson Observatory, near Pasadena, California, where they had the famous 100-inch telescope which was at that time the largest in the world. Hubble's Law said that the greater the distance between two galaxies, the faster they would be moving apart, and fit this into the kind of solution to Einstein's relativistic equations which Friedman had proposed. Or in other words, it was not just the galaxies themselves which were moving away from one another. All of space itself was in fact expanding in a homogeneous, isotropic fashion.

By observing distant galaxies at the Mount Wilson Observatory, Hubble had come up with observational evidence to show that the Big Bang theory was a possible solution to the origin of the universe, but not ironclad evidence to prove that it was the only possible solution. That did not happen until the discovery thirty-five years later, in 1964, of the cosmic microwave background radiation which the theory of the Big Bang had predicted.[218] But the existence of this radiation proved that none of the other theories about the origins of the universe which were being debated by scientists of that time could be right.[219] It now became clear that the Big Bang theory was correct: that this universe had a beginning in time (before which there was no universe at all), and that it came into being *out of some kind of mysterious ground* which had created space and time themselves 13.7 billion years ago, along with all the matter and energy in the universe, in an event which had violated some of what were regarded (in all other contexts) as the fundamental laws of the universe.

That has been over forty years ago now. One would have expected enormous public excitement at that discovery. But I remember that back at the time, the discovery of the cosmic microwave background radiation in 1964 did not get anything like the kind of newspaper coverage that had been given earlier in the century to Einstein's discovery of the theory of relativity. I think that the average person did not at all realize the significance of what this discovery meant: that there was now hard evidence, good scientific data which could be measured with great numerical precision, showing that the theory of the Big Bang was correct. And what was so especially important about this, was that it was the necessary piece that had to be put in place in order to put God back into the picture of the universe.

Because being able to prove that the Big Bang had taken place meant that we now had good scientific evidence showing that *the ground of being*—whatever that mysterious reality was out of which this universe had exploded into existence 13.7 billion years ago—also of necessity had to exist. We cannot make a precise scientific "measurement" of God (the mysterious ground which lay prior to the creation of this universe), but we *can* measure the "echo" as it were of God's mighty act of creation still reverberating through the entire cosmos, and show that the Creator must of necessity have existed.

God as the ground of being

I do not believe that there are many physicists today who would doubt that such a ground of being has to exist. There has to have been *something* there out of which this universe came into being, even if we have as yet no direct scientific access to it. Granted that modern science can work back almost to the very instant of the Big Bang itself, this *almost* is not the same as *all the way there*. So we cannot describe the preexistent ground of being in any but the most general terms.

Nevertheless, what comes out of this general description is clearly identical with that ultimate reality which the ancient tradition, both East and West, refers to as the supreme principle: unknowable, inexpressible, incomprehensible, beyond all space and time. The ground of being is what the gospel of John calls the Unknown Father, the one who can only become knowable by reflection into our box of space and time in the person of the Cosmic Christ principle. In the Jewish Kabbalah, the ground of being is that which is above all knowledge and understanding, that is, the divine mystery which (in the theory of the ten *Sephirot*) lies above both *Hokhmah* (Wisdom, Being from nothingness) and *Binah* (Reason or Intellect). In ancient gnosticism, it was called the Unknowable Father. In ancient pagan Neo-Platonism, the ground of being was called the unknowable One.

In medieval Muslim philosophy and mysticism, this Neo-Platonic One (the unknowable ground of being) was of course identified as Allah, the God of Islam. In Hinduism, the ground of being (whether thought of as God or as an impersonal Godhead) is called Brahman.

St. Gregory of Nyssa:
God as the unknowable abyss

Does the ground of being exist? Of course. The universe had to explode *out of something* in the Big Bang. There has to have been *something* there.

But can modern science describe the ground of being? Of course not. Or at least not by ordinary scientific methods, because the ground of being is outside of both space and time. It operates in a realm where many (perhaps even all) of the ordinary laws of nature do not apply (such as the laws of thermodynamics). It operates in a realm where ordinary mathematics cannot be employed, because it is a realm of infinities. Attempting to multiply or divide by infinity, or to add or subtract infinity, turns a mathematical formula into nonsense.

But this is what the great thinkers of the past meant when they talked about God. What the modern world has forgotten is how much of the philosophy and theology of the ancient and medieval world was built on a conception of a ground of being which was described as an unknowable abyss of nothingness (in the literal sense of no-thing-ness, not a specific physical object or sense phenomenon).

In the fourth and fifth century A.D., at the height of the patristic period, two important authors helped give birth to two different kinds of western spiritual teaching. One of these theologians was St. Gregory of Nyssa (c. 330 - c. 395). In many of his spiritual writings, St. Gregory eagerly embraced the idea that we saw God in the vision of the abyss of nothingness which lay outside the box of space and time in which our human minds were normally imprisoned.[220] This was a vision of God which was awe-inspiring, disconcerting, humbling, but also oddly freeing and liberating.

Instead of being frightened out of our minds by the radical unknowability of the ground of being, and—with cries of despair—proclaiming this unknowability as "the death of God,"[221] we need instead to turn back to the ancient tradition, and learn to see this well of impenetrable mystery as an overflowing fount from which gush forth all the things which can fill our spirits with good things, and create in us the highest kind of humanity.

It is not really an empty abyss anyway. It is an infinite depth from which we can see pouring out upon us a world of perpetually changing beauty and goodness and novelty and creativity. The tiny spring flowers, the towering thunderstorm, the starry galaxies extending outward as far as our telescopes can peer, songbirds singing for pleasure on hot summer days, and the joy of a human artist painting a new work of art, are all part of this explosion of novelty and creativity and beauty. One human being hugging another human being who feels sad is an expression of the kind of heights of goodness which can spontaneously appear in this constantly changing creation. There are enormous healing powers in the created world as well, ranging from the natural processes which mend broken bones and cut fingers, to the spiritual healing forces which heal injured souls.

But there is real evil in this universe too. The four horsemen of the Apocalypse ride forth from the throne of God every day: the white horse of conquest and defeat, the red horse of warfare and conflict, the black horse of want and starvation, and the pale horse whose rider is named Death.[222] Even among the most saintly of us, though we have the souls of angels (which are creatures of divine light), we will always have the dark side in us too: the reptilian brain that wants to rip and tear and taste blood, and rape and ravage, and rise to the top of a pecking order based on the vicious subjugation of those weaker than us.

It is nevertheless possible to develop a truly good spirituality based on our encounter with the impersonal God whom we meet in the vision of the unknowable abyss, a spirituality which puts the light soul in charge of our lives, and keeps the dark side of us as domesticated as possible.

It is time to listen to our ancestors, and to quit saying that "if the ground of being is an impersonal and unknowable abyss, then God does not exist and trying to live a spiritual life is nonsense." Our ancestors knew better than that, in both the East and the West, and it is time for us to recover some of their ancient wisdom. This is as true for Christianity as it is for the Hindu and Buddhist traditions, because we have almost two thousand years worth of Christian theologians and great spiritual teachers who believed in a God who was, at the most essential level, a totally or almost totally impersonal absolute: St. Gregory of Nyssa and St. Denis belonged in that company, and even St. Thomas Aquinas (with his theory that God is literally describable and knowable only as Being Itself) had a far more impersonal view of God than many people assume. But the list is far longer than just those three: St. Bonaventure, Meister Eckhart, Johann Tauler, the author of the Theologia Germanica, Friedrich Schleiermacher, Rudolf Otto, Emmet Fox, and Paul Tillich, to name just a few, were thinkers who showed us ways of understanding the spiritual life which will work even if we believe that God is totally impersonal. This requires an intelligent reader, of course, who is willing to do some honest work, and especially one who has some real reservoirs of courage inside. Looking fully into the abyss of no-thing-ness is as scary as it gets.

Modern atheists try to pretend that they are the ones who are intelligent, while those ancient people who believed in God were all ignorant and stupid. It appears to me that the real difference is that, all too frequently, these modern atheists are cowards who react to everything frightening by running away in fear, while those ancient people who believed in God were people of real courage. They were willing to look into the abyss without losing their nerve.

It is time now to quit taking the fact that the vision of the ground of being is extremely frightening, and trying to turn that into the atheist's statement that "God does not exist." The ground of being obviously does exist. Modern science has now explored, using powerful particle accelerators, almost all the way back to the very moment of creation. The echo of the act of creation still reverberates throughout the universe in the cosmic microwave background radiation.

In that relatively brief period of history which began in the 1840's and ran for perhaps two or three generations, atheism seemed to make sense to lots of western intellectuals, and seemed "scientific." But the sweeping changes in modern science which occurred over the course of the twentieth century, have undermined the roots of all those atheistic arguments. And in particular, from 1964 on, no one has had any excuse for trying to deny the existence of the unknowable abyss (underlying everything else in the cosmos) which the ancient and medieval world called "God."

Remember the title to one of Paul Tillich's major works? *The Courage to Be.* Real faith, Tillich said, can look openly into the abyss of non-being and still courageously affirm the power of being. Let us quit pretending we are atheists, if the truth is that we are just scared, or in a snit because everybody and everything else in the universe does not automatically and instantly follow our commands and do our will. There are spiritual answers which can heal that fear, and can also pull us out of our pettish snits!

The intimately personal God of St. Macarius

At the other extreme from the impersonal God which we see in some of the passages in St. Gregory of Nyssa's spiritual writings, is the intimately personal God proclaimed by St. Macarius the Homilist, who was his rough contemporary.[223] The two men make a good contrast, and we can trace those two very different ways of looking at God down through all the subsequent centuries of the Christian tradition.

St. Macarius had a profound influence on the Eastern Orthodox tradition, particularly figures like St. John Climacus (the author of the *Ladder of Divine Ascent*), and the monks of Mt. Athos and those later theologians in the hesychast tradition like St. Symeon the New Theologian and St. Gregory Palamas. But he also had an influence on the western Christian tradition in part of the Lutheran pietist tradition, and above all in John Wesley, who was one of the founders of the modern evangelical tradition. The religion of the heart when it is fully and unselfconsciously expressed in the Wesleyan and Methodist tradition is an evangelical Christian echo of the teaching of the great Eastern Orthodox mystics.[224]

St. Macarius and the image of the Throne Chariot in Ezekiel

St. Macarius, in the first of his *Fifty Spiritual Homilies*,[225] used the description of the *Merkabah* or Throne Chariot in the first chapter of Ezekiel as an image of the human soul. Four angelic beings are described, made of divine fire and light, whose job it is to pull the heavenly chariot. The four angelic beings represent "[1] the will, [2] the conscience, [3] the intelligence, and [4] the faculty of love. By these the chariot of the soul is controlled, and upon these God rests." Macarius is telling us that these four different parts of the human mind, in other words, function at the angelic level. Like the angels, we have [1] the ability to choose between good and evil, [2] the ability to recognize the fundamental difference between right and wrong, [3] the ability to think at a higher intellectual level, and above all, [4] the ability to show genuine love. We are effectively super angels in fact, far more complex and multifaceted than any of the ordinary angels around God's heavenly throne.

When I allow God to be the one who rides upon the chariot of my soul and directs all its movements, and when I allow the chariot of my soul to rest with full faith upon the divine hand which is extended below it and holds it up and enables it to fly through the heavens, then my transcendent self will be filled with a radiant white light and turned into what St. Macarius elsewhere calls the Man of Light, that is, the Heavenly Human Being.

Who are the human beings who bring us the message which saves us? We have already described them in Chapter 12. They are the God-bearers, the ones who allow God to ride upon the chariot of their souls.

Macarius's image also speaks of what the Oxford Group and the twelve step program calls divine guidance. As is also said in Ignatian spirituality, by allowing God to hold the reins and steer the chariot of our souls, we are increasingly given the power of *discernment*, where we are given an internal divine guide to what we should say and do, and become increasingly guided by God in all our actions.

As we come to sense more and more that the hand of God is always underneath, holding us up—for as it says in Deuteronomy 33:27, "and underneath are the everlasting arms"—we discover that the vision of the underlying abyss no longer has the power to totally unglue us. Instead of falling screaming into the nightmares of our greatest fears, we learn to "float" on top of our fear, to use a metaphor which St. Macarius employed in another of his sermons.

But what is most important of all in the Macarian vision of God is that it shows how the relationship between the human soul and God becomes the most intimate and personal kind of relationship which could possibly exist between two personal beings. In my association with other human beings, I and the other person always remain fundamentally external to one another. I cannot truly enter into somebody else's head, nor can that other person enter into my brain, not really. But God can and does. It is the most intimate kind of relationship which can occur. It is more intimate than sex, even though there is a long Roman Catholic, Eastern Orthodox, and Jewish tradition of interpretation of the Song of Songs which uses human sexuality as a metaphor for speaking about the divine-human encounter.

When we talk about the mystical "union" between God and a human being, we do not mean (or we certainly do not mean in Macarian spirituality) that I can no longer tell the difference between me and God. That would be absurd. I do not have God's powers, nor can I "become a God," nor can any other human being. But the union between God and the human soul is closer, more intimate, and more immediate that any kind of relationship at all between two human beings, no matter how much they love one another.

And the God who rides upon the chariot of my soul, and upholds it with his loving hand, is the most deeply personal being that it would be possible to imagine.

Personal or impersonal?

Where do you the reader stand at this point? My first piece of advice to you would be to suggest that you quit fussing around "trying to decide whether God exists or not." God exists. Your problem is figuring out how to deal with God, where if you are like most human beings, you have an incredible amount of misunderstandings to put away, and an equally large number of truths about God that you need to learn.

You do not need to begin by believing in a personal God. There are an enormous number of spiritual techniques which do not require belief in anything other than an impersonal absolute, a ground of being, a vision into the abyss of no-thing-ness. And many of them are very sophisticated, and can yield very successful results.

As far as I can see—but this is just me—there is no way of really conclusively proving that God is personal by using the kinds of intellectual arguments that the philosophers and natural scientists use, although in Chapter 13 of this book, I talk about some of these arguments, and point the reader to some very good theologians and philosophers who have gone at it that way. To me, though, it seems as though something equivalent to the Turing test, which I described in Chapter 18, is the best route to a deep belief in a personal God. It takes a good deal of time and experience in the spiritual life to carry out this sort of Turing test, however, so many newcomers to the spiritual life may feel more comfortable regarding God as an impersonal absolute, at least in the beginning.

And remember that in the ancient and medieval world, there were large numbers of good people who led very satisfying spiritual lives, thinking about the ground of being in totally impersonal terms, for all of their lives.

If you are a beginner, you do not need to make a decision on that. You *do need* to make a decision to commit yourself to actually living the spiritual life in a concrete way. That means finding a spiritual method and a spiritual community which is congenial, and a teacher or spiritual director, and it also requires engaging in regular prayer and meditation, and becoming involved in some kind of discipline which will deal with all the resentment and fear which is locked up in your soul.

Appendix:

Time, Eternity, God's Temporality, Love, and Immortality

St. Augustine's static and fatalistic concept of eternity

Western European thinking about the nature of God's temporality was set upon a bad course at the beginning of the Middle Ages by the most important philosopher in the west at that time: St. Augustine, in his *City of God*, said explicitly that what was called "God's providence" by Christians was simply the same thing as what had been called Fate (*fatum*) in the writings of the old pagan Roman Stoics like Seneca. It was the decree of God which specified exactly how all events were going to happen. In fact, Augustine went on to say, he would have used the word Fate in his own writings, were it not for his fear that the common people of his own time—who had no knowledge of Stoic philosophy but often had a superstitious belief in astrology—would assume that his use of that word meant that he believed that, not the decree of God, but the aspects between the planets at the time of birth completely determined the course of human lives.

Like those ancient Stoic philosophers, Augustine believed that the whole course of the universe was predetermined. Each new event was caused to take place, in exactly the way that it happened, by all the events which had preceded it, and this new event in turn would act as a cause which precisely determined how the next event was going to happen. What we meant by the word "time" (*tempus*) was this mechanical sequence of events happening one after another, in long chains of cause and effect which stretched from the beginning of the universe all the way to its end. God dwelt in "eternity" (*aeternitas*), sitting up above the course of events and seeing them all simultaneously as it were.

The seventeenth and eighteenth century Deists, at the beginning of the Early Modern Period, believed that God created the universe in 4004 B.C., and that the first set of physical objects which were created in that precise millisecond gave rise to all the succeeding things in the universe, by a process of scientific cause and effect. God started the universe off at the beginning, but then dropped out of the picture and let the universe run by itself, like a well-made pocket watch which had been wound up and then left to tick away the hours and minutes. You needed a Divine Creator to set things off in the beginning, but past that point, scientists like Sir Isaac Newton could explain everything that happened without any reference to God.

But this was not Augustine's view. To him, God was not closer to events at the beginning of time, but equally close to all times: when God created the universe, he created all the events which have ever happened and ever will happen, in one single act of creation. St. Thomas Aquinas, during the High Middle Ages, believed the same, which was why he believed that philosophy *could* prove that the universe was created by God, even though philosophy *could not* prove that the universe had a beginning in time (that is, on the basis of natural reason alone and without appealing to the supernaturally revealed truths of the Bible). Modern university students are often confused when they first hear Aquinas' position—how could he believe that he could prove that God created the universe, if he did not believe that he could prove that the universe had a beginning in time?—because they do not understand the underlying Augustinian perspective of Aquinas' thought.

To give a very crude metaphor, we might think of the image of two people, one of them standing at a railroad crossing and watching the railroad cars go past one by one, and the other person sitting on top of a hill and looking at the train from on high, where he or she can see the entire train all at once, from the locomotive at its beginning to the last car at the end of the train. The person who is standing at the railroad crossing is seeing time fly past *from within time,* as it were, where events take place one moment after another, in such a way that all we can immediately see is what is happening at the present moment. But the person sitting on the hill is seeing time from the viewpoint of eternity—*sub specie aeternitatis* so to speak—where everything in the predetermined course of events can be seen all at once: "Ah, I see that the red box car with its doors open is going to be passing the railroad crossing in exactly five seconds, and that this is going to happen necessarily because of the way the cars are coupled in order."

This metaphor should not be pressed too far, and is meant to be suggestive only, because in the medieval Western European understanding of the nature of eternity, there is no way that we human beings, who are temporal creatures, can go outside the box of space and time in which our minds are enclosed, and truly comprehend what the eternal is like. But I might be tempted to say here that the very fact that we cannot possibly imagine what this kind of eternity would be like first hand, may arise from the fact that it is an impossible concept—medieval philosophers playing with words that did not really mean anything comprehensible! Charles Hartshorne believed that the understanding of time which was connected with this static concept of eternity likewise could not be truly imagined, and in fact turned time into an illusion instead of adequately explaining how the flow of time could be a reality.

There are also two consequences of adopting this Augustinian view of time and eternity which must be mentioned. First, it means that there is no real human free will, and that the question as to whether each of us human beings is going to be saved or damned is a matter of divine predestination, and was decided by God even before the creation of the universe. This was a consequence which Augustine embraced and was perfectly willing to accept, as did John Calvin at the end of the Middle Ages. John Calvin's first published work (in 1532) was not on any Christian theological theme, but was a commentary on the pagan Stoic philosopher Seneca's *De Clementia.* It is important to remember that belief in predestination (and the denial of human free will necessarily associated with this doctrine) is, in the case of both St. Augustine and John Calvin, an idea that arose far more from their early training in Stoic philosophy than from anything truly in the Bible.

A second consequence of accepting the Augustinian view of the relationship between time and eternity, is that it becomes simply impossible to understand any kind of life after death in which we could continue to have meaningful personal experiences. In medieval Western Europe, the orthodox Catholic belief was that our souls traveled after death to the eternal realm. But eternity in the Augustinian sense is a static state in which nothing ever changes in the slightest. So going to heaven would be what? Sort of a timeless orgasm of pure pleasure that just went on forever? And hell would then become something truly insanely and unimaginably cruel.

There could be no purgatory, no second chance, in a realm where nothing ever changed. And the near death experiences where people find their dead relatives and other loved ones welcoming them to the next life could never take place in anything but our imaginations, because a decision to travel through the land beyond and welcome us could never take place in a realm where nothing ever changes. Likewise, those who have preceded us in death can know nothing whatever about our continually changing lives in this realm of time. Let us remember that a mind which knew about changes taking place elsewhere, also by that very fact would have changes going on in itself. So my deceased father or mother, if their souls are living in an Augustinian eternity, can know nothing about either my successes or my failures. Nor could I speak to their souls at a séance, if one believes (as Bill and Lois Wilson did, and apparently Dr. Bob and Anne Smith did too) that it is sometimes possible to speak with the souls of the dead. And in the Catholic tradition, it would seem pointless to pray to saints who are locked into total unchangeability, nor could saints of that sort appear to us in visions or intercede in any other way in our lives.

These are all things that we should remember would be consequences, if we wish to continue to adhere to the medieval Western European conception of the nature of time and eternity.

The ancient Greek concept
of chronological time (chronos)

Augustine's concept of time (*tempus* in Latin) went back to the ancient Greek understanding of *chronos* or chronological time. This referred to a very specific kind of temporality.[226] When our minds go back into the realm of memory in an attempt to draw up a narrative of the past, they select what are in fact only a small number of memories which we objectify as phenomena. We arrange this partial collection of memories into what we think is an appropriate chronological order, where—as Immanuel Kant pointed out—our minds attempt to portray each specific event as leading logically to the next one in a long chain of cause and effect.

Now in fact, as Kant also observed, we can never exhaustively lay out all the causes of the events which we are describing. And it must also be noted that, even if we make use of written documents and set up the most precise scientific instruments for observational purposes, we can never give all the details about everything that happened at any particular moment in the past. We usually only think consciously about the facts that seem important to us because they fit into our pre-established theories about what "makes sense to us," or because they "ought to be important" according to all the things we have been taught by our teachers, or because they are able to get through the filters of our denial systems and our subconscious mental censors, or simply because that was the direction we were looking at the time. And some things we simply forget with the passage of time, or no documents survive which record what happened. So for example, here at the age of seventy, I can no longer remember the name of a single teacher whom I had for the first five years of my schooling, not a one of them, until I had the good and wise Mrs. Collie for my teacher in the sixth grade. And no one in my family saved any of my old report cards or made any written notes about my schooling, so that although it is possible that records still exist somewhere naming these teachers and linking my name to theirs as a student, there are no written documents to which I have access which preserve their names.

But if we can recover enough in the way of facts about the past, and work out a scheme for arranging them in cause-effect chains, we can do something extremely useful with them. We can then project these chains of events into the realm of that-which-has-not-yet-happened, and if we do it properly, we can predict the future. If I have successfully completed the first five grades in elementary school, then I can safely predict that the next grade I will enter if I continue my schooling, will be the sixth grade. If every time in the past when I mixed a solution of silver nitrate with a solution of sodium chloride, an insoluble white precipitate of silver chloride formed and slowly settled to the bottom of the beaker—and especially if, furthermore, my knowledge of chemistry gives me a well constructed theoretical framework for understanding all the cause-effect relationships involved—I can safely predict that exactly the same thing will happen the next time I perform that experiment.

So organizing the events of the past in *chronos* (chronological time) not only allows us to make sense of the past, it also gives us the possibility of predicting the future. In real life, sometimes our predictions of the future come true and sometimes they do not. Chemists and physicists usually have impressive records of success at predicting the future as long as they stick to a relatively small scale. Scientists who are attempting to predict larger and more complex phenomena (such as the effect of carbon dioxide production from the burning of fossil fuels on global warming) have to be much more approximate in their predictions. At the time I am writing this, for example, the shrinking of the ice cap at the North Pole is taking place even more quickly than the climatologists had been warning. Political scientists who are hired by politicians who are running for public office tend to have a much more checkered success rate than chemists or physicists or even climatologists. Sometimes their suggestions work and sometimes they do not. If there were mechanical rules for winning an election in the United States, any candidate who hired a competent political scientist for advice, and rigidly followed that advice, would automatically win any election which was entered.

Nevertheless, organizing the events of the past into chains of cause and effect can often lead to theories and observations that are extremely useful in predicting and controlling the future, and sometimes impressively accurate. I am the first to emphasize that modern science has done marvelous things in devising laws governing the changes in physical objects over the course of chronological time, and as a professional historian, of course, I made my living for most of my adult life teaching students about the course of human history and making observations about the causes of various historical events.

So I am not saying that *chronos* is a pure and totally meaningless illusion, as is done in some Asian philosophies (and as was also done in some versions of ancient Greco-Roman Platonism and Neo-Pythagoreanism). Nevertheless, *chronos* (chronological time) is in fact an artificial construct. The realm of *chronos* will always be to some degree an over-simplification of reality. A map of the world would become useless if we tried to map everything, which is why the most useful maps concentrate on specific areas of knowledge: a road map for driving automobiles, a geological map for petroleum or mining research, a topological map showing the elevations of mountains and hills of the sort which is designed for airplane pilots, a map showing local political orientations used by those planning political campaigns, maps in bird watchers' guide books displaying the normal ranges of different bird species, and so on.

But even beyond that, *chronos* is not totally real. Its partially illusory nature is based on something more fundamental than simply the fact that chronological analysis always deals in simplified sets of partial information. So for example, let us ask, can the human mind cure illnesses in the human body simply by learning to think about the situation differently? That is, can I heal my physical body merely by reframing the cause-effect scheme which I am using to organize the realm of *chronos*? The best medical experimenters in the world acknowledge this as a fact every time they run tests on newly developed drugs and keep statistics on the placebo effect. Even if the new drug cures 60% of the people who take it, another 5% or more will frequently end up being cured just as effectively by a sugar pill which they *think* is the new drug. *That* the placebo effect occurs can be described scientifically within the realm of *chronos*, but *why* this effect takes place—how the mind, just by thinking differently about the world, can affect the physical and biochemical processes going on in the body in precisely this fashion—cannot be accounted for by an analysis of things going on within the realm of *chronos* alone.

Because the world of chronological time is always an over-simplification of reality, and because even beyond that point, changes in the way our minds think about the phenomenal world can change the objective facts we are observing, we cannot use theories describing the causal connections within the chronological realm to tell us what the truly basic realities are. Whether we are attempting to discuss human free will or the nature of God, or anything else truly basic like that, looking only at the realm of *chronos* gives us no help in deciding what is real and what is illusion.

The early Greek Christian concept of
the Eternal Now as vital force

The understanding of time taught by Augustine (354-430 A.D.)—the one which he bequeathed to the Western European middle ages—was very similar to the ancient Greek concept of *chronos*. But Augustine does not seem to have known how to read Greek very fluently, definitely did not enjoy reading Greek (he tells us that he detested his classes in that language when he was a schoolboy), and in the various cities in Italy and Africa where he lived over the course of his life, he had little or no access to Greek literature. As a result he knew relatively little about the ideas of the great Greek Christian theologians who had preceded him, and had to work out a number of philosophical and theological issues on his own, with sometimes notably different results.

In particular, his understanding of eternity was very different from the early Greek Christian concept. Even though both the Latin word for eternity (*aeternitas*) and the classical Greek word for eternity (*aiôn*) came from the same ancient Indo-European root—the word *aiw-* which meant vital force, life, long life, or someone filled with youthful vigor—the Greek word had preserved a good deal more of the original root meaning. This was particularly true in the hands of the most important fourth century Greek Christian theologians such as Gregory of Nyssa (c. 330 - c. 395 A.D.) and Eusebius of Caesarea (c. 260 - c. 340). Their understanding was totally different from Augustine's. For them, the eternal was a dynamic concept, not a static concept.

The concept of *aiôn* in early Christianity referred to what is called in modern English the Eternal Now—definitely in the writings of the fourth century Christian theologians who immediately preceded Augustine, but in my interpretation going all the back to the gospel of John,[227] which was written in the Greek-speaking eastern end of the Mediterranean at the end of the first century A.D.

If you ask me what I was doing at 8:00 yesterday evening, I can search back in my memory and tell you that "I was sitting in a meeting in Osceola, Indiana, with Frank Nyikos to my left, Karen Z. to my right, Submarine Bill Correll and Sam S. across from me, and four or five other people sitting around the far end of the table." But the "I" which *was sitting* in that meeting, and the "I" which *is remembering* sitting in that meeting, is not the same "I."[228] When I am in the act of remembering what was happening, the first "I" is the object and the second "I" is the subject. The first "I" is not only an object—a "me" actually instead of an "I"—it is a phenomenon contained in the artificially constructed world of chronological time. It is merely a mental construct, invariably oversimplified and partial.

Where and what then is the other "I," the one which is the present tense conscious subject? This is the one which is in the Now. This "I" is the only one which really exists as a concrete reality. And it exists in the realm of *aiôn*, the Eternal Now. This may seem quite startling to those who have for years unconsciously assumed the old Augustinian and western medieval understanding of eternity as the static and unchanging ground of a fatalistic universe. And I hope it does startle people enough to get them thinking in a very different direction.

We must remember what was pointed out several paragraphs back, that is, that the classical Greek word for eternity (*aiôn*) came from—and often still preserved some of the sense of—the ancient Indo-European root *aiw-* which meant vital force, life itself, and youthful vigor. It was a dynamic concept, not a static one. We must remember one of the most famous and oft-quoted passages from the *Meditations* of Marcus Aurelius (121-180 A.D.):

> The *aiôn* is like a river, consisting of all things that come into being, aye, a rushing torrent. No sooner is a thing sighted than it is carried past, and lo, another is passing, and it too will be carried away.[229]

But it is extremely difficult to talk about the nature of the *aiôn*, because the minute we start trying to describe it, we of necessity objectify it and turn it into *chronos*. The "I" which is me as conscious present tense subject is certainly not appropriately described as static. It is obviously in some way incredibly dynamic and filled with energy. My "I" as conscious subject is the seat of decision, will, choice, freedom, and creativity—perhaps not most of the time, when I am mechanically following habitual and learned procedures and ways of evaluating the things around me—but certainly at those points in my life when I enter what the Tibetan Buddhists call a *bardo* state, that is, the sort of transitional, intermediate, liminal, or in-between state where I am poised between two possible ways of framing the basic cognitive structures of my mind, or caught in a sort of vacuum where my old way of thinking has clearly become untenable, forcing me to realize that I have no other choice than to set up some sort of totally new mental framework for my life. It is in these *bardo* states that I am able to make life-changing decisions about myself. It seems clear that the "I" which can do that is certainly not properly described as static or caught in the unbreakable chains of Fate.

But still we have the problem of describing what this dynamic, living "I" actually is. To use the example I gave slightly earlier, the "I" who was at a meeting in Osceola, Indiana, at 8:00 p.m. yesterday evening, was a conscious subject in the realm of the *aiôn* at that point. But the minute I start trying to remember or describe it, it turns from subject into object, and becomes a phenomenon embedded in the chains of *chronos*. For that matter, if I try to actually think about or describe the "I" which is (at this point) myself-as-present-tense-conscious-subject, it immediately ceases being the subject and becomes the object, and moves from the living realm of the *aiôn* into the lifeless phenomenal abstractions of the realm of *chronos*.

Nevertheless, we must at least attempt to describe it, even if the words we use are filled with paradoxes and (in the final analysis) inadequate to the description. Eusebius of Caesarea in the fourth century A.D. described the *aiôn* as the ground upon which we construct our human concept of "before" and "after." It was what we might call *pure process* itself, a dynamic process which is "stretched out in a straight line and stretches onward into infinity." Eusebius said that God created the universe by hypostatizing it upon the pure undifferentiated flow of the *aiôn* like embroidery sewn upon a ribbon. First God created matter (*hylê*) and placed it in that flow, then added form (*eidos*), and created three-dimensional space by combining matter and form into body (*sôma*).[230]

Now I think we can easily see here, that if we take Eusebius' words literally, we have turned *aiôn* into *chronos*, that is, we have converted reality-as-it-is-in-itself into phenomenal abstractions. But in terms of pointing our thoughts in the right direction, Eusebius's language is (I believe) a good deal more useful than Augustine's static and fatalistic imagery.

The "I" which is myself-as-present-tense-conscious-subject is filled with vital force, the power of life itself, freedom, and the energy of love, which is able to embody itself in true creativity and novelty just for the sake of the joy which exercising this ability produces. This is the fundamental nature of the *aiôn*. This is also where God dwells. Gregory of Nyssa said that God in his essence or ownmost being (*ousia*) was in the *aiôn*, but in his outflowing love he created the world of *chronos* and the phenomena as his temporal *energeia* (his act or energy or temporal operation). So God in his essence is not in time, but God in his activity operates in time.

If both the subjective "I" (that spiritual core which is at the center of my own being as a person) and God's ownmost being are in the realm of the *aiôn*, then my spirit truly participates in God's divinity in some real and concrete way. As Richmond Walker said in *Twenty-Four Hours a Day*, a spark of the divine exists in each human being.

A process philosophy, but not quite the same as Charles Hartshorne's

Now the position I am laying out here is like the one associated with Charles Hartshorne's name, in that what I am arguing is also a kind of process philosophy. Like him, I believe that it is totally inappropriate to describe God and the eternal realm as static. Ultimate reality is dynamic and filled with an endless energy which can never run out.

But my position is also very different from his, because, to my way of thinking, he failed to adequately distinguish between *chronos* and *aiôn*. Hartshorne (and also Alfred North Whitehead before him) believed that God must be within the flow of chronological time in the same way as all the other phenomena which make up the world. Their God was in time (*chronos*), a series of actual events moving from one moment in the world's history to the next, prehending all things at each point in time and creatively assimilating all the world's events into an always new and creative cosmic whole.

Love and immortality

Now if love is the energy of the realm of the *aiôn*, this leads to an interesting observation. The laws of thermodynamics, and in particular the law of entropy, which says that all energy eventually runs down or wears out, are laws which apply only to the realm of *chronos*. Love on the other hand, which is the vital force within the realm of the *aiôn*, does not automatically run down in the process of giving it to others. In fact, those human beings who love the most, seem to grow ever greater in their supply of love, the more they give it to others.

Certainly in the case of God, the *aiôn* is not only a realm where the energy of love and creativity and novelty never wears out or decays, it is also (for that reason) a realm where there is no death, not as an automatic necessity. What this might say about the life of the human spirit and its capacity for immortality (since the conscious center of the human spirit is also part of the *aiôn*) is not something that we ought to get into in this book, which has already gotten long enough at this point. But I would suggest that this is a matter for serious thought on your part as the reader.

As Carl Jung pointed out, all of the rich symbolism in the world's religions seems to point towards things which can be demonstrated to be perfectly real, whenever they are things which we can check out in scientific research. Jung said that this was the strongest evidence he knew of for a life after this one. Almost all the world's religions speak either of going to a heaven or land of the dead, or undergoing some kind of series of transmigrations from one existence to the next. Even perfectly ordinary people have experienced moving into a realm of light in near-death experiences. Spiritual adepts (like Dante and Bill Wilson), but also many perfectly ordinary people, have undergone the experience of being absorbed for a moment into that realm of light and overwhelming love during the normal course of life, without any need for a near-death situation. So a good way of ending this book might be, I think, to quote from the prayer which Bill and Lois Wilson would recite together in the morning:[231]

> Oh Lord, we thank Thee that Thou art,
> that we are from everlasting to everlasting.
> Blessed be Thy holy name and all Thy benefactions
> to us of light, of love, and of service ....
> Oh Lord, we know Thee to be all wonder,
> all beauty, all glory, all power, all love.
> Indeed, Thou art everlasting love.
> Accordingly, Thou has fashioned for us a destiny

> passing through Thy many mansions,
> ever in more discovery of Thee
> and in no separation between ourselves.

To understand the full nature of that hope, I think that we should read that prayer together with the concluding lines to the first part of the Big Book, with its famous reference to the Road of Happy Destiny which leads from this world into the path of light which runs through the house of many mansions and all the amazing new dimensions of reality waiting to be discovered in the unending eternal world beyond:[232]

> Abandon yourself to God as you understand God. Admit your faults to Him and to your fellows. Clear away the wreckage of your past. Give freely of what you find and join us. We shall be with you in the Fellowship of the Spirit, and you will surely meet some of us as you trudge the Road of Happy Destiny.
>
> May God bless you and keep you—until then.

Notes

1. NOTES TO CHAPTER 1: Augustine, *Confessions*, trans. R. S. Pine-Coffin (Baltimore, MD: Penguin Books, 1961) 8.12. The bible verse (Rom. 13:13–14) reads "Not in reveling and drunkenness, not in lust and wantonness, not in quarrels and rivalries. Rather, arm yourselves with the Lord Jesus Christ; spend no more thought on nature and nature's appetites."

2. For psychological profundity and intuitive depth, none can match Peter Brown, *Augustine of Hippo: A Biography* (London: Faber & Faber, 1967).

3. John Wesley, *Journal* for May 24, 1738, in Albert C. Outler, ed., *John Wesley*, Library of Protestant Thought (New York: Oxford University Press, 1964), 66.

4. Among other things he read Jonathan Edwards' *Faithful Narrative*, and also Archbishop Thomas Cranmer's sermonic essay on justification by faith. See Outler's volume on *John Wesley* 15–16, 52, 121–123. His contact with the Moravian missionaries gave him no important new intellectual ideas, but did give him firsthand contact with the *feeling tone* of a deep and real faith in God's love and goodness. The periodic bouts with depression which he recorded in his *Journal* after returning to England from colonial Georgia also provided the pressure needed to break through his psychological shields of rigid self-control and over-intellectualization. On the depression, see Wesley's *Journal* for May 19–24 and June 3, 1738 (in Outler 59–67 and 68), but also see Outler's observation on p. 51.

5. William James, *The Varieties of Religious Experience*, Gifford Lectures on Natural Religion Delivered at Edinburgh in 1901–1902 (New York: Modern Library, 1994), Preface xiv.

6. I am not sure why, but people sometimes jump to the conclusion that this story of the drunken English professor was actually a story about me. No, it was not I. The real person knows a good deal more about English literature than I do, a fact which is essential to the story, because that knowledge allowed him to observe something and teach me something that I had never noticed before.

7. *Alcoholics Anonymous*, 3rd ed. (New York: Alcoholics Anonymous World Services, 1976).

8. The x-factor which appears at the point of conversion or significant spiritual transformation is of course what a theologian would call the appearance of God's grace. Jonathan Edwards, in his sermon "A Divine and Supernatural Light," makes the point in classic fashion: the saving light comes when, how, and where God wants it to come, and can be withdrawn whenever God chooses. Jonathan Edwards, *Basic Writings*, ed. Ola Elizabeth Winslow (New York: New American Library, 1966) 123–134. As Edwards pointed out, when God's grace intervened to save the person, this was an additional factor not included in the this-worldly analysis of the person's character and earthly circumstances.

9. Karl Barth (1886-1968) exploded onto the theological scene when he published his first book in 1919, a commentary on the Apostle Paul's epistle to the Romans, entitled simply *Der Römerbrief.* Reinhold Niebuhr (1892-1971) was an American from Missouri who taught at Union Theological Seminary in New York City from 1928 until his retirement in 1960. Paul Tillich (1886-1965) was a German theologian who was forced to leave Germany in 1933 by the rise of the Nazi movement (which he had publicly opposed as evil and demonic). He came to New York and taught at Union until he reached their mandatory retirement age in 1955, then went to teach at Harvard and later at the University of Chicago. The four best American Protestant seminaries at that time were Union, Yale, Harvard, and Chicago, so every well-read Protestant pastor in the United States knew who the key theologians were at all four of those places, and what they taught. Barth, Niebuhr, and Tillich were all considered members of the Neo-Orthodox movement which was trying to return Protestantism to the central insights of the original sixteenth-century Protestant Reformation, including the realization that we were saved *sola gratia,* by grace alone, and not through our own unaided human efforts to pull ourselves out of the spiritual miry pits into which our souls had fallen.

Bill Wilson and Dr. Bob met and began putting together the A.A. system of treating alcoholism in 1935, *Alcoholics Anonymous* (the Big Book) was published in 1939, and the *Twelve Steps and Twelve Traditions* was published in 1952-53. All of this took place during the period when Reinhold Niebuhr and Paul Tillich were the two great theologians at Union Theological Seminary in New York City.

10. John Baillie, *Our Knowledge of God* (London: Oxford University Press, 1939) 15 ff.

11. Karl Barth, *The Epistle to the Romans*, trans. E. C. Hoskyns (London: Oxford University Press, 1933; the orig. German ed. was pub. in 1919 as *Der Römerbrief*), 29 and 37.

12. In classical Hindu philosophy, the ground of Being (which is sometimes described as a personal God and sometimes as an impersonal absolute) is likewise viewed as the ultimate reality. Nontheistic Buddhism uses an interesting strategy: since it is impossible to speak adequately about the ground of Being in terms of natural human concepts, Buddhist spiritual literature in this tradition refuses to speak of it at all, and talks instead about how human beings must live in a world where human thoughts and desires can never be ultimate. Salvation comes from surrendering the belief that we could ever control either our lives or the world around us by our human physical power or the keenness of our human intellects. Speaking about the role of grace in bringing about human salvation is more complicated when God is believed to be an impersonal absolute instead of a personal being, and requires even more careful discussion in nontheistic systems which refuse to talk about the ground of Being directly at all, even by using symbolic language or analogies or the *via negativa*.

13. NOTES TO CHAPTER 2: That is the way the Bible is written. It is filled with a prodigious number of helpful metaphors and analogies: God is our Friend, the good Father (who holds his little child in his arms, and feeds him from a spoon, and holds his hands when he is first learning to walk, and hugs and kisses him and consoles him when he falls and hurts himself), the Good Boss for whom we work, the Farmer (where we are the farm animals, the donkeys and camels and the oxen who pull the plow). God's power is described as Lady Wisdom giving birth to the sun, moon, stars, earth, trees, flowers, and animals. In the Christian tradition, we see God portrayed metaphorically as the King or Mighty Lord whom we serve gallantly and honorably as knights and ladies and warriors, a two-edged Sword, the Rock of Ages, and the great ocean of Love in which we live and move and have our being.

Friend (Exod. 33:11, 2 Chron. 20:7, Isa. 41:8, James 2:23), good father (Hosea 11:1–4), good boss (passages like Matt. 20:1–15, for in current American English we say boss and employee instead of master and servant), Lady Wisdom (Prov. 8:22–31, Sirach [Ecclesiasticus] 1:4–9, Wisdom of Solomon 7:22–27), two-edged sword (Heb. 4:12–13), rock (Pss. 18:2, 28:1, 31:2–3, 42:9, 62:2, 71:3; Matt. 7:24–25; in the phrase "Rock of Ages, cleft for me, let me hide myself in thee" there is an allegorical linkage to Isa. 2:10 and 19).

Mighty lord with his knights and ladies: the repeated Old Testament references to God as "the Lord of Hosts," i.e., Yahweh of the Warriors, and similar militant metaphors, were interpreted in the language of chivalry in the western European middle ages, see Glenn F. Chesnut, "Eusebius, Augustine, Orosius, and the Later Patristic and Medieval Christian Historians" in Harold W. Attridge and Gohei Hata (eds.), *Eusebius, Christianity, and Judaism* (Detroit: Wayne State University Press, 1992) 687–713.

One finds the ocean metaphor, which I believe is especially useful and helpful, as early as the eighteenth century in John Wesley, Sermon 36, "The Law Established through Faith, Discourse II," 2.3, in *The Works of John Wesley*, Vol. 2, *Sermons II: 34–70* (Nashville: Abingdon Press, 1985). "Love existed from eternity, in God, the great Ocean of Love. Love had a place in all the children of God, from the moment of their creation. They received at once from their gracious Creator to exist, and to love." By the time of William James' *Varieties of Religious Experience*, at the beginning of the twentieth century, this metaphor had become very widely used in western spirituality. Sigmund Freud commented on it (negatively of course, but the fact that he singled it our for special attack was a mark of how widely known the metaphor had become).

14. In Exodus 33:18, the Prayer of Moses is, "I pray you, show me your glory," and towards the very end of his story, God grants him that request. This is the light and glory of the infinite sacred and holy reality which shines through in all the works of creation. It is what is sung about in the Song of the Seraphim in Isaiah 6:3, "Holy, holy, holy is the Lord of hosts; all the world is filled with his glory." Bill Wilson came into its presence in Winchester Cathedral, and Bill's grandfather felt it when he gazed up into the starry heavens at night. It shines in the faces of some of the A.A. good old timers.

15. NOTES TO CHAPTER 3: John Locke, *An Essay Concerning Human Understanding*, 2 vols., ed. A. C. Fraser (New York: Dover. 1959), 3.4.11. In his *Essay* Locke argued that all human knowledge was based on experience and reflection—he was the father of modern scientifically-oriented empiricist philosophy—but many today forget his insistence that words can be meaningless without immediate personal experience, and his observation that some meaningful experiences have no words to describe them.

16. *Ibid.*, 2.18.5, referring to compounded (as opposed to simple) tastes and smells.

17. Michael Polanyi, *Personal Knowledge: Towards a Post-Critical Philosophy* (New York: Harper & Row, 1964; orig. pub. 1958).

18. Polanyi, *Personal Knowledge* 4.1–4 (pp. 49–55); also his preface to the 1964 edition (pp. ix–xi)—tacit knowing is more fundamental than ex-

plicit knowing: *"we can know more than we can tell and we can tell nothing without relying on our awareness of things we may not be able to tell."*

19. Augustine, *Confessions*, trans. Albert C. Outler, Library of Christian Classics (Philadephia: Westminster Press, 1955) 10.8(12)–26(38). I have quoted the famous concluding lines (my trans.) in the text.

20. Polanyi, *Personal Knowledge*, pp. ix-xi.

21. NOTES TO CHAPTER 4: *Dictionary of Latin and Greek Theological Terms: Drawn Principally from Protestant Scholastic Theology*, ed. Richard A. Muller (Grand Rapids, Michigan: Baker Book House, 1985).

22. Rudolf Otto, *The Idea of the Holy: An Inquiry into the Non-Rational Factor in the Idea of the Divine and Its Relation to the Rational*, 2nd ed., trans. John W. Harvey (Oxford: Oxford University Press, 1950). Quotes from the German original are from *Das Heilige: Über das Irrationale in der Idee des göttlichen und sein Verhältnis zum Rationalen*, 11th ed. (Stuttgart: Friedrich Andreas Perthes, 1923).

23. Mircea Eliade, *The Sacred and the Profane: the Nature of Religion*, trans. Willard R. Trask (New York: Harcourt Brace Jovanovich, 1959) is a classic work on this subject.

24. John H. Flavell, *The Developmental Psychology of Jean Piaget* (Princeton, New Jersey: D. Van Nostrand, 1963), p. 260. "Physics-chemistry relates to biology by interdependence; one causal system (biology) can be 'reduced' to another, more general and elementary one (physics-chemistry)." On the other hand, "logic-mathematics relates to physics-chemistry by correspondence—a deductive series of implications isomorphic to an empirical system of causes." The relationship between the sacred realm and the ordinary, everyday world is not exactly that kind of correspondence, but it is better described as a correspondence than as an interdependence, because events in the sacred realm cannot be "reduced" to a scientific analysis of the sequence of causal factors operating within the this-worldly realm.

25. *Alcoholics Anonymous*, 3rd ed., 25 and 8.

26. Ibid., 1.

27. Ibid., 10-13.

28. Seneca, *Epistulae morales*, ed. and trans. Richard M. Gummere, 3 vols., Loeb Classical Library (Cambridge MA: Harvard University Press, 1917–25), ep. 41.

29. William James, *Varieties of Religious Experience*, Lecture III, "The Re-

ality of the Unseen," pp. 76–7. See also Glenn F. Chesnut, *Images of Christ: An Introduction to Christology* (Seabury Press/Harper & Row, 1984), ch. 4, "The Vision of God," pp. 50–67.

30. Otto, *The Holy*.

31. Rudolf Otto, *The Philosophy of Religion Based on Kant and Fries*, trans. E. B. Dicker (London: Williams & Norgate, 1931).

32. Apollo was attempting to commit violent rape upon the young woman Daphne when she was turned into a laurel tree, Kronos castrated his own father Uranus with a jagged flint sickle, Zeus took the form of an eagle to carry off the little boy Ganymede in order to perform homosexual acts upon him, Hephaestus the blacksmith of the gods discovered his wife Aphrodite (the goddess of love) in bed with the war god Ares in yet another myth, Apollo defeated a mortal named Marsyas in a musical contest and then skinned him alive for revenge, and so on.

33. Otto, *The Holy*, pp. 5–6 (Ger. 5–6): *gegen das Ethische . . . gleichgültig*.

34. Ibid., pp. 6–7 (Ger. 6–7).

35. Ibid., p. 13 (Ger. 13): the numinous as *mysterium* was something that dwelt *im unsagbaren Geheimnis*; it was *das Verborgene*, the *nicht Offenkundige, nicht Begriffene und Verstandene, nicht Alltägliche, nicht Vertraute*.

36. Ibid., pp. 19 (Ger. 19), 60 (Ger. 72); see also p. 34 (Ger. 41).

37. NOTES TO CHAPTER 5: Otto, *The Holy*.

38. Ibid., pp. 13-18 (Ger. 13-18).

39. *Alcoholics Anonymous*, 4th ed. (New York: Alcoholics Anonymous World Services, 2001; orig. pub. 1939), 53—"When we became alcoholics, crushed by a self-imposed crisis we could not postpone or evade, we had to fearlessly face the proposition that either God is everything or else He is nothing."

40. Harry M. Tiebout, M.D. "Surrender Versus Compliance in Therapy: With Special Reference to Alcoholism," *Quarterly Journal of Studies on Alcohol* (Yale University) 14 (1953): 58-68. Available as reprint from National Council on Alcoholism, 733 Third Avenue, New York NY 10017.

41. Otto, *The Holy*, pp. 19-21 (Ger. 20-21).

42. *Alcoholics Anonymous*, 4th ed., 85. Compare pp. 67 and 88, where this prayer is shortened to simply "Thy will be done."

43. Rudolf Otto, *The Philosophy of Religion Based on Kant and Fries*.

44. St. John of the Cross, *Ascent of Mount Carmel*, trans. E. Allison Peers (Liguori, Missouri: Triumph Books, 1983), and *The Dark Night of the Soul*, trans. and abridged by Kurt F. Reinhardt (New York: Frederick Ungar, 1957). St. Gregory of Nyssa, *From Glory to Glory: Texts from Gregory of Nyssa's Mystical Writings*, introd. Jean Daniélou, trans. Herbert Musurillo (Crestwood NY: St. Vladimir's Seminary Press, 1961). St. Teresa of Ávila, *Interior Castle*, trans. E. Allison Peers (Garden City NY: Image Books/Doubleday & Company, 1961), the Spiritual Marriage as described in "Seventh Mansions" (the concluding section of the book). Hannah Hurnard, *Hind's Feet in High Places* (Wheaton, Illinois: Tyndale House Publishers, 1975; orig. pub. 1955).

45. The Greek word *agapé* was originally simply a translation, devised by Hellenistic era Jewish rabbis, of the old Hebrew word *hesed*.

46. Beginning with *Cardinal Sins* (1981), *Thy Brother's Wife* (1982), *Ascent into Hell* (1983), and *Lord of the Dance* (1984). Some of Andrew Greeley's more recent novels are *Irish Gold, A Midwinter's Tale, Irish Stew, Irish Mist, The Bishop in the Old Neighborhood, Irish Lace, Younger than Springtime, The Bishop Goes to the University, Star Bright: A Christmas Story*, and so on. His ideas about the divine Eros as a feminine, seductive love are better developed in the later novels, but in all his novels he recognizes that erotic love between man and woman are reflections (Platonic images) down here on earth of one part of the divine love.

47. In the New Testament, see for example Luke 11:49 (it was Holy Wisdom who sent the prophets and apostles), 1 Corinthians 1:24 ("Christ the power of God, and the wisdom of God"), 1 Corinthians 1:30 ("Christ Jesus, who of God is made unto us wisdom, and righteousness, and sanctification, and redemption"), 1 Corinthians 2:7 ("But we speak the wisdom of God in a mystery, even the hidden wisdom, which God ordained before the world unto our glory"), and James 3:17 (the reference to "the wisdom that is from above").

48. Whom we see in western Catholic Christianity in the figure of Mary as the Mystical Rose at the end of Dante's *Paradiso*, and in eastern Orthodox Christianity in many of the powerful verses of the Acathist Hymn (the office of praise of the Mother of God), where she is hailed as the one who has opened the gates of Eden, the fountainhead, the bridge to heaven, the key to the doors of Paradise, the radiance of the mystical day, the sea which drowned Pharaoh, the pillar of fire which guided those in darkness, the one who flows with milk and honey, the tree from whom believers feed, the shady glen in which we shelter, space of the spaceless God, gate of the sublime mystery, the

sacred chariot which bears the Godhead, lamp of knowledge, beam of the mystical sun, opener of the stream of the waters of life, flowing water which cleanses the conscience, holy vessel overflowing with joy, wall of the kingdom of heaven, and healer of our bodies and savior of our souls.

49. Anger: the Thugee cult in India was commanded by the sometimes murderous goddess Kali to waylay travelers on the highway and strangle them to death, the Greek gods and goddesses would become angered at a human being (e.g. Odysseus, Arachne, Psyche) and do that unfortunate person great harm (cf. Otto, *The Holy*, pp. 23-24 [Ger. 24-25]). Grief: the goddess Demeter grieved for her daughter Persephone every winter, and the women of Syria and Lebanon ritually mourned with Aphrodite for the death of Adonis once a year.

50. Otto, *The Holy*, pp. 26-30 (Ger. 28-32) and 16 (Ger. 16). On existential anxiety in the face of nonbeing, see also the classic work by Paul Tillich, *The Courage to Be* (New Haven: Yale University Press, 1952), e.g. ch. 2 (pp. 32–63).

51. Viktor E. Frankl, *Man's Search for Meaning: An Introduction to Logotherapy*, rev. ed. (New York: Washington Square Press, 1963; earlier title of English version was *From Death Camp to Existentialism*, 1959; orig. German version was entitled *Trotzdem Ja zum Leben sagen: Ein Psychologe erlebt das Konzentrationslager* [Nevertheless Say "Yes" to Life: A Psychologist's Experience of the Concentration Camp], 1946). Tillich, *The Courage to Be*.

52. Otto, *The Holy*, pp. 31-36 (Ger. 38-45) and 38-39 (Ger. 47-48).

53. Contrary to what Otto said at one point in his book. He must have been interpreting Plato in a different way than I do, but I feel fairly confident that I am reading Plato correctly concerning the nature of the Good.

54. Otto, *The Holy*, pp. 50-57 (Ger. 61-69).

55. Vladimir Lossky, *The Vision of God*, trans. A. Moorhouse (Crestwood NY: St. Vladimir's Seminary Press, 1963) 56–7 and 86, see also 115 and 117. Jean Daniélou's introd. to Gregory of Nyssa, *From Glory to Glory*, sect. 2, "Gregory's Doctrine on the Image of God in Man" (pp. 10–23). For the Lutheran and Reformed understanding, see *Dictionary of Latin and Greek Theological Terms: Drawn Principally from Protestant Scholastic Theology*, s.v. *imago Dei* (pp. 143–6). For the idea of the image of God in christology, see also Glenn F. Chesnut, *Images of Christ: An Introduction to Christology* (San Francisco: Harper & Row/Seabury, 1984).

56. Teresa of Ávila, *Interior Castle*, First Mansions, chapter 2, pp. 40-

41.

57. Plato, *Republic*, 2 vols., trans. Paul Shorey, Loeb Classical Library (London: William Heinemann, 1935–7), 7.1.514A–3.518B. In 7.3.517B-C he said that the sun stood metaphorically for "the idea of the Good" (*hê tou agathou idea*), which was that which enabled us to see what is right (*orthos*) and beautiful (*kalos*), to recognize truth (*alêtheia*) and intelligible meaning (*nous*), and to act in a manner which was sane and sensible (*emphrôn*). This central concept therefore linked together the Good (and truth and beauty), and the establishment of the the the noetic realm (where the fundamental organizing concepts and cognitive structures of our minds were fitted together in a way which enabled us to think intelligibly and coherently about both internal and external things).

58. Jonathan Edwards, "A Divine and Supernatural Light," pp. 123-134 in Jonathan Edwards, *Basic Writings*.

59. Earl Marlatt, "Spirit of Life, in This New Dawn." It is Hymn No. 462 in *The Methodist Hymnal* (Nashville, Tennessee: Methodist Publishing House, 1966), but can be found in numerous American Protestant hymnals. Earl Marlatt taught at Perkins School of Theology at Southern Methodist University in Dallas, Texas, where I did my seminary degree, although he was born in 1892 and was no longer on their faculty when I became a student there in 1961. When I quote from his hymns, I do so with a certain twinge of what I suppose is guilt, because I got myself through one summer there by repainting faculty offices. Marlatt had been in charge of choosing the paint scheme when the structure was newly built, and he had chosen a deep purplish maroon color for a good many of the offices, which the other faculty deeply detested, and referred to as "Marlatt mauve." I was instructed to repaint them in a light tan color called adobe (the color of Mexican sun-dried bricks). Having spent many weeks undoing that part of the man's work, I am not totally sure that I have the right to quote from his work, but he did produce some very good hymns, and I sometimes find that his way of putting things is very useful for explaining my own thoughts!

60. NOTES TO CHAPTER 6: *Brave New World* was the title of a novel by Aldous Huxley, 1894-1963 (Garden City, New York: Doubleday, Doran & Company / Garden City Publishing, 1932), which described a rather grim future utopia, a hedonistic society which was driven by the pleasures of promiscuous sex and drugs, particularly an imaginary new drug which he called "soma" in the novel. It was described as a powerful stimulant which washed away pain and unpleasant memories with hallucinatory fantasies. Many years

later, he was one of the people who talked Bill Wilson, the cofounder of Alcoholics Anonymous, into taking experimental doses of the newly discovered hallucinogen called LSD.

61. A. A. Penzias and R. W. Wilson, "A Measurement of Excess Antenna Temperature at 4080 Mc/s," *Astrophysical Journal* 142 (1965), 419.

62. See for example Richard D. McKirahan, Jr., "Zeno," in A. A. Long, ed., *The Cambridge Companion to Early Greek Philosophy* (Cambridge: Cambridge University Press, 1999), pp. 140-141.

63. Augustine, *On Free Will*, ed. and trans. Richard McKeon, *Selections from Medieval Philosophers*, I. *Augustine to Albert the Great* (New York: Charles Scribner's Sons, 1929), 2.15.39—"Moreover you had conceded that if I should show you that there is something above our minds, you would confess that it is God, provided there were nothing still loftier. I had said, acceding to this concession of yours, that it would be sufficient to demonstrate this. For if there is something still more excellent, that rather is God: if however there is nothing, then truth itself is God. Whether therefore that more excellent something is or is not, you nevertheless can not deny that God is: which was the question set to be discussed and treated by us." Seneca, *Naturales Quaestiones* 1, preface, 13 (trans. Thomas H. Corcoran in the Loeb Classical Library, Cambridge: Harvard University Press, 1971)—"After all, how great is the distance from the farthest shores of Spain all the way to India? Only the space of a very few days—if a good wind drives the ship." But suppose the mind travels out into the heavenly regions, to the realm of the farthest star? There we encounter a God who is bigger and greater even than the whole visible universe, and contains the universe within his own being, as a part of himself. "Here, finally, the mind learns what it long sought: here it begins to know God. What is God? The mind of the universe. What is God? All that you see, all that you do not see. In short, only if he alone is all things, if he maintains his own work both from within and without, is he given due credit for his magnitude; nothing of greater magnitude than *that* can be contemplated." The crucial part of Seneca's Latin reads: *Quid est deus?... Sic demum magnitudo illi sua redditur, qua nihil maius cogitari potest ....*

64. The Latin word *sublimis* means literally "under the lintel," and came to mean high or exalted. The famous work known as Longinus, *On the Sublime*—written during the Roman imperial period by an unknown author, probably in the first century A.D.—laid out a theory describing how rhetoricians could develop a high and exalted style in their speeches. But the Kantian notion of the sublime derived from Edmund Burke's treatise on aesthetics, published in 1757, called *A Philosophical Enquiry into the Origin*

of Our Ideas of the Sublime and Beautiful. The Beautiful is that which is well-formed and aesthetically pleasing, while the Sublime is that which has the power to compel us and destroy us. We love the beautiful, Burke said, but fear the sublime. The sublime has a greatness with which nothing else can be compared, which is beyond all calculation, measurement or imitation. We are above all confronted with the sublime when we encounter the greatness of nature and its vastness.

65. NOTES TO CHAPTER 8: Probably written around 150 A.D. roughly, because so many of its ideas fit most smoothly into the mid-second century world of Justin Martyr and the Shepherd of Hermas.

66. Gregory of Nyssa, *From Glory to Glory: Texts from Gregory of Nyssa's Mystical Writings.* The long introduction (pp. 1-78) by Jean Daniélou is an excellent analysis of the major themes in Gregory's understanding of the mystical vision.

67. The river of *aiôn.* This is a Greek word which refers to endless time or eternity, and means something quite different from the word *chronos,* which also refers to time, but time objectified as a sequence of things and events. The word *aiôn* refers to pure process itself, whereas *chronos* refers to our human attempts to make sense out of it by constructing chains of events connected by cause and effect, in such a way that things will appear to proceed in logical fashion from one event to the next.

68. Writings of authors who had been publicly condemned as heretics, like Apollinarius or Nestorius, were sometimes preserved by putting another author's name on the title page, but the Dionysian corpus contains no "heresies" of the sort which were publicly controversial at that time. Claims that his writings contained "monophysite" ideas are nonsense. In order to get labeled as a "monophysite heretic" by the Chalcedonians, an author had to strongly defend the doctrine of one nature in the incarnate Christ and viciously attack those who held the doctrine of two natures, and do it in fully explicit and open fashion. Chance and careless remarks that could have been labeled as potentially monophysite in their implications can be found in the writings of all the major orthodox writers of that period, including all three of the great Cappadocian Fathers! In addition, the ideas and writing style in the Dionysian corpus do not correspond with those of any widely recognized heretical author of that period. One scholar has argued that Severus of Antioch actually wrote the Dionysian mystical writings, but this has been rejected by all the sensible modern scholars in the field, because Severus can only be described as a narrow logic-chopper, totally lacking in that kind of mystical vision and skill with poetic imagery. And there are no other possible candi-

dates either, among the heretical authors of that period.

69. Big Book = *Alcoholics Anonymous*, 4th ed., 60-61.

70. Dr. Paul Ohliger (Laguna Niguel, California, sober July 1967, died May 19, 2000 at the age of 83). His story appeared in the Big Book, 3rd ed., as "Doctor, Alcoholic, Addict," pp. 439-452, see p. 449. In the 4th ed., his story was retained but retitled "Acceptance Was the Answer," pp. 407-420, see p. 417. His story has become the only part of the story section of the Big Book which has achieved a status equal to, and is quoted from as frequently as, the first 164 pages of the Big Book.

71. If one could take the Serenity Prayer and translate it back into ancient Greek and transport it somehow to the period of the early Roman empire, it would have been immediately recognized as obviously and blatantly a statement of fundamental Stoic philosophical principles: "*Zeus* grant me the *apatheia* to accept *ta ouk eph' hêmin*, the *andreia* to change *ta eph' hêmin*, and the *sophia* to know the difference." Philosophy was *philo-sophia*, the love of the wisdom which allowed us to know the difference. The great Stoic heroes were not people who passively accepted everything which was thrust upon them, but courageously attacked the world when they had to, because above all good Stoics must remain true to themselves at all costs, and were warned that the greatest sin was to betray yourself and who you really were, simply because you were afraid of being injured or killed. Hercules and Socrates were two of their greatest heroes, along with some of the brave souls who carried out assassination attempts against some of the crueler and wickeder Roman emperors of the first century. The good Stoic, they taught, was the lion who would rather die than be caged. The good Stoic was the hunting dog who would courageously attack the lion even at the risk of being killed by the lion's claws. The good Stoic was the bull who instinctively, without even having to think about it, moved to the front to defend the rest of the herd from the attack of the lion.

72. Ernest Kurtz, *Not-God: A History of Alcoholics Anonymous*, expanded edition (Center City, Minnesota: Hazelden, 1991; orig. 1979). Ernest Kurtz and Katherine Ketcham, *The Spirituality of Imperfection: Modern Wisdom from Classic Stories* (New York: Bantam Books, 1992).

73. In the Greek Orthodox spiritual tradition of the hesychastic monks of Mount Athos, this was called *hêsychia* (quietness, peace), while in the heretical gnostic sects of the second and third centuries it was called the divine *sigê* (silence).

74. Ephesians 2:12, *epida mê echontes kai atheoi en tô kosmô*.

75. NOTES TO CHAPTER 9: This was one of the things St. Thomas Aquinas pointed out in his five proofs for the existence of God, and it is still a valid philosophical observation.

76. What the ancient Greeks called the *aiôn*, pure process itself. There are three different words for time in Greek. *Chronos* means the kind of time which we see in history books or novels, where certain events are selected and abstracted from the flow, and arranged in a chronological series, with an attempt to show the causal connections between them and the logical progression from one event to the next. In writing any kind of historical account or connected story, we are forced to be highly selective, and leave out most of the things that happened during the years covered by the story. We have to make decisions about which events were "important" and which were not, which may either illuminate or falsify the story, depending on how well we choose. Eusebius of Caesarea, whose style of historiography dominated most of the historical works written during a thousand years of western history writing, said that *chronos* was embroidery sewn onto the endless ribbon of the *aiôn*. The third Greek word for time was *kairos*, the opportune moment. *Kairos* was portrayed in sculpture as a running man, whose head was shaved except for a long forelock at the front. When *Kairos* ran at us, we had a single moment in which we could "seize the opportunity" by grasping and hanging onto his long, dangling forelock. If we waited a moment too long, however, *Kairos* continued to run his race through time, and would be past us, so that our fingers would slip ineffectually down the back of his smooth-shaven head. The Greek patristic authors (the Christian theologians in the eastern half of the Mediterranean world during the first seven or eight centuries) had a synergistic doctrine of divine grace. We were indeed saved *sola gratia*, by grace alone, because fallen human beings could not save themselves by their own efforts. But a synergistic element was also present, because saving grace was offered to us by God at specific points during our lives, where we had to "grasp" the moment of grace and the kind of grace which was being offered, before that brief window of opportunity had passed. So even though we were basically saved by grace alone, human action and human decision and responsible human behavior were also necessary before we could be saved.

77. There is a long and distinguished chain of Christian theologians who spoke of God as the epistemological ground of being; they formed a great ancient and medieval western tradition that went back through Meister Eckhart, St. Thomas Aquinas, St. Bonaventure, Hugh and Richard of St.-Victor, John Scotus Erigena, St. Denis, St. Gregory of Nyssa in the fourth century, and Origen in the third century, all the way back to St. Justin Martyr, the first Christian philosophical theologian, in the second century A.D.

78. There have been many debates over how best to label Heidegger, where one prominent contemporary commentator argues that he started out in *Being and Time* (1927) as to some degree an ontological idealist and then later became what that author calls a temporal idealist. But I think it is still correct to refer to him as an idealist, even if there is a difference of opinion about exactly what kind of idealist to call him.

79. Richmond Walker, the second most published early A.A. author, offered the possibility in one of his readings in *Twenty-Four Hours a Day* that everything was made up of ideas, including even what were apparently solid physical objects, although he did not press the point.

80. Rudolf Otto, *The Holy*, pp. 37-38.

81. NOTES TO CHAPTER 10: In the works of the existentialist psychologist Rollo May, who was a close friend of Tillich's, we can see an excellent picture of the basic healing process from a psychological perspective. Like Tillich, he took the tragic dimensions of human existence seriously. See, e.g., Rollo May, *Love and Will* (New York: W. W. Norton, 1969) and *The Courage to Create* (New York: W. W. Norton, 1975), whose title was modeled after Tillich's *The Courage to Be*.

82. Paul Tillich, *My Search for Absolutes* (New York: Simon and Schuster, 1967), Chapter 1, "What Am I: An Autobiographical Essay: Early Years," available on the internet at http://www.religion-online.org/showchapter. asp?title=1628&C=1595 (January 31, 2007). He did manage to also gain a position from 1927 to 1929 as *Honorarprofessor für Religionsphilosophie und Kulturphilosophie* at the University of Leipzig, so he did not totally abandon university teaching.

83. Paul Tillich, *The Courage to Be* (New Haven: Yale University Press, 1952) and *Dynamics of Faith* (New York: Harper & Brothers, 1957).

84. Incorporating material from the Gifford lectures which he gave in 1952-54: Paul Tillich, *Systematic Theology*, 3 vols. (Chicago: University of Chicago Press, 1951-63; repr. 1967 as three vols. in one).

85. NOTES TO CHAPTER 11: Paul Tillich, *Theology of Culture* (New York: Oxford University, 1959), Chapter 9, "The Idea of a Personal God."

86. Albert Einstein, "Religion and Science," *New York Times Magazine*, 9 November 1930, 1-4. Reprinted in Albert Einstein, *Ideas and Opinions*, based on *Mein Weltbild*, ed. by Carl Seelig and other sources, new translations and revisions by Sonja Bargmann (New York, Crown Publishers, 1954), 36-40, and also in Albert Einstein, *The World as I See It* (New York: Philosophical

Library, 1949), 24-28. It may also be read online (February 2007) at www.geocities.com/HotSprings/6072/1einstein.html

87. This was the book written by Canadian psychiatrist Richard Maurice Bucke (1837-1902), *Cosmic Consciousness: A Study in the Evolution of the Human Mind* (Philadelphia: Innes & Sons, 1901). Its influence was so great that we already see a long discussion of it right after its publication in William James' *Varieties of Religious Experience*, in 1901-1902, in his chapter on mysticism, pp. 294-6. Alcoholics Anonymous historian Mel Barger, one of the foremost experts on the life of Bill Wilson, has emphasized to me the importance of Bucke's work for understanding Wilson's ideas and experiences.

88. Paul Tillich, *Systematic Theology*, vol. 1, 206.

89. Paul Tillich, *My Search for Absolutes*, ch. 1, "What Am I: An Autobiographical Essay: Early Years."

90. On the lamed vavers, see the section entitled "Judaism and other religions" in Chapter 12, "The God-Bearers and the Analogy of Being."

91. NOTES TO CHAPTER 12: My italics. Luke 7:47 says in the original Greek, *hou charin, legô soi, apheôntai hai hamartiai autês hai pollai, hoti êgapêsen polu*, which would literally be translated, "By grace of which, I tell you, her many sins are forgiven, because she loved so much." This sentence in isolation could be read to mean grammatically that her gracious and loving actions after coming to Jesus, had eventually *earned* her forgiveness for her past sins. But the story of the two debtors which Jesus told the Pharisee just a few verses earlier, in 7:41-43, makes it clear that God's forgiveness precedes the restoration of our ability to show *agapê* love. For Jesus, we are able to love only because God loved us first, just as in the Apostle Paul's teaching, and the epistles of John (see e.g. 1 John 4:19-20, also 4:7, 4:10, and 4:16b).

92. Glenn F. Chesnut, *The First Christian Histories: Eusebius, Socrates, Sozomen, Theodoret, and Evagrius*, 2nd ed., rev. and enlarged (Macon GA: Mercer University Press, 1986). [Orig. pub. in Paris by Éditions Beauchesne in 1977.] Chesnut, *Images of Christ: An Introduction to Christology*.

93. The people called the "Lamed Vavers" or "Lamed Vavniks" were the Thirty-Six Righteous Ones, the *lamed vav tzadikim*. The Talmud states that in every generation thirty-six righteous people "greet the *Shechinah*," the Divine Presence (Tractate Sanhedrin 97b; Tractate Sukkah 45b). For their sake, God keeps the world in existence, no matter how evil the rest of the human race has become. But should there ever be less than thirty-six of these Righteous Ones—should the number be even one short—God will instantly destroy the entire world, just as he once destroyed the cities of Sodom and

Gomorrah. In Jewish *gematria* (numerology) the number 18 represents the concept of "life" because the numerical values of the two letters that spell the Hebrew word *chai* ("living") add up to that number (the letter *chet* = 8 and the letter *yod* = 10). Since 36 is two times 18, it symbolically represents the idea of "two lives."

94. Taking this verse a bit out of the context, because Hosea 11:8-9 is actually stating that God is far more forgiving and compassionate than human beings, and finds it far harder to hold an implacable grudge.

95. Fox, who was Irish, eventually came over to the United States and became a minister in what was called the Divine Science Church, serving as pastor of the Church of the Healing Christ in New York City. The name of the denomination stressed the idea of an orderly set of scientific laws governing spirituality, which could be "demonstrated" in experiments which we performed during the course of our everyday lives.

96. Emmet Fox, *The Sermon on the Mount: The Key to Success in Life* and *The Lord's Prayer: An Interpretation* (San Francisco: HarperSan Francisco, 1938), in his commentary on the fourth clause in the Lord's Prayer ("Thy kingdom come, Thy will be done, in earth as it is in heaven"), pp. 158-159.

97. My translation, from the Italian text in Dante Alighieri, *The Divine Comedy*, trans. and comm. Charles S. Singleton, *Paradiso* 1: Italian Text and Translation (Princeton: Princeton University Press, 1975), Canto 33, lines 115-120.

98. Ibid., lines 130-131.

99. NOTES TO CHAPTER 13: Mary Whiton Calkins, who published ten books over the course of her long career, was educated at Harvard and taught philosophy at Wellesley for forty-two years, as well as being one of the pioneers who (along with William James) worked to establish the study of psychology as a separate academic field. She became the first woman to serve as president of the American Psychological Association (1905-06), as well as serving as the first woman president of the American Philosophical Association (1918-19), of which she had been a charter member.

100. Thomas A. Langford, *Practical Divinity: Theology in the Wesleyan Tradition* (Nashville: Abingdon Press, 1983), 119-124.

101. Borden Parker Bowne, *The Immanence of God* (New York: Houghton Mifflin, 1905).

102. Selections from Bowne's *The Immanence of God* in Thomas A. Langford, *Wesleyan Theology: A Sourcebook* (Durham, North Carolina: Labyrinth

Press, 1984), 151-161.

103. See Langford, *Practical Divinity*, 175-177.

104. Selections from Edgar S. Brightman, *The Problem of God* (New York: Abingdon Press, 1930) in Langford, *Wesleyan Theology: A Sourcebook*, 182-193.

105. Perkins School of Theology at Southern Methodist University in Dallas, Texas, where I was a student from 1961 to 1965.

106. The word "eternal" did not necessarily have that kind of totally static connotation in the Greek philosophy and theology of the eastern Mediterranean. Eusebius of Caesarea for example, who lived in the fourth century and provided the only sophisticated alternative in the ancient and medieval world to Augustine's philosophy of history, described the *Aiôn* (eternity) as *chronos achronos*, that is, as "nonchronologically-organized chronological flow," or pure process itself. Chronological time arose, Eusebius said, when this pure undifferentiated process—the *Aiôn*, which was the flow of ultimate reality as it was in itself—was organized by the human mind by turning it into a sequence of objectified phenomena arranged in chronological order, linked by cause and effect.

107. This is not necessarily impossible. But Whitehead's disciple Charles Hartshorne argued that it was impossible to do without creating the idea of an omniscient and omnipotent God who had both foreseen and foreordained everything that was to take place in a universe in which no true novelty could ever appear. Human free will and choice would of necessity be no more than an illusion in a world ruled by that kind of static and unchanging God, and one can certainly question whether time itself would be much more than an illusion of some sort, if no true novelty could ever appear.

108. Charles Hartshorne, *The Darkness and the Light: A Philosopher Reflects Upon His Fortunate Career and Those Who Made it Possible* (Albany: State University of New York Press, 1990), pp. 124-125.

109. Ibid., pp. 150-151.

110. Randall E. Auxier and Mark Y. A. Davies, eds., *Hartshorne and Brightman on God, Process, and Persons: The Correspondence, 1922-1945* (Nashville: Vanderbilt University Press, 2001).

111. Langford, *Wesleyan Theology: A Sourcebook*, p. 184; see also Langford, *Practical Divinity*, p. 177.

112. Charles Hartshorne and W. L. Reese, *Philosophers Speak of God*

(University of Chicago, 1953).

113. Charles Hartshorne, *The Darkness and the Light: A Philosopher Reflects Upon His Fortunate Career and Those Who Made it Possible* (Albany: State University of New York Press, 1990).

114. Charles Hartshorne, *Omnipotence and Other Theological Mistakes* (State University of New York Press, 1983), p. 18.

115. Charles Hartshorne, *The Logic of Perfection and Other Essays in Neoclassical Metaphysics* (LaSalle, Illinois: Open Court Publishing Company, 1962), p. 316.

116. NOTES TO CHAPTER 14: The need for making a distinction between Logos and Nomos was realized as early as the eighteenth century by the theologian John Wesley, from whom I picked up the idea of making this distinction. For Wesley, the Nomos was part of the created world, while the Logos was part of the uncreated godhead. The Nomos was a Platonic image of the Logos. But for Wesley, the Nomos seems to refer to the laws and structures of nature as understood within the human mind, whereas I am using the term to refer to those actual laws and structures of nature as they exist in themselves, shaping and directing what actually happens in ordinary natural processes, whether there is any human mind present to understand them or not. Human science is the best approximation we can come up with for understanding the workings of Nomos (natural law).

117. Thomas S. Kuhn, *The Structure of Scientific Revolutions* (Chicago: University of Chicago Press, 1962).

118. Flavell, *Developmental Psychology of Jean Piaget*.

119. In the first book of his *Elements*, the Greek mathematician Euclid (active around 300 B.C. roughly) gave five fundamental axioms, from which he would deduce all the other theorems in his system of geometry: (1) Any two points can be joined by a straight line. (2) Any straight line segment can be extended indefinitely in a straight line. (3) For any straight line segment, a circle can be drawn having the segment as its radius and one endpoint of that segment as its center. (4) All right angles are congruent to one another. (5) The parallel postulate: if two lines intersect a third in such a way that the sum of the inner angles on one side is less than two right angles, then the two lines must intersect each other on that side if extended indefinitely.

120. An ancient Stoic aphorism.

121. NOTES TO CHAPTER 15: Flavell, *Developmental Psychology of Jean Piaget*, 260.

122. Eric Berne, M.D., *Games People Play: The Psychology of Human Relationships: The Basic Handbook of Transactional Analysis* (New York: Ballantine Books, 1964).

123. Ibid., 105-108.

124. My translation, from the Italian text in Dante's *Divine Comedy*, Canto 33, lines 115-120.

125. Exodus 33:11.

126. Chesnut, *First Christian Histories*.

127. Teresa of Ávila, *Interior Castle*.

128. Now Teresa here makes an interesting contrast to Dante. Teresa's seven mansions were clearly intended to refer to the medieval concept of the seven heavens which surrounded the earth. And in the medieval picture of the world, as it was portrayed in Dante's *Paradiso*, the seventh heaven, which was the sphere of the planet Saturn, was the level closest to Heaven and therefore closest to God, the level where the souls of the great contemplative mystics dwelt. For both Teresa and Dante, the seventh sphere or region referred to the level where the highest and most important kind of human contact with God took place. For Dante, this was an ecstatic vision of overwhelming light, but for Teresa (if my interpretation is correct), it was instead a warm and reassuring awareness that I am being held in God's arms and am living in God's immediate presence at all times and places.

Or to put it another way, I do not believe that Bernini's famous seventeenth-century sculpture, *The Ecstasy of St. Teresa*, which stands in the church of Santa Maria della Vittoria in Rome, is a very good interpretation of the spiritual marriage, certainly at its most important level. Let us remember that Bernini was not a saint, but a very romantic and sensual Italian artist. Observe, for example, the way in which Pluto's fingers sink lasciviously into the soft buttocks of Proserpina in another of Bernini's famous sculptures, *The Rape of Proserpina*. That is the way Bernini looked at the world. St. Teresa on the other hand indeed had some extraordinary ecstatic experiences during the course of her spiritual life, but this was not what the concept of the spiritual marriage was referring to (or certainly not primarily).

129. NOTES TO CHAPTER 16: Justin Martyr's two most important surviving writings are his *Dialogue with Trypho* and his *First Apology*.

130. Justin also based his ethics upon *logos* (reason and logic alone). Acting ethically meant treating other human beings the way we would wish to be treated. This was what is called a natural law ethics. We did not in fact

need any kind of revealed truth in order to understand the moral standards by which God would judge us at the Last Judgment.

131. See Frankl, *Man's Search for Meaning*.

132. NOTES TO CHAPTER 17: *Dictionary of Latin and Greek Theological Terms*, s. v. *liberum arbitrium*. Some scholastic theologians attempted to make a distinction between *voluntas* (will) and *arbitrium* (choice), but this is not useful for our purposes here.

133. Macarius was victimized in the western world in the twentieth century by a small handful of academics who produced some of the poorest excuses for critical scholarship I have ever seen. I am appalled to see some of this nonsense still being repeated today in the scholarly literature. In the middle ages, it is true that the Macarius who wrote the *Fifty Spiritual Homilies* was mistakenly identified with a famous Egyptian desert father from the same period, and often incorrectly referred to as Macarius the Egyptian. It is clear that referring to him as Macarius "the Egyptian" is in fact incorrect. I therefore prefer to call him Macarius the Homilist to distinguish him from his rough contemporaries Macarius the Egyptian (c. 300-c. 390), Macarius of Alexandria (fourth century, also an Egyptian), and Macarius of Jerusalem (d. c. 334). The name Macarius, which means "blessed," was a common one among pious Christians of that period. But there is no serious evidence whatsoever that his "real name" was Symeon (that was a later medieval copyist's error in one document), nor that the name Macarius was a pseudonym used by someone pretending to be Macarius the Egyptian. So we do not properly refer to him as "Macarius-Symeon" or "Pseudo-Macarius." It is only because of contempt for and hostility towards the Eastern Orthodox tradition in certain circles that this particular small handful of twentieth-century western academics was allowed to publish such contrived trash without being called on it by more competent scholars.

In terms of dating, on internal grounds the *Fifty Spiritual Homilies* of St. Macarius were clearly written after the Arian controversy came to a resolution during the latter part of the fourth century, but before the christological controversy began affecting everything eastern theologians wrote during the course of the latter fifth century. So we would need to date him as a rough contemporary of St. Augustine, active somewhere in the late fourth to the earlier fifth century.

134. In John Wesley's letter of 1749 to the Cambridge deist Conyers Middleton, he refers to a number of early Christian theologians whom he regards as model representatives of "true, genuine Christianity." He says that "I mean particularly Clemens Romanus, Ignatius, Polycarp, Justin Martyr,

Irenaeus, Origen, Clemens Alexandrinus, Cyprian, to whom I would add Macarius and Ephraim Syrus." See Gordon Wakefield, "John Wesley and Ephraem Syrus," *Hugoye: Journal of Syriac Studies* 1, no. 2 (July 1998).

135. Glenn F. Chesnut, *Images of Christ* 35–9; *The First Christian Histories* 39, 43–5, 48n, 100, 109, 143, and *passim*.

136. See for example Romans 2:15, 9:1, 13:5; Acts 23:1, 24:16; and so on in the New Testament. This particular Greek word got taken over into medieval Latin theology as *syneidesis, synderesis,* and *synteresis,* but to talk about the natural human conscience (and the natural human consciousness of God), not to talk about personal consciousness *per se.*

137. See Roberta C. Chesnut, "The Two Prosopa in Nestorius' Bazaar of Heracleides," *Journal of Theological Studies* (Oxford) N.S. 29 (1978) 392–409.

138. So in the third-century pagan Neo-Platonic philosophy of Plotinus, for example, the highest levels of reality were spoken of as layered into three hypostases (substrata) called the One, *Nous* (Mind), and Soul—see A. H. Armstrong, *An Introduction to Ancient Philosophy* (London: Methuen, 1965), 180–194. And in the fourth century, the Cappadocian Fathers persuaded Athanasius to accept the language of three hypostases for speaking of God's threefold nature, which was ratified at the Council of Constantinople in 381-383.

139. In the fourth century, one of the great Cappadocian theologians, St. Gregory of Nyssa, made the statement in one of his writings that the word hypostasis could *also* be used to represent the substratum of defining characteristics which enabled us to distinguish one human being (such as James) from another human being (such as Paul), with the result that in the fifth century, in the Christological controversy leading up to the Council of Chalcedon, it was decided by some of the leading theologians that hypostasis *in this sense* was what ought to be used to refer to the unifying factor in the union of God and man in Christ—the incarnate Christ, as the Chalcedonian formulation eventually put it in 451 A.D., was made up of "two natures united in one hypostasis." A decision was also made that Christians in the Latin speaking western half of the Roman empire could translate the Greek word *hypostasis* by the Latin word *persona,* which introduced considerable confusion since that word had originally meant an actor's mask, or the role someone played in a stage play, in addition to being used to refer to someone's character (i.e., the Latin word *persona* was in many of its usages far closer in meaning to the Greek word *prosôpon*). This was the reason that the word hypostasis, when it came into English as a loan word many centuries later, took

on so many of the meanings associated with the modern European ideas of person and personality and "personification."

But this was only in the specific context of talking about the union of humanity and divinity in the person of Jesus Christ. When speaking of God in himself, the Cappadocian formulation was accepted as the orthodox one: there were not three "personalities" or three different conscious personal beings in God, in the modern English sense of those words. There were three hypostases in the sense of *substrata* within the Godhead (Father, Logos, and Holy Spirit), all equally partaking in the attributes of divinity (so that no Arian subordinationism was involved), but since there was in the undivided Godhead only one will and one action (*energeia*), there was only one God—not three gods—with a single consciousness and personhood in the English sense of those words. See Gregory of Nyssa, *An Answer to Ablabius: That We Should Not Think of Saying There Are Three Gods*, trans. Cyril C. Richardson, in *Christology of the Later Fathers*, ed. Edward Rochie Hardy, Library of Christian Classics (Philadelphia: Westminster Press, 1954), pp. 256–67.

140. See John Herman Randall, Jr., *Aristotle* (New York: Columbia University Press, 1960) 61, 68, and 76.

141. Thucydides, ed. and trans. Charles Forster Smith, 4 vols., Loeb Classical Library (Cambridge MA: Harvard University Press, 1921–30), 1.67–88.

142. See Gordon Leff, *Medieval Thought: St. Augustine to Ockham* (Baltimore MD: Penguin Books, 1958), chapt. 6, "The Philosophy of Islam" (pp. 141–67); and *Oxford Dictionary of the Christian Church*, 2nd ed., ed. F. L. Cross and E. A. Livingstone (London: Oxford University Press, 1974), s.v. "Averroism" and other related articles for a full bibliography. Also consult Arthur O. Lovejoy, *The Great Chain of Being: A Study of the History of an Idea* (New York: Harper & Row, 1936), Lecture 3, "The Chain of Being and Some Internal Conflicts in Medieval Thought," pp. 67–98.

143. S. Körner, *Kant* (Baltimore MD: Penguin Books, 1955) 118–22; Frederick Copleston, *A History of Philosophy*, Vol. IV. *Descartes to Leibniz* (Westminster MD: Newman Press, 1958), ch. 18, pp. 320–32.

144. Etienne Gilson, *History of Christian Philosophy in the Middle Ages* (New York: Random House, 1955).

145. NOTES TO CHAPTER 18: Andrew Hodges, *Alan Turing: The Enigma* (New York: Simon and Schuster, 1983).

146. A[lan] M. Turing, "On computable numbers, with an application

to the Entscheidungsproblem," *Proc. London Maths. Soc.*, ser. 2, 42 (1936): 230-265. [Also available online] This raises interesting issues for the kind of Thomistic doctrine of God which one sees described in Bernard Lonergan, *Insight: a Study of Human Understanding* (New York: Philosophical Library, 1957). That is, if God as Being Itself is described as "all the possible answers to all the possible questions" (which Lonergan argues would be a good translation of Thomas' doctrine into modern philosophical language) are we not forced to say that the combination of Gödel's proof and this paper by Alan Turing proves that some of these possible questions either have contradictory answers or lead us into infinite unresolvable chains of reasoning? On the other hand, since Lonergan very carefully said "all the *possible* answers," one could argue that his definition is still valid. It is neither a meaningless nor an impossible statement, because it does not necessarily imply that God knows answers which are meaningful, complete, and internally logically coherent, to all the possible questions which could be asked. See Chapter 20 of this present volume, "Why the Future Cannot Be Totally Predicted."

147. Alan M. Turing, "Computing Machinery and Intelligence," *Mind* (October 1950) 59: 433-460, repr. in Alan Ross Anderson, ed., *Minds and Machines* (Englewood Cliffs, N.J.: Prentice-Hall, 1964). [Also available online] See also Douglas R. Hofstadter, *Gödel, Escher, Bach: an Eternal Golden Braid* (New York: Vintage/Random House, 1979) 594–599 *et passim*.

148. In more recent years, a good philosophical theologian named William P. Alston realized that the same kind of simple, common sense reasoning could be applied to the question of whether God existed. See William P. Alston, "Religious Experience and Religious Belief," *Nous* 16 (1982) 3-12, an epistemological defense of the immediate personal religious experience of God by an extremely competent philosopher in which he discussed such issues as norms, reliability, justification, and comparison with the epistemological limitations of sense experience. I am not sure whether Alston was aware of the Turing test, but he used closely parallel reasoning, and argued that if the kind of experiences which we have (over a number of years) when we are living the spiritual life leads us to the conclusion that we have been encountering a real God, then we are completely justified in concluding that God does in fact exist. The reason I believe that there is a maple tree in my front yard is based upon a number of direct experiences of that tree, not upon philosophical argument and intellectual debates over the nature of "treeness." It is more difficult to build up experiences of God, Alston acknowledges, but the fundamental principle is the same. In good empiricist philosophy, theories have to be based on actual experience, as opposed to being used to try to deny our experiences.

149. See Glenn F. Chesnut, *The Higher Power of the Twelve-Step Program: For Believers & Non-Believers*, Hindsfoot Foundation Series on Spirituality and Theology (San Jose: Authors Choice/iUniverse, 2001), Chapter 1, which was originally a lecture given on this topic to the Northern Indiana Counselors Association on October 21, 1999.

150. This was an adaptation of the fundamental principles involved in the experiential religion developed by Jonathan Edwards and John Wesley, the eighteenth-century founders of the modern evangelical tradition, see Glenn F. Chesnut, *Changed by Grace: V. C. Kitchen, the Oxford Group, and A.A.*, Hindsfoot Foundation Series on Spirituality and Theology (New York: iUniverse, 2006).

151. Martin Heidegger, *Being and Time*, trans. John Macquarrie and Edward Robinson (San Francisco: Harper, 1962).

152. Martin Buber, *I and Thou*, trans. Walter Kaufmann (New York: Charles Scribner's Sons, 1970; orig. pub. 1923 as *Ich und Du*). When Buber began studying Hasidic Judaism (the Jewish movement which began in eastern Europe in the eighteenth century under the leadership of Rabbi Israel ben Eliezer, 1698–1760, known as the Ba'al Shem Tov) he learned how to see God as an intensely personal presence pervading everything in the universe, including all physical objects as well as all living beings.

153. Note the amazingly complex social interactions uncovered by Elizabeth Marshall Thomas in *The Hidden Life of Dogs* (New York: Houghton Mifflin, 1993). In this little gem of a book, she applied the same ethnological observational techniques to understanding the thoughts, feelings, and wants of dogs which she had previously used in her excellent anthropological studies of Bushmen and Dodoth tribesmen (*The Harmless People* and *Warrior Herdsmen*).

154. NOTES TO CHAPTER 19: See 2 Corinthians 3:17-18, "Now the Lord is the Spirit, and where the Spirit of the Lord is, there is freedom. And we all, with unveiled face, beholding the glory of the Lord, are being changed into his likeness from glory to glory; for this comes from the Lord who is the Spirit."

155. Werner Jaeger, *Two Rediscovered Works of Ancient Christian Literature: Gregory of Nyssa and Macarius* (Leiden: E. J. Brill, 1954), Part One, Chapter 5 (pp. 70-114) describes St. Gregory of Nyssa's use of a synergistic doctrine of free will instead of a doctrine of predestination in his discussion of Gregory's theology and its background. See also Jean Daniélou, Introduction (pp. 1-78) to Gregory of Nyssa, *From Glory to Glory: Texts from Gregory of*

Nyssa's Mystical Writings, ed. Herbert Musurillo (New York: Scribner, 1961).

156. The other major strand within the modern evangelical tradition is more affected by Calvinism, and tends to accept, in whole or in part, some sort of rigid Calvinistic doctrine of predestination. John Wesley taught classics and theology at Oxford University. What an undergraduate degree in theology at Oxford meant, not only in the eighteenth century, but when I was a student there in the 1960's, was a strong concentration on the New Testament and on patristic theology down to the Council of Chalcedon in 451 A.D. It should be emphasized very firmly that Wesley's synergistic doctrine came from the early patristic period, not from the Philippist heresy taught by Philipp Melanchthon (1497-1560) in the Lutheran tradition, nor from the Arminian heresy taught by Jacobus Arminius (1560-1609) in the Reformed (Calvinist) tradition. For more about those two figures, see the article on "synergismus" in the *Dictionary of Latin and Greek Theological Terms: Drawn Principally from Protestant Scholastic Theology*, ed. Richard A. Muller (Grand Rapids, Michigan: Baker Book House, 1985). Wesley's synergistic doctrine was structured very differently from either of those two theological positions, although when Wesley found himself accused of Arminianism by the eighteenth-century English Calvinists, he found it more expedient to simply challenge the basic underlying Calvinist doctrine of predestination head on, than to get involved in endless scholastic squabbles about the actual differences between his teaching and Arminius's. In fact, to bait the Calvinists, Wesley began the publication in 1778 of a Methodist periodical called *The Arminian Magazine*. Albert Outler, the greatest Wesley scholar of the twentieth century, once told me however that he had found no evidence that Wesley had ever read a single word which Arminius wrote, so studying that figure, and the Calvinist heresy by that name, is not a useful way of investigating Wesley's position on free will and grace. It will do nothing but point you in wrong directions.

157. The one possible exception in the Big Book of Alcoholics Anonymous comes in a line in one of the stories added in the third edition, which came out in 1976, called "Doctor, Alcoholic, Addict," where the author (Paul Ohliger, M.D.) said on page 449, "When I am disturbed ... I can find no serenity until I accept that person, place, thing or situation as being exactly the way it is supposed to be at this moment. Nothing, absolutely nothing, happens in God's world by mistake." This third edition came out five years after Bill Wilson's death, and I have often wondered whether he would have allowed that last line into the book without further elaboration. Ohliger's story was also included in the fourth edition of the Big Book which came out in 2001, retitled "Acceptance Was the Answer," but with the text un-

changed (see page 417). As the A.A. author Father Ralph Pfau says, however, everything that happens in the universe happens either because God decreed it to be so, or *allowed it* to be so, which provides a way of giving a Catholic interpretation of this passage, as opposed to having to read it in terms of some kind of Calvinist doctrine of predestination and foreordination. *Alcoholics Anonymous* (New York: Alcoholics Anonymous World Services, 3rd edit. 1955, 4th edit. 2001).

158. See Brown, *Augustine of Hippo: A Biography*.

159. This seems to have been a collection of Latin translations of Neo-Platonic works, perhaps some written by Plotinus (c. 205-270 A.D.), although some scholars see definite signs that Augustine had read at least one work either written by (or influenced by) the later Neo-Platonic philosopher Proclus, one of the most famous heads of Plato's Academy in Athens, whose life overlapped with Augustine's—Proclus lived down to 485, shortly after Augustine arrived in Milan.

160. One of the best studies of the developments of Augustine's ideas in this area is J. Patout Burns, *The Development of Augustine's Doctrine of Operative Grace* (Paris: Études Augustiniennes, 1980). See also Glenn F. Chesnut, "The Pattern of the Past: Augustine's Debate with Eusebius and Sallust," pp. 69-95 in John Deschner, Leroy T. Howe, and Klaus Penzel (eds.), *Our Common History as Christians: Essays in Honor of Albert C. Outler* (New York: Oxford University Press, 1975), on the City of God and the Earthly City, original sin, and providence in Augustine's theology of history.

161. Chesnut, *First Christian Histories*.

162. Chesnut, *First Christian Histories*, p. 43. Eusebius *PE* 7. 10. 1-3 (314bd); *De laud.* 12. 5; cf. 11. 17. For a more complete discussion of what the Logos concept meant in the ancient Christian world, see Chesnut, *Images of Christ*, pp. 35-38, 44-47, 52-53, 92-93, 99, 139.

163. Chesnut, *First Christian Histories*, pp. 43-44. Eusebius *Contra Hier.* 6. Cf. *De laud.* 12. 5, duplicated in *Theoph.* 1. 23.

164. Chesnut, *First Christian Histories* p. 47.

165. Chesnut, *First Christian Histories*, p. 41. Aristotle, *Physics* 2. 5. 197a.

166. Cf. Plutarch, "On Fate," 568cd and 569d-570a.

167. Chesnut, *First Christian Histories*, p. 44.

168. Taken from the title of a talk by American mathematician and me-

teorologist Edward Lorenz at the meeting of the American Association for the Advancement of Science in 1972.

169. Chesnut, *First Christian Histories*, p. 42.

170. Emmet Fox, *Sermon on the Mount*.

171. James Allen, *As a Man Thinketh* (orig. pub. 1902), in Mel B., *Three Recovery Classics: As a Man Thinketh (by James Allen), The Greatest Thing in the World (by Henry Drummond), An Instrument of Peace (the St. Francis Prayer)*, Hindsfoot Foundation Series on Spirituality and Theology (New York: iUniverse, 2004).

172. Richard M. Dubiel, *The Road to Fellowship: The Role of the Emmanuel Movement and the Jacoby Club in the Development of Alcoholics Anonymous*, Hindsfoot Foundation Series on the History of Alcoholism Treatment, ed. Glenn F. Chesnut (New York: iUniverse, 2004).

173. The other three were Bill Wilson, Richmond Walker, and Ed Webster. Ralph Pfau was the author (under the pseudonym Father John Doe) of the set of booklets called the Golden Books: the *Spiritual Side* (1947), *Tolerance* (1948), *Attitudes* (1949), *Action* (1950), *Happiness* (1951), *Excuses* (1952), *Sponsorship* (1953), *Principles* (1954), *Resentments* (1955), *Decisions* (1957), *Passion* (1960), *Sanity* (1963), *Sanctity* (1964), and *Living* (1964). He also published three larger volumes: *Sobriety and Beyond* (1955), *Sobriety Without End* (1957), and an autobiography, which he entitled *Prodigal Shepherd*, in 1958. They were all originally published by SMT Guild in Indianapolis, Indiana, but are kept in print now by Hazelden in Center City, Minnesota.

174. The story that follows is taken from Ralph Pfau and Al Hirshberg, *Prodigal Shepherd* (Indianapolis, Indiana: SMT Guild, 1958).

175. Jean Piaget (1896-1980) was one of the great figures in the study of how human beings gain knowledge about the world. The best introduction which I know to Piaget's theories of knowledge was written by the American psychologist John H. Flavell (now professor emeritus at Stanford University), who is also recognized for his own research into childhood development in the area of metacognition (knowing about knowing). On the distinction Piaget made between correspondence and interdependence see Flavell's *Developmental Psychology of Jean Piaget*, p. 260.

176. Ernest Kurtz, *Shame & Guilt*, Hindsfoot Foundation Series on Treatment and Recovery, 2nd rev. ed. (New York: iUniverse, 2007; orig. pub. 1981), Part II, Ch. 1, page 15.

177. Chesnut, *First Christian Histories* 50-51.

178. Sally Brown and David R. Brown, *A Biography of Mrs. Marty Mann: The First Lady of Alcoholics Anonymous* (Center City, Minnesota: Hazelden, 2001) 107-108.

179. Ibid., pp. 107-108 and 336 n 10. Also see Marty's story, "Women Suffer Too," in *Alcoholics Anonymous*, 4th ed. (New York: Alcoholics Anonymous World Services, 2001) 200-207.

180. NOTES TO CHAPTER 20: A physicist whom I studied under at Iowa State University devised a way of calculating the orbit of the single outer electron in an ionized molecule of oxygen, where the electron and the two oxygen nuclei formed a three-body system, by using elliptical coordinates where the oxygen nuclei were placed at the two foci of the ellipses. The energy levels of the orbits which he and his graduate student calculated in fact matched up with the experimentally observed lines in the spectrum of ionized oxygen. And there are a handful of other kinds of special situations where the equations for a three-body system can be set up and solved. But these are the kinds of exceptions which prove the general rule that a three-body problem cannot be solved.

181. Stephen Hawking, "Gödel and the end of physics," at: http://www.damtp.cam.ac.uk/strings02/dirac/hawking/ (September 2007).

182. Hofstadter, *Gödel, Escher, Bach.*

183. It appeared as a two-part article in the July and October 1948 issues of the *Bell System Technical Journal.*

184. NOTES TO CHAPTER 21: That human beings share a common ancestor with the great apes had already been established on the grounds of comparative anatomy, and was an intrinsic part of many of the new atheistic systems which began developing in western thought in the mid-nineteenth century. Charles Darwin, in his book *On the Origin of Species* (1859), made only one brief allusion to the topic of human evolution—"light will be thrown on the origin of man and his history"—but Victorian controversialists understood the implications of what he was saying about the evolution of species by natural selection, and almost immediately began attacking him on the grounds that he was teaching that human beings were descended from apes. Darwin's *The Descent of Man, and Selection in Relation to Sex* (1871) made it much clearer and more explicit that human beings were also part of the evolutionary process, and have helped keep his name at the focus of conservative Christian attacks on the doctrine of evolution ever since.

185. The scientific evidence demonstrating that human beings are descended from apelike ancestors moved in the mid-twentieth century from the study of comparative anatomy to new discoveries in biochemistry, when it was found that a kind of molecule called DNA (deoxyribonucleic acid) contained the genetic instructions used in the development of all known living organisms. The link between DNA and heredity was established in work carried out between 1953 and 1958, when I was in high school and just beginning college. This was another of the great twentieth-century discoveries that has so revolutionized our picture of the world. DNA studies carried out in the latter half of the twentieth century gave chemical measurements for working out the basic ancestral tree of human beings and the great apes. Human beings are not descended from chimpanzees or gorillas. It is rather that we and the great apes share a common remote ancestor. Modern human beings are descended from early primates like Proconsul (the fossil evidence for this species was first discovered in 1909) which lived from 27 to 17 million years ago. A comparison of the DNA from modern primates shows that the gibbons split off and formed their own family between 18 and 12 million years ago, and the line of evolutionary development that produced modern orangutans split off about 12 million years ago. The ancestors of modern gorillas split off about 8 million years ago, and that of the chimpanzee only about 4 million years ago. The part of the genetic code which distinguishes us from the latter is extremely small. Human DNA is 98.4 percent identical to the DNA of chimpanzees.

186. The story in Genesis 1:1-2:3 (which originally came from the picture of the universe taught by the priests in the Babylonian city-states) has human beings created after all of the other living creatures on earth. The story in Genesis 2:4-24 (which originally was recited by the Israelite tribes while they were still wandering as nomads, shepherding their little flocks of sheep and goats around the margins of the areas in the Near East which could be turned into settled farms), gives a different order of creation: it has the first man created, then all the animals and birds, and then the first woman. Among the great Greek philosophers later on, the Epicureans stayed closer to the Babylonian theory, and taught (like modern scientists) that life first appeared in the oceans, then the first land animals appeared, and finally human beings evolved out of animal ancestors. The Epicurean philosophers said (again fundamentally like modern scientists) that this evolution occurred due to random selection produced by the chance movement and recombination of atoms.

187. The actual phrase "the ghost in the machine" was coined by the British philosopher Gilbert Ryle in his book *The Concept of Mind* (New York:

Barnes & Noble, 1949) as a derogatory description of Descartes' philosophy of mind-body dualism.

188. Flavell, *Developmental Psychology of Jean Piaget.*

189. The idea that the soul cannot see the world of ideas clearly as long as it is imprisoned in a material body was a prejudice, inherited from the world of ancient Platonic and Neo-Pythagorean philosophy, which influenced Kant at an extremely basic level in spite of his attempts in his critical philosophy to shake himself out of his earlier "dogmatic slumbers." One of the earliest of the Kantian interpreters, Jakob Friedrich Fries (1773-1843), pointed that out very clearly and, I believe, quite correctly. For a good introduction to Fries' interpretation of Kant, see Rudolf Otto, *The Philosophy of Religion Based on Kant and Fries.* See also Jakob Friedrich Fries, *Knowledge, Belief, and Aesthetic Sense*, ed. Frederick Gregory, trans. Kent Richter (Köln: Jürgen Dinter Verlag für Philosophie, 1989).

190. We can in fact illustrate the distinction between interdependence and correspondence by looking at Kant's philosophy. Kant's categories were *in correspondence with* the basic principles of logic. Every category could be connected with a specific type of logical statement, in a strict isomorphic relationship. So for example, every time my mind takes the category of causality and schematizes it onto the phenomenal world to make a causal observation, what I am observing can be put in the form of an "if ... then" logical statement. I might say, in one situation, "Be careful, IF you drop that bag of groceries, THEN you will break the eggs that are sitting in the bottom of the bag." But I think that almost all modern philosophers are agreed that Kant's categories cannot be *deduced* from that set of different kinds of logical statements. That is, an "if ... then" statement does not necessarily logically imply the fundamental understanding that is involved when we say that the occurrence of one event is the efficient cause of the occurrence of another event ("when the batter hit the ball, it went flying through the air"). The concept of efficient causality means something *more than* a simple "if ... then" relationship. If as a philosopher, you understand why Kant's categories are in correspondence with certain basic types of logical statements, but cannot be mechanically derived from them, then you understand what is meant by the distinction between correspondence and interdependence. If Kant's categories could be derived from the principles of pure logic, then and only then could we say that the Kantian categories and those logical principles were in a relationship of interdependence.

191. Douglas R. Hofstadter, *I Am a Strange Loop* (New York: Basic Books, 2007), see pages 37-39 and further discussions later on in the book. See also

his earlier extremely thought-provoking book *Gödel, Escher, Bach* (1979).

192. Martin Heidegger, *Being and Time*, trans. John Macquarrie and Edward Robinson (San Francisco: Harper, 1962).

193. NOTES TO CHAPTER 22: On the continent of Europe, the Protestant scholastic theologians (sixteenth-eighteenth centuries) attempted to deal with this by distinguishing between different kinds of "faith": the faith of a devil (James 2:19) could be termed *fides historica*, as opposed to *fides salvifica*, that is, saving faith. The latter (saving faith) involved intellectual components (*notitia* or knowledge of the actual contents of the saving message, and *assensus* or intellectual assent or acknowledgment of its truth), together with a volitional component (*fiducia* or trust). The intellectual component could be referred to as the *fides quae creditur* (the faith which is believed) to distinguish it from the *fides qua creditur* (the subjective faith by which it is believed by the believer). See *Dictionary of Latin and Greek Theological Terms*.

194. James 2:18-19 and 26, my translation.

195. The first Book of Homilies contained twelve sermons, nos. 3, 4, and 5 (on salvation, faith, and works) by Thomas Cranmer, the Archbishop of Canterbury. It was officially released in July 1547 and became one of the traditional doctrinal standards of the Church of England. S.v. "Homilies, the Books of" in the *Oxford Dictionary of the Christian Church*, 2nd ed., ed. F. L. Cross and E. A. Livingstone (London: Oxford University Press, 1974). John Wesley drew up an abridged version of the first five homilies and published it under the title "The Doctrine of Salvation, Faith and Good Works, Extracted from the Homilies of the Church of England," which may be found in *John Wesley*, Library of Protestant Thought, ed. Albert C. Outler (New York: Oxford University Press, 1964) 121–33. See also John Wesley, Sermon 7, "The Way to the Kingdom," 1.6 and 2.10, in *The Works of John Wesley*, Vols. 1–4, *Sermons*, ed. Albert C. Outler (Nashville: Abingdon Press, 1984–7).

196. Still one of the clearest introductions to Luther is Philip S. Watson, *Let God Be God! An Interpretation of the Theology of Martin Luther* (Philadelphia: Fortress, 1947).

197. *Alcoholics Anonymous*, 4th ed., pp. 64-67.

198. Ibid. p. 68.

199. In the early 1300's, Dante had attempted the same task in his *Divine Comedy*. As we can see, in the last part, the *Paradiso*, although he gave the place of highest honor (the sphere of the planet Saturn) to the great contemplative mystics (like St. Bernard) from the monasteries and convents, he

gave places of honor to men and women living in the secular world in the spheres of the other six planets. Or in other words, the great majority of the people in heaven, according to Dante, would be laypeople—not priests, monks, and nuns.

200. Evelyn Underhill, *Mysticism: A Study in the Nature and Development of Man's Spiritual Consciousness* (London: Methuen, 1911).

201. Richmond Walker, *Twenty-Four Hours a Day*, Compiled by a Member of the Group at Daytona Beach, Fla., rev. ed. (Center City, Minnesota: Hazelden, 1975; orig. pub. 1948).

202. Wesley used this terminology throughout his many writings, but see for example John Wesley, *Explanatory Notes upon the New Testament* (London: Epworth, 1958; orig. pub. in London by William Bowyer, 1755) in the commentary on 1 John 4:18: "'There is no fear in love; but perfect love casteth out fear: because fear hath torment. He that feareth is not made perfect in love.' There is no fear in love—No slavish fear can be where love reigns. But perfect, adult love casteth out slavish fear: because such fear hath torment— And so is inconsistent with the happiness of love. A natural man has neither fear nor love; one that is awakened, fear without love; a babe in Christ, love and fear; a father in Christ, love without fear."

203. John Wesley, one of the two great eighteenth-century Christian thinkers who helped found the modern evangelical tradition, put this very bluntly: "salvation is not the going to heaven." Wesley certainly believed in the life of the world to come—he was in no way denying that—he was simply pointing out that in real New Testament Christianity, salvation meant having God come into our hearts and fill us with his divine light here in this world.

204. First in Galatians 3:6-7, and then in Romans 4. A pair of modern American Jewish authors uses the same motif, echoing the biblical stories of Abraham leaving Ur and Moses and the Israelites making their exodus from Egypt, but with the additional poignant invocation of the way in which so many present-day American Jews are alive only because their grandparents somehow got out of Poland or Germany or Hungary as the onslaught of the Nazi holocaust swept through central Europe: "Our grandparents! In the darkness of night, they packed their bags and fled in fear for their lives and those of their families. Yet, somehow our people always have known that they had to take the first step if they were to improve their lot. Powerlessness does not have to be passivity. As Jews, we do not believe in chaos. Rather, order is what anchors us in this world . . . . When the world we have built and the family we have nurtured are threatened because of our dependence [on some addictive substance or behavior], we should act." Rabbi Kerry M.

Olitzky and Stuart A. Copans, M.D., *Twelve Jewish Steps to Recovery: A Personal Guide to Turning from Alcoholism and Other Addictions* (Woodstock VT: Jewish Lights Publishing, 1991).

205. A very free but I believe totally accurate translation of what is actually being said in that verse— *estin de pistis elpizomenôn hypostasis, pragmatôn elenchos ou blepomenôn*—rendered in the King James Version as "Now faith is the substance of things hoped for, the evidence of things not seen." *Hypostasis* means in this case, not the abstract philosophical technical term "substance," but the concrete notion of the "substratum" which lies below everything else, such as (in particular in ancient Greek usage) the row of stones at the bottom of a structure which serve as the supporting "foundation" for everything else. *Elenchos* means in Greek, not "evidence" *per se*, but refers to any "proof" or "verification," or anything we can point to, which can give us the positive "sense of truth" about what we assert to be so. "Things not seen," in this theological context, clearly refers to the invisible realm of the heavenly spirit, as opposed to the visible world of matter (as in the phrase "maker of heaven and earth, and of all things visible and invisible" in the Nicene Creed, which sets out the same symbolic dichotomy).

206. John Calvin, *Institutes* 3.2.14 and 3.2.19-20, my translation. St. Bernard of Clairvaux was the one medieval Catholic teacher whom Calvin deeply respected: we can see some of the technical terminology of Cistercian mysticism being borrowed and adapted by Calvin here.

207. 2 Corinthians 3:18.

208. Dennis E. Tamburello, *Union with Christ: John Calvin and the Mysticism of St. Bernard*, Columbia [Theological Seminary] Series in Reformed Theology (Louisville: Westminster John Knox Press, 1994). See also the review of this book by Dagmar Heller in the *Ecumenical Review* (July 1996).

209. See also Walker, *Twenty-Four Hours a Day*, readings for April 30, "there is a spark of the Divine in every one of us," and March 4, "we start out with a spark of the Divine Spirit but a large amount of selfishness."

210. *Alcoholics Anonymous*, 4th ed., pp. 8 and 25.

211. NOTES TO CHAPTER 23: All the excerpts that follow in this chapter are taken from the tape recording of this talk which Ed Pike gave on August 23, 1980. The tape recording was discovered in the A.A. Archives in Elkhart, Indiana. A full transcript is given, along with a description of the historical context, in Glenn C[hesnut], *The St. Louis Gambler & the Railroad Man: Lives and Teachings of the A.A. Old Timers*, 2nd ed., Hindsfoot Foundation Series on Alcoholics Anonymous History (New York: iUniverse, 2005;

orig. pub. 1996). See also its companion volume, Glenn C[hesnut], *The Factory Owner & the Convict: Lives and Teachings of the A.A. Old Timers*, 2nd ed., Hindsfoot Foundation Series on Alcoholics Anonymous History (New York: iUniverse, 2005; orig. pub. 1996).

212. Compare John Wesley, Sermon 34, "Original, Nature, Properties, and Use of the Law" 4.1–2, in *The Works of John Wesley* Vol. 2.

213. The tape recording of Ed Pike from 1980.

214. This is NOT the same as the medieval scholastic notions of a *fides implicita* or *fides carbonaria* (the "faith of charcoal burners"), which was a willingness on the part of uneducated laborers to believe "whatever the church says you should believe" without even knowing much about its contents. See under those terms in the *Dictionary of Latin and Greek Theological Terms*. The kind of proto-faith or tacit faith that I am talking about here shows itself in a willingness to make a commitment, to trust enough to start walking the spiritual path, even though the one so committed may be confused enough about theological terminology at the rational level that he does not understand that he has already obtained the first small seed of genuine faith, and has already begun to walk in the light. This proto-faith is in one sense *unconscious* as opposed to fully conscious, but not in the Freudian sense of that word, so I would rather not create additional possibilities for confusion by calling it an "unconscious faith."

215. Currently, many people in A.A. in the St. Joseph river valley area make the same distinction by referring to faith in the first sense as "religion" and faith in the second sense as "spirituality." John Wesley in the eighteenth century, in closely similar manner, made a contrast between (1) "formal religion" (which, together with the mere "outward form of religion" did not truly save or help anybody) and (2) true "inward religion" and "the religion of the heart," which alone would truly bring us into the saving and healing presence of God.

216. Michael Polanyi, *Personal Knowledge*, preface to the 1964 edition (pp. ix–xi)—"tacit knowing is more fundamental than explicit knowing: we can know more than we can tell and we can tell nothing without relying on our awareness of things we may not be able to tell." See also 4.1–4 (pp. 49–55).

217. 2 Corinthians 3:18, an important passage in the spiritual teaching of St. Gregory of Nyssa and in later Eastern Orthodox spirituality.

218. NOTES TO CHAPTER 24: A. A. Penzias and R. W. Wilson, "A Measurement of Excess Antenna Temperature at 4080 Mc/s," *Astrophysical*

Journal 142 (1965): 419.

219. The steady state theory held that the universe had always existed and had never had a beginning in time. The oscillatory universe was a theory which saw the universe going through an endless sequence, in which a big bang started an expansion which extended outwards only so far before the universe began contracting, ending in a big crunch which in turn served as the source of the next big bang.

220. For a good collection of passages from St. Gregory and an excellent introduction to this aspect of his spiritual teaching, see Jean Daniélou, Introduction (pp. 1-78) to Gregory of Nyssa, *From Glory to Glory*.

221. As was done by the mid-twentieth-century "death of God theologians"—Thomas J. J. Altizer, Rabbi Richard L. Rubenstein, and their comrades.

222. Revelation 6:1-8.

223. We can date St. Gregory of Nyssa to c. 330 - c. 395 A.D. In the case of St. Macarius the Homilist, dating is more difficult, but as one reads his sermons, one can see on internal grounds that he was living in a world where the Arian controversy had finally been completely settled, hence well after the First Council of Constantinople in 381, because his statements about the Trinity are expressed unselfconsciously and automatically in terms of the kind of interpretation of the Nicene doctrines which the Cappadocian theologians got Athanasius to accept at that council. On the other hand, he ignores the issues which arose in the christological controversy which began with the condemnation of Nestorius in 431—a dispute which had totally polarized eastern Christianity by the time of Severus of Antioch (c. 465-538), Philoxenus of Mabbug (c. 440-523), and Jacob of Sarug (c. 451-521). So Macarius could have preached during the very late fourth century, but was (I believe) more likely an early to mid-fifth century figure. In the middle ages, St. Macarius the Homilist was confused with two slightly earlier desert monks, and for that reason became referred to (inaccurately) as St. Macarius the Egyptian. In fact however, by looking at his sermons, one can tell on internal grounds that he was the archimandrite (abbot) of a small Orthodox monastery somewhere in the deserts of eastern Syria or western Mesopotamia. During the past few decades, some of the worst patristic scholarship that I have ever seen has produced some truly bad publications about him. There is no reason to doubt, for example, that his name really was Macarius, nor is there any reason to believe that this was a pseudonym used to disguise the writings of some terrible Messalian heretic. To give you an idea of how really bad some of the current scholarship is, there is one work claiming to be a fresh,

new translation of Macarius' *Fifty Spiritual Homilies* where, once the author got past the first few homilies, he took A. J. Mason's translation and simply changed the words slightly *without even bothering to look at the original Greek*, which produced some laughable mistakes—using words that appeared to be near synonyms in English of some of Mason's words, but which in fact were not possible translations of the original Greek at all. It is a total cheat and a fraud by a completely unscrupulous person, and the thing I marvel at, is that this pseudo-translation is still being used today by some so-called Macarius experts. Macarius is direly in need of some really first-rate scholar to rescue him from all of this nonsense.

224. John Wesley taught theology at Oxford University, where the study of that subject meant the same thing in the eighteenth century that it did when I was a student there in the mid-twentieth century: principally courses and exams on the New Testament and on the Catholic and Orthodox theology of the first through fifth centuries. Wesley mentioned Macarius explicitly as one of the great spiritual masters from that period, and published a translation of some of Macarius's writings for his Methodists to read and learn from.

225. Macarius the Homilist, *Fifty Spiritual Homilies of St. Macarius the Egyptian*, trans. A. J. Mason (London: S.P.C.K., 1921).

226 NOTES TO APPENDIX: Part of what I am saying here is also noted, interestingly enough, in some comments made in a book which Charles Hartshorne published when he was 93 years old, called *The Darkness and the Light: A Philosopher Reflects Upon His Fortunate Career and Those Who Made It Possible* (Albany: State University of New York Press, 1990). I am referring here to the first chapter of that work, where Hartshorne made some very interesting observations as he discussed the nature of human memory. The concept of time and eternity which I am laying out in this Appendix is not at all the standard Hartshornean one, the one which appears in his earlier writings. But I would argue that my interpretation of the relationship between time and eternity makes better sense out of the things which the elderly Hartshorne was noting here in this masterpiece of his later years.

227 It has long been recognized by biblical scholars that the gospel of John teaches what is called a realized eschatology. In John 17:3, for example, the author of the gospel says "And this is eternal life, that they know thee the only true God." Salvation does not mean going to heaven at some point in the far off future, it means learning to live here in the Now in the conscious awareness of God's presence and eternal reality.

228 Again see the first chapter of Hartshorne, *The Darkness and the Light.*

229 Marcus Aurelius, *Meditations* 4.43, as quoted in the discussion of time and eternity in Chesnut, *First Christian Histories* 91-93.

230 Chesnut, *First Christian Histories* 91-93, including extended notes 106, 107, and 109.

231 *Pass It On: The Story of Bill Wilson and How the A.A. Message Reached the World* (New York: Alcoholics Anonymous World Services, 1984), 265.

232 *Alcoholic Anonymous* (the Big Book), 4th edit., p. 164. See also p. 8—even in this life, Bill W. says, "I was soon to be catapulted into what I like to call the fourth dimension of existence" and p. 25 "We have found much of heaven and we have been rocketed into a fourth dimension of existence of which we had not even dreamed." The image of the world to come as a house of many mansions comes from John 14:2 "In my Father's house are many mansions: if it were not so, I would have told you. I go to prepare a place for you."

Bibliography

Alcoholics Anonymous, also known as the Big Book. New York: Alcoholics Anonymous World Services, orig. pub. 1939; 3rd ed. 1976; 4th ed. 2001.

Allen, James. *As a Man Thinketh* (orig. pub. 1902), in Mel B., ed., *Three Recovery Classics: As a Man Thinketh (by James Allen), The Greatest Thing in the World (by Henry Drummond), An Instrument of Peace (the St. Francis Prayer).* Hindsfoot Foundation Series on Spirituality and Theology. New York: iUniverse, 2004.

Alston, William P. "Religious Experience and Religious Belief," *Nous* 16 (1982) 3-12.

Armstrong, A. H. *An Introduction to Ancient Philosophy.* London: Methuen, 1965.

Augustine. *Confessions.* Trans. Albert C. Outler. Library of Christian Classics. Philadephia: Westminster Press, 1955.

_____ . *Confessions.* Trans. R. S. Pine-Coffin. Baltimore, MD: Penguin Books, 1961.

_____ . *On Free Will.* In Richard McKeon, ed. and trans., *Selections from Medieval Philosophers*, I. *Augustine to Albert the Great.* New York: Charles Scribner's Sons, 1929.

Auxier, Randall E. and Mark Y. A. Davies, eds., *Hartshorne and Brightman on God, Process, and Persons: The Correspondence, 1922-1945.* Nashville: Vanderbilt University Press, 2001.

Baillie, John. *Our Knowledge of God.* London: Oxford University Press, 1939.

Barth, Karl. *The Epistle to the Romans.* Trans. E. C. Hoskyns. London: Oxford University Press, 1933; orig. pub. as *Der Römerbrief*, 1919.

Berne, Eric. *Games People Play: The Psychology of Human Relationships: The Basic Handbook of Transactional Analysis.* New York: Ballantine Books, 1964.

Big Book: see *Alcoholics Anonymous*

Bowne, Borden Parker. *The Immanence of God.* New York: Houghton Mifflin, 1905.

Brightman, Edgar S. *The Problem of God.* New York: Abingdon Press, 1930.

Brown, Peter. *Augustine of Hippo: A Biography.* London: Faber & Faber, 1967.

Brown, Sally and David R. Brown. *A Biography of Mrs. Marty Mann: The First Lady of Alcoholics Anonymous.* Center City, Minnesota: Hazelden, 2001.

Buber, Martin. *I and Thou.* Trans. Walter Kaufmann. New York: Charles Scribner's Sons, 1970; orig. pub. 1923 as *Ich und Du.*

Bucke, Richard Maurice. *Cosmic Consciousness: A Study in the Evolution of the Human Mind.* Philadelphia: Innes & Sons, 1901.

Burke, Edmund. *A Philosophical Enquiry into the Origin of Our Ideas of the Sublime and Beautiful.* New York: Oxford University Press, 1990; orig. pub. 1757.

Burns, J. Patout. *The Development of Augustine's Doctrine of Operative Grace.* Paris: Études Augustiniennes, 1980.

Calvin, John. *Institutes of the Christian Religion.* 2 vols. Ed. John T. McNeill. Trans. Ford Lewis Battles. Philadelphia: Westminster, 1960.

Chesnut, Glenn F. *Changed by Grace: V. C. Kitchen, the Oxford Group, and A.A.* Hindsfoot Foundation Series on Spirituality and Theology. New York: iUniverse, 2006.

_____ . "Eusebius, Augustine, Orosius, and the Later Patristic and Medieval Christian Historians." Pp. 687–713 in Harold W. Attridge and Gohei Hata, eds., *Eusebius, Christianity, and Judaism.* Detroit: Wayne State University Press, 1992.

_____ . *The Factory Owner & the Convict: Lives and Teachings of the A.A. Old Timers.* 2nd ed. Hindsfoot Foundation Series on Alcoholics Anonymous History. New York: iUniverse, 2005; orig. pub. 1996.

_____ . *The First Christian Histories: Eusebius, Socrates, Sozomen, Theodoret, and Evagrius.* 2nd ed., rev. and enlarged. Macon, Georgia: Mercer University Press, 1986; orig. pub. in Paris by Éditions Beauchesne, 1977.

_____ . *The Higher Power of the Twelve-Step Program: For Believers & Non-Believers.* Hindsfoot Foundation Series on Spirituality and Theology. San Jose: Authors Choice/iUniverse, 2001.

_____ . *Images of Christ: An Introduction to Christology.* San Francisco: Harper & Row / Seabury, 1984.

_____ . "The Pattern of the Past: Augustine's Debate with Eusebius and Sallust." Pp. 69-95 in John Deschner, Leroy T. Howe, and Klaus Penzel (eds.), *Our Common History as Christians: Essays in Honor of Albert C. Outler.* New York: Oxford University Press, 1975.

_____ . *The St. Louis Gambler & the Railroad Man: Lives and Teachings of the A.A. Old Timers.* 2nd ed. Hindsfoot Foundation Series on Alcoholics Anonymous History. New York: iUniverse, 2005; orig. pub. 1996.

Chesnut, Roberta C. "The Two Prosopa in Nestorius' Bazaar of Heracleides," *Journal of Theological Studies* (Oxford) N.S. 29 (1978) 392–409.

Copleston, Frederick. *A History of Philosophy.* Vol. IV. *Descartes to Leibniz.* Westminster, Maryland: Newman Press, 1958.

Daniélou, Jean. Introd. to Gregory of Nyssa, *From Glory to Glory: Texts from Gregory of Nyssa's Mystical Writings.* Trans. Herbert Musurillo. Crestwood NY: St. Vladimir's Seminary Press, 1961.

Dante. *The Divine Comedy.* Trans. and comm. Charles S. Singleton. *Paradiso* 1: Italian Text and Translation. Princeton: Princeton University Press, 1975.

Dictionary of Latin and Greek Theological Terms: Drawn Principally from Protestant Scholastic Theology. Ed. Richard A. Muller. Grand Rapids, Michigan: Baker Book House, 1985.

Dubiel, Richard M. *The Road to Fellowship: The Role of the Emmanuel Movement and the Jacoby Club in the Development of Alcoholics Anonymous.* Hindsfoot Foundation Series on the History of Alcoholism Treatment. Ed. Glenn F. Chesnut. New York: iUniverse, 2004.

Edwards, Jonathan. *Basic Writings.* Ed. Ola Elizabeth Winslow. New York: New American Library, 1966.

Einstein, Albert. "Religion and Science," *New York Times Magazine*, 9 November 1930, 1-4. Reprinted in Albert Einstein, *Ideas and Opinions*, based on *Mein Weltbild*, ed. by Carl Seelig and other sources, new translations and revisions by Sonja Bargmann (New York, Crown Publishers, 1954). Also reprinted in pp. 24-28 of Albert Einstein, *The World as I See It* (New York: Philosophical Library, 1949). It may also be read online (February 2007) at www.geocities.com/HotSprings/6072/1einstein.html

Eliade, Mircea. *The Sacred and the Profane: The Nature of Religion.* Trans. Willard R. Trask. New York: Harcourt Brace Jovanovich, 1959.

Flavell, John H. *The Developmental Psychology of Jean Piaget.* Princeton, New Jersey: D. Van Nostrand, 1963.

Fox, Emmet. *The Sermon on the Mount: The Key to Success in Life* and *The Lord's Prayer: An Interpretation.* San Francisco: HarperSan Francisco, 1938.

Frankl, Viktor E. *Man's Search for Meaning: An Introduction to Logotherapy.* Rev. ed. New York: Washington Square Press, 1963; orig. title of English version was *From Death Camp to Existentialism*, 1959; orig. German version was entitled *Trotzdem Ja zum Leben sagen: Ein Psychologe erlebt das Konzentrationslager* (Nevertheless, Say "Yes" to Life: A Psychologist's Experience of the Concentration Camp), 1946.

Fries, Jakob Friedrich. *Knowledge, Belief, and Aesthetic Sense.* Ed. Frederick Gregory. Trans. Kent Richter. Köln: Jürgen Dinter Verlag für Philosophie, 1989.

Gilson, Etienne. *History of Christian Philosophy in the Middle Ages.* New York: Random House, 1955.

Greeley, Andrew. *Ascent into Hell.* New York: Warner Books, 1983.

_____ . *Cardinal Sins*. New York: Warner Books, 1981.

_____ . *Lord of the Dance*. New York: Warner Books, 1984.

_____ . *Thy Brother's Wife*. New York: Warner Books, 1982.

Gregory of Nyssa. *An Answer to Ablabius: That We Should Not Think of Saying There Are Three Gods*. Trans. Cyril C. Richardson. Pp. 256–67 in *Christology of the Later Fathers*. Edited by Edward Rochie Hardy. Library of Christian Classics. Philadelphia: Westminster Press, 1954.

_____ . *From Glory to Glory: Texts from Gregory of Nyssa's Mystical Writings*. Introd. Jean Daniélou. Trans. Herbert Musurillo. Crestwood NY: St. Vladimir's Seminary Press, 1961.

Hartshorne, Charles. *The Darkness and the Light: A Philosopher Reflects Upon His Fortunate Career and Those Who Made it Possible*. Albany: State University of New York Press, 1990.

_____ . *The Logic of Perfection and Other Essays in Neoclassical Metaphysics*. LaSalle, Illinois: Open Court Publishing Company, 1962.

_____ . *Omnipotence and Other Theological Mistakes*. Albany: State University of New York Press, 1983.

_____ and W. L. Reese. *Philosophers Speak of God*. Chicago: University of Chicago Press, 1953.

Hawking, Stephen. "Gödel and the end of physics." http://www.damtp.cam.ac.uk/strings02/dirac/hawking/ (September 2007).

Heidegger, Martin. *Being and Time*. Trans. John Macquarrie and Edward Robinson. San Francisco: Harper, 1962.

Heller, Dagmar. Review of Dennis E. Tamburello, *Union with Christ: John Calvin and the Mysticism of St. Bernard*, in *Ecumenical Review* (July 1996).

Hodges, Andrew. *Alan Turing: The Enigma*. New York: Simon and Schuster, 1983.

Hofstadter, Douglas R. *Gödel, Escher, Bach: an Eternal Golden Braid.* New York: Vintage/Random House, 1979.

_____ . *I Am a Strange Loop.* New York: Basic Books, 2007.

Hurnard, Hannah. *Hind's Feet in High Places.* Wheaton, Illinois: Tyndale House Publishers, 1975; orig. pub. 1955.

Huxley, Aldous. *Brave New World.* Garden City, New York: Doubleday, Doran & Company / Garden City Publishing, 1932.

Jaeger, Werner. *Two Rediscovered Works of Ancient Christian Literature: Gregory of Nyssa and Macarius.* Leiden: E. J. Brill, 1954.

James, William. *The Varieties of Religious Experience.* Gifford Lectures on Natural Religion Delivered at Edinburgh in 1901–1902. New York: Modern Library, 1994.

John of the Cross. *Ascent of Mount Carmel.* Trans. E. Allison Peers. Liguori, Missouri: Triumph Books, 1983.

_____ . *The Dark Night of the Soul.* Trans. and abridged by Kurt F. Reinhardt. New York: Frederick Ungar, 1957.

Kant, Immanuel. *Critique of Pure Reason.* Trans. Norman Kemp Smith. London: Macmillan & Co., 1933.

Körner, S. *Kant.* Baltimore, Maryland: Penguin Books, 1955.

Kuhn, Thomas S. *The Structure of Scientific Revolutions.* Chicago: University of Chicago Press, 1962.

Kurtz, Ernest. *Not-God: A History of Alcoholics Anonymous.* Expanded edition. Center City, Minnesota: Hazelden, 1991; orig. pub. 1979).

_____ . *Shame & Guilt.* 2nd rev. ed. Hindsfoot Foundation Series on Treatment and Recovery. New York: iUniverse, 2007; orig. pub. 1981.

_____ and Katherine Ketcham. *The Spirituality of Imperfection: Modern Wisdom from Classic Stories.* New York: Bantam Books, 1992.

Langford, Thomas A. *Practical Divinity: Theology in the Wesleyan Tradition.* Nashville: Abingdon Press, 1983.

_____ . *Wesleyan Theology: A Sourcebook.* Durham, North Carolina: Labyrinth Press, 1984.

Leff, Gordon. *Medieval Thought: St. Augustine to Ockham.* Baltimore, Maryland: Penguin Books, 1958.

Locke, John. *An Essay Concerning Human Understanding.* 2 vols. Ed. A. C. Fraser. New York: Dover. 1959.

Lonergan, Bernard. *Insight: A Study of Human Understanding.* New York: Philosophical Library, 1957.

Lossky, Vladimir. *The Vision of God.* Trans. A. Moorhouse. Crestwood, New York: St. Vladimir's Seminary Press, 1963.

Lovejoy, Arthur O. *The Great Chain of Being: A Study of the History of an Idea.* New York: Harper & Row, 1936.

Macarius the Homilist. *Fifty Spiritual Homilies of St. Macarius the Egyptian.* Trans. A. J. Mason. London: S.P.C.K., 1921.

Marlatt, Earl. "Spirit of Life, in This New Dawn." Hymn No. 462 in *The Methodist Hymnal.* Nashville, Tennessee: Methodist Publishing House, 1966.

May, Rollo. *The Courage to Create.* New York: W. W. Norton, 1975.

_____ . *Love and Will.* New York: W. W. Norton, 1969.

McKirahan, Richard D., Jr. "Zeno." Pp. 140-141 in A. A. Long, ed., *The Cambridge Companion to Early Greek Philosophy.* Cambridge: Cambridge University Press, 1999.

Mel B., ed., *Three Recovery Classics: As a Man Thinketh (by James Allen), The Greatest Thing in the World (by Henry Drummond), An Instrument of Peace (the St. Francis Prayer).* Hindsfoot Foundation Series on Spirituality and Theology. New York: iUniverse, 2004.

Ohliger, Dr. Paul (Laguna Niguel, California). "Doctor, Alcoholic, Addict." Pp. 439-452 in *Alcoholics Anonymous* (the Big Book), 3rd ed. Subsequently retitled "Acceptance Was the Answer" and printed as pp. 407-420 in the 4th ed.

Olitzky, Rabbi Kerry M. and Stuart A. Copans, M.D. *Twelve Jewish Steps to Recovery: A Personal Guide to Turning from Alcoholism and Other Addictions.* Woodstock, Vermont: Jewish Lights Publishing, 1991.

Otto, Rudolf. *Das Heilige: Über das Irrationale in der Idee des göttlichen und sein Verhältnis zum Rationalen.* 11th ed. Stuttgart: Friedrich Andreas Perthes, 1923.

_____. *The Idea of the Holy: An Inquiry into the Non-Rational Factor in the Idea of the Divine and Its Relation to the Rational.* 2nd ed. Trans. John W. Harvey. Oxford: Oxford University Press, 1950.

_____. *Kantisch-Fries'sche Religionsphilosophie und ihre Anwendung auf die Theologie.* Tübingen: J. C. B. Mohr, 1909.

_____. *The Philosophy of Religion Based on Kant and Fries.* Trans. E. B. Dicker. London: Williams & Norgate, 1931.

Outler, Albert C., ed. *John Wesley.* Library of Protestant Thought. New York: Oxford University Press, 1964.

Oxford Dictionary of the Christian Church. 2nd ed. Ed. F. L. Cross and E. A. Livingstone. London: Oxford University Press, 1974.

Pass It On: The Story of Bill Wilson and How the A.A. Message Reached the World. New York: Alcoholics Anonymous World Services, 1984.

Penzias, A. A. and R. W. Wilson. "A Measurement of Excess Antenna Temperature at 4080 Mc/s." *Astrophysical Journal* 142 (1965), 419.

Pfau, Ralph and Al Hirshberg. *Prodigal Shepherd.* Indianapolis, Indiana: SMT Guild, 1958.

Plato. *Republic.* 2 vols. Trans. Paul Shorey. Loeb Classical Library. London: William Heinemann, 1935-7.

Polanyi, Michael. *Personal Knowledge: Towards a Post-Critical Philosophy*. New York: Harper & Row, 1964; orig. pub. 1958.

Randall, John Herman, Jr. *Aristotle*. New York: Columbia University Press, 1960.

Ryle, Gilbert. *The Concept of Mind*. New York: Barnes & Noble, 1949.

Seneca. *Epistulae morales*. Ed. and trans. Richard M. Gummere. 3 vols. Loeb Classical Library. Cambridge, Massachusetts: Harvard University Press, 1917–25.

_____ . *Naturales Quaestiones* Books 1-3. Trans. Thomas H. Corcoran. Loeb Classical Library. Cambridge, Massachusetts: Harvard University Press, 1971.

Tamburello, Dennis E. *Union with Christ: John Calvin and the Mysticism of St. Bernard*. Columbia [Theological Seminary] Series in Reformed Theology. Louisville: Westminster John Knox Press, 1994.

Teresa of Ávila. *Interior Castle*. Trans. E. Allison Peers. Garden City NY: Image Books/Doubleday & Company, 1961; orig. pub. 1577 as *El Castillo Interior*.

Thomas, Elizabeth Marshall. *The Hidden Life of Dogs*. New York: Houghton Mifflin, 1993.

Thucydides. Ed. and trans. Charles Forster Smith. 4 vols. Loeb Classical Library. Cambridge, Massachusetts: Harvard University Press, 1921–30.

Tiebout, Harry M. "Surrender Versus Compliance in Therapy: With Special Reference to Alcoholism." *Quarterly Journal of Studies on Alcohol* (Yale University) 14 (1953): 58-68. Available as reprint from National Council on Alcoholism, 733 Third Avenue, New York NY 10017.

Tillich, Paul. *The Courage to Be*. New Haven: Yale University Press, 1952.

_____ . *Dynamics of Faith*. New York: Harper & Brothers, 1957.

_____ . *My Search for Absolutes*. New York: Simon and Schuster, 1967. Available on the internet at http://www.religion-online.org/showchapter. asp?title=1628&C=1595 (January 31, 2007).

_____ . *Systematic Theology*. 3 vols. Chicago: University of Chicago Press, 1951-63; repr. 1967 as three vols. in one.

_____ . *Theology of Culture*. New York: Oxford University Press, 1959.

Turing, Alan M. "Computing Machinery and Intelligence," *Mind* (October 1950) 59: 433-460. Reprinted in Alan Ross Anderson, ed. *Minds and Machines*. Englewood Cliffs, New Jersey: Prentice-Hall, 1964.

_____ . "On computable numbers, with an application to the Entscheidungsproblem," *Proc. London Maths. Soc.*, ser. 2, 42 (1936): 230-265.

Underhill, Evelyn. *Mysticism: A Study in the Nature and Development of Man's Spiritual Consciousness*. London: Methuen, 1911.

Wakefield, Gordon. "John Wesley and Ephraem Syrus," *Hugoye: Journal of Syriac Studies* 1, no. 2 (July 1998).

Walker, Richmond. *Twenty-Four Hours a Day*. Compiled by a Member of the Group at Daytona Beach, Fla. Rev. ed. Center City, Minnesota: Hazelden, 1975; orig. pub. under the sponsorship of the local A.A. group in Daytona Beach, 1948. Hazelden has made changes in the book since Rich's death in 1965.

Watson, Philip S. *Let God Be God! An Interpretation of the Theology of Martin Luther*. Philadelphia: Fortress, 1947.

Wesley, John. *Explanatory Notes upon the New Testament*. London: Epworth, 1958; orig. pub. in London by William Bowyer, 1755.

_____ . *John Wesley*. Ed. Albert C. Outler. Library of Protestant Thought. New York: Oxford University Press, 1964.

_____ . *The Works of John Wesley*, Vols. 1–4, *Sermons*. Ed. Albert C. Outler. Nashville: Abingdon Press, 1984–7.

Index

539

R

random 1, 16, 26, 114, 173, 274, 275,
    276, 321, 366, 367, 368, 388,
    392, 508, 509, 515, 527, 529
responsibility 41, 87, 159, 192, 235,
    239, 241, 291, 299, 376, 377,
    378, 379, 431
river of eternity 147, 148, 157, 159,
    161, 163, 173, 174, 176, 177,
    178, 182
river of time 149, 173, 223
Roman vii, 1, 2, 3, 60, 62, 71, 76, 80,
    84, 139, 150, 157, 160, 187,
    219, 226, 234, 240, 295, 303,
    305, 323, 340, 351, 352, 353,
    361, 374, 379, 406, 435, 454,
    470, 473, 479, 496, 498, 507

S

sacramental view of the universe 219,
    443
sacred 27, 42, 66, 68, 69, 70, 71, 72,
    73, 74, 75, 76, 77, 78, 79, 80,
    82, 84, 85, 86, 87, 89, 90, 91,
    92, 95, 98, 99, 100, 101, 102,
    104, 105, 106, 107, 109, 110,
    119, 121, 140, 143, 146, 166,
    167, 182, 184, 204, 208, 215,
    220, 226, 227, 231, 236, 244,
    443, 490, 491, 494, 527
Sartre 101, 149, 150
self-referential 395, 397, 405, 406,
    407, 408, 425
self-transcendence 402, 408, 409, 410,
    411, 421, 425, 445
Seneca 76, 139, 351, 352, 473, 475,
    491, 496, 532
Serenity Prayer 160, 162, 181, 498
silence 42, 77, 165, 498
Sinai 23, 24, 26, 29, 37
Southern Methodist University vii, 3,
    219, 495, 503
spark of the divine 446, 484, 519

spirit 15, 30, 32, 44, 47, 53, 58, 59,
    64, 65, 70, 73, 74, 76, 77, 84,
    94, 97, 103, 104, 105, 107, 109,
    110, 159, 183, 192, 218, 220,
    233, 242, 243, 244, 282, 346,
    349, 358, 426, 427, 428, 432,
    434, 439, 444, 445, 455, 456,
    461, 466, 484, 485, 486, 495,
    508, 510, 519, 530
spirituality 2, 17, 51, 52, 64, 65, 69,
    105, 107, 112, 117, 119, 130,
    132, 143, 144, 146, 147, 150,
    152, 153, 154, 155, 157, 160,
    163, 164, 169, 170, 173, 174,
    178, 179, 184, 190, 201, 208,
    220, 227, 231, 232, 233, 237,
    286, 314, 320, 323, 324, 329,
    383, 423, 432, 433, 434, 435,
    444, 466, 470, 490, 498, 502,
    510, 513, 520, 524, 525, 526,
    529, 530
spiritual marriage 307, 308, 493, 505
static 91, 92, 95, 246, 350, 404, 473,
    475, 476, 481, 482, 483, 484,
    503
steady state theory 128, 262, 521
sublime 70, 140, 141, 142, 143, 169,
    170, 173, 174, 178, 182, 256,
    493, 496, 497, 525
suffering 10, 29, 47, 148, 173, 183,
    185, 190, 191, 192, 193, 205,
    229, 235, 246, 250, 253, 254,
    256, 373, 406
supernatural 28, 70, 108, 129, 236,
    358, 370, 374, 444, 445, 446,
    488, 495
symbol 24, 36, 37, 79, 80, 81, 82, 83,
    107, 118, 124, 142, 202, 203,
    204, 207, 208, 209, 211, 213,
    235, 360, 441, 448
symbolic 41, 80, 151, 207, 209, 210,
    213, 241, 304, 360, 489, 519
synchronicity 359, 360, 362, 363, 365
synergism 102, 350

T

U

CPSIA information can be obtained
at www.ICGtesting.com
Printed in the USA
BVOW08s1253251017
498626BV00001B/87/P